NOIR IN THE NORTH

NOIR IN THE NORTH

Genre, Politics and Place

Edited by
Stacy Gillis and Gunnthorunn Gudmundsdottir

BLOOMSBURY ACADEMIC
NEW YORK • LONDON • OXFORD • NEW DELHI • SYDNEY

BLOOMSBURY ACADEMIC
Bloomsbury Publishing Inc
1385 Broadway, New York, NY 10018, USA
50 Bedford Square, London, WC1B 3DP, UK

BLOOMSBURY, BLOOMSBURY ACADEMIC and the Diana logo are
trademarks of Bloomsbury Publishing Plc

First published in the United States of America 2020
This paperback edition published 2022

Volume Editors' Part of the Work © Stacy Gillis and Gunnthorunn Gudmundsdottir, 2020
Each Chapter © of Contributors, 2020

Cover design by Eleanor Rose
Cover photograph © Dagur Gunnarsson

All rights reserved. No part of this publication may be reproduced or
transmitted in any form or by any means, electronic or mechanical, including
photocopying, recording, or any information storage or retrieval system,
without prior permission in writing from the publishers.

Bloomsbury Publishing Inc does not have any control over, or responsibility for,
any third-party websites referred to or in this book. All internet addresses given
in this book were correct at the time of going to press. The author and publisher
regret any inconvenience caused if addresses have changed or sites have
ceased to exist, but can accept no responsibility for any such changes.

Library of Congress Cataloging-in-Publication Data
Names: Gillis, Stacy, 1972- editor. | Gudmundsdóttir, Gunnthórunn, editor.
Title: Noir in the North : gender, politics, and place / edited by Stacy Gillis and Gunnthorunn Gudmundsdottir.
Description: New York : Bloomsbury Academic, 2020. | Includes bibliographical references and index. | Summary: "In this timely and vital account of the transnational cross-media phenomenon that is often loosely described as 'Nordic noir', leading scholars and three crime writers unpick precisely what is noir and what is northern about this genre, and discuss its transnational significance"– Provided by publisher.
Identifiers: LCCN 2020013040 | ISBN 9781501342868 (hardback) | ISBN 9781501342882 (pdf) | ISBN 9781501342875 (ebook)
Subjects: LCSH: Detective and mystery stories, Scandinavian–History and criticism. | Scandinavian fiction–20th century–History and criticism. | Scandinavian fiction–21st century–History and criticism. | Crime in literature. | Politics in literature. | Scandinavia–In literature.
Classification: LCC PT7083.5.D48 N65 2020 | DDC 839/.5–dc23
LC record available at https://lccn.loc.gov/2020013040

ISBN:	HB:	978-1-5013-4286-8
	PB:	978-1-5013-6928-5
	ePDF:	978-1-5013-4288-2
	eBook:	978-1-5013-4287-5

Typeset by Integra Software Services Pvt. Ltd.

To find out more about our authors and books visit www.bloomsbury.com
and sign up for our newsletters.

CONTENTS

List of Figures	viii
Notes on Contributors	ix
Foreword *Yrsa Sigurðardóttir*	xiii
Acknowledgements	xvi

Chapter 1
INTRODUCTION: NOIR IN THE NORTH
Gunnthorunn Gudmundsdottir and Gerardine Meaney 1

Part I
GENDER AND TRANSNATIONAL DIMENSIONS

Chapter 2
THE WOMAN BETWEEN: A SOCIAL NETWORK ANALYSIS OF *THE FALL* AND *THE BRIDGE*
Gerardine Meaney, Derek Greene, Karen Wade and Maria Mulvany 23

Chapter 3
ADAPTING NORDIC NOIR: FROM *FORBRYDELSEN* TO *THE KILLING*
Delphine Letort 41

Chapter 4
LILYHAMMER'S 'LAND OF SECOND CHANCES': MASCULINITY, VIOLENCE AND CORRUPTION
Catherine Ross Nickerson 57

Part II
SPACE AND PLACE

Chapter 5
VIEWS FROM *THE BRIDGE*: PANORAMAS, STREETSCAPES AND THE OPTICS OF *NOIR*
Graeme Gilloch 73

Chapter 6
COMPLEX NOSTALGIAS: NORTH, PASTNESS AND COMMUNITY SURVIVAL IN ARNALDUR INDRIÐASON'S *STRANGE SHORES* AND ANN CLEEVES' *BLUE LIGHTNING*
Daisy Neijmann   85

Chapter 7
NORDIC NOIR AND THE 'POST-COLONIAL' NORTH: THE LEGACIES OF DANISH COLONIALISM IN THE NORDIC REGION
Christinna Hazzard   101

Part III
POLITICS AND MORALITY

Chapter 8
CRIME'S CARTOGRAPHY: USING SJÖWALL AND WAHLÖÖ'S *STORY OF A CRIME* TO MAP SWEDEN'S CO-ORDINATES WITHIN GLOBAL NEOLIBERALISM'S UNEVEN SPREAD
Patrick Kent Russell   117

Chapter 9
KID STUFF: NORDIC NOIR, POLITICS AND QUALITY
Andrew Nestingen   133

Chapter 10
DARK NIGHTS AND MORAL DIVERSITY: RE-THINKING MORALITY IN NORDIC NOIR
Mary Evans   149

Part IV
GENEALOGY AND GENRE

Chapter 11
WHAT'S IN A NAME? THE THORNY THREAD OF NORDIC NOIR
Björn Nordfjörd   165

Chapter 12
BLEAKNESS AND TENACITY: NORDIC NOIR AND *FIN-DE-SIÈCLE* FRENCH DECADENT LITERATURE
Christopher James   183

Chapter 13
DRAGON TATTOOS, CRIME AND THE CITY: THE
CONTEMPORARY EPIC
   Giti Chandra199

Chapter 14
THE NEW SWEDISH POLICE THRILLER OF THE 2010s
   Kerstin Bergman211

Chapter 15
'SAFE LITTLE NORWAY': NORWEGIAN NOIR AND THE ROOTS OF
SUBVERSIVE SOCIO-POLITICAL COMMENTARY
   Nina Muždeka221

VAL MCDERMID ON NOIR IN THE NORTH
   Interview by Lorna Hill239

CODA
   Gunnar Staalesen245

Index249

FIGURES

2.1	Social Network Map, S1E1, *Bron/Broen*	26
2.2	Social Network Map, S1E1, *The Fall*	27
2.3	Social Network Map, Chapter 1, *The Sign of Four*	29
2.4	Social Network Map, Chapter 1, *The Mysterious Affair at Styles*	29
2.5	Stella and Spector dominate the social network in *The Fall*	32
2.6	Saga's networks at the beginning of *Bron/Broen*	34
2.7	Saga between the police and the victims on the Öresund Bridge, image © 2011 FILMLANCE INTERNATIONAL AB, NIMBUS FILM	35
2.8	Stella and Spector, image courtesy of Fables and Artists Studio (an Endemol Shine company)	36

CONTRIBUTORS

Kerstin Bergman is an affiliated researcher of comparative literature at Lund University, Sweden. She is an expert on Swedish crime fiction and Nordic noir, a literary critic and a member of the Swedish Academy of Crime Fiction. She is the author of *Swedish Crime Fiction: The Making of Nordic Noir* (2014), and numerous popular and scholarly articles on Swedish and international crime fiction (in English and Swedish). As an expert on crime fiction, a writer and lecturer, she runs CrimeGarden and blogs (in Swedish) about crime fiction at crimegarden.se.

Giti Chandra is an affiliated scholar with the United Nations University, Gender Equality Studies and Training programme, at the University of Iceland. She is the author of *Narrating Violence, Constructing Collective Identities: To Witness these Wrongs Unspeakable* (2009), and she is currently working on *In Visible Texts: Hidden and Spectacularised Violence in Colonial India and Africa*. She has written and published on issues of violence, the body, gender and collective identity formation.

Mary Evans is currently a Leverhulme Emeritus Professor in the Department of Gender Studies at the London School of Economics (LSE). Her work has discussed issues in feminist and sociological theory, and her most recent work is a study of contemporary European detective fiction, with Sarah Moore and Hazel Johnstone entitled *Detecting the Social: Order and Disorder in Post-1970s Detective Fiction*, published in 2019.

Stacy Gillis is Lecturer in Modern and Contemporary Literature at Newcastle University, UK. She is the editor of four books, including Feminism, Domesticity and Popular Culture (co-edited with Joanne Hollows, 2009).

Graeme Gilloch is Professor of Sociology at Lancaster University. He is the author of *Myth and Metropolis: Walter Benjamin and the City* (1995); *Walter Benjamin: Critical Constellations* (2002); *Siegfried Kracauer: Our Companion in Misfortune* (2015) and co-author (with Bülent Diken and Craig Hammond) of *The Cinema of Nuri Bilge Ceylan* (2018). His work focuses on critical social and cultural theory, with particular reference to the intersections of the city, visual culture and memory. His latest book (with Jaeho Kang) is *Siegfried Kracauer: Selected Writings on Media, Propaganda and Political Communication* (2018).

Derek Greene is Assistant Professor at the School of Computer Science, University College Dublin, and a Funded Investigator at the Science Foundation Ireland (SFI) Insight Centre for Data Analytics and the SFI VistaMilk Research Centre. He currently leads a research group which is focusing on developing algorithms for social network analysis and text mining.

Gunnthorunn Gudmundsdottir is Professor of Comparative Literature at the University of Iceland. She has published widely on contemporary literature and life writing. Her most recent book is *Representations of Forgetting in Life Writing and Fiction* (2017).

Christinna Hazzard is an Associate Lecturer in the Department of English and Cultural History at Liverpool John Moores University. She is currently preparing a monograph proposal for her doctoral thesis titled "Semi-Periphery Realism: Nation and Form on the Borders of Europe" and has an article forthcoming in a special issue of the *Journal of Postcolonial Writing* on the European peripheries.

Christopher James is Assistant Professor of French at Bridgewater College (Virginia, USA) in the Department of World Languages and Cultures. His research interests focus on space in literature and film studies, as well as work on memory studies. His dissertation concerned proper names in fiction as bearers of cultural memory, and most recently he guest edited a special issue of the *International Journal of Humanities Arts and Computing*, concerning the spatial humanities.

Delphine Letort is a Professor of American Studies at Le Mans University. Her latest book is entitled *The Spike Lee Brand: Documentary Filmmaking* (2015). She has published numerous articles on film noir, film adaptation, African American cinema and documentaries.

Val McDermid is a Scottish crime writer and best known for a series of suspense novels featuring Dr Tony Hill. Her novels have been translated into forty languages. She received the Crime Writers' Association Gold Dagger for Best Crime Novel of the Year in 1995 for *The Mermaids Singing*.

Gerardine Meaney is Professor of Cultural Theory and Director of the Centre for Cultural Analytics in University College Dublin's School of English Drama and Film. She is the author of *Gender, Ireland and Cultural Change* (2010), *Nora* (2004), *(Un)like Subjects: Women, Theory, Fiction* (1993, 2012) and co-author with Mary O'Dowd and Bernadette Whelan of *Reading the Irish Woman: Cultural Encounter and Exchange, 1714–1960* (2013).

Maria Mulvany is a postdoctoral fellow at the University College Dublin Centre for Cultural Analytics. Her research interests include gender and sexuality studies, the historical novel, diaries and crime fiction. She co-edited (with Gerardine Meaney and Karen Wade) a new multimedia edition of James Joyce's *A Portrait of the Artist as a Young Man* (www.joyceportrait100.com).

Nina Muždeka is an associate professor of Anglophone literatures at the University of Novi Sad, Serbia. Her research interests include contemporary literatures in English with particular focus on genre theory, gender theory, identity construction, transnational studies and global literature. She has published on contemporary British and American fiction, as well as fiction in translation, in Australia, the USA, Finland, Croatia, Hungary, Romania, Montenegro and Serbia. Dr Muždeka is also the author of monographs on the issue of genre in Julian Barnes' novels (2006) and magical realism in Angela Carter's work (2017).

Daisy Neijmann teaches Icelandic literature and culture at the University of Iceland. She is the author of *The Icelandic Voice in Canadian Letters* and *Colloquial Icelandic* (2000, 2013), editor of *A History of Icelandic Literature* (2006), and has published widely on Icelandic-Canadian literature, modern Icelandic fiction, Icelandic literary historiography, war memory and trauma texts, and Icelandic as a second and heritage language. She is also a fan of crime fiction.

Andrew Nestingen is Professor of Scandinavian Studies at the University of Washington (Seattle, USA) and Department Chair. He has published numerous books and articles on Scandinavian film and literature, especially Nordic noir, including *Crime and Fantasy in Scandinavia* (2008) and *Scandinavian Crime Fiction* (co-edited with Paula Arvas, 2011). He teaches courses on Nordic noir, Scandinavian cinema and cultures of childhood in Scandinavia. He is working on a book about Nordic noir.

Catherine Ross Nickerson is Associate Professor of English at Emory University (Atlanta, USA). Her research and teaching focus on issues of gender in crime narratives (fiction, history, film and television) and in gothic literature. She is the author of *The Web of Iniquity: Early Detective Fiction by American Women* (1999) and editor of the *Cambridge Companion to American Crime Fiction* (2010).

Björn Nordfjörd is Associate Professor at St. Olaf College (Minnesota, USA) in the Department of English. His research interests focus on crime fiction, Nordic cinema and world cinema more broadly. He has published widely on Icelandic and Nordic cinemas, including work on crime films, and is working on a book project devoted to world cinema.

Patrick Kent Russell is a PhD candidate in the English Department at the University of Connecticut. His research focuses on the relationship between popular culture and the state, particularly pop-cultural representations of crime and their impact upon public perception of state problems. He has published and presented on crime fiction's potential for social and political commentary.

Yrsa Sigurðardóttir is an Icelandic author of crime fiction and children's books. Her work has been translated widely. She is a two-time winner of *Blóðdropinn* (The Drop of Blood), the annual Icelandic crime fiction prize. She received the prize in 2011 for *Ég man þig* (I Remember You) and in 2015 for *DNA*. Yrsa maintains a full-time job as a civil engineer alongside writing her books.

Gunnar Staalesen is a Norwegian author and is best known for his work on the crime series about the Bergen private investigator, Varg Veum. The Varg Veum books have been translated into twelve languages. Staalesen won the 1989 Norwegian Booksellers' Prize for *Falne engler* (Fallen Angels).

Karen Wade is a postdoctoral fellow in the University College Dublin Centre for Cultural Analytics. Her research interests include social-network analysis of nineteenth-century fiction, literary letters, gender, blogging and the intersection of medical and digital humanities. Her recent papers have focused on word embedding in and the semantic analysis of literary corpora.

FOREWORD

Yrsa Sigurðardóttir

Ever since the appearance of crime fiction in the 1800s, novels that fall into this genre have been immensely popular with readers in most corners of the world. The reason behind this popularity is hard to pinpoint precisely, although numerous theories have been set forth. Crime novels are said to provide a safe thrill, that is easily turned off by putting the book down. They are also said to appeal to the human longing to know and understand everything. Before the reader is a puzzle of sorts, and between the reader and the writer, an unspoken agreement that all will be cleared up at the end. This in itself is not the only aspect that keeps readers turning the pages, the novel must also be well written and the characters engaging and relatable. It is at least obvious that if murder and mayhem were the only appeal, readers could get their fix from reading the news.

Crime fiction novels are as varied as the authors that write them. Various sub-genres exist: everything from what is referred to as cosy crime to psychological thrillers, and even cat crime novels, wherein a cat features prominently in the investigation. There is certainly something for everyone. A further distinction is often made between crime novels and thrillers, a classification that in most part is dependent on the novel's pacing. In a crime novel, the story often begins with the awful event, almost always a murder, and the reader is led through the pages, along the path of discovery until all is settled and the villain is unmasked and apprehended. This path can be littered with further bodies, but make no mistake, the reader is headed for the restoration of normality. In thrillers, however, the awful incident is about to happen. Is it going to happen, or is it not going to happen? Usually it does not.

As unlikely as it may be, the peaceful Nordic countries have somehow managed to become a powerhouse of the crime fiction market. Sweden, Norway, Denmark, Iceland and Finland usually find themselves aligned side-by-side at the top of lists such as the most peaceful countries and the happiest countries. Yet their crime authors are regularly seen in the top spots of bestseller lists the world over. Despite many years foretelling the demise of this popularity, Nordic noir has not let go of its strong foothold, and there are no indications that it is losing ground. Much like in thrillers, the predicted doomsday occurrence will probably not take place.

The popularity of Nordic noir is a prevalent topic in the crime fiction world. Nordic noir authors are more frequently asked for their views on the subject, and they are asked where they get their ideas. And that is saying something. The reason why this question is so often posed is because there is no sole, definitive and correct answer. Taste, be it in literature, food or art, is very hard to pinpoint. It varies greatly between individuals, and furthermore, evolves and changes for reasons that are not always easily identifiable. That being said, the most commonly referred to aspects of Nordic noir that are said to influence its popularity are the sparse writing style, the focus on social issues, the inkling of an underside to a seemingly perfect society, the often well-drawn 'defective detective' protagonist and the presence of snow. Yes, snow. Preferably speckled with blood. But even snow is not present in every crime novel that comes out of the Nordic countries, much less all of the other factors. If you randomly pick a Nordic noir crime novel off a bookshelf, however, you are more likely to find some, if not all, of these factors within its pages than you would if the book had originated from other countries.

With respect to the characteristics above, many of those asked tended to sway to the side of social commentary when it came to the popularity of Nordic crime fiction. It is of course not present in every novel written by every Nordic crime author, but it is very often present, in a very apparent way or more subtly. The origin of its injection is no mystery. Anyone familiar with Nordic noir knows of Maj Sjöwall and Per Wahlöö, heralded as the first authors to utilize the crime novel as a vehicle for social criticism. They managed to entertain their readers and keep them enthralled, while simultaneously raising their awareness of injustice or dangerous social trends. It is no wonder then, that the Nordic noir authors who followed them aspire to achieve the same. Some writers manage to do this very well, others not at all. As mentioned, the authors writing crime fiction, be it Nordic noir or other sub-genres, are an extremely diverse bunch. They come from various different countries, all age groups, all genders, all levels of society and tend to have a much more varied educational background than authors in other branches of literature. This ensures that the genre presents an extremely broad horizon, which is possibly why it is still thriving.

When it comes to gender, crime fiction has welcomed female writers on a much grander scale than most other types of literature, aside from romance novels. Many of the widest read contemporary crime authors are female, and Agatha Christie is not only the most important author of golden age crime fiction, she is also the world's bestselling author of all time. With the increased popularity of the psychological and domestic thriller, it is now more likely that an initialled crime author's name is a male author, while until recently it was a given that this author was a woman hoping to be perceived as a man by hiding their given name. Hopefully, in future, an author's gender will be a non-issue and such initials will only be used to mask a very 'un-sellable', complex or unappealing name, as all genders are just as capable of writing quality crime fiction, and any other type of fiction come to that.

I am unable to leave the gender aspect without mentioning an anomaly in Icelandic society regarding female authors. My home country has warmed the top seat of the gender gap index for almost a decade, meaning that the status of women is considered the best in the world with respect to the factors that contribute to the score. Local female fiction authors are not, however, as popular as their male counterparts when it comes to sales. The bulk of the sales of Icelandic hardcover fiction are in the weeks leading up to Christmas, as books are a traditional present. The bestseller lists during this period are, thus, best reflective of local book sales, and to my great sadness, women usually represent a mere 10 to 20 per cent of the top ten books, despite writing around 40 per cent of the fiction titles. I cannot but conclude from this that the average Icelandic book purchaser believes that men are better writers than women. To make this even sadder, Icelandic women buy more books than Icelandic men. It is my sincere hope, then, that we as a nation of readers are able to amend this oddity, and it is not unlikely that crime fiction will lead us to a path of additional equality, where each author is judged by the quality of their writing, not their gender.

The above is quite obviously very general in all respects. Crime fiction as a topic is a more complex discussion than a foreword allows for. Thankfully, the chapters that follow address it in a more thorough manner. Read on and enjoy.

ACKNOWLEDGEMENTS

Thanks are due to the editors' institutions, Newcastle University and the University of Iceland for facilitating the work on this volume. Special thanks go to the Centre for Research in the Humanities, University of Iceland, in particular to Margrét Gudmundsdottir, and also to The British Embassy in Reykjavik and Reykjavik UNESCO City of Literature, who all provided assistance at the start of this project. Thanks also to University College Dublin's (UCD) Research Visiting Professor scheme which hosted Gudmundsdottir in 2018, and where part of the work was carried out. Thanks also to the Humanities Institute at UCD and its director Anne Fuchs where Gudmundsdottir was a visiting fellow. A grant from EDDA, Centre of Excellence, at the University of Iceland, was instrumental in securing the work on this volume, with special thanks to Irma Erlingsdóttir and Valur Ingimundarson. The initial co-operation with the festival of crime fiction, 'Iceland noir', proved very fruitful, and thanks go to Lilja Sigurðardóttir, Quentin Bates and Ragnar Jónasson. Thanks also to the crime writers who so generously agreed to take part in this project: Val McDermid, Yrsa Sigurðardóttir and Gunnar Staalesen. Vera Knútsdóttir, our editorial assistant, provided essential support and her work has been of immense help. Gerardine Meaney's invaluable contribution has made all the difference in the last stages, and to her we are extremely grateful. Haaris Naqvi and Amy Martin at Bloomsbury have been supportive and encouraging throughout the, at times, challenging development of the volume. Finally, thanks to our families for all their help during this process. Thank you Dagur and Flóki.

Chapter 1

INTRODUCTION: NOIR IN THE NORTH

Gunnthorunn Gudmundsdottir and Gerardine Meaney

Transnational noir

Crime fiction is both a distinctive genre and a global transmedia form. As is abundantly evident from the contributions to this volume, it is a dynamic and hybrid genre, deeply intertwined with the history of film and the novel, and is a mainstay of television production. A transnational form, it is embedded in national cultures and canons, regularly ascribed conservative and even cultural imperialist tendencies, while constantly evolving in response to social change, and local, national and transnational concerns. A noir sensibility has, by contrast, always been associated with subversion and disturbance. While noir fiction, in the form of American writers like James M. Cain and Dashiell Hammett, preceded its cinematic form, the name comes from transatlantic film studies, specifically a French avant-garde reconstruction of American cinema which foregrounded its murky, discontented, scandalous edges. In its European context, noir was re-purposed not only as an interrogation of the dark underbelly of the American Dream, but of the human condition. In some ways, however, European influences were already there, as Delphine Letort draws attention to in Chapter 3, with the 'influence of European immigrant directors in the development of Hollywood noir [...] although many of them have adapted American hard-boiled novels and scripts'. Patrick Raynal, editor of Gallimard's *Série noire*, proclaimed as late as 1995 that:

> If we can broadly define noir writing and noir inspiration as a way of looking at the world, at the dark, opaque, criminal side of the world, shot through with the intense feeling of fatality we carry within us due to the fact that the only thing we can know for certain is that we will inevitably die, then it can indeed be said that Oedipus Rex was the first noir novel.[1]

Raynal's understanding of literary noir as part of the tradition of tragedy is in keeping with some of the earliest reception of 'Nordic noir', which positioned it as a response to the inevitable failure of optimistic social democracies to fundamentally alleviate human suffering, a thread highlighted in several chapters of this volume. In its current usage, however, the term is not without its own contradictions and complications, as Gunnar Staalesen elucidates in the Coda to this volume and Björn Nordfjörd addresses in detail in Chapter 11, where he points to the 'whole-hearted adoption of the term by the scholarly community' as somewhat surprising. Both Staalesen and Nordfjord are mainly concerned with the problematic use of the term 'noir', but the lumping together of all crime fiction from many countries and cultures is not without its problems either.

The regional differences – social, cultural and literary – within the Nordic countries should not be underestimated, each having their own particular trajectory (as Kerstin Bergman and Nina Muždeka make clear in Chapter 14 on Swedish crime fiction and Chapter 15 on Norwegian noir respectively), with certain transnational markers such as the pan-Nordic influence of Maj Sjöwall and Per Wahlöö, and the development of Nordic film and television. Denmark has a long tradition of high-quality film and television making, which has also been influential in the other Nordic countries, and then further afield when *Forbrydelsen* (*The Killing*, 2007–12), broke the transnational barrier. The change from when it was unthinkable to show subtitled series on primetime UK television, such as when Lars von Trier's *Riget* (*The Kingdom*, 1994–97) was shown on BBC2 at 11pm on Tuesday evenings in the late 1990s, should not be underestimated. With the advent of streaming services such as Netflix the distribution game has completely changed with Spanish series such as *La casa de papel* (*Money Heist*, 2017–) and Belgian series *Beau Sejour* (*Hotel Beau Sejour*, 2016–) suddenly having instant global distribution. And although not exactly threatening Anglo-Saxon hegemony, these productions knock forcefully on its door, adding new angles, languages and traditions.[2]

The transnational and transmedia spread of Nordic noir can be categorized into different modes of representation: there are remakes of Nordic TV series, such as Kenneth Branagh's *Wallander* (2008–16) and the US remake of *The Killing* (2011–14); series produced elsewhere but set in the North, such as *Fortitude* (2015–18); co-productions, such as the French/Swedish production *Midnatssol* (*Midnight Sun*, 2016–); series that make use of the aesthetics and tone, such as the UK series *The Fall* (2013–16) and *River* (2015); novels set in the Nordic countries, such as the British author Quentin Bates' novels set in Iceland and Will Dean's crime novel set in Sweden (*Dark Pines*, 2017); and crime fiction set in other northern locations such as Tartan noir, Irish noir, etc. Catherine Nickerson analyses a deeply self-referential, and perhaps unusual instance of this by the transnational Norwegian/US TV series *Lilyhammer* (2012–14) in Chapter 4, accentuating its connections with what, by some, is termed the first 'quality' TV series, *The Sopranos* (1999–2007).

In this volume we seek to expand the concept of the North beyond the geographical boundaries of the Nordic countries and map how themes and images from Nordic crime fiction and television have spread and travelled in the last decade, not least in Britain and the US. The Nordic countries are still firmly at the centre of the aesthetics and themes of noir in the North, so their image is important for our discussion and it is worthwhile tracing some of the geographical, historical and imagined images of the North.

The sections in this volume reflect the concerns and preoccupations of noir in the North, focusing on gender, place, politics and genre respectively, although with significant thematic overlap. In Part I gender issues are seen through the prism of transnational influences and adaptations in noir TV series. It is apt that the volume begins with a discussion of TV adaptations and series, as they have been a prominent feature of Nordic noir, with the Swedish series *Beck* (1997–), an adaptation of Sjöwall and Wahlöö's novels, being one of the earliest. Through an innovative use of social network analysis, Meaney et al. show the difference between the main protagonists in *Bron/Broen* (*The Bridge*, 2011–18) and *The Fall*, while Nickerson explores the masculine values at play in the transnational co-produced TV series, *Lilyhammer*. The section concludes with Letort's analysis of the gendered differences in the US adaptation of *Forbrydelsen*.

Part II focuses on another crucial aspect of noir in the North, that of the significance of place, location, settings and its visual characteristics. Graeme Gilloch analyses the visual imagery of *Bron/Broen* and the US version *The Bridge* (2013–14), while Christinna Hazzard examines an often overlooked feature of the North, the case of Danish colonialism and how it manifests in Nordic noir. Neijmann is concerned with place where she looks at one of the central characteristics of the genre, that is representations of the North in the works of Arnaldur Indriðason and Ann Cleeves.

Part III addresses the politics of Nordic noir, frequently described as the genre's distinguishing feature. Patrick Russell examines the neoliberal dangers to the welfare state described in Sjöwall and Wahlöö's series, while Andrew Nestingen investigates the political dimensions of the figure of the child in Nordic noir, and its connection to the image of 'quality' television. Mary Evans looks at Nordic noir through the prism of its treatment of ethics, morality and current trends in world politics.

Part IV, the volume's longest section, takes to task the genealogy of the genre, where Nordfjörd addresses the difficulties and trapfalls involved in the wholesale application of the term 'noir' to Nordic crime fiction, and Christopher James and Giti Chandra examine crime fiction's relationship to other genres, French Decadence and the epic. As mentioned above, Bergman and Muždeka address regional generic markers and developments in Sweden and Norway respectively.

This book was initially conceived in response to the lively, productive dialogue between crime fiction writers and researchers. Sigurðardóttir's Foreword, Staalesen's Coda, and Lorna Hill's interview with Val McDermid are timely interventions and ruminations from practitioners of the genre, which appropriately set the tone for the book and complete it.

Crime fiction

While there are significant differences in the trajectories that have made the novel the dominant literary form in so many countries and contexts in the nineteenth and twentieth century, the origins of the modern novel are deeply intertwined with crime fiction in many traditions, a connection that Chandra remarks upon in Chapter 13, while also relating the genre firmly to the classical form of the epic. The connection to the modern novel is most notable in the English language tradition, where the *Chronicles of Newgate* both shaped the development of narrative fiction and fed the press with content sensational enough to capture a wide readership for the nascent novel form. These often-faked memoirs of notorious criminals situate the fascination with crime and criminality at the heart of the development of the novel in English. It also marks a point of convergence between literature, reportage and the hidden influence of the ballad tradition. This genealogy is not specifically replicated in other language traditions, but such points of convergence recur. Schiller's 'philosophy of crime' and contribution to the true crime genre have attracted considerable critical attention.[3] The preoccupation with deception and intrigue in Laclos, Dostoyevsky's delving into the criminal mind and Strindberg's fascination with the occult, indicate that transgression and investigation, crime, mystery and punishment have been central to the evolution and vigour of the European novel from the eighteenth century onwards. The investigative framework in crime fiction roots it firmly in the picaresque and the 'network' novel.[4] At heart, however, all detective fiction has elements of a heroic quest, another strand which ties it to the epic. That quest is initiated in most cases by the commitment of the ultimate crime – murder – which ruptures the social fabric and requires a social remedy. Its object is truth, a resolution of the mystery, and justice, which ideally restores social equilibrium. That goal is frequently reached by circuitous routes and only partially realized. This trajectory partly aligns it with classical tragedy, not least when the execution of the perpetrator was the inevitable outcome of a successful murder investigation. Contemporary crime fiction in Europe operates in a different judicial and social context, however, and noir in the North is characterized by the interrogation of the social origins of violence, not its disavowal. Part III on politics and morality in this book provides ample evidence of this.

Traditionally, crime fiction has been decried by critics for its conservative tendencies and moral certitude. Roland Barthes' much-cited praise for Agatha Christie's *The Murder of Roger Ackroyd* (1926) predicates this compliment on the assumption that the crime genre is not usually, or indeed often capable, of such complex narrative manoeuvres. In the last decade, the burgeoning field of crime fiction criticism has challenged such assumptions, influenced by Tzvetan Todorov's structuralist analysis of the narratological characteristics of crime fiction. In part, this has also been fuelled by literary criticism's rejection of the modernist legacy which constructed an oppositional relationship between literature as art produced by singular genii and popular fiction as a mass produced commodity. Influenced by sociologists of culture such as Raymond Williams and Pierre Bourdieu, a rich field of literary criticism has begun to replace this opposition with an understanding of the dynamic relationship between all forms of culture along a continuum of cultural practices from fashion to abstract sculpture. Tanya Norman, for example, has argued that:

> despite the very different tone and style of [Agatha] Christie's oeuvre to what we traditionally consider as examples of modernism, her texts are haunted by many of the same anxieties that permeate the works of canonical modernist writers such as T.S. Eliot, Virginia Woolf, Joseph Conrad, and Rebecca West – including, but not limited to, technological and scientific innovation, the aestheticization of the everyday, psychology, urbanization, shifting global roles, and the First World War.[5]

This historical understanding of crime fiction – and high modernism – as different, but nonetheless related forms of the novel in the early twentieth century retains some elements of the old polarized approach: 'Unlike Woolf, Conrad, Eliot, or West, in the early Poirot texts, Christie alleviates these extratextual realities and provides escape'.[6] The consensus of this new wave of criticism, reading crime fiction on its own terms, increasingly emphasizes that the genre's particular strength is its ability to negotiate between the binary oppositions that structure the crime narrative. A recent reappraisal of the work of Agatha Christie states that 'Detective fiction is located in a field of binaries: structure versus innovation, stability versus mobility, the one final solution versus the many possibilities of the beginning. These binaries suggest that this genre ... is less settled than is commonly assumed'.[7] These reassessments of the complexity of detective fiction as a genre require a re-evaluation of the origin myth of Nordic noir in the politically engaged Swedish crime fiction of the 1960s and 1970s.

Maj Sjöwall and Per Wahlöö are usually considered to be the originators of a distinctively Scandinavian form of crime fiction that is rooted in Swedish politics and culture, and influenced by American hardboiled and noir. Reflecting on their contribution to the crime genre in 2009, Sjöwall was very clear about their objectives:

> We wanted to describe society from our left point of view. Per had written political books, but they'd only sold 300 copies. We realised that people read crime and through the stories we could show the reader that under the official image of welfare-state Sweden there was another layer of poverty, criminality and brutality. We wanted to show where Sweden was heading: towards a capitalistic, cold and inhuman society, where the rich got richer, the poor got poorer.[8]

What has tended to set the Nordic countries apart is indeed what Sjöwall terms the official image of the welfare state and the associated social conditions, or the so-called 'Scandinavian exceptionalism'. It is common to think of these countries as model societies, to refer to the incredible rise (and now fall) of the welfare state and the strides these countries have made in gender equality, which can be seen in Nordic noir's representation of women. Some, of course, are romanticized visions, a utopian hope for the rest of the world, and in the reception of Nordic noir one can also detect a certain pleasure in debunking this social optimism, where the works explore the dark side of the Nordic ideal.

This new social fiction was not created *ex nihilo*, however. Sweden had its own golden age of crime fiction, where authors such as Stieglitz Trenter and Maria Lang competed with popular translations of Simenon, Dürrenmatt and Christie. Lang, whose female detective Puck tackles much darker and psychologically complex familial and small-town secrets than Miss Marple, has been cast as the Swedish Agatha Christie, who publicly quarrelled with Sjöwall and Wahlöö's re-invention of the rules for detective fiction. However, her psychoanalytically informed stories are as much part of the evolution of the region's crime narrative tradition as Sjöwall and Wahlöö's prioritization of social critique. The disavowal of continuity between noir in the contemporary north and the popular fiction traditions of the twentieth century is so extreme that accounts of 'Nordic noir' frequently describe Sjöwall and Wahlöö as 'the beginning'.[9] Yet at the heart of the argument between Lang and Sjöwall and Wahlöö is the creative tension between the demands of genre and the impulse towards social and psychological inquiry that has influenced the global evolution of crime fiction since the genre established itself in the nineteenth century.

The recurrent argument in recent years that critics need to debunk assumptions about the crime genre's tendency to simplify complex social, ethical and narrative problems needs to be updated in a period when transmedia circulation of the many texts and varieties of noir in the North has become such an important part of the genre. Pearson and Singer, introducing a recent collection on crime fiction in a postcolonial and transnational framework, argue that the 'detective novel is generically, structurally, and historically suited for creating precisely the kind of dynamic interplay between the modern and postmodern, the material and the metaphysical, the investigation of truth and of investigation itself, that local understanding within a postcolonial and transnational world demands', arguing that, 'the detective novel's existence within generic and discursive borderlands – between literary and popular culture, between narrative and meta-narrative, between inquest and epistemic critique – highlights the need to perceive ideology even as we deduce criminal guilt, and especially when the crime is abetted or supported by institutions that traverse the internal complexity'.[10] This sense of crime fiction's capacity to not only stimulate social critique but undermine the hold of ideology itself is indicative of a new critical respect for the genre. No longer a historical and sociological symptom, neither is it a cure nor escape from social ills. This capacity for stimulating debate is the focus of Chapter 10, where Mary Evans maintains that what 'Nordic noir asks is perhaps one of the fundamental questions of the twenty-first century, that of how to define what individual competition is for and how that might build social solidarity'.

The positioning of crime noir fiction (whether Nordic, Mediterranean or Celtic) in opposition to old-fashioned, socially and formally conservative detective fiction is reductive and obscures both the continuity within the genre and its hybridity. Some of the distinctive elements of noir in the North derive from the modernization of elements from the gothic tradition. Others are indicative of the influence of the atmosphere and style of film noir, with bleak winter landscapes replicating its monochrome palette and bleak networks of corruption and violence replicating its moral spectrum. Anne Mari Waade has convincingly argued, however, that the traditions of Nordic melancholy are also evident in the colour scheme, visual style and scene composition of televisual Nordic noir, as well as in its content.[11]

Images of the North

The international reception of Nordic crime fiction in the last two decades has reflected and been influenced by histories of images of the North through the ages. Mysterious, remote, desolate and ghostlike landscapes, marked by absence and death have long since been associated with the North, along with, but in some ways contradictory to, images of prosperous, egalitarian societies. A particular visual aesthetics is one of the identifying markers of Nordic noir and is primarily identifiable by landscape and colour. The landscape is more often than not isolated, rural, bare, cold and characterized by blue, grey and white colours, much in the same vein as the cover image of this book. This is not a coincidence and has both historical and contemporary foundations. The weather, the colours of twilight, hint at something hidden, a mystery, even ghosts which Peter Davidson boldly claims are northern by nature, 'the revenant narrative is essentially of the north, and is a product of occluded weather and broodings upon the fate of the dead'.[12] One might say it lends itself particularly well to modern crime fiction, even though the colour palette has much older historical roots as Davidson describes: 'Scandinavia is much concerned with the colours of twilight, with the early winter dark, with the colours of the infinitely protracted summer evenings. [...] A crepuscular grey is the recurring colour of the painted rooms of eighteenth-century Sweden, of the autumnal landscapes of the Nils Kreuger and of the numinous twilight houses of Vilhelm Hammershøi'.[13] These colours and this particular type of light, the viewers of Nordic crime TV series are intimately familiar with.

From nineteenth-century paintings of twilight, to the 'Nordic' colours of Ikea, from the mid-twentieth century onwards, the Nordic countries have long since been associated with design and architecture; from great innovators in post-war design such as the Finnish architect Alvar Aalto (1898–1976) to the global spread of the Ikea brand in the last few decades. In discussing the image of New Nordic design which emerged from ca. 2005, Skou and Munch explain that it was, in part, a way to 'reassure an international audience that this is still Nordic Design'.[14] And they explain how its promotion is based on '"self-exotication" of Scandinavian Design' where the advertising emphasizes 'landscape and ancestors, challenging climate and modesty, handing down a tradition'.[15] As Letort points out in Chapter 3, US remakes and adaptations of Nordic television series have incorporated the characteristic Scandinavian colour palette firmly into their aesthetic.

The 'North' has long circulated as a cultural space to explore the edges of society and the challenging borders between the human and natural worlds, as is evident in Neijmann's interrogation of the North in Arnaldur Indriðason's and Ann Cleeve's works in Chapter 6. The identification between a region and a narrative genre like this has interesting twentieth-century precursors, such as the identification of Latin America with magical realism. Images of the North have developed primarily through the visitor's eye, and James Buzard describes how domestic travel took off in late eighteenth- and early nineteenth-century Britain, with the Highlands of Scotland attracting much real and imagined travel, when 'the barren, forbidding, and ominous character of the region [...] became part of the attraction'. This was part of a new aesthetic, a move away from the 'fertile, gentle landscapes' favoured by the Continental Grand Tourist to the 'mist, mountains, and waterfalls' to which the Ossianic pilgrims were drawn.[16] The British captivation with the Nordic countries in the nineteenth century drew on this new aesthetic and was influenced by the search for a rugged, simple life, such as sparked William Morris' fascination with Iceland. Although primarily a nineteenth-century phenomenon, this interest carried on well into the twentieth century. Peter Davidson has reflected on the many manifestations and representations of the North in literature and art and discusses for instance W. H. Auden's attraction to it. In tracing the various influences and origins of Auden's interest, Davidson counts crime fiction as one deciding factor:

> Thrillers and spy fiction were [...] crucial. The essential thriller text for Auden was John Buchan's *The Thirty-Nine Steps* with the revelatory northward journey of its mining engineer hero, its narratives of pursuit through lonely places and its disorienting sense of a society infiltrated by an enemy to the extent that nobody can be accepted to be what they seem.[17]

From the north of Britain to the remotest northern fringes of the Nordic countries, all has been fodder for the imagination, and crime fiction today continues to work with these imaginings as Davidson explains: 'Greenland is powerful as an idea, one of the most powerful ideas of north. Even to Scandinavians, it was the true *ultima Thule* – a perception that is powerfully evoked in *Miss Smilla's Feeling for Snow*, in which the half-Inuit Smilla's return to Greenland is a journey into an ultimate strangeness'.[18]

This fascination with a particular Northern aesthetic, which with time has crystallized into cliché, accentuates remoteness, isolation, tough, adverse conditions, snow and cold weather, and a picture of a people close to nature, rural, characterized by depressive tendencies, dourness and melancholia. These tropes have found their way into art, cinema and fiction repeatedly since the nineteenth century. As Neijmann explores in an essay on fiction by foreign writers set in Iceland, the clichés permeate contemporary writing as well:

> Fiction, it seems, does not change the image of Iceland in foreign literature, but rather incorporates it. Iceland in foreign fiction continues to serve as a mystical, natural or Northern, peripheral, wild Other to an urban, cultured, central self, 'the Other within,' thereby perpetuating, albeit self-consciously, literary conventions, discursive traditions, and images of Iceland at home – creating fictional Icelands.[19]

It is important to note that images of the North are not necessarily uniform across countries or global in nature. Certain areas or countries have adopted a particular history of reception of the North. There are also many contradictory notions of Nordic countries that crop up in the media and elsewhere, from the exulted status of liberal, egalitarian societies, and the inventors of the welfare state, to the dark, desolate and barbaric icy fringes of civilization. Arnaldur Indriðason's first translations into German – which marked the first forays of Icelandic crime writing onto the international stage, had a highly dated image of rural Iceland on their covers, even though the novels in question were for the most part urban tales of murders in the city. Gauti Kristmannsson explains that judging by the covers, Indriðason's novels were set in cosy nineteenth-century turf houses despite their late twentieth-century urban setting, employing stale clichés of the country in the German imaginary.[20] According to Sumarliði Ísleifsson, such stereotypical images of the North evoke the Utopian North or the Original North. Other stereotypes Ísleifsson recounts and still finds common in the twenty-first century are the Creative North, the Progressive North, the Unfeeling North, the Wealthy North and the Evil or Immoral North.[21] Nickerson in Chapter 4 finds these views echoed in the TV series *Lilyhammer* in the American characters' utopian vision of Norway as 'clean' and 'pure', and 'high ideals associated with the Olympics'.

One of the ways in which to frame these images and clichés is by employing the term *borealism*. Kristinn Schram makes use of it to describe 'the cultural practices involved in exoticizing the inhabitants of the North. Originating in the Latin, *borealis* (the North), it is an appropriation of Edward Said's term *Orientalism*'. In travel literature, fiction, art, design and many other types of discourse, one can see a tendency to place the Nordic countries apart, as separate, distant and different from the rest of Europe. These ideas of the Nordic countries also lump them together into one entity; topographically, politically and culturally. Schram elucidates: 'The image of one's ethnicity or regional background plays a significant role in the negotiation of power in transnational encounters. So making sense of images of the North in general [...] is in many ways a study of relations between the centres and margins of power'. As 'crossnational power relations reveal the fluctuating agency and appropriation that is the experience of people from the margins of regional power bases or the "fringes of the North"',[22] Hazzard's chapter in this volume on the colonial past is also an important intervention into the power relations *within* the Nordic countries themselves.

The self-exoticization mentioned by Munch and Skou can also be found in fiction. In his study of Scandinavian crime fiction, Jakob Stougaard-Nielsen maintains that: 'Scandinavian crime novels are ripe with "overdetermined" eccentric locations, which are constantly refracted through a wider world of crime and insecurity'.[23] The same contradictions can be seen in the reception of Nordic television series, where the rural and the desolate are often highlighted, while the most popular of these series, such as *Forbrydelsen* and *Broen/Bron* are set in some of the most densely populated areas of Scandinavia: Copenhagen and Malmö. Thus, images, ideas and clichés of the North colour the reception, but also a continuous and perhaps increasing self-exoticization of the North.

Transnational depictions can also lead to stereotypes and formulas, as when a country is represented deliberately for the global market. The Icelandic television series *Ófærð* (*Trapped*, 2015–), Kristín Loftsdóttir, Katla Kjartansdóttir and Katrín Anna Lund maintain 'draws from historically generated images of otherness, and the recent capitalization of these images in the tourism industry'.[24] They argue that:

> the visual representation of *Trapped* and its association of natives with a hostile, strange landscape not only takes place in the series itself but is further engaged with in foreign media discussion of the series. These discourses engaging with each other also become part of mediascapes already saturated by the tourism industry's emphasis on Iceland as an exotic destination with strange people and rough empty nature.[25]

Waade and Jensen, whom they quote, have made a similar point as regards the production values of Danish television series. They argue 'that the Nordic noir production values [...] arguably perceived as essentially Nordic and even at times essentially *Danish* – are actually a consequence of the increasingly international orientation and ambition of Denmark's public broadcaster DR to win international prizes in order to attract international funding'.[26]

Identifications between narrative forms and regions are almost always oversimplifications, but they also illuminate the preoccupations of the international global media marketplace, and how regional images are determined in a negotiation between national and regional identities, and transnational reception. As this volume amply demonstrates, the crime genre is at the centre of a global transmedia web, where translation, adaptation and distribution networks circulate texts, forms and products. In this context, authors and nations or regions become brands just as much as the publishers, platforms and media providers who circulate the series of novels and crime dramas. Hedling, Hansen and Waade have argued that writers of noir in the North are producing and interrogating a new European popular culture and European identity.[27] It is tempting to proclaim that in the world of Netflix and Amazon, popular culture is already global as mentioned above, but this ignores the residual presence of national and regional borders that inform the way these global providers organize their marketing and the ways in which their market is regulated. Postcolonial perspectives on the crime genre offer interesting insights into the multiple layers of how texts and identities are circulated, produced and consumed in this transnational context, which has important implications for the understanding of European noir:

> Transnational studies [...] shares with recent postcolonial theory a need to move beyond nationally circumscribed and center/periphery models of cultural and economic development toward models, and worldviews, that effectively comprehend not just liminal states, but liminal forms of statehood, and that articulate or legitimize multiple trajectories of belonging and identity.[28]

The preoccupation with liminal spaces in the texts this book explores is one of the characteristics which aligns noir in the North with gothic traditions. Sometimes these liminal spaces challenge not just the boundaries of realism, but of reality itself. In contrast to its social-realist origins, supernatural elements are widespread. This is particularly evident in crime narratives deriving from national traditions influenced by gothic fiction, for example in Icelandic writer Yrsa Sigurðardóttir's use of ghost-story elements and Ian Rankin's co-option of elements from the Scottish gothic tradition, but it is also evident in the Swedish TV series *Jordskott*'s (2015–) use of Swedish folklore and the Danish supernatural series *Heartless* (2014–). Intriguingly, *Jordskott* was broadcast on a horror channel in the US, while *Heartless* was specifically marketed there as being influenced by American gothic traditions. This would seem to indicate that the 'Nordic noir' brand is more restrictive in television than in fiction, where a thriving sub-genre at the intersection of crime and supernatural fiction has developed.

Settings and locations

Liminality remains a key feature of narratives which observe the boundaries of realism, however. In *Forbydelsen*, Sarah Lund spends the first series in a kind of suspended animation between Denmark and Sweden, to which she plans to move when she solves the crime. In *Bron/Broen* the crime scene is literally international, the victim(s) located exactly halfway across the bridge between Denmark and Sweden. The centrality of these countries to these narratives is not incidental. Sweden is central to the development of the Northern European crime fiction which became an international phenomenon, though Henning Mankell's publisher is clear that the publishing trail was opened up by the Danish writer Peter Hoeg's *Frøken Smillas fornemmelse for sne* (1992, *Miss Smilla's Feeling for Snow*, 1993),[29] another liminal narrative, situated between Greenland and Denmark, where postcolonial concerns are highly relevant as Hazzard discusses in Chapter 7. Danish television production was similarly central in opening up the international audience for the sub-genre that would be marketed as 'Nordic noir'. In both instances migration is equally, but differently, central. Sarah Lund's planned move to Sweden promises a move into a personal life which is more conventionally feminine, and with a more familiar nuclear family structure. Mankell's breakthrough novel in English and internationally was *Mördare utan ansikte* (1991, *Faceless Killers* 1997), which explores the impact of migration on Sweden. The extent to which these two narratives drove the international response to and characterization of 'Nordic noir' immediately raises the question of why this sub-genre became so influential in international popular culture. Mankell's exploration of the ripple effect of the Balkan conflict across Europe is barely mentioned in reviews and criticism, in comparison to his depiction of the impact of mass migration on Swedish culture and society. On the one hand, this is indicative of the impact of a large-scale Anglophone market and readership on the reception of this transnational genre, but also of the impact of that readership's preoccupation with how the question of migration itself is understood. The specificity of a crime narrative's response to local, national and regional conditions is frequently subsumed with ease into apparently 'universal' or 'global' issues.

In terms of location, the texts explored in this volume are frequently much closer to the golden age fiction of Christie and Lang than the mean streets of film noir, Hammett or Sjöwall and Wahlöö. This use of location is closely aligned with the European tradition, characterized by an intellectual and observant detective who interprets the mystery, in contrast to the American hardboiled detective who characteristically intervenes and whose actions are a catalyst towards the resolution of the plot and revelation of the perpetrator. It is this strong sense of place which James finds Nordic noir shares with novels of French Decadence and which he explores in Chapter 12. The advantage of rural settings, country houses and self-contained communities in creating a knowable community, a shortlist of suspects and challenging exercises in deduction are obvious. A distinctive characteristic of noir in the North is the blending of these characteristics with elements of urban noir made possible by smaller cities such as Edinburgh and Malmö and smaller nations like Iceland and Ireland, where the protagonists have a greater degree of proximity to each other, despite the apparent social gulf that can divide them. The usual understanding of the use of isolated locales or limited communities in classic crime fiction is that such fiction depends on the representation of a stable society which is shattered by murder, with the process of detection functioning to restore its original stability. Structurally, however, classic detective fiction depends on an event or ritual that brings together people from a wider world, who have a shared past, objective or hidden connection. Some of the key texts of golden age crime fiction are excellent examples of the way that the genre exploits the concatenation of significant events and self-contained communities and settings to create the ideal crime scene.[30]

Both Agatha Christie and Maria Lang were particularly fond of using holidays and festivities to bring together families, old friends or enemies, and to justify their detectives' proximity to the scene of the crime. (Seasonal settings also make excellent sense from a marketing point of view, a reminder of the influence of commercial considerations on the genre.) Much darker and wide-ranging forces have always functioned in the crime genre to bring suspects and victims together, however, which challenges the idea that these communities are initially stable. In Christie's *The Mysterious Affair at Styles* (1920), the First World War functions analogously to the Balkan conflict in *Faceless Killers*, moving characters around Europe as soldiers and refugees, impacting on small villages and farm life. It is notable that Christie found her detective among the refugees, not her perpetrator. While the rural settings of crime fiction frequently look idyllic, the investigation quickly establishes that this is misleading. Beneath the surface, the breach in security and stability has long been established. Murder does not create it, but reveals it.

The development of the modern novel is deeply intertwined with the development of modern nations. Shared languages, shared marketplaces, shared copyright laws all contributed to the development of canons of fiction which are still *de facto* organized for the purposes of publication and teaching within national boundaries. Translation, circulation and sheer power have always ensured that certain texts have transcended these boundaries. This is as true for *The Count of Monte Cristo* as it is for *Crime and Punishment*, but popular fictions have a different relationship to national cultures. Crime fiction developed very rapidly from the mid-nineteenth century onwards in response to transnational phenomena: industrialization, urbanization, migration and globalization. The primary canonical categories remain continental rather than national: American hardboiled, Golden Age and now Nordic noir. Race and/or migration, social borders and mobility are at the heart of the genre. In his introduction to Arthur Conan Doyle's *The Sign of Four*, Peter Ackroyd vibrantly describes how the narrative defines the trajectory that would lead to urban noir:

> the urban fog has become part of the mystery of the Holmes adventures; it represents the impenetrability of the city, its viscous materiality as well as its pallid obscurity ... The world can be read and interpreted; the veils of fog can be lifted ... It is a city of fitful illumination by gas and naphtha, where in the

flickering light faces pass by as if in a procession of lost souls. It is a world of strange citizens, quixotic or malformed, and of odd out-of-the-way places.[31]

The strangeness and impenetrability are, though Ackroyd does not mention it, revealed in the novel as products of the global web of trade, violence and exploitation which serve the imperial centre. The trail Holmes follows through the warren of London streets reaches back to the first Indian War of Independence and across the Indian Ocean to the Andaman Islands. The plot reveals a network of colonizer and colonized, displaced by wars, greed and persecution. In short, it reveals the presence, marginalization, agency and exploitation of migrants, with which much Nordic crime fiction is preoccupied, as Muždeka shows in Chapter 15. Crime narratives are preoccupied with the limits of any given society, the point where violence erupts and must be managed or expelled. Since the nineteenth century, it has recurrently identified those limits with the point at which newcomers become – or fail to become – one of us. The international fascination with Nordic narratives' exploration of such crises of rapid social change and increasing diversity is rooted in this primal function of crime fiction.

The foreignness of the setting creates a safe, even exotic distance for an international audience from the social and historical circumstances so painstakingly described, and leaves open the possibility of mythic resolution. Part of the appeal is that a distinctive feature of the Nordic societies under the microscope is their relative lack of diversity, particularly in the rural and small-town settings which predominate in Henning Mankell, Ann Cleeves, Jørn Lier Horst and others. In this respect, it is easy for metropolitan readers and audiences to initially position the locations as historically anterior to urbanization and migration, but noir in the North has a habit of undermining these assumptions. This is very striking in the way in which understanding the past is crucial to solving the crime in so many of these texts. Far from offering a glimpse of a simpler past, rural locations are frequently the scene of suppressed and traumatic personal and national memory. *Män som hatar kvinnor* (2005, *The Girl with the Dragon Tattoo*, 2008), where the country house hides both a history of fascism and incest, is an influential example, but this pattern is also evident in Yrsa Sigurðardóttir's representation of an isolated Icelandic farm as the location and motive for child murder in *Sér grefur gröf* (2006, *My Soul to Take*, 2009); in the rural commune in Season 3 of *Bron/Broen*, which is a scene of pervasive surveillance and threat as well as child abduction; in the nightmare rural landscape where the victim runs for her life at the beginning of *Forbrydelsen*. This pattern recurs in the home towns and places to which so many detectives return to confront their demons, including Sweden's Rebecca Martinson; Finland's Lauri Räiha; Scotland's Rhona MacLeod; Ireland's Frank Mackey.[32] Nestingen points out in Chapter 9 that the child in Nordic noir 'has come to be definitive of domestic space, serving to bring the complexity of family melodrama, and by extension "quality", into the texts of Nordic noir'.

Nestingen argues that one characteristic of Nordic crime fiction, is how the 'child sensitively handled, is a figure who draws on the regionally distinct cultural construction of the child, while also seeking to appeal to an ever-broadening audience readers and viewers by differentiating these texts from other forms of crime fiction'.

The past is never innocent in crime fiction. 'I like a good detective story,' comments Agatha Christie's Mr Treves. 'But, you know, they begin in the wrong place! They begin with the murder. But the murder is the end. The story begins long before that – years before sometimes – with all the causes and events that bring certain people to a certain place at a certain time on a certain day'. His comments get Mr Treves killed, they draw our attention to one of Christie's narrative arabesques in the novel, but they also illuminate the particular strength of detective fiction in dealing with cultural memory. The process of detection is necessarily retroactive, as Todorov's narratological analysis demonstrated. It brings the past back to life to explain the present. The peculiar temporality of noir in the North is very closely linked to this process. The scene of the crime is always after the fact. Even if the faceless killers come from the east or the victims from the south, the footprints in the snow always lead back to causes and events that began in the past, to forces that are neither new nor foreign to that place, to 'that class of the terrifying which leads back to something long known to us, once very familiar'.[33]

Genders, families and nations

If noir in the North is deeply concerned with social and geopolitical change, it is also an important transmitter of cultural memory and a site to interrogate social change, not least because of the continued explorations of the past. The influence of historical events and large-scale social movements is mediated in many of these narratives through the personal, and especially the family histories of the protagonists. The family is where the consequences of the past are most immediately and powerfully experienced. This is evident in hugely popular crime fiction, like Stieg Larsson's *The Girl with the Dragon Tattoo* trilogy and Jo Nesbø's *Rødstrupe* (2000, *The Redbreast*, 2006), where resolution of mysteries in the present demand simultaneous confrontation with hidden, shameful histories and traumatic family secrets. Arnaldur Indriðason's Erlendur is haunted by the family trauma of his brother's disappearance. Trauma, loss and violence are literally entwined in the DNA of the victims and perpetrators in *Mýrin* (2000, *Jar City*, 2004, later known as *Tainted Blood*), the first of the series to be translated into English. Tana French's *The Wych Elm* (2018) engages in an extended exploration of the tension between self-absorbed privilege, and love, loyalty and kinship, but it is the latter which provides the motive and alibi for murder. In Ann Cleeves' *Wildfire* (2016), the English family seduced by the idea of Shetland as a supportive community in tune with nature find themselves next door to an apparently successful but utterly dysfunctional local family. Once again in this novel, murder is motivated by love, as one sister seeks to protect another from abuse.

These investigations identify the home as the origin of violence rather than a refuge from it. If noir in the North is characteristically concerned with the rupture in the social fabric created by violence and its repair, it frequently situates these processes within the most basic social unit, the family. It is worth remembering that the origins of both noir fiction and film noir are inextricable from 'maternal melodrama'.[34] Both the singular hero and femme fatale in noir express anxieties about fixed gender identities which the post-war era sought so eagerly to restore after the extended integration of women into the workforce during the Second World War. The figure of the suffering mother, the lynchpin of maternal melodrama, is crucial in the first series of *Forbrydelsen,* which so influentially established the 'Nordic noir' brand. The conflict between mother and daughter, another staple of maternal melodrama, becomes increasingly central to Seasons 3 and 4 of *Bron/Broen,* where Saga's most challenging criminal adversary is her manipulative mother. The detectives in both these series are often referenced as indicative of Nordic noir's progressive gender politics, but each in their different ways are associated with a crisis in the maternal function. The constant pressure of negotiating between the demands of detection and motherhood has become almost as characteristic of detectives in noir in the North as alcoholism and broken marriages in more conventional TV detectives. Sarah Lund is in many respects the prototype, but the theme has been widely reproduced. The female detective has become a significant cultural channel for exploring society's ambivalence towards working mothers, but part of the reason these texts appeal to women readers is the seriousness with which this highly recognizable problem is addressed across the genre from the point of view of a woman who is committed to her profession, a subject matter which is also at the heart of the popular political series *Borgen* (2010–13). While American critics have commented rather wistfully on the maternity leave and parental employment rights enjoyed by women detectives in Nordic noir, there is a very strong transnational trend *within* it to critique persistent prejudices against working women. In the Finnish television series *Karppi* (*Deadwind,* 2018–20), the recently widowed Sofia Karppi is patronizingly advised by her boss to go home to her children. In both the Danish series *Dicte* (*Dicte: Crime Reporter,* 2013–16)[35] and the Icelandic *Pressa* (*Cover Story,* 2007–), the investigating journalists struggle to combine their parenting and professional roles in complex blended-family situations. Both of these series are unusually direct about the fact that motherhood increases the financial pressures on these women and that this impacts their career choices. In Aline Templeton's series of crime novels set on the Scottish coast, Detective Margery Fleming agonizes over her tendency to prioritize her job over her family. While her husband and son respect and support her, her daughter utterly rejects her mother and her values.

Intractable daughters are a recurrent feature for the genre's male detectives, from the runaway turned detective Linda Wallander, through Wisting's adversarial journalist daughter in Jørn Lier Horst's series of novels, to Detective Erlendur's addiction-troubled daughter, Eva Lind, in Arnaldur Indriðason's novels. Ian Rankin's Rebus in contrast enjoys a warm and reciprocal relationship with the daughter with whom he always fails to spend enough time, though his role as her protector leads him to serious errors of judgement. Implicit in these fraught father–daughter relationships is a crisis in the paternal role which is almost as pervasive as ambivalence regarding the maternal one. The collapse of paternal authority is embodied in Wallander, Erlendur and Wisting's errant daughters and the absence of Rebus's. Their role as fathers persists, however, although it must be recuperated through a surrender of control, mutual respect and small acts of care and kindness. Just as the female detectives provide an opportunity to explore the pressure of combining maternal nurture with professional strength, the male ones provide a critical space in popular culture for the exploration of the changing meaning of fatherhood and the cost of affiliation to older modes of masculine responsibility. The stereotype of the detective as failed family man persists, but the nature of the failure has become more complex.

As discussed above, the transnational reception of Nordic noir sometimes reveals a utopian vision of Nordic societies, not least of gender equality. As Muždeka points out in Chapter 15, the narratives of the immigrant woman muddy the waters considerably. She explains that Karin Fossum's *Den onde viljen* (2008, *Bad Intentions*, 2010) and *Elskede Poona* (2000, *The Indian Bride*, 2005) 'feature two women who left their home countries (Vietnam and India) to seek this better, Norwegian life', but instead find discrimination, racism, and violence and the immigrant woman's murder in the latter text is 'an example of gendered abuse in a supposedly multicultural, tolerant, and affluent society'. It is clear from Fossum's texts that gender equality is far from being a universal given in these countries, but is conditioned by race, ethnicity, citizenship and class.

Christopher Browning maintains that the Nordic model and 'particularly "Nordic" approaches to economic and international affairs, has been important in Nordic and national *identity* construction for the Nordic states'. He also explains that 'there has been the idea that Nordic practices represent a *model* that might be exported and copied by other societies. In both instances, Nordic identity and the Nordic model have been associated with being *different* from others [...] with the Nordic brand ultimately being about what it is to be a "good state"'. He posits, however, that:

> the exceptional aspects of Nordicity and the Nordic model are becoming increasingly less clear. In terms of ideas of Nordic peacefulness, bridge-building, internationalist solidarism and the economic model, two processes are apparent. First, some of the Nordic states are finding it difficult (or simply do not want) to continue to adhere to previous 'Nordic norms'.[36]

The re-negotiation of regional and national identities at the same time as familial structures and gender roles are changing, and static or declining monocultural populations are growing and becoming more ethnically diverse, is the context out of which noir in the North has emerged as a global transmedia phenomenon. The characteristic panning shots over serene landscapes which come to rest on discordant images of death and bloodshed in the television series associated with the Nordic noir brand suggest that this violence is an interruption, a blot on the landscape that can be erased by the forensic application of narrative exposition and resolution. This is part of the appeal to an international and especially Anglophone audience which characteristically overestimates the level of crime and violence on its doorstep. Yet, these narratives ultimately insist otherwise. The source of violence is close to home. The preoccupation with liminal spaces – bridges, coastlines, the edge of the forest or the town – is a preoccupation with the border zones where identities are redrawn. These are the scenes of the action. 'The story begins long before that', in apparently perfect families and stable nations, where things seem so much simpler, and where complex motives for murder have their origin.

Notes

1. Patrick Raynal, 'Le Roman noir et l'avenir de fiction', *Les Temps Modernes* 595 (1997), 88–99.
2. See Mareike Jenner, *Netflix and the Re-invention of Television* (London: Palgrave Macmillan, 2018).
3. See for example Gail Kathleen Hart, *Friedrich Schiller: Crime, Aesthetics, and the Poetics of Punishment* (Newark: University of Delaware Press, 2005).
4. Nancy Armstrong and Leonard Tennenhouse, 'The Network Novel and How It Unsettled Domestic Fiction', *A Companion to the English Novel*, eds Stephen Arata, et al. (Hoboken: John Wiley and Sons, 2015), 306–21.
5. Taryn Norman, 'Gothic Stagings: Surfaces and Subtexts in the Popular Modernism of Agatha Christie's Hercule Poirot Series', *Gothic Studies* 18, no. 1 (May 2016): 86.
6. Ibid., 88.
7. Alistair Rolls and Jesper Gulddal, 'Reappropriating Agatha Christie: An Introduction,' *CLUES: A Journal of Detection* 34, no. 1 (2016): 6–7.
8. Louise France, 'The Queen of Crime,' Interview with Maj Sjöwall in *The Guardian*, 22 November 2009. Available at: www.theguardian.com/books/2009/nov/22/crime-thriller-maj-sjowall-sweden (accessed 23 February 2020).
9. Barry Forshaw (2013), who entitles the first chapter of *Nordic Noir* 'Beginnings': Mark Tapper does the same at the national level in (2014) *Swedish Cops: From Sjöwall and Wahlöö to Stieg Larsson*.
10. Nels Pearson and Marc Singer, *Detective Fiction in a Postcolonial and Transnational World* (New York: Routledge, 2016), 12.
11. Anne Marit Wade, 'Melancholy in Nordic Noir: Characters, landscapes, light, and music,' *Critical Studies in Television* 12, no. 4 (2017): 380–94. doi:http://dx.doi.org.ucd.idm.oclc.org/10.1177/1749602017729629

12 Peter Davidson, *The Idea of North* (London: Reaktion Books, 2016), 156.
13 Ibid., 185.
14 Niels Peter Skou and Anders V. Munch, 'New Nordic and Scandinavian Retro: Reassessment of Values and Aesthetics in Contemporary Nordic Design', *Journal of Aesthetics & Culture* 8, no. 1 (2016): 32573. DOI: 10.3402/jac.v8.32573, 11.
15 Ibid., 10.
16 James Buzard, 'The Grand Tour and after (1660–1840)', in *The Cambridge Companion to Travel Writing*, eds Peter Hulme and Tim Youngs (Cambridge: Cambridge University Press, 2002), 37–52, 43.
17 Peter Davidson, 93–4.
18 Ibid., 172.
19 Daisy Neijmann, 'Foreign Fictions of Iceland', in *Iceland and Images of the North*, ed. Sumarliði Ísleifsson (Québec: Presses de l'Université du Québec and Reykjavík: Reykjavíkurakademían, 2011), 481–511.
20 Gauti Kristmannsson, 'Þjóðsagan um þýðingar: Er Erlendur innlendur eða erlendur?' A paper given at the Humanities Conference at the University of Iceland, 3 November 2011, and published on the website *Bandalag þýðenda og túlka*, 13 June 2012. http://thot.is/thot.is/v8f90.html?page=44&Article_ID=65. (accessed 19 February 2020).
21 Sumarliði Ísleifsson, 'Introduction: Imaginations of National Identity and the North', in *Iceland and Images of the North*, 3–22, 17–18.
22 Kristinn Schram, 'Banking on Borealism: Eating, Smelling, and Performing the North', in *Iceland and Images of the North*, 305–28, 310.
23 Jakob Stougaard-Nielsen, *Scandinavian Crime Fiction* (London: Bloomsbury, 2017), 114.
24 Kristín Loftsdóttir, Katla Kjartansdóttir and Katrín Anna Lund, 'Trapped in clichés: Masculinity, films, and tourism in Iceland', *Gender, Place & Culture* 24, no. 9 (2017): 1225–52, DOI:10.1080/0966369X.2017.1372383, 1237.
25 Ibid., 1238.
26 Anne Marit Waade and Pia Majbritt Jensen, 'Nordic Noir Production Values: *The Killing* and *The Bridge*', *Akademisk Kvarter* 7 (2013): 188–201, 197.
27 Olof Hedling, 'Notes on Nordic Noir as European Popular Culture', *Frames Cinema Journal* (2014), 201–14. Kim Toft Hansen and Anne Marit Waade, *Locating Nordic Noir: From Beck to the Bridge* (Basingstoke: Palgrave Macmillan, 2017).
28 Nels Pearson and Marc Singer, *Detective Fiction in a Postcolonial and Transnational World* (New York: Routledge, 2016), 9.
29 See Stephanie Craighill, 'Henning Mankell: European Translation and Success Factors', *Publishing Research Quarterly* 29 (2013): 201–10. https://doi.org/10.1007/s12109-013-9319-2.
30 Examples include Marjorie Allingham's 1931 *Look to the Lady*, where an annual ritual provides both opportunity to steal the Gyrth Chalice and an event which brings the protagonists together, and the return of alumni to a troubled and dangerous Shrewsbury college in Oxford in Dorothy Sayers' 1935 *Gaudy Night*. Sometimes the shared objective is simply a destination, for example, of the passengers on a ship in Ngaio Marsh's 1959 *Singing in the Shrouds* who become prey for a serial killer on a voyage to South Africa. The continued popularity of this format was evident when the British Library Crime Classic, J. Jefferson

Farjohn's 1937 *Mystery in White* which combines a railway journey, snow storm, Christmas and an isolated farmhouse became a seasonal bestseller again in the UK in 2017. Norwegian Anna Holt used a similar device in *1222* (2007).
31 Peter Ackroyd, introduction to *The Sign of Four*, by Arthur Conan Doyle (London: Penguin, 2001), viii.
32 In the novels of Asa Larson, the TV series *All the Sins*, the novels of Lin Anderson and the novels of Tana French, respectively.
33 Sigmund Freud, 'The "Uncanny"' [1919], in *The Complete Psychological Works*, Vol. XVII (London: Hogarth Press, 1955 & Edns.) [trans. Alix Strachey, in Freud, C.P., 1925, 4] 369–70.
34 For the origins of this term, see Linda Williams, '"Something Else besides a Mother": "Stella Dallas" and the Maternal Melodrama'. *Cinema Journal* 24, no. 1 (1984): 2–27. www.jstor.org/stable/1225306 (accessed 21 February 2020).
35 Based on Elsebeth Ekholm's novels.
36 Christopher S. Browning, 'Branding Nordicity: Models, Identity and the Decline of Exceptionalism', *Cooperation and Conflict: Journal of the Nordic International Studies Association* 42, no. 1 (2007): 27–51, 44.

Part I

GENDER AND TRANSNATIONAL DIMENSIONS

Chapter 2

THE WOMAN BETWEEN: A SOCIAL NETWORK ANALYSIS OF *THE FALL* AND *THE BRIDGE*

Gerardine Meaney, Derek Greene, Karen Wade and Maria Mulvany

This chapter focuses on the figure of the female detective in two collaborative, cross-country productions, Stella Gibson in *The Fall* (Acorn Productions for BBC 2 UK and RTE Ireland, 2013) and Saga Norén in *Bron/Broen* (*The Bridge*) (Sveriges Television Sweden and Danmarks Radio Denmark, 2011). Both series have distinctive noir characteristics and use crime narratives to explore societies on the edge, characterized by uncertain identities in the present and long, destructive shadows from the past. Both detectives embody an in-between space where anxieties about national and gender identities are investigated. There is a productive tension in the case of both these detectives between their status as outsiders to the social norms of those around them and the extent to which investigators are characteristically central to the social networks of detective fiction as well as focal points for audience identification. It is illuminating to explore that tension by mapping the social networks established at the outset of each series and identifying how Stella and Saga are positioned within them. Previous critical discussion of these series has focused on misogyny in *The Fall*'s representation of sexual violence, and the challenge to gender stereotypes from *Bron/Broen*'s female detective, Saga Norén, who combines analytic intellect and forensic levels of observation skills with an almost complete lack of emotion, empathy and social skills.[1] This chapter will seek to change the focus, exploring how Stella is connected to other women in the narrative and how Saga operates within a complex and supportive framework, using the techniques of social network analysis. Social network analysis offers a rich interpretative framework for analysis of how long-form crime drama works and, in particular, the ambiguities and tensions in Nordic and other forms of noir's engagement with gender and national identities, their intersections and borders. Through analysis of the exposition which maps out the social networks of *Bron/Broen* and *The Fall*, the extent to which crime narrative (re)produces the idea of society as a network of intimate connections and responsibilities becomes apparent.[2] This emphasis on exposition in the first few episodes is useful not just for practical purposes, such as creating readable visualizations, but also because it identifies the social world to which the viewer is introduced, and allows us to map these contemporary narratives on to the history of crime fiction in an illuminating way.

We have adopted a co-linear approach to the social network analysis of the opening episodes of both series. This approach quantifies the proximity between each named entity in the text, rather than their interactions. Named entities in these instances include all named individual characters, unnamed characters (e.g. the pathologist), collectives (e.g. ambulance staff, the Jennings kids), and some inanimate objects (e.g. cars whose drivers are not known, but whose presence may be significant to the plot). Previous attempts to map interactions between fictional characters have had mixed results.[3] For television drama, social network analysis based on identifying which characters are in shot together has real potential, but this has limitations in relation to crime drama where connections between named entities are often withheld for the purposes of suspense and only become apparent at the conclusion of the narrative when the mystery is solved. Contiguity, where apparently disconnected entities appear in consecutive shots or scenes, pushes the audience to make connections and engage with the puzzle. Consequently, we have used episode scripts to construct the social network analysis.[4]

In both of these series the connection between the main plot and sub-plots are important parts of the mystery. This narrative drive to uncover connections between apparently disconnected social contexts is central to the way in which long-form crime narrative imagines society as a web of connections, histories, and consequences. In this respect, it is very close to the traditions of nineteenth-century social realism and somewhat at odds with modernist fiction and its legacy in the twentieth century. This social realist impulse is evident if we focus on the inter-connectedness of the nodes or named entities, especially on *betweenness centrality*. Social network analysis measures the centrality of characters in a variety of ways, but a key indicator of the density of social connection within a text is *betweenness centrality*, a measure used to determine the extent to which each character plays a hub or gatekeeper role in the complete character network, connecting disparate groups of characters to one another.[5] In the highly networked social world of *Bleak House,* an example frequently cited in network analyses of fiction, there is 0.188 difference in betweenness among the top ten characters and 0.214 in the top twenty. In the alienated stream of consciousness, first person narrative, *A Portrait of the Artist as a Young Man*, there is a much greater difference (0.727) in betweenness among the top ten characters.

There are several different forms of social network analysis, but the priority for our research was the generation of a map of all the relationships between named entities in the texts. The entities are represented by nodes, with certain pairs of individuals connected to one another by relations called edges. Depending on the semantics of the network, these edges could represent friendships, co-locations or some other form of association between individuals (e.g. victim–perpetrator). In a weighted network, a numeric value is assigned to each edge, which typically represents the strength of association between two individuals. In this type of network, each node represents a distinct character in a given novel, while an edge between a pair of characters indicates that the pair co-occur at least once within the novel. The weight on an edge indicates the number of co-occurrences between a pair of characters. Using co-occurrences rather than direct conversation between a pair of characters allows us to capture associations as well as interactions between characters. For example, Stella Gibson, Paul Spector, the serial killer, and Sarah Kay, the victim, form a key triangular relationship at the centre of the network in *The Fall* episode 1, though Stella does not meet either. To identify co-occurrences, we applied a sliding window across the words in the text, which was manually annotated.[6] The size of the window (40 words) was determined algorithmically for each annotated script.[7] If a pair of characters appeared within the same window, an edge was created between those two characters in the character network for the chapter. If such an edge already existed, the weight on that edge increased incrementally with each instance of contiguity. The edge between Saga and Martin, her Danish counterpart, is represented in Figure 2.1 by a thick, heavily weighted line, for example, as they frequently co-occur, while that between Saga and Göran Söringer (who is only significant in the narrative when his wealth makes his widow a target for the Truth Terrorist) is represented in Figure 2.2 by a thin line as they are only once closely associated in the script for this episode, as he is transported by ambulance past her on the Öresund bridge. Once the scripts were processed in this way, a character network for each of the episodes was produced.

The opening episodes of the two series are crucial to understanding their social networks as they offer both narrative and social exposition. Figure 2.1, which illustrates the network in the first episode of *Bron/Broen*, has strong correlations with the social networks in the opening chapters of genre-defining examples of crime fiction, *The Sign of Four* and *The Mysterious Affair at Styles*. Saga and Martin occupy analogous positions to Holmes and Watson, connecting police and suspects and the main plot and sub-plots. As in *The Mysterious Affair at Styles*, the perpetrator will eventually be found to be part of one of the detectives' existing social network, but that information is very much withheld. The Truth Terrorist is no more than a voice and an implied agency in the first episode. In contrast, the two most influential nodes in episode 1 of *The Fall* are Stella Gibson, the detective, and Paul Spector, the serial killer. The heavily weighted connection between Stella, her junior female colleague, Danielle, and the victim, Sarah, are in marked contrast to Saga. Saga's networks are overwhelmingly professional and predominantly masculine. Apart from Martin, her strongest professional relationship is with her boss, Hans. The mentoring relationship which Stella establishes with Danielle, who is below her in the professional hierarchy and for whom she provides a role model in

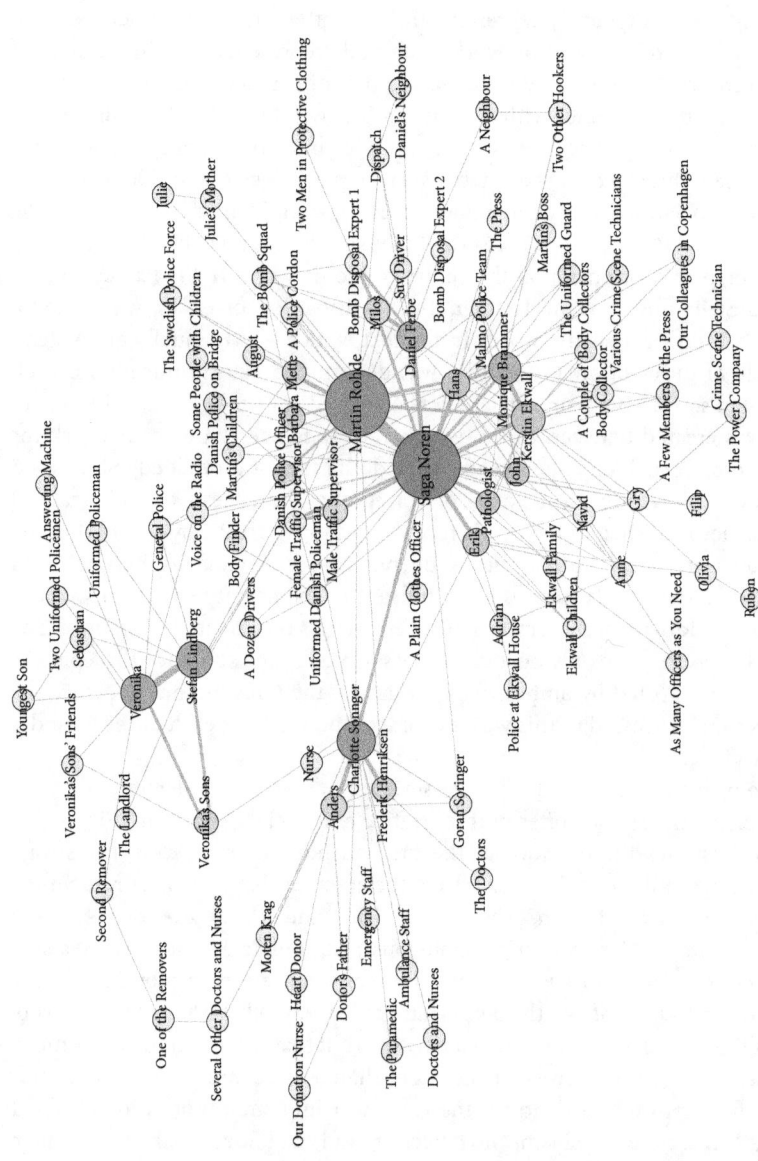

Figure 2.1 Social Network Map, S1E1, *Bron/Broen*.

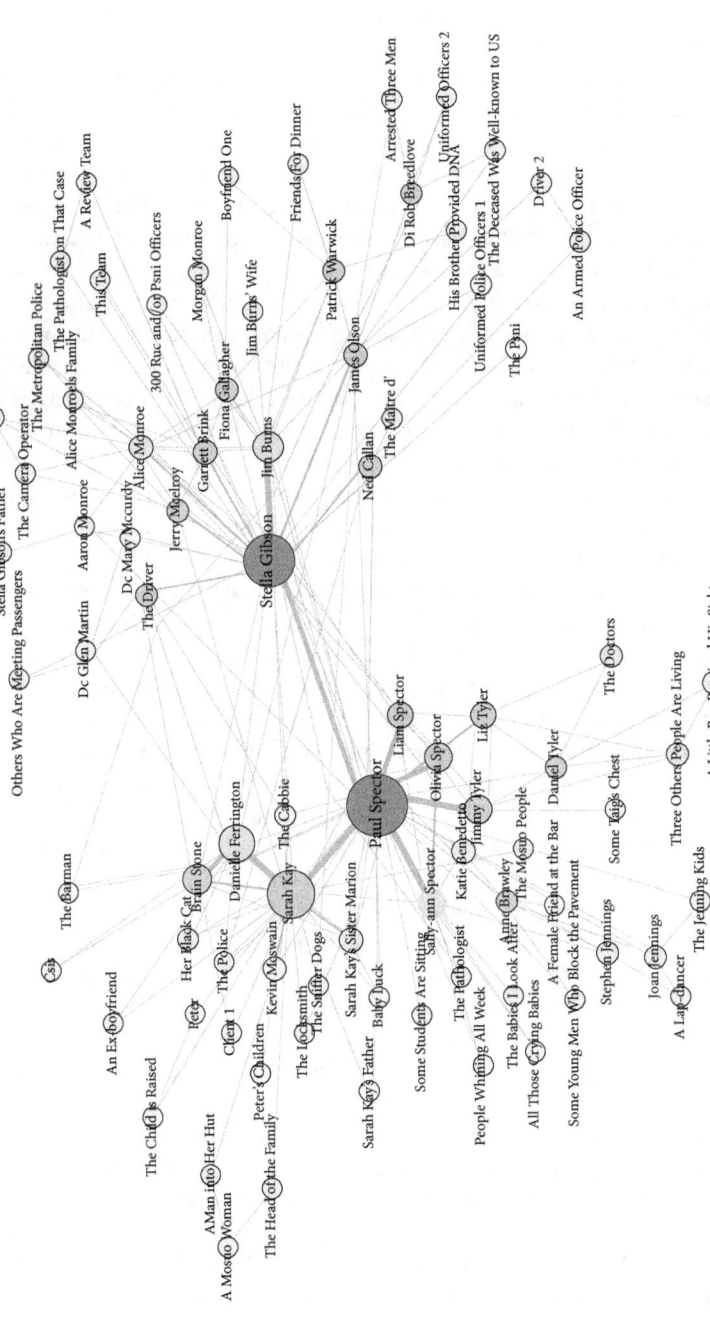

Figure 2.2 Social Network Map, S1E1, *The Fall*.

a very masculine environment, is stronger than that between Saga and her female colleagues. The women with whom Saga is most strongly connected are the victims, the powerful politician Kersten and the disregarded and marginal prostitute Monique, and Charlotte, later a target of the Truth Terrorist's extortion, who challenges Saga's authority at the crime scene on the bridge. Charlotte's imperiousness mirrors Saga's, but she also represents an extreme contrast to Saga's hyper-rationalism. Demanding that her husband's ambulance can cross the bridge and bullying a grief stricken father to allow his son's organs to be used for her husband's unsuccessful transplant, Charlotte is quickly established as equally passionate in love and hate, entirely motivated by emotion and quite amoral. Martin's positive response to Charlotte on the Öresund bridge is an important indicator of his character and sets up another opposition, between his and Saga's style of policing, and also establishes the possibility of his relationship with Charlotte later. The constellation of connections around Charlotte have a function later in the plot, but they also flesh out the ethical, social and sexual worlds of the protagonists.

In the visualization of the social network analysis of Chapter 1 of *The Sign of Four,* (Figure 2.3) Holmes and Watson are very obviously at the centre in their Baker Street rooms, connecting the plot and police. In this novel, the murderer, his very different world and their connections to the protagonists in Chapter 1 will be gradually revealed. Figure 2.4, which visualizes the networks in Chapter 1 of *The Mysterious Affair at Styles* illustrates the similarities and differences in the social and narrative worlds of Christie and Doyle and the origins of patterns which are repeated and revised in *Bron/Broen* and *The Fall*. In *The Mysterious Affair at Styles,* the relationship between Poirot and Hastings parallels that between Holmes and Watson, but it is enmeshed in a tangle of relationships between the detectives, the victim, and the potential suspects. Hastings connects and involves Poirot in the victim, Mrs Inglethorp's, relationships: this is very different to the clear lines between professional and personal initially established in *The Sign of Four.* In classic crime fiction, the ordinary human perspective supplied by sidekicks such as Watson and Hastings is comically inadequate to solving the fiction's central mysteries, but essential to mediate between the reader and the almost inhuman detachment of the great detective. In Peter Ackroyd's vivid introduction to Arthur Conan Doyle's *The Sign of Four,* he argues that the London evoked in the novel is 'a maze and a labyrinth, to which only the famous detective holds the thread'.[8] Social network analysis of the novel shows how the detective moves towards the perpetrator at the centre of the maze, as the connections between the apparently strange and alien murderer and his victim are exposed and the detective moves closer to his prey. *Bron/Broen* replicates this classic pattern as the Truth Terrorist is gradually revealed to have known his victims and chosen them for personal motives rather than as representatives of social 'problems', as he initially claims. Serial killer fictions can be understood to express both nostalgia for, and fear of, the social web that binds apparently disparate and disconnected individuals

2. *The Woman Between* 29

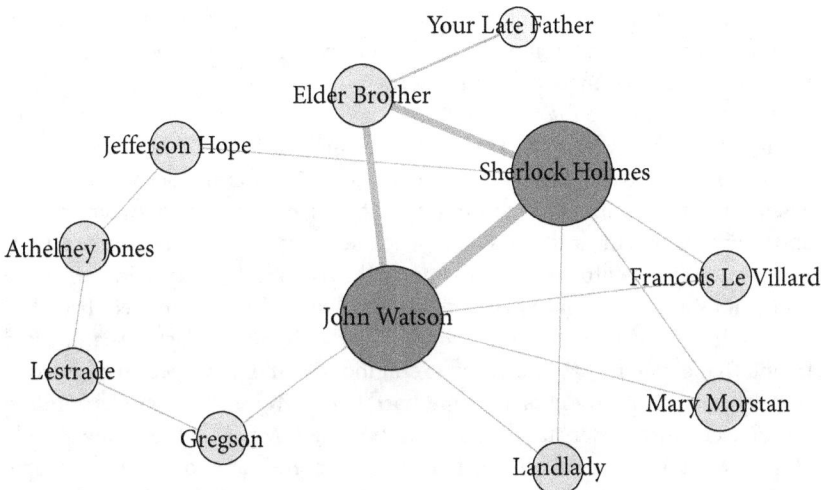

Figure 2.3 Social Network Map, Chapter 1, *The Sign of Four*.

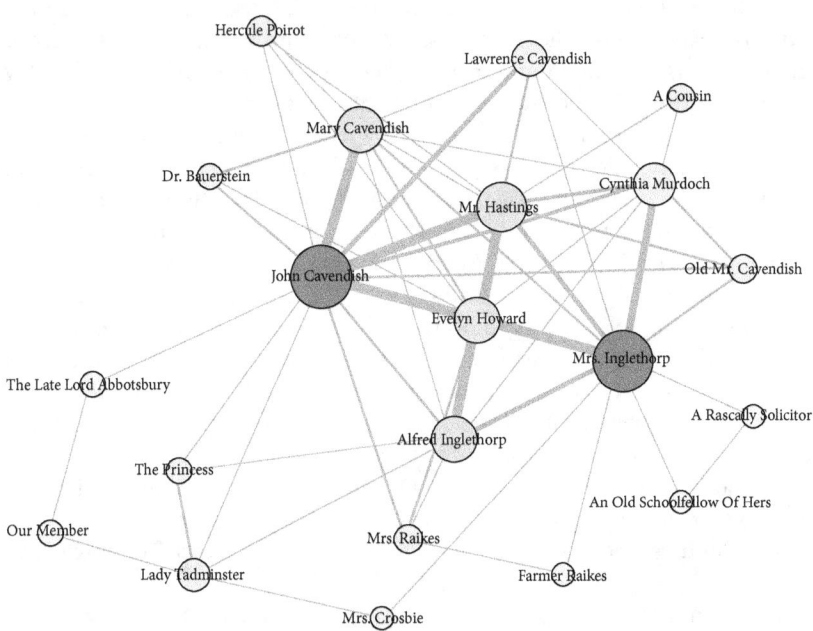

Figure 2.4 Social Network Map, Chapter 1, *The Mysterious Affair at Styles*.

into a single narrative, a single community. The focus of the detectives in both *Bron/Broen* and *The Fall* is initially on the connection between the victims, as an indicator of their connection to the murderer and a clue to his identity. In this respect, they continue the work of Sherlock Holmes, teasing out the threads of the intertwined narratives that connect the inhabitants of the urban labyrinth. The emphasis in Nordic noir on the social contexts of crime derives from and extends a genre-defining interest in exploring the connections between victims and criminals, and the intricate and inescapable complexities of social interaction. *Bron/Broen* will eventually perform one final twist on this, when it identifies the criminal as a former policeman and a once close, although betrayed, friend of Martin. In Agatha Christie's *The Mysterious Affair at Styles*, Hastings is shocked to find that a man he has known since childhood could be suspected of murder. At the heart of the traditional crime narrative, however, is an understanding that reflects the murder statistics. People are killed by people they know. While Hastings' childhood friend is not guilty, the murderers are none the less people with whom he has sat down to dinner and whom the victim regarded as her nearest and dearest.

Both Stella and Saga are usually understood as outsiders, but their crucial role in the narrative puts them at the centre of complex social networks. Both women are agents of law, order and meaning in border zones, between countries, cultures, moralities, and mores. Stella is a London-based detective, called in to solve a crime that has baffled the local force, but this cliché of the detective genre is complicated by the fact that this locality is Belfast, part of the UK's jurisdiction, but also external, on another island and part of a very different history. While Stella forges relationships with her PSNI (Police Service of Northern Ireland) colleagues, she is very much in charge of the investigation, however much her institutional status is undermined at times. While Martin is ostensibly Saga's partner and of equal weight in the networks, she is very much the leader. Asked who is in charge of the crime scene, she assumes control: 'The victim is Swedish, the car that dumped her came from Sweden, so it should be me'. Saga and Martin are cast in episode 1 as variations on Holmes and Watson respectively. The process that gradually undercuts our identification with Martin and re-centres our identification with Saga is barely hinted at in episode 1, where Saga is only marginally more central to the networks. The inter-territorial space which Saga and Martin occupy is more clearly defined than that negotiated by Stella. The action begins and ends on the bridge between southern Sweden and Denmark. Such a space, connecting and dividing territories, has some parallels with Stella's hunting ground in Belfast, which is understatedly presented as both Irish and British, each in complicated, alienated ways.

Social network analysis by its nature creates connections; nodes or characters that connect other nodes are called hubs or bridges. As a technique it is particularly good at identifying in-between spaces, such as the scarcity of connections between the three networks centred on Saga–Martin, Charlotte and Stefan–Veronica respectively, and the two closely linked triangles of Stella–Sarah–Paul and Stella–Danielle–Sarah. It is a crucial aspect of social networks in crime fiction that they include the dead as well as the living, and that the dead continue to connect the living. In this respect, contemporary crime drama has a considerable affinity with the traditions of gothic fiction, especially in its focus on liminal spaces. Emma Grey's reading of *Bron/Broen* as borderline gothic focuses on the use of liminality in the narrative:

> Liminality, as a key feature of Gothic texts, is characterised by narrative devices that cross thresholds and explore the notion of in/between spaces [...] the show explores liminality through the literal and allegorical bridges: the Öresund Bridge that gives the show its title and is the setting of much of the action; the relationship between protagonists Martin Rohde and Saga Norén, with Martin attempting to act as a bridge between the socially awkward Saga and the world; and finally through the show's villain, the Bridge Killer/Truth Terrorist/Jens Hansen who acts as a bridge between Martin Rohde and his estranged son, August.[9]

This sense that the narrative unfolds in a liminal, complex territory plays out differently in *The Fall*. Northern Ireland is a strangely indefinite territory: politically part of the UK, geographically part of the island of Ireland, with a scarcely visible, open border with the other Ireland in the south. These external borders are only vaguely alluded to in *The Fall*, but the traces of internal borders and barriers are quite visible. We follow Stella's gaze as she observes the colourful street murals from her car which cover a 'peace wall', which kept unionists and nationalists apart. The peace wall marks a history of violence, hidden beneath a cheerful veneer. 'This is Belfast' is the only explanation local senior officer, Jim Burns, gives Stella when she demurs when he tells her to get down to the firing range and pick up a gun. The liminality of *Bron/Broen*'s crime scenes and investigations creates a space to explore the borders where social responsibility, the nature of justice and the importance of truth are negotiated. *The Fall*, through its use of point-of-view shots, mirroring and crosscutting, makes it difficult to identify the dividing lines between hunter and hunted, violence and justice, society and its others.

There are many parallels drawn between Spector and Stella. Rapid cuts in the editing that are reflected in short scenes in the script create heavily weighted edges between them. They may not meet, but they are uncannily close in the narrative network (see Figure 2.5). The parallels between how these two predators look at the world is not captured by this network analysis, but they are apparent in plot and visual style. Both need to observe details, make connections, and anticipate. We see Spector looking at his next victim while Stella looks at photographs of his previous ones. His crimes turn his victims into a perverse network of the dead: as she investigates, she uncovers both the network and its meaning, 'misogyny – age-old male violence against women'.

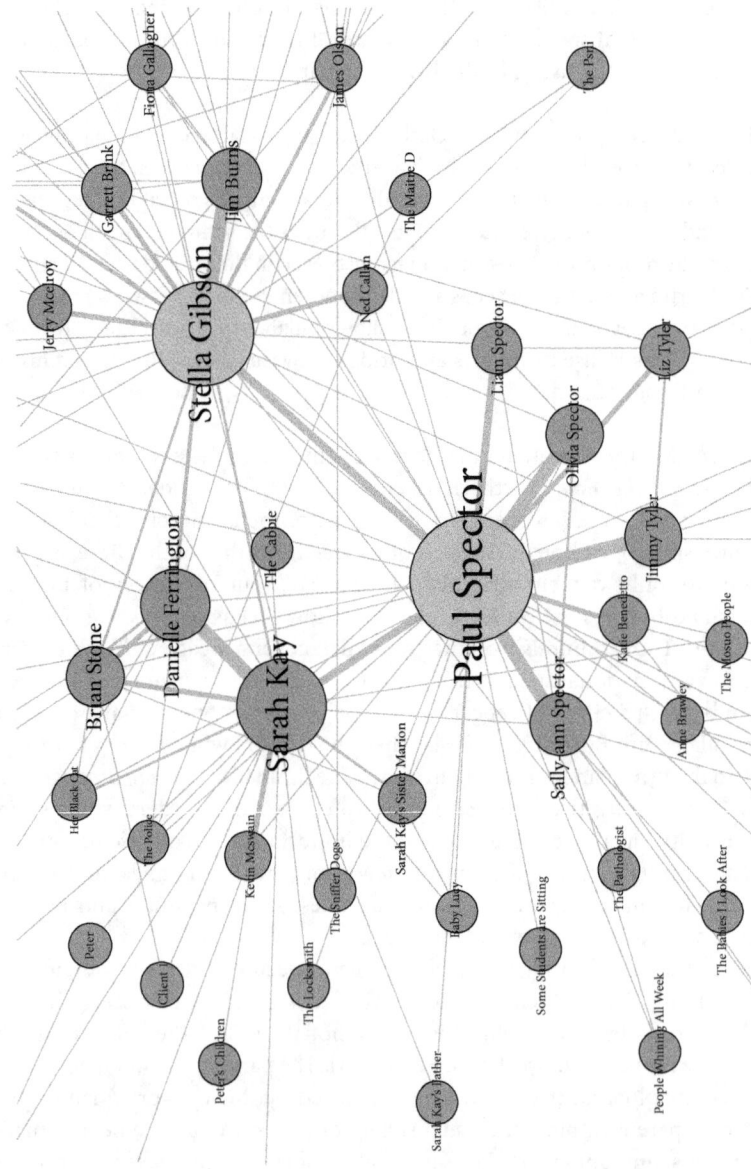

Figure 2.5 Stella and Spector dominate the social network in *The Fall*.

Given that it is a much longer narrative, *Bron/Broen* can afford a more complex and leisurely set up. Saga's strongest connection by far is with Martin, and it will be a very long time before his close connection to the killer is revealed. While Martin initially functions as partner and foil to Saga in the network, he is also a hub linking her to the murderer. Saga was always just one edge away from the Truth Terrorist. The grotesque physical fusion of Monique and Kersten's bodies both re-enacts and changes crime drama's exploitation of violence against women. The crime draws attention to the contrast between the resources and social value attached to their relative disappearances, a contrast which Saga is quick to classify as a police failing. The nature of the crime also of course creates a relationship between three women from very different social groups and creates a connective space in-between them. Initially, Kersten and Monique's bodies are inscribed with meaning by the Truth Terrorist. Saga, situated between the two women in the networks, as she is when the bodies come apart on the bridge (Figure 2.6), re-inscribes them in a different narrative (see Figures 2.6 and 2.7).

The preoccupation with liminality is repeated and reflected in both series in relation to gender. Both women detectives occupy and negotiate spaces outside of traditional gender roles. 'Links between corporeality, pathology, women, and the relationship of the individual to the state are apparent in depictions of the single, professional woman in contemporary "quality television" more generally', argues Alex Bevan.[10] Saga's lack of emotion, Stella's steely professionalism, and both characters' aggressive and unsentimental sexuality put them at odds with conventional femininity in ways which startle their male colleagues. Yet both operate within a highly structured, complex organization: the police force. In Stella's case, that force is both patriarchal and misogynistic, withholding information on the basis of masculine networks of power and privilege that corrupt its operations and apply egregious double standards to her one-night stand with a married man. To a large extent these female detectives are strangers within the states, societies, and communities which they serve. While Saga represents the Swedish police force in the criminal investigation, her colleagues are clear she does not represent Swedish normality. They react to the news that she is working with a Danish policeman with the question, 'Does he know she is a little odd?' In a much more direct way, Stella's sexuality is pathologized and challenged by the police hierarchy: 'the patriarchal institutions of Belfast law enforcement make her adulterous promiscuity the object of more scrutiny than the murder itself'.[11] In the opening episode, the visual style of *The Fall* establishes this focus on Stella's sexuality. Steenberg argues that, the opening sequence 'demonstrates how *The Fall* interconnects its fetishization of Stella Gibson (and her professional power) and Paul Spector, the only character whose viewpoint is shared by the camera in a handheld style that suggests the "killer cam" of the horror genre'.[12] Noting Stella's dismissal of Spector's violence as a refusal to 'accept many of the ways that the show frames Spector's crimes', Steenberg argues that 'the visual and narrative economy of the

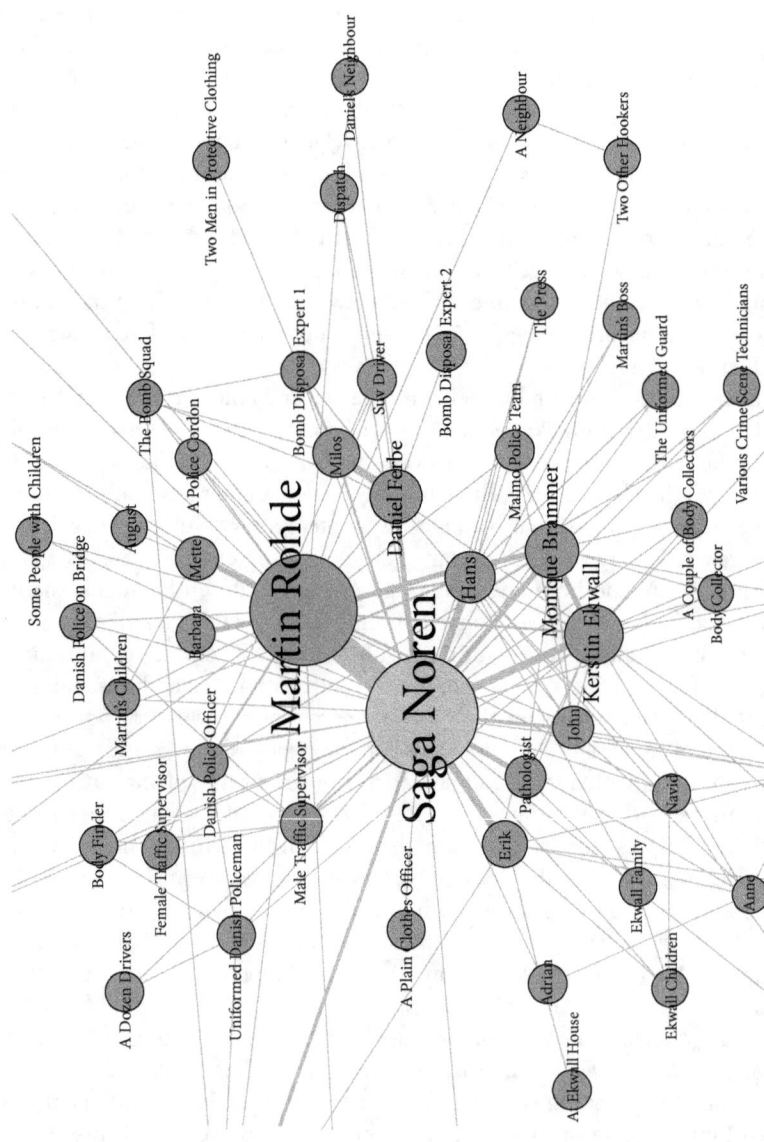

Figure 2.6 Saga's networks at the beginning of *Bron/Broen*.

Figure 2.7 Saga between the police and the victims on the Öresund Bridge, image © 2011 FILMLANCE INTERNATIONAL AB, NIMBUS FILM

television series, however, is at odds with Gibson's politics'.[13] Stella is dressed and shot as a femme fatale (see Figure 2.8). Yet social network analysis indicates that she has a heavily weighted, strong relationship with female colleagues, as well as the victims. In short, it illuminates the centrality of female solidarity to the narrative, a centrality at odds with the visual representation of the female characters. Saga in contrast, completely undermines the 'to-be-looked-at' status of her body by unselfconsciously taking her top off in the office, just as a male detective of crime drama would, in order to put on a clean shirt to interview a suspect. Paradoxically, the social network analysis indicates that this character who profoundly challenges stereotypes of femininity renounces female solidarity (we will later learn that she still mourns her long-dead sister and was rejected by her mother). Saga's most heavily weighted connections are to her male colleagues, though her connections to the victims, Kersten and Monique in episode 1, are similarly weighted to the link between Stella and Sarah. Saga's representation parodies social anxieties about women in authority: her conversation with Martin casually rejecting motherhood is associated with his discomfort after a vasectomy, in turn associated with emasculation in an earlier conversation. That authority, her dismissal of emotion and her personal history nonetheless isolate Saga from other women. The Saga-centred section of the network (see Figure 2.6) is almost exclusively professional and its living members are predominantly male. Yet, the full network represents an extensive set of transnational, cross-class, gender-balanced web of relationships, some

Figure 2.8 Stella and Spector, image courtesy of Fables and Artists Studio (an Endemol Shine company).

entirely unconscious or fortuitous. That full network is intelligible only by the decidedly neuro-divergent Saga and it survives because she, rather than the revenge-driven serial killer, ultimately gains control of the narrative. The network functions and coheres through its diversity.

One legacy of the emergence of film noir in the post-World War II period when gender, national and social identities were all undergoing re-negotiation is a generic predisposition to explore crises of representational borders. 'The post-9/11, "post"–Iraq War climate is characterized by a crisis of national representability,' argues Bevan, 'drone wars violate the integrity of national borders; war is declared on individuals rather than nations; perceived threats from the "outside" (terrorist attacks like 9/11) merge with those that come from within (the 2013 Boston Marathon bombings, the escalation of mass shootings in the United States), including violence that defies physicality and territory, like cyberterrorism'.[14] Social network analysis offers a fresh perspective on the noirish cultural negotiations within these texts and the chord which their female detectives seem to strike in the global social imaginary. The vast difference in trust in the state and justice between the two programmes is eventually very clear in the endings to the first series of each, where Saga re-instates the social order the Truth Terrorist had challenged, using limited legitimate force to wound both him and Martin and thus asserting the rule of law. She does not, however, prevent the terrible death by suffocation of Martin's son, August.

The serial killer may be captured, but he has achieved his revenge, leaving Martin desolate and grieving. Saga saves Martin's social role as a policeman, but cannot prevent his emotional agony. Nonetheless, as Bruce Robbins has influentially argued, when she shoots Martin to prevent him from taking his own revenge, *Bron/Broen* asserts the social basis of justice and a belief in the legitimacy of the legal framework.[15] In *The Fall*, the conclusion to series 1 offers the possibility of an end to Spector's killing spree, but no more than that. Stella is closing in, but Spector not only escapes justice, he holds on to his family. Some of this narrative inconclusiveness is determined by the practicalities of television commissioning. A consequence of making the murderer as central as the detective, as *The Fall* does, is that he cannot simply be captured and sent to trial at the end of series 1 if series 2 is to deploy the same stars and dynamic. The narrative setup precludes justice and narrative resolution. The long-term patterns in the plots of both series are evident in the social network structure set out in their first episodes. The ongoing hunt for Spector by Stella which drives all three series of *The Fall* indicates a primal struggle between the forces of atavistic misogyny and violence on the one hand, and reason and justice on the other, complicated by the role of violence and misogyny in the very structures which the crime genre usually relies on to provide reason and justice.

In a 2013 interview, crime writer Tana French stated that:

> I have this theory that crime writing is one of the places where the crucial issues of any nation's identity get explored. I think it's because crime writing is so high stakes – you're dealing with the worst thing that one human being can do to another, because it's almost always murder that you're dealing with in the crime novel. But also you deal with something that's very culturally specific, because the kind of murder you get is determined by the society in which it takes place.[16]

Through its focus on a crime which marks the breakdown of all legal constraints and communal norms, crime fiction is particularly adept at situating key questions about how societies, laws, institutions and individuals function and how they should function within a particular national and cultural moment. The social function of crime fiction has featured prominently in discussions of Nordic noir, with both Slavoj Žižek and Andrew Nestingen identifying it as symptomatic of a breakdown in trust in Scandinavian social democracy.[17] Bruce Robbins offers a more compelling diagnosis of the origins and global popularity of Nordic noir, one which is closer in sentiment to French and supported by the contrast between *Bron/Broen* and *The Fall*: 'The success of Nordic noir both domestically and for export contains an important component of Nordic progressivism. In order to see that progressivism, you have to look at the texts themselves, not just as symptoms of the Zeitgeist, but – if you will forgive the expression – as works of art, in strenuous dialogue with themselves.'[18] Robbins' challenge to criticism to engage fully with the moral, political and social complexity of these works is also a challenge to many assumptions about how realism operates in crime narrative. It is striking that French, as an influential crime writer, argues that the crime genre explores national identity and 'big themes' as well as capturing the culturally and historically specific context, as doing much more than *reflecting* social reality. Like Robbins, she sees it as interrogating and engaging with multiple realities, forcing us to re-appraise our assumptions about those realities and our responses to them. Crime narrative is an artistic practice engaged with society, not just a social and cultural symptom.

The application of social network analysis to *The Bridge* and *The Fall* illuminates that engagement and maps contemporary Nordic noir and noir-influenced crime drama on to the history of the genre. It also illuminates the extent to which crime fiction, which occupies a central role in contemporary popular culture, has a changing, complex, locally nuanced function in relation to the social imaginary. There are significant differences in the way in which international relationships are mapped in the border zones represented by the Öresund Bridge and Belfast. The high degree of betweenness centrality given to the villain from the start of *The Fall* and the invisibility of the avenging serial killer in the initial exposition of the social networks in *Bron/Broen* indicate a clear difference between the Nordic and the Anglo-Irish narratives. Both Saga and Stella are strangers, liminal figures but also guardians of the networks and flow around the post-territorial borders of states and social relationships. In *Bron/Broen*, Saga, as both a woman and a detective, functions to explore change, assert difference and to reassure the audience that, however strong the forces of violent disruption, someone is ultimately capable of holding the social plot together. In *The Fall*, despite Stella's heroic efforts, intellect and aura of feminine power, much darker forces dictate the plot. The possibility of meaningful resolution remains uncertain. Both *Bron/Broen* and *The Fall* offer the pleasures of suspense, of the hunt through the labyrinth to identify the murderer, but in their conclusions both resist, in very different ways, the resolution of conflict and the restoration of order which might allow their viewers to escape into the certainty or the fantasy that knowledge can impose order on social relations and guarantee safety.

Acknowledgements

Images from the Nation, Genre, Gender SNA Project by Gerardine Meaney, Derek Greene, Karen Wade, Maria Mulvany, Siobhan Grayson and Jennie Rothwell are licensed under a Creative Commons Attribution-NonCommercial 4.0 International License. The project was made possible by funding from the Irish Research Council and University College Dublin (UCD) Insight Centre for Data Analytics. For further information see www.nggprojectucd.ie.

Notes

1. Lindsay Steenberg, '*The Fall* and Television Noir', *Television & New Media* 18, no. 1 (2017): 58–75; Gunhild Agger, 'Nordic Noir – Location, Identity and Emotion', in *Emotions in Contemporary TV Series*, ed. A.N. Garcia (New York: Palgrave Macmillan, 2016); Isadora García Avis, 'Adapting Landscape and Place in Transcultural Remakes: The case of *Bron/Broen*, *The Bridge* and *The Tunnel*', *International Journal of TV Serial Narratives* 1, no. 2 (2015): 127–38.
2. This approach is an experimental one, a pilot on television drama deriving from a larger project, 'National, Genre, and Gender' (www.nggprojectucd.ie) which analysed the social networks of characters in Irish and English fiction across a wide range of genres from the early nineteenth to early twentieth centuries.
3. See, for example, Apoorv Agarwal, Augusto Corvalan, Jacob Jensen, Owen Rambow, 'Social Network Analysis of *Alice in Wonderland*', *Workshop on Computational Linguistics for Literature* (2012), 88–96; Mariona Coll Ardanuy, Caroline Sporleder, 'Clustering of Novels Represented as Social Networks', *LiLT* 12, no. 4, (2015); David K. Elson, Nicholas Dames and Kathleen R. McKeown, 'Extracting social networks from literary fiction' *Proceedings of the 48th Annual Meeting of the Association for Computational Linguistics* (2010), 138–47.
4. We are extremely grateful to Anders Landström at Filmlance and Niklas Ahlgren at SVT International who very kindly provided access to the script of the opening episode of *Bron/Broen* and to Patrick Irwin at Artists Studio who very kindly provided access to the script of the opening episode of *The Fall*, and who collectively facilitated work on this chapter and on the presentation on which it was based at the 'Noir in the North' conference in 2016.
5. The other forms of centrality measured by the 'National, Genre and Gender' project were: *degree centrality*, a count of the number of unique other characters with which a given character interacts, across the complete novel; *weighted degree centrality*, a count of the total number of interactions involving a given character, across the complete novel; *closeness centrality*, which measures the average 'social distance' from each character to every other character in the network for the complete novel; and *Eigenvector centrality*, a measure that considers a character to be important if they frequently interact with other important characters.
6. Testing has shown that the manual production of a character dictionary is much more accurate for this corpus than, for example, Stanford Named Entity Recognition software. The open source tool Gephi (Bastian et al., 2009) was used to produce network diagram visualizations, where the relative position of the nodes is determined using a standard force-directed layout algorithm.
7. The average window size in the 'Nation, Gender, Genre' corpus of novels is approximately 100 words.
8. Peter Ackroyd, introduction to *The Sign of Four*, by Arthur Conan Doyle (London: Penguin, 2001), p. viii.
9. Emma Grey, 'In/between Places: Connection and Isolation in *The Bridge*', *Aeternum: The Journal of Contemporary Gothic Studies* 1, no. 1 (June 2014).
10. Alex Bevan, 'The National Body, Women, and Mental Health in *Homeland*', *Cinema Journal* 54, no. 4 (Summer 2015): 145–51.
11. Ibid.

12 Lindsay Steenberg, 5.
13 Ibid., 6.
14 Alex Bevan, 'The National Body, Women, and Mental Health in *Homeland*,' 145.
15 Bruce Robbins, 'The Detective Is Suspended: Nordic noir and the Welfare State' *Post45*, 18 May 2015. Available at: http://post45.research.yale.edu/2015/05/the-detective-is-suspended-nordic-noir-and-the-welfare-state/ (accessed 17 December 2018).
16 Clare Coughlan, 'An Interview with Tana French', in *Down These Green Streets: Irish Crime Writing in the Twenty First Century*, ed. Declan Burke (Dublin: Liberties Press, 2013).
17 Slavoj Žižek, 'Parallax', *London Review of Books* 25, no. 22 (20 November 2003); Andrew Nestingen, *Crime and Fantasy in Scandinavia* (Seattle: University of Washington Press, 2008).
18 Bruce Robbins, 'The Detective is Suspended: Nordic noir and the Welfare State'.

Chapter 3

ADAPTING NORDIC NOIR: FROM *FORBRYDELSEN* TO *THE KILLING*

Delphine Letort

While film noir is originally associated with films made in 1940s America, signifying a trend of crime fiction that is characterized by noir aesthetics and archetypal characters (including the femme fatale, the private eye, the loser), the genre has influenced the visuals of murder on both cinema and television screens across many countries. The aesthetics of film noir convey, according to Jon Tuska, a 'darkling vision of the world, a view from the underside, born of fundamental disillusionment perhaps, but also invariably the result, no matter how timid, of a confrontation with nihilism'.[1] This philosophical interpretation of the genre arises from an analysis of the gloomy atmosphere that pervades the bleak cityscape of film noir and its narrative of loss, and emphasizes the powerlessness of characters confronted with forces that they cannot master. Jean-Pierre Esquenazi argues that film noir originally expressed an existential crisis linked to the experience of modernity, symbolized by the growth of cities into megalopolises and the frantic development of capitalism into a globalized economy.[2] Scholars have noted the influence of European immigrant directors in the development of Hollywood noir (Billy Wilder, Edgar Ulmer, Robert Siodmak, Jacques Tourneur, etc.), although many of them have adapted American hardboiled novels and scripts written by the likes of Raymond Chandler, James M. Cain, Cornell Woolrich and William Faulkner, among others.[3] The noir aesthetic therefore seems to result from an encounter between artists from different countries – writers delved into the dark corners of crime and plumbed the depths of the criminal soul in their books, which filmmakers fleeing Nazi Europe adapted for the screen through the lens of expressionism.[4]

The appeal of noir goes beyond borders, thriving on the human, economic, cultural and political exchanges between Europe and the United States.[5] Film noir provides a source of inspiration and creation that has given rise to nostalgic neo-noir in the United States and in Europe, and Nordic noir provides further illustration of its enduring influence. Nordic noir has both absorbed the conventions of American film noir and contributed to rejuvenating the genre by adding a Nordic touch, which is rooted in the Scandinavian literary tradition initiated by Maj Sjöwall and Per Wahlöö's ten-book series on Swedish detective Beck in the 1960s and 1970s. This fictional focus on social flaws characterized the Nordic appropriation: Sjöwall and Wahlöö interpreted individual flaws and criminal behaviour as resulting from the very specific political and social conditions created by the development of the welfare state, its strengths and its drawbacks. Andrew Nestingen observes that Scandinavian crime fiction typically uses the investigation to 'reveal histories and circumstances that make [the protagonists] question the apparent facts, and often come to regard them as shaped by economic and social forces'.[6] Nowadays, those forces include the consequences of globalization, xenophobic and anti-immigrant sentiment, a sense of social injustice, and the 'erosion of the welfare state infrastructure and the solidarity and egalitarianism ostensibly underpinning it'.[7] The development of Nordic noir seems to translate a sense of uncertainty, responding to the doubts and fears caused by the development of a neoliberal globalized economy that offers little protection to anyone.

In addition to this thematic shift which illustrates the legacy of Nordic noir literature, Pia Majbritt Jensen and Anne Marit Waade aptly observe that the Scandinavian genre displays 'a specific use of Nordic imagery and a feeling of melancholy [that] are created through landscapes, climate, architecture, colours, and light'.[8] The noir philosophy feeds into the construction of melancholy landscapes, which translate into drab colours and long wide shots of grey scenery in Nordic noir. Nordic filmmakers have brought in new features; Gunhild Agger remarks that 'the Scandinavian touch can be labelled contemporary crime fiction with a social conscience and a Nordic setting', in reference to the bleak urban and rural settings used as backdrops in crime stories with social relevance.[9] The grey, flat Nordic scenery reflects the sense of loneliness of the detectives that fight corruption at every social level – as exemplified by Kurt Wallander, played by Kenneth Branagh in a BBC-produced TV series (*Wallander*, BBC1, 2008–16), which itself is a remake of a Swedish series (*Wallander*, TV4, 2005–13).

The international success of Nordic noir has spawned new adaptations from abroad, especially in TV series. Glen Creeber argues that international remakes and adaptations of Scandinavian series have propagated Nordic noir features across European and US screens by helping to reinvent the narrative form of the miniseries: 'Nordic noir has been instrumental in shaping both its form and content, helping TV drama to adapt to the unique conditions of this new broadcasting age.'[10] A number of TV series in Europe (*Broadchurch, Le Tunnel*) and in the United States (*The Bridge, True Detective*) exhibit the appeal of Nordic noir TV series (*Forbrydelsen, Broen*) by adopting similar aesthetic features and plotlines. Not only do these TV series build on the visual legacy of Nordic noir, introducing landscape shots that replicate the colour tones seen in Scandinavia (most notably the grey cloudy skylines), but their narratives also include the same type of sinister and complex characters. Television executive

Christian Wikander (head of Sweden's SVT Drama department) accounts for this international success by explaining that 'viewers abroad are especially taken by the universal relevance of the narratives'.[11] Although Wikander believes that the local aspects of Nordic noir do not undermine the international appeal of a genre which tackles issues that have universal resonance, the US remake of *Forbrydelsen* seems to prove the contrary. Indeed, the TV series was adapted or 'remade' to fit US television rather than broadcast in its original form as in European countries. This adaptation process suggests the limited appeal of the Nordic brand in the United States.[12]

Considering the US remake of *Forbrydelsen* underlines significant shifts that indicate cultural and political nuances underlying the concept of noir on Danish and American screens, this chapter analyses the creative aspects and the limits of transnational adaptations through comparing the Danish TV series *Forbrydelsen* (Danmarks Radio, 2007–12) and its US version *The Killing* (AMC, 2011–14). This comparison allows us to observe the extent to which national cultural production contexts have some bearing on the showrunners' creative freedom and interpretive framework. The influence of the TV series produced by the Danish Broadcasting Corporation (DR) on US television goes beyond 'geographically relocated adaptations or reworkings' and reveals a set of cultural differences that impact the narrative constructions of the criminal cases investigated.[13] The cultural and social politics of gender differ from one country to another and shape plot dynamics by determining the characters' codes of behaviour. The comparison between the Danish and US versions points out a shift in female characterization: the woman investigator experiences more intensely the constraints of gender definitions in the US version.[14] The political underpinning of the narrative also betrays a distinct ideological context by redefining the detective's mission in a country where individual action is seen as key to collective progress.

The influence of Nordic noir on The Killing

The first season of the *The Killing* foregrounds intertextual references to *Forbrydelsen* as characters model their speech and behaviour on their Danish counterparts: Sarah Linden's (Mireille Enos) clothing style replicates Sarah Lund's (Sofie Gråbøl), most notably her thick sweater and jeans; her new colleague Stephen Holder (Joel Kinnaman) displays the same sense of deadpan humour as Jan Meyer (Søren Malling); and the Pacific Northwest region of the United States, the chosen location for the remake, creates a landscape that recalls the overcast setting of Copenhagen and its surrounding areas. A child's drawing of a wooded landscape provides a clue to an unsolved murder and crops up as a recurrent sign of Linden's failed investigation in *The Killing*; the drawing also serves as an intertextual link to the woods where Nanna is hunted down by her killer in the first season of *Forbrydelsen*. This drawing is a pictorial representation of Lund's subjective and intrigued gaze at the wooded horizon in the first minutes of the series, thereby inscribing the Danish setting and crime story (the *hypotext* in Gérard Genette's terminology) as a narrative matrix of the remake. The drawing generates plot when the case it refers to is re-opened in the third season, when a serial murderer is suspected of following the same killing pattern revealed in this unresolved case.

While the outside settings of *The Killing* depict a cloudy Seattle skyline that darkens the atmosphere of the series and recalls the greyish tones used to create the Nordic noir cityscape typical of Copenhagen in *Forbrydelsen*, most changes happen at a narrative level and affect the sense of rhythm in the US version. The Danish twenty-episode series is a slow procedural drama, consisting of sixty-minute episodes; it involves many red herrings and false leads that allow the detectives to uncover hidden or repressed motives below the surface of appearances. *Forbrydelsen* also includes many scenes that slow the narrative down, lingering on detective Lund's inquisitive gaze and highlighting the Birk Larsen family's efforts to cope with the demise of their daughter. Silence often prevails over speech in the Danish series as the camera dwells on Lund's enigmatic face, suggesting that her theories often prove intuitive rather than grounded in fact. The narrative of *Forbrydelsen* incorporates scenes of briefings and discussions that offer guidance through an elliptic narrative, compensating for the complex deduction process followed by the uncommunicative detective. The slow pace of the Danish series highlights the detective's strenuous efforts and makes her exceptional determination stand out by avoiding digging into her past and focusing on her professional engagements instead.

In counterpoint, the US thirteen-episode remake has forty-five-minute episodes, which has the effect of accelerating the pace of the series. *The Killing* comparatively and proportionally devotes more space to the emotional drama by restricting the number of plotlines, which enables the directors to dramatize the plight of Rosie Larsen's family. The investigation moves ahead more rapidly as the characters act without discussing their decisions. The ominous silence of *Forbrydelsen* disappears in musical sequences that help to accelerate the narrative's pace by dramatizing its emotional climate. *The Killing* does not linger on the same existential questions as *Forbrydelsen*; Lund ponders the actions of murderers who take advantage of their social position, whereas Linden's quest looks for individual patterns of criminal behaviour.

Mike Hales emphasizes the tonal differences between Danish restraint and American expressiveness, noting the greater reserve with which grief and anger are expressed in *Forbrydelsen*:

> The children who act out do so more politely; adults who scheme and fight do so with more compunction. Some of this may be national temperament and some of it, again, may be the exigencies of short-season character development. As the victim's mother, the Danish Pernille Larsen starts out

shell-shocked and gradually builds to anger while the American Mitch Larsen starts out in a rage and stays there.[15]

Emotions are portrayed with significant differences in the two series, responding to distinct cultural and televisual codes. A melodramatic tone prevails on US television, drawing on soap opera codes of acting, which favour the expression of overwrought feeling. These dramatic conventions particularly affect the characterization of the main protagonists: Sarah Lund in *Forbrydelsen* and Sarah Linden in *The Killing*. Lund remains a silent, mysterious character throughout the three seasons of *Forbrydelsen*, and she often seems to act on impulse, making decisions for which she gives no verbal explanation. Lund is distinguished by her unbending decision-making, which conveys her professional commitment to the values of justice, for she would rather sacrifice her personal well-being than abandon a case where the perpetrator might go unpunished. Her actions and life choices define her character as uncompromising: this is often framed by emphasizing her singular status in groups as she follows her own train of thoughts instead of participating in collective discussions.

The Killing relies more on melodrama as it delves into Linden's backstory as a woman whose childhood in care makes it hard for her to assume her role as a mother; her colleague Stephen Holder is a former drug addict who struggles with his life as a divorcee. The past seems to bear on the protagonists' present, which the drawing used in the first episode and mentioned above constantly recalls, as it signifies Linden's failed attempt at solving a case – the memory of which undermines her self-confidence. Linden's personal life interferes with her professional career, most notably when the criminal investigation becomes secondary to her search for her missing son (S1E11). Her private troubles frequently overshadow her professional life, distracting her from an investigation that she fails to conduct without feeling overwhelmed by personal worries. *The Killing* does not relinquish the soap dimension that characterizes many US TV series – including the use of long filmed conversations which are 'a serious matter on soaps' according to Louise Spence.[16] Spence adds that 'conversations seldom take place while the speaker is doing something else (washing dishes, watching television, knitting, shelling beans). They are shown in close-up, both literally and figuratively'.[17] *The Killing* introduces soap-opera elements by dwelling on tearful moments in Linden's everyday life, whereas Lund avoids gossip in *Forbrydelsen*; her reflective character undercuts the soap opera atmosphere.

Sarah Lund embodies the noir perspective on life, sacrificing her own career and family to pursue a sense of justice that turns her into a Philip Marlowe figure – 'a knight errant maintaining his code of honour in a deceitful and corrupt world'.[18] By the end of season 3, she shoots at point blank range the murderer who brags about the impunity granted him by his upper-class social status. The Danish series incorporates noir elements on narrative and visual levels, creating an environment that reflects Lund's enigmatic character. Lund is often seen as a backlit figure in dark settings, a lone detective fighting for justice and truth. Creeber observes that the symbiotic relationship between character and environment is symptomatic of Nordic noir:

> The dark and gloomy shots of Copenhagen reflect not just the sombre and desolate mood of its gruesome murder, but also the personality and disposition of its central detective. Indeed, Sarah Lund is a particularly mysterious figure who is given precious little backstory and remains consistently reserved and uncommunicative throughout.[19]

The long shots of the Copenhagen skyline and the night settings point out the isolated status of the detective in a world where every character hides deep secrets about themselves and others. Darkness enshrouds the woman in a web of mysteries, heightening the abstract determination behind her every move.

The US remake portrays Linden as a doubt-ridden character whose personal plight interferes with her investigation, and her psychological fragility is used against her by her detractors. Jonathan Bignell underlines that US television series' focus on dialogue and character tends to privilege performance, capturing 'the rhythm of psychological revelation through facial expression, gesture and movement that are characteristics of American actor training based on Actors Studio Methods'.[20] Close-ups of actress Mireille Enos' facial features highlight the depth of the emotions worrying her, whereas Sofie Gråbøl remains expressionless and displays little emotion whatever happens. This filmmaking strategy underlines the melodramatic intent of *The Killing*, which the Danish version eschews by foregrounding Lund's silent character. Her detachment conveys her strength of character as a detective who remains in control of her emotions in the face of danger. While Lund's insight allows her to disclose the shadowy underpinnings of the political world, Linden's perceived weaknesses seem to undermine her reasoning. She looks, and is trapped in her own dark world, thus bearing responsibility for misleading the investigation. Rather than reveal the extent of corruption around her, the investigation unveils Linden's own frailties – thereby downplaying the political and social analysis that underpins Nordic noir. While the rainy streets and grey skies of Seattle convey a touch of 'Nordic-ness', it seems that the gender values espoused by Danish society have not transferred to US screens.[21] Lund's strength of will counterpoints Linden's weaknesses; Lund's successes and failures point at the failings of the welfare state, whereas Linden's mis/handlings of an investigation appear as the results of a personal failing and/or achievement. Lund's cases relate to institutional powers (political figures in S1, the army in S2, the welfare state in S3), whereas Linden's are rooted in individual flaws.

Women investigators in the limelight

The main influence of Nordic noir concerns its innovative portrayal of women, who are not just to be looked at but assume an active narrative role. As a detective animated by a professional conscience and sense of moral justice, Lund takes action and guides every step of the investigation to uncover the truth. She is an example of 'Nordic feminism', maintaining distance between her private and professional life and refusing to let her love affairs or her family life interfere with the cases she is investigating.

Gerard Gilbert celebrated Lund, 'this penetrating, half-obsessed woman', as the television character of 2011, arguing that '[f]or just as *The Killing* has revolutionized what can be done with that most hackneyed of all genres, the whodunit, so Sarah Lund has redefined the female police detective – indeed female protagonists generally'.[22] Lund relinquishes the usual feminine props and social positions, among them a commitment to traditional domesticity and family, to commit herself to pursuing justice. Lund is not driven by her ambition to rise in the police ranks, but by an empathy for her victims whose murderers she will not let go, assuming a feminist sense of empowerment and control. It is striking to note that the murderers she deals with typically occupy positions of social power, which enables them to abuse their weaker victims. Lund stands for the powerless and aims to restore a sense of order by fighting moral and social corruption as embodied by a male sexual predator (S1 and S3) and an army officer in a mission abroad (S2).

Forbrydelsen enhances Lund's appeal by making her the dominant character of the series throughout its three seasons. Nordic noir challenges the conventions of the detective story which, according to Gabeba Baderoon, exploits gender roles to reinforce the masculine and the feminine:

> The detective story rehearses the division of masculine and feminine, and mind and body, by investing the woman's body as the sign of excess and disruption to the masculine unconscious. [...] The masculine protagonist enacts the power of looking, and controlling through seeing [...]. He seeks resolution in both its senses: as solution and as clear vision.[23]

The Nordic noir frame reverses gender roles by making Lund fulfil the formal and thematic role of the masculine. She enacts the power of looking in *Forbrydelsen*, which many subjective shots underline by capturing her observing stance, which is key to the decision-making process that helps to piece the narrative together (even though it also sometimes leads her astray). She offers an empowering model of womanhood by inviting the spectator to see through her eyes. The camera lingers on her intrigued gaze by standing by her in the woods in the first episode of season one, while a few musical notes are added to convey Lund's extraordinary intuition. The musical theme creates a link of complicity between the character and the viewers whose attention is aroused by its return at crucial moments in the narrative. Lund is never seen crying and her own personal life is secondary to her job; she walks out on a family gathering to resume her work (S3) and leaves her recently born grandson before she even has time to see him in person for instance (S3). Actress Sofie Gråbøl compared Lund's dedication to her mission to Harry Callahan's sense of professional duty in *Dirty Harry* (1971), a man who conflates his investigation with a personal quest.[24] Her character has exercised fascination and inspired her fans to adopt the same clothing style by wearing similar woolly Faroese jumpers, which returned to fashion in the months following the broadcasting of the series. Lund's casual clothing style bespeaks her complete lack of personal vanity; she is a woman who is not concerned by her looks as much as by her possibility to act.

The international success of *Forbrydelsen* may well be related to the singularity of its female protagonist, a woman who exhibits all the qualities deemed necessary for her to become a television heroine. Sue Turnbull explains that the long-term success of a TV series depends on the characters' potential to develop into attractive heroes:

> One of the key factors in the success of such series is clearly the 'attractiveness' of the hero, or indeed, the heroine. This does not necessarily equate with physical attractiveness, although that may well matter, but rather their 'appeal' as long running characters with whom the viewer becomes familiar.[25]

Lund's enigmatic character endows her with the power to shape her own life and craft a different type of crime narrative. When she relinquishes a life of peace and quiet in the company of her Swedish boyfriend (S1), she asserts an independence of spirit that allows her to pursue her own destiny. It opens up more narrative possibilities which the series can subsequently develop. Scandinavian television has created new models of womanhood and Patrick Kingsley argues that series such as *Broen* and *Forbrydelsen* star 'a strong woman in a position of authority – a reflection of Scandinavia's slightly more enlightened attitude to gender equality'.[26] The first season of *Forbrydelsen* begins with a sequence that illustrates the meaning of gender parity in Danish society: Lund's colleagues have set up a fake crime scene with an inflatable male doll to which they have added a plastic penis. The scene points to a sense of humour that overcomes gender boundaries, suggesting that Lund has managed to fit in with the male world of the police. While the Danish series presents Lund's professional commitment as a strength, enabling her to see beyond appearances and to sometimes challenge orders, the US version weakens Linden's charisma by making her share the main role with recurrent male characters. In *The Killing*, the inflatable female doll of the opening sequence (S1) is attired with a blonde wig and a cigarette dangling in her mouth, representing a caricature of Linden herself. In this case, the woman detective is the butt of a joke that undermines her authority.

While s TV series such as *Cagney and Lacey* (1982–88) and *Charlie's Angels* (1976–81) offered original portrayals of female detectives at a time when male investigators dominated the procedural genre on US television, new female character types have emerged in US television series that may illustrate the influence of Nordic noir. *Cagney and Lacey* depicted female friendship and solidarity in a police department for which they worked without compromising their family life; the series was nonetheless imbued with a soap opera atmosphere as the two women regularly discussed their personal situations at work. The Nordic woman represents a distinct model of womanhood, however, which may have spawned new character types on US screens – among them Carrie Mathison in *Homeland* (2011–16). Steenberg and Tasker compare the female investigator of *Homeland* with the hardboiled hero of film noir, arguing that she exhibits the 'ambiguity and irreverent toughness' that make her stand out as an outsider inside the CIA.[27] However, Carrie's unstable mental state casts persistent doubt over her ability to uncover the truth; she is repeatedly on the verge of losing her sanity when her theories collapse, shattering the sense of reality she has carefully constructed. Suffering from bipolar disorder which she attempts to control through anti-psychotic medication, she undergoes several relapses that demonstrate her fragility in the face of deception.[28] Even her liberated sexuality is portrayed as indicative of a pathological state, enclosing her in a conspiratorial narrative that limits her power of action.

Homeland and *The Killing* show that the psychopathological slant introduced to the remakes and in the avatars of Scandinavian TV limits the women's narrative role. Lund eschews personal intimacy at work, focusing all her attention on professional matters, which endows the series with increased critical power, whereas *The Killing* lingers on the melodramatic elements of the story and dilutes the political critique that prevails in *Forbrydelsen* by extending the Rosie Larsen investigation over two seasons. The US version presents Linden crying over her own inability to raise her son (S2E9) and her obsessive devotion to the case she has not solved causes her to be admitted to a psychiatric ward (S2E10). Linden continuously juggles looking after her son and solving her case, which the US series portrays as 'bad' mothering. Kim Akass contends that *The Killing* reveals a negativity that does not exist in the Danish version when dealing with women 'who choose self-fulfilment and/or a return to work after childbirth over domestication'.[29] *Forbrydelsen* questions the failure of the welfare system to protect young women who fall prey to sexual predators (S3), whereas *The Killing* points out that the plight of abandoned teenagers living on the streets of Seattle is due to their status as victims of dysfunctional families (S3). This shift of focus has significant political meaning.

Politics from Nordic noir to US noir

Three seasons of *Forbrydelsen* convey a complex portrait of Danish society. Lund's criminal investigations expose shady characters among the individuals who hold public office (S1) and reveal crimes and misdemeanours committed by Danish soldiers during a mission in Iraq (S2). The second season broaches issues of foreign relations by centring on small-scale terrorist attacks staged to accuse Muslim extremists of plotting against the army. Such allegations prompt questions about the Danish army's involvement in Iraq and Afghanistan; the series then entertains the possibility that far-right activists perpetrated the attacks. The third season questions the impact of globalization on the proliferation of crime, suggesting that the nation is endangered from outside. Globalization has encouraged the free circulation of goods: traveling from one port and one country to another, container ships symbolize a growing global market that nations fail to control. The privatization of maritime transport services has permitted new forms of criminality to flourish by making it more difficult to control routes, crews and cargo. The investigation of the abduction of a girl whom the kidnapper claims to have hidden inside a traveling container allows Lund to retrace the labyrinthine routes of international commerce (S3). The criminal investigations of *Forbrydelsen* reveal structural problems rather than individual flaws, portraying a society that grapples with issues of immigration, racism, terrorism and globalization (S1). The detective's errors are in bringing to light the extent of corruption across every layer of society. Girls are often the main victims of a system that exposes them to danger instead of protecting them; the family breeds its own dangers (S1) whereas the welfare system cannot compensate for failing parenthood (S3).

From the second to the fourth seasons onwards, *The Killing* departs from *Forbrydelsen* on thematic and narrative levels.[30] The investigation of Rosie Larsen's murder does not end with season 1 in the US version, which enables the producers to eschew the subject of crimes and culpabilities during the Iraq War. *Forbrydelsen* addresses the notion of war crimes by exposing the inner workings of the military in season 2; the fact that the name of the murderer is kept secret until the last episode permits the detective to avoid personalizing the case. Rather than focus attention on a few rotten apples, Lund discovers political manoeuvring behind a military operation that led to the killing of civilians. Season 2 levels criticism at the politicians' complicity with the military in a hidden case of military abuse. *The Killing* downplays the political content by drawing on the pleasures of melodrama, including the moral conflicts between good and bad that characterize the genre, which usually involves stories resolved through individualized solutions rather than collective measures. The ambiguity that prevails in *Forbrydelsen* gives way to a clear delineation between moral positions, and opposes the good and the bad in the US version. For example, *Forbrydelsen* points out the difficulty of integrating Muslims into a society that views them with suspicion: season 1 shows the racist implications of an accusation levelled against an Arab professor whose religion both raises and questions prejudice against the Muslim community. Rama may be innocent of the crime he is suspected of; however, his secret intervention to save a girl from a forced marriage reinforces the idea that some Muslims fail to conform to Danish standards. *The Killing* downplays the political critique by framing Bennet Ahmet's sexual behaviour as suspect; he is a Somalian professor who married a former student of his. Ahmet's sexual attraction to a former student weakens the racist argument and casts doubts on his morality as a professor who has crossed a moral line, whereas the introduction of Somali customs, and more precisely a case of circumcision, further designates him as the Other. While Rama is portrayed as a model of integration in *Forbrydelsen*, Ahmet becomes a signifier of the exclusion of his ethnic community – and so does the attack on the mosque which he attends. Season 2 of *The Killing* also portrays the indigenous US community as the Other by making the Wapi Eagle reservation casino the place where the murder happened and by characterizing the Native American chief Nicole Jackson as a corrupt authoritarian female figure.

While the Danish TV series appropriates the detective story to question crimes that have resulted from the structural inequalities of neoliberalism, the US version turns social and political issues into personal ones. The female character embodies this shift of perspective: Lund accomplishes her mission as a civil servant, whereas Linden constantly interweaves the personal and the professional. Bruce Robbins extols the qualities of Lund as a detective whose professional commitment is best understood in terms of politics rather than gender, noting that her lack of socialization reflects a national trait in a country where collective interest prevails over personal satisfaction. He contends that Lund's behaviour reflects a welfare-state mentality, privileging the common good over individual interests and gains:

> All these women [i.e. female detectives in Nordic noir series] manifest some failure of socialization. This failure can be read as the mark of a loss or lack. But it makes more sense if seen as a voluntary sacrifice, a sacrifice of personal life, even of personality or personhood, in the interest of the public welfare. This may not seem plausible in the US, where the god on whose altar the woman's sacrifice is made is more often seen as work, which is to say money-making or career. Since the dimension of publicness is missing or muted, the woman's choice can look like the very reverse of sacrifice: pure self-interest. In Scandinavia, however, it seems important that whatever doubts may be expressed about the high cost of this sacrifice, the higher good itself is never thrown into question. In that sense what audiences are identifying with is in fact the legitimacy of the state as the proper recipient of personal sacrifice, the site where you can see the results of your work in the lives of other people and where work therefore becomes something that it might not otherwise be: worth doing. They are working for the common good.[31]

Lund remains focused on the cases that she investigates and her social life revolves around the police station she belongs to. Her concern with right and wrong gives meaning to a life which she dedicates to solving crimes instead of raising a family. Close-ups repeatedly focus on her silent face and show her resolve to not abandon a case that remains unsolved when she orders the flight bound for Sweden to stop during take-off (S1E5). This scene exposes her determination, a character trait that Linden does not display. In the US version, a phone call informing her of forged evidence urges the detective to disembark from the plane that was to take her to San Diego. This narrative change affects the television show's gender discourse by creating a causal link between her decision to act and an external event. While Lund is empowered by a decision-process she assumes on her own, Linden's behaviour is determined by outside forces. As illustrated by this example, the characters' actions are not motivated by the same reasons or situations. Lund intervenes in the public sphere by searching into the private life of political figures, whereas Linden reveals domestic and personal issues that are not directly related to the political.

The atmosphere of *The Killing*'s third season darkens as Linden walks out on her boyfriend after reopening the file of the unsolved case, relinquishing the peaceful life that she had achieved. The season questions the critical shortage of welfare services for the youth in a city like Seattle by showing the fate of runaway teenagers who prostitute themselves to survive. The girls are easy prey for a serial killer who happens to be the police chief with whom Linden has an affair. This personal story once again overshadows the political critique that *Forbrydelsen* articulates throughout each season. While Lund kills a paedophile before he can fly away because his privileged position as a man of power enables him to circumvent accusations, Linden kills her superior out of personal anger for a man who has deceived her, and she even manages to gain absolution from her superiors once the truth has come to light. One woman marginalizes herself by aiming for restorative justice, whereas the other turns into a hero and her audacity is celebrated as an individual's power to bring justice. Lund is the ultimate loser in *Forbrydelsen*, for there is no place for individual risk-taking in the context of a society where the detective should first and foremost follow her hierarchy's orders. Although her choice to disappear and escape the law brings an end to the Danish series, it is also a sign of her radical feminist engagement with advocating for the oppressed.

Conclusion

Comparing *Forbrydelsen* and *The Killing* points out cultural and sociological differences between the two countries, showing that adaptation goes beyond the visual to signify political shifts. The change of setting and characters undergirds a different set of values, which the narrative explores as it unfolds. The social issues that take prominence in the Danish series are discarded by the personal concerns that testify to the soap opera's enduring influence on US television series. External conflicts become internal to the characters when adapted to US screens, portraying individuals haunted by traumatic memories of the past, whereas danger testifies to structural defects in the Nordic series – including the failings of the welfare state (S2) and the crimes committed within the military (S3). The comparative approach also highlights gender differences; the female protagonists exhibit distinct character traits that impact the unfolding of the narrative. Lund does not distinguish her personal from her professional commitments; her dedication to work is born from her sense of ethics and nourished by it. The US series portrays a woman whose complex family life often interferes in a negative way with her professional judgement. Narrative choices testify to the varying social and political values embodied by the characters themselves. Lund is empowered by welfare state ideals which dictate her personal devotion to cases where the victims are the powerless, whereas Linden's authority is repeatedly undermined by her maternal duties or sentimental affairs. *The Killing* does not sexualize its main female character, whose masculine dress code de-eroticizes the female body; however, she is not empowered by her rejection of a post-feminist ethos that demands women 'embrace professional competitiveness while prioritizing domestic life, exhibit sexual independence while foregrounding the search for heterosexual romance, and embrace consumerism while remaining loyal to non-market values'.[32] The image of femininity conveyed by Linden resonates with her personal and professional failures, confining her to the margins of society as a role model not to follow.

Notes

1. Jon Tuska, *Dark Cinema: American Film Noir in Cultural Perspective* (Westport: Greenwood Press, 1984), xvi.
2. Jean-Pierre Esquenazi, *Le Film noir: Histoire et significations d'un genre populaire subversif* (Paris: CNRS, 2012).
3. See for example Vincent Brooks, *Driven to Darkness: Jewish Emigré Directors and the Rise of Film Noir* (New Brunswick: Rutgers University Press, 2009); Mark T. Connard (ed.), *The Philosophy of Film Noir* (Lexington: University Press of Kentucky, 2006).
4. Thomas Pillard, 'Une histoire oubliée: la genèse française du terme "film noir" dans les années 1930 et ses implications transnationales', *Transatlantica, revue d'études américaines*, Vol. 1, 2012. Available online: https://journals.openedition.org/transatlantica/5742 (accessed 7 September 2018).
5. Delphine Letort (ed.) *Panorama mondial du film noir, CinémAction n° 151*, (Condé sur Noireau: Charles Corlet, 2014).
6. Andrew Nestingen, 'Scandinavian Crime Fiction and the Facts: Social Criticism, Epistemology, and Globalization', in *Globalization and the State in Contemporary Crime Fiction: A World of Crime*, eds. Andrew Pepper and David Schmid (London: Palgrave Macmillan, 2016), 160.
7. Ibid., 170.
8. Pia Majbritt Jensen and Anne Marit Waade, 'Nordic Noir Challenging the "Language of Advantage": Setting, Light and Language as Production Values in Danish Television Series', *Journal of Popular Television* 1, no. 2: 262.
9. Gunhild Agger, 'Approaches to Scandinavian Crime Fiction', *Crime Fiction and Crime Journalism in Scandinavia*, Working Paper no.15, 2010, 2.
10. Glen Creeber, 'Killing us Softly: Investigating the Aesthetics, Philosophy and Influence of Nordic noir Television', *The Journal of Popular Television* 3, no. 1 (2015): 32.

11 Ib Keld Jensen, 'The Nordic Welfare Model makes Good TV', *Nordvision Annual Report*, 2012–13, 24.
12 Gunhild Agger explains that the label 'Nordic noir' was coined by the Scandinavian Department at University College London in 2010, thereby emphasizing cross-Nordic characteristics that can be exported. Gunhild Agger, 'Nordic Noir: Location, Identity and Emotion', in *Emotions in Contemporary TV Series*, ed. Alberto N. Garcφa, (Basingstoke: Palgrave McMillan, 2016), 138.
13 Olof Hedling, 'Notes on Nordic Noir as European Popular Culture', *Frames Cinema Journal*, available online: http://framescinemajournal.com/article/notes-on-nordic-noir-as-european-popular-culture/ (accessed 18 April 2018); 'Mondo Pop: Rethinking Genre Beyond Hollywood', Issue 6, 201–14.
14 *Forbrydelsen*, [TV series] (Denmark: DR1, 2007–12); *The Killing* [TV series] (USA: AMC, 2011–13) and (USA: Netflix, 2013–14).
15 Mike Hales, 'The Danes do Murder Differently', *The New York Times*, 28 March 2012, available online: www.nytimes.com/2012/04/01/arts/television/comparing-the-killing-to-the-show-forbrydelsen.html?_r=0 (accessed 18 April 2018).
16 Louise Spence, *Watching Daytime Soap Operas: The Power of Pleasure* (Middletown: Wesleyan University Press, 2005), 123.
17 Ibid.
18 Gene D. Phillips, *Creatures of Darkness: Raymond Chandler, Detective Fiction and Film Noir* (Lexington: University Press of Kentucky, 2000), 134.
19 Glen Creeber, 'Killing us Softly', 26.
20 Jonathan Bignell, 'The Police Series', in *Close-up 3*, eds John Gibbs and Douglas Pye (London and New York: Wallflower Press, 2009), 6.
21 Pia Majbritt Jensen and Anne Marit Waade, 'Nordic noir Production Values: *The Killing* and *The Bridge*', *Akademisk Kvarter*, no. 7 (Fall 2013), 194.
22 Gerarg Gilbert, 'Ten People who Changed the World: Sofie Grabol, Star of *The Killing*', *The Independent*, 31 December 2011. Available online: www.independent.co.uk/arts-entertainment/tv/features/ten-people-who-changed-the-world-sofie-grabol-star-of-the-killing-6282315.html (accessed 18 April 2018).
23 Gabeba Baderoon, 'Happy Endings: The Story of *Twin Peaks*', *Journal of Literary Studies* 15, no. 1–2 (1999): 97.
24 Gerarg Gilbert, 'Ten People Who Changed the World'.
25 Sue Turnbull, *The TV Crime Drama* (Edinburgh: Edinburgh University Press, 2014), 98.
26 Patrick Kingsley, *How to Be Danish: A Journey to the Cultural Heart of Denmark* (New York: Marble Arch Press, 2012), 144.
27 Lindsay Steenberg and Yvonne Tasker, '"Pledge Allegiance": Gendered Surveillance, Crime Television, and *Homeland*', in *Focus: Homeland. Cinema Journal, The Journal of the Society for Cinema and Media Studies* 54, no. 4 (2015): 136.
28 Delphine Letort, 'Conspiracy Culture in *Homeland* (2011–2015)', *Media, War and Conflict* 10, no. 2 (2016): 152–76. Available online: http://mwc.sagepub.com/content/early/2016/07/04/1750635216656968.full.pdf?ijkey=1Zh9sS4kwp1g3cP&keytype=finite (accessed 23 November 2016).
29 Kim Akass, 'The Show that Refused to Die: The Rise and Fall of AMC's *The Killing*', *Continuum* 29, no. 5 (2015): 745. Available online:https://doi.org/10.1080/10304312.2015.1068724 (accessed 23 August 2018).

30 The term 'remake' is used to refer to a very specific form of adaptation, sustained by Thomas Leitch's definition of film remakes as 'adaptations of a given story to a new discursive incarnation within the same mode of representation'. Therefore, the specificity of remakes resides in the adaptation of a story (or fable) within the same mode and medium (which, in this particular case, is long-form television). Thomas Leitch, 'Twice-Told Tales: The Rhetoric of the Remake', *Literature Film Quarterly* 18, no. 3 (1990): 138–49.
31 Bruce Robbins, 'The Detective Is Suspended: Nordic Noir and the Welfare State', *Post 45*, 18 May 2015. Available online: http://post45.research.yale.edu/2015/05/the-detective-is-suspended-nordic-noir-and-the-welfare-state/ (accessed 8 December 2016).
32 Clara Bradbury-Rance, 'Querying Postfeminism in Lisa Cholodenko's *The Kids Are All Right*', in *Postfeminism and Contemporary Hollywood Cinema*, eds Joel Gwynne and Nadine Muller (Basingstoke: Palgrave Macmillan, 2013), 30.

Chapter 4

LILYHAMMER'S 'LAND OF SECOND CHANCES': MASCULINITY, VIOLENCE AND CORRUPTION

Catherine Ross Nickerson

The Norwegian television series *Lilyhammer* (2012–14) proposes an intriguing if absurd thought experiment: what would happen if a mid-level American mafioso were located to Lillehammer under a witness protection programme and asked to begin a new life as an ordinary immigrant?[1] The show proposes Norway as a society of rules, rules that form a social contract based on a sense of national belonging, ideals of peaceful civic engagement, prosperity for all, egalitarianism and well-intentioned efforts at inclusivity. The show's version of the Mafia, on the other hand, is aligned with American principals of ambition, competition, ingenuity and loyalty to the 'family'. The results of the experiment are at first comic, but later turn darker. Frank Tagliano, played by Steven Van Zandt, lands in Lillehammer with a thin cover story and an unlikely new name, Giovanni Henrickson. What unfolds at first is the comedic premise of this 'fish out of water' story. There are so very many things that Frank doesn't understand: that a sheep's head might be someone's dinner, why he has to wear shoe covers in a hospital, why no one finds the concept of a male midwife odd. On the first morning Frank awakes in Norway, he is so ill-prepared for the frigid temperatures that he roots about in his rented home and finds snow boots, a thick sweater emblazoned with a leaping stag, and a knit hat that reads 'I heart NY-norsk'. This image of Frank in a Norwegian ski sweater under his good New York overcoat with peak lapels and velvet-trim captures the awkward fit between Frank's American mafioso style and the culture of Lillehammer.

Though required to take an acculturation class for immigrants called 'New Start', it is clear from the beginning that Frank has no intention of going straight. He has smuggled in a handgun, a nice pile of cash and a lot of ideas about how to get things done. He doesn't take to the culture of assent that undergirds social and institutional relationships in Norway. He does not like to hear advice like 'here, one just has to accept,' or 'that's just the way it is' (1.4). It is impossible for him to accept that no one is allowed to shoot a bothersome wolf, or that the local civilian patrol talk respectfully to teenage vandals instead of breaking their kneecaps. By the end of the series, he tells one girlfriend, 'When I first came here, I learned that it was the land of second chances' (S3E7). At first, that 'second chance' is about starting over as a criminal in a new territory. By the end of the show, Frank means something more profound, something about being a slightly different kind of man.

Upon arrival in Lillehammer, Frank begins disrespecting all norms of the Norwegian social contract. Frank's first concern is getting a licence to open a nightclub, a virtual impossibility for a new immigrant. He attempts to bribe Jan, the NAV (Norwegian Labour and Welfare Administration) employment counsellor assigned to help him get a job; when that doesn't work, he finds a way to blackmail the man. Once he has the nightclub, The Flamingo, in place, Frank sets up the same kind of multifaceted criminal enterprise that he ran as a Mafia underboss in New York City. He recruits a crew of local young men who are bored out of their minds while living on unemployment benefits or working low-paying jobs. He quickly gets his hand into bootleg alcohol sales, into poker games, into money laundering – and he also violates other points of Norwegian law, like refusing to hire waitresses he finds unattractive, and conducting extortion to get papers for an immigrant chef he favours. He is also very successful at corrupting the Norwegians around him. In the first season, he blackmails, bribes or otherwise draws in: two immigration officers, a midwife, a driver's licence examiner, a biker gang, a real estate developer and lawyer, a nursery school teacher and the chief of police. He corrupts children: he teaches his girlfriend's son to fight back with weapons when bullied, instead of following the peace-making protocols in place at the school, and he edits the boy's National Day speech on the value of diversity into a rant on nativism. He is so incensed by a puppet show at his children's nursery school that promotes ideas of non-competition, the abolition of the profit motive and the benevolence of the state that he bribes two older children to trash the puppets and set.

Mafia on ice

The show includes characters who are infatuated with American popular culture, like the local policeman who works as an Elvis impersonator. Characters share a common set of references to American television and film, from *Dexter* to *The Three Stooges*. But by far, their favourite type of film involves gangsters and wise guys. Torgeir, Frank's hapless right-hand man, finally realizes what Frank used to do for a living after watching *Goodfellas* and recognizing Frank's tough-guy declarations in the movie's dialogue. There are multiple references to *The Godfather*, including the horse head scene (once with a sheep's head (S1E1), once with a chicken (S1E3)) and a parody of the famous wedding-day appeal to Don Corleone in which a local man appeals to Frank for relief from troublesome immigrant neighbours (S2E1). The show emphasizes its point that the vocabulary of gangster films has permeated Norwegian culture in a sub-plot about an autistic boy who communicates with others only by quoting lines from old James Cagney movies (S3E1).

More centrally, the show is itself a consumer of American popular culture. Its premise takes a character from *The Sopranos* and transplants him into *Lilyhammer*. The main character, Frank, is played by the American actor and musician Steven Van Zandt, whose first, and only, previous acting job was playing *consigliere* Silvio Dante on *The Sopranos*. Frank is only moderately distinguishable from Silvio: they both run nightclubs, they were both confidantes of bosses; the main difference is that where Silvio tends to sulk, Frank has a brutal vivacity. In a big wink to fans of *The Sopranos*, Maureen Van Zandt, who is married to Van Zandt in real life and played Silvio's wife on the earlier show, plays Frank's ex-wife and Tony Sirico, who played fellow gangster Paulie Walnuts, is Frank's brother. And in a final dizzying touch, the show has Bruce Springsteen, Steven Van Zandt's bandmate, play his other brother, a lugubrious hitman. There are multiple shared music cues and plot points across the two shows and, moreover, it is clear that characters within the show watched and loved *The Sopranos*. In the third season, when Frank's Norwegian crew gets to travel to the United States, Torgeir takes great delight in playing the theme music from *The Sopranos* as they drive the streets of New York City.

The return of a Soprano, through the casting of Steven Van Zandt, is more than a in-joke for fans of both shows. Frank is a snitch, a rat, someone who took revenge on his enemies by giving information to the FBI (Federal Bureau of Investigation). The threat of the turncoat haunts *The Sopranos*, and part of the show's extended lament on the decline of mid-century American masculinity is the rise of the snitch. Tony Soprano complains, 'You know how many mobsters are selling screenplays and screwing everything up?'[2] The Mafia is premised on the idea of safety in numbers, of layers of soldiers who alibi each other and their bosses, of sticking to the script when questioned by police. While much is made in Mafia stories about '*omerta*' as a code of silence, it is also an oath to perpetuate a series of cover stories and fronts that shield criminal enterprise from view. Maintaining the web of lies, keeping everyone safe, rises to the level of honour in Mafia stories, the level of something that defines a man for life.

The figure of the snitch threatens to destabilize the narrative of a Mafia story, just as the co-operating informant threatens to send his comrades to jail. The person who turns into a snitch has decided to transfer knowledge from the world of criminal enterprise to the world, in the American context, of the FBI task force. The snitch has the capacity to alter both worlds – sending people to jail, getting agents promotions. Snitches are a force of volatility. If criminals are the authors of their crimes, and cops are the authors of the investigation, the snitch rivals them both, able to unexpectedly alter both their narratives. In most Mafia stories, the snitch is killed by the Mafia, even when they are a beloved member of the family. Rarely does the snitch survive (with *Goodfellas* as a notable exception). *Lilyhammer* does something else with the snitch – it lets him live on, and it imagines a whole new world for him to conquer.

Frank, the successful snitch, decides that it is possible to slip the identity of honourable keeper of oaths and to lead another life. From past experience in extortion, he knows that everyone has a secret and has things they will pay a high price to protect. He also gambles that identities and allegiances can easily be faked and that whole selves can be dropped and acquired. His first criminal act on Norwegian soil, after all, is the attempted bribery of a NAV employment counsellor to get the job opportunity he wants – an extreme version of the ingenuity the newcomer must use in negotiating a new economy and making a new life. Frank's instinct for the vulnerable points in the Norwegian system and his absolute delight in exploiting them is why Torgeir exclaims near the end of the series, 'you are still the most awesome immigrant I ever met' (S3E8). Not everyone warms to the stranger in their midst. Frank piques the interest of one local cop, Geir, who is the Elvis impersonator. Initially annoyed that Frank won't allow him to perform at the club, he figures out that Frank is not who he claims to be, though he fixates on the wrong category of criminal. Geir, an Islamophobe, believes Frank to be an Al-Qaeda terrorist in hiding. Geir is a fan of the American television programme *24*, and becomes quite unglued in his attempts to imitate its hero, Jack Bauer, searching Interpol files and conducting surveillance on Frank. It is notable that Geir's fears of terrorism are couched entirely in terms of 9/11 and itinerant Islamists, not in terms of the mass shooting by native Norwegian Anders Breivik in 2011. When Geir starts nosing around in New York City, he unwittingly reveals Frank's location and is killed by members of Frank's old crime family.

Frank's presence thus draws dangerous American mafiosi to Lillehammer as two of his former associates track him down to seek revenge. His crew, including the faithful Torgeir, still do not know about Frank's past, even as they try to help retrieve Frank's girlfriend's son, who is being held hostage by the two American hitmen. Things come to a head on National Day, when the assassins make a move on Frank at an outdoor party packed with locals in traditional costume. An extended, comic chase ensues through the Norwegian Troll Park, an amusement park that puts the folk symbols of Norway front and centre. When Laila, the local chief of police, shows up to the scene in her National Day *bunad* (national costume), it begins to dawn on us that the show is trying to make a point about the intersection of Norwegian identity and errant New York mobsters. What Laila discovers, in a stand of birch trees, is the aftermath of a gunfight that has left one of the hitmen dead. Frank persuades the remaining hitman to return to New York with the story that Frank was also killed. Laila needs to be convinced to remain quiet about the killing of the hitman, and Frank successfully plays upon her emotions by explaining that the dead man was responsible for the death of Geir, who is like a son to her.

Laila, the very soul of community-minded decency, a stickler for the law, the guardian of common-sense values, standing there in her *bunad*, agreeing to cover up a murder out of a sense of vengeance and lack of faith in the Norwegian justice system, has been utterly corrupted and demoralized by

Frank. At this moment, we realise that *Lilyhammer* isn't simply a story about an emigrant mafioso infecting Lillehamer with the virus of organized crime. The show's more unexpected point is that there is something already there in Norwegian culture that welcomes a man like Frank. We probably should have seen it coming. Frank's first crime on Norewegian soil is a relatively minor case of assault that subtly indicates much about Frank's future role in Lillehammer. On the train from Oslo that will bring Frank to his new life, a pair of Norwegian teenagers are acting up, snatching an old man's hat and playing music loudly on their boom box. Everyone around them is clearly annoyed, but nobody does anything – until Frank follows one of the boys to the lavatory, mashes his head into a wall, and demands that he make apologies and restitution. His alpha-male behaviour wins gratitude from the old man and admiring looks from the beautiful young mother seated across from him. The old man, a town commissioner, later refuses to testify against Frank on another matter. The beautiful woman ends up romantically involved with Frank and has twins with him. Frank's pugnacious style, developed in the world of the American mob, finds a receptive audience amongst the citizens of Norway.

Over the course of seasons two and three, Frank is drawn back into the orbit of the New York Mafia, eventually being restored to the good graces of the upper-level Commission of the Five Families and officially being given all of Scandinavia as his territory for racketeering and other enterprises. At one point, he travels back to New York to perform a hit on his old nemesis, aided by his new Norwegian crew. To get close to his target, Frank needs a disguise, something that will make him invisible to his old associates. Ruefully, he realizes, with the help of Torgeir and others, that his best bet is a traditional Norwegian national costume, with plaid vest, knee-pants, and wide-brimmed hat. The choice is both effective and befitting, as Frank is by this point falling deeply in love with Norway, the place he now calls home. By the third season, a young mafioso from New York attempts to criticize Frank by declaring: 'You're becoming too Norwegian. All this commie government safety-net bullshit is turning you soft and weak' (S3E7). Later, he claims Frank's managerial style is overly protective of his crew, making him less profitable than he should be. Frank is unperturbed; he accepts his change of national identity and cultural style.

Violence and Norwegian identity

The visual iconography of Norwegianness on the show includes not only trolls and traditional dress and folk costumes, but also vernacular architecture and the venues built for the 1994 winter Olympics. When Frank explains to the FBI why he chose Lillehammer as the place to start over, he declares his attraction in mostly visual terms, asking 'didn't you see the Olympics in '94? It was beautiful. Clean air, fresh white snow, gorgeous broads' (S1E1). To a local, he explains

'I fell in love with your Olympics'. For Frank, reflexive reference to 'broads' aside, Norway is a landscape of purity and Olympian high ideals. Much later, he tells Torgeir that 'Norway is a fairytale' (S2E8). But if Frank sees Norway as an innocent land, about which he can have fond feelings while corrupting everyone around him, the show suggests early on that there is already a darker side to even the Olympic legacy Frank extols. In the second episode, Frank and Torgeir torture a member of a rival biker gang (who will eventually become part of their crew) by forcing him onto skis and pushing him down the Olympic ski jump ramp. Like so much else in the show, the scene is both funny and cruel. We later learn that Torgeir was an Olympic hopeful in ski-jumping, suggesting that this bit of brutality was a collaboration of a dormant Norwegian fantasy and the inciting can-do spirit of the criminal immigrant.

Perhaps the most prevalent visual marker of Norwegianness on the show is the parade of traditional and contemporary Scandinavian knitwear. We see traditional black-and-white *lusekofte*, or Sedestal, jumpers, with their intricate graphic designs and pewter clasps; Marius jumpers with bold cross and diamond patterns across the chest; Fana cardigans with geometric patterns and stripes; Selburose mittens with combinations of large flowers and small tracework; jumpers with stags, or reindeer, or trees, or snowflakes, or floral bands. Babies, children and adults are all marked as Norwegian by these distinctive garments; even the more contemporary designs with stripes, blocks of bright color or soft yarns underline the importance of knitwear in the Nordic wardrobe on the show. Sigrid, Frank's girlfriend, often knits, as do extras and minor characters in several scenes. Knitting and wearing sweaters is a visual reminder of the deep cultural values of tradition, national belonging and cheerful industry. It is a mark of Torgeir's fierce loyalty to Frank that he decides to knit traditional jumpers and pants for Frank and Sigrid's twins, for whom he will serve as godfather. Though he is teased by his peers and called 'Auntie Torgeir', he seems driven to accomplish this rite of welcome for the new babies, to knit them into the fabric of Norwegianness. But again, as with the Olympics, the show finds a darker side to this trope of Norwegian festivity. In a crucial scene, Torgeir will have cause to use his knitting needle, that iconic instrument of a technology of affection, to kill a man.

The man Torgeir murders is the most brutal and depraved figure in the series. Duncan, an English gangster, is incensed when his attempt to fence a Ferrari with Frank's crew ends badly. Armed with the improvised weapon he learned to make as a soccer hooligan, the Millwall brick, he goes to The Flamingo to bust as many heads as possible. The scene pits national styles of masculine rage and violence against each other. Duncan insults the Norwegians by declaring 'Vikings! I fucking shit 'em'; Frank refers to Duncan's 'limey ass', and Duncan proposes a toast to 'one less American' (S2E1). One of the crew locates Frank's American handgun behind the bar and brandishes it to try to stop Duncan's rampage, but is so unskilled with it that Duncan is not the least bit cowed and takes it from him easily. The only weapon left to save Frank from Duncan is

Torgeir's circular knitting needles, which he fashions into a sort of garrote, eventually stabbing Duncan through the throat. One could argue that Torgeir kills Duncan in the most Norwegian way possible.

This killing, which happens in the first episode of the second season, affects Torgeir deeply and casts a long shadow over the rest of the series. It creates a typically Nordic noir crisis for Torgeir: he has done something that makes him feel irredeemable. In a conversation with Frank shortly after the killing, Torgeir sounds despairing, ('I always fuck things up') and expresses his fear that Frank will replace him as the godfather to his children with another member of the crew, Jan. He expresses the horror of his experience in the language of the traumatized: 'did you see his eyes?' Frank answers with a more pragmatic 'did you see his gun? You did what you had to do in there' (S2E1). But as we learn over the rest of the series, Torgeir is psychologically overwhelmed by the killing of the Englishman.

Immigrants and 'discrimination-ball'

The fact that Torgeir sees Jan as a rival for Frank's loyalty is a mark of how much Jan has been incorporated into the rise of criminal enterprise in Lillehammer. Jan, who is the employment counsellor that Frank blackmails at the beginning of the series, was never an innocent. He is a long-time and pernicious harasser of women, using his position as an employment officer to extract sexual favours from them. But at first, Jan comes across as a giggly government functionary. He teaches classes for new immigrants on adjusting to Norwegian culture and preaches that they offer 'a fresh start [...] a chance to get the know the multi-headed but basically pleasant troll we call Norwegian society' (S1E2). Jan himself appears to be 'basically pleasant' and well-meaning, offering cheerful if slightly manic advice. It isn't long, however, before Frank discovers that Jan has a secret – he has sex parties with the female immigrants he supervises, whose consent is unclear. Frank, knowing a useful piece of information when he sees it, forces Jan to get him the permits he needs to open a nightclub.

Over the course of the first two seasons, we learn that just below Jan's warm and pleasant welcome to immigrants lies a stern condition of acceptance: immigrants must conform to Norwegian norms of social enlightenment. He embodies a sort of pernicious cluelessness about the racism that immigrants from Africa and the Middle East face in Norway. He favours an exercise where he sits in a circle with immigrants, tossing a 'discrimination-ball' while calling out racial epithets. 'We can make fun of everything by kidding around [...] the bad words lose all meaning'. But this exercise goes as poorly as we might expect, and when Jan decides that one Nigerian immigrant, Odera, has said something unacceptable, he gives a paternalistic scolding: '[There are] rules you need to learn if you want to be Norwegian' (S2E2).

That Nigerian immigrant is one of the most developed characters of colour on the show. Odera, nicknamed Balotelli during the seven years he spent as a refugee in Sicily, is an accomplished chef with an impressive repertoire of Italian dishes. Frank goes to great lengths to extort an immigration official so that Balotelli can stay in Lillehammer and cook at Frank's club. Frank cares a great deal about good food and good music, and Balotelli cooks pasta with *élan* and sings Italian opera like an angel. Balotelli and Frank joke around about the inferior palates of the 'Norskis,' and Torgeir develops a tormented crush on him. He is well-liked and quite safe in the club. But he was not that way when he was in the hands of the Norwegian government and a privatized refugee centre, under the direction of Jan. The cold opening of the episode that introduces his storyline has him reading a letter to his nephew back in Nigeria:

> Hope you haven't resorted to piracy yet. Although after three years in Norway, I wish I had. Like the albinos of Lagos, we are isolated from the rest of the society, and they break our spirits by humiliating us, a process they call 'integration'. They say Norway is a cold country. So far the worst cold I have felt has not come from the climate, but from the hearts of the Norwegians. (S2E2)

Under this reading is a montage of shots showing Jan laughing hysterically while presenting Balotelli with a t-shirt emblazoned with the phrase 'Integration Works', the official letter refusing him asylum, and locals running Balotelli off the road next to the refugee centre and beating him in the snow. It is one of the most serious moments in all three seasons, and clearly states the critique the show wants to make of social attitudes and official Norwegian policy towards non-white immigrants, even as it includes many characters with entrenched resistance to difference.

When Jan is fired from the NAV for his record of sexual harassment, he goes to work for Frank. He is a quick study of Mafia strong-arm techniques, and combines them with what he already knows, figuring out how to make money out of the business of refugee resettlement. He sums up the financial opportunities in a sector where there are both charitable donations and government subsidies by telling Frank, cynically, 'there's a lot of money in integration' (S2E1). Jan's first move is to blackmail his lover, Randi, getting her to sign over ownership of a refugee resettlement centre to Frank, thus allowing the crew to siphon off money, goods and services in a classic Mafia takeover. Jan cracks under the strain of working for Frank, kills Randi and uses his past connections to flee to Iraq, where he converts to Islam. Whether or not we are to understand his conversion as sincere, we do see him return later to Lillehammer. He becomes, by returning to Norway with a beard and skullcap, exactly the kind of immigrant that he himself used to help on behalf of the state. He is shunned by both native Norwegians and Muslim immigrants.

In the second half of the last season, Jan, who began as 'basically pleasant,' becomes an embodiment of masculine rage and resentment. He angrily laments the decline of the Norwegian welfare model, ranting that the social safety net 'has started to rot'. In a speech that reveals his deep misogyny as well as his stubborn nostalgia, he says, 'We used to say it was typically Norwegian to be good', paraphrasing the famous declaration of Prime Minister Brundtland about the success of the 1994 Olympics. 'Do you know what we should say now? It's typically Norwegian to be a fucking cunt' (S3E5). He decides to become a suicide bomber, targeting the government offices he once worked in. In the video he makes to explain his planned crime, he says, 'I happen to be a man who dedicated his adult life to the welfare state and Norwegian values, such as compassion, integration and raising competence. Desperate measures are necessary to wake Norway up' (S3E5). In the end, he aborts his suicide mission, and is embraced and brought back into the fold of the NAV by his old boss, who accepts him precisely under the terms of 'compassion, integration and raising competence', pointing out that his experience as an outcast will make him a better counsellor to minorities.

But there is no happy ending for Jan; even as he shaves his beard and goes back to work at the NAV, Randi's murder is still a legal and moral liability for him. Nothing can hold him together, and he ends up killing another woman who, like Randi, refused to be controlled by him. In the final episodes of the show, he is taken out by Frank's crew, because he framed one of them for Randi's murder and because he was in a car accident that killed Frank's father-in-law. Jan's complex trajectory, which tangles together government work and violent crime, shows that the veneer of pleasantness and the gestures toward multiculturalism cannot contain the rage and insistence on tradition that form the core of Jan's identity as a citizen of Norway. His story highlights the ways that xenophobia and fear of difference are always fears about the self or the nation.

Torgeir, one of those who flew

Torgeir, when he meets Frank, is aimless and unemployed, but it isn't entirely clear why he turns so readily to a life of crime or why he sticks with it. Something of an answer comes in the third season, when we learn about Torgeir's childhood dream of being an Olympic ski jumper. 'For me, being a ski jumper was better than being prime minister of Norway. It was a chance for a guy like me to be somebody. One of the ones who get noticed. One of those who flew' (S3E4). In the Norwegian context, Torgeir's hopes are transgressive, and become a source of shame to him; he is injured just before the 1994 Olympics and cannot compete. Norwegian novelist Karl Ove Knausgaard writes of this feature of twentieth-century Scandinavian culture: 'You are not to think you are anything special [...] You are not to convince yourself that you are better than we are [...] You are not to think you are good at anything'. Knausgaard argues that these 'commandments', which were articulated by novelist Aksel Sandemose, express 'the mentality of a community in which everyone controls everyone else, the collective suffocates the individual and the price of individual freedom is ostracism.[3] Torgeir seems to understand, partly based on his consumption of American popular culture, and partly on his buried wish to fly high, that partnership with swaggering, preening, rule-breaking Frank is just the thing he needs to break free from his sense of suffocation. But it is of course a very bad idea to search for a sense of self in a life of crime, as its forms of validation all come soaked in blood. Torgeir's trajectory shows us how dark that path becomes.

Torgeir begins his criminal training as Frank's right-hand man. On paper, he is the owner of Frank's nightclub; in a typical Mafia arrangement, Frank creates some legal distance between himself and the criminal activities going on at the club. Torgeir, too naïve (perhaps willfully naïve) to discern Frank's Mafia past, is a young man who willingly, eagerly tries out various criminal personae, which are mostly played for comic effect by Trond Fausa Aurvåg. Torgeir begins his missions for Frank with a lot of nervous bluster, as when he confronts a local farmer who has been overcharging the club. In a Mafia-style retaliatory shakedown Torgeir takes over the farm, including its herd of reindeer. Other members of the crew decide that they should collect the insurance on the herd by dynamiting a slope and burying the animals in the snow. But Torgeir's tender heart won't let himself or the gang go through with it, and he stampedes the reindeer to safety. This pattern holds on other occasions when Torgeir feels that innocent people need protection; his self-doubt makes him compassionate. At the same time as we see his lack of self-confidence, we see how much more calloused he becomes under Frank's influence, perfectly willing to leave rivals to freeze to death on the ice, to torture other criminals to extract confessions, to kidnap and imprison anyone perceived as a threat, to participate in hits on Frank's behalf. He draws his brother Roar into the criminal enterprise of The Flamingo early on, wanting to spread the wealth, and the two become almost lethally estranged in the gang wars of the last season.

Of all Torgeir's acts of violence against other people, the killing of Duncan the Englishman affects him most. In the third season, where the show becomes a lot less funny and a lot more noir, he begins to have hallucinations where Duncan appears and talks to him. Duncan first appears in the attic of Torgeir's house when Torgeir, having learned his girlfriend Birgitte is pregnant, goes in search of his childhood toys to celebrate. Duncan is a very gothicized ghost, looming out of the attic darkness when Torgeir lights a candelabra, and an angry one. He complains, 'nothing prepared me for the indignity of being killed with a couple of knitting needles. By a Norwegian' (S3E5). He points out the similarities between them, claims that it was he who impregnated Birgitte and ensconces himself in Torgeir's mind as a double. He begins interfering with Torgeir and Birgitte's sex life, inciting Torgeir to hit her and call her names. The filming of scenes with Duncan makes it clear that only Torgeir can see him, though other people seem to hear Duncan's words coming out of Torgeir's mouth. To other people, Duncan is Torgeir, and Torgeir begins to feel the same way, finding it more and more difficult to distinguish between himself and the ghost of the man he killed. In one intensely violent scene, Duncan attempts to kill, or force suicide, upon Torgeir using Birgitte's knitting needles, resulting in a bizarre dance that makes her think Torgeir has gone mad. After an all-night rampage, Torgeir is hospitalized and diagnosed with a blood clot. However, the medical diagnosis of the source of the hallucinations doesn't address the deep fracture in Torgeir's soul, and thus doesn't last. Duncan shows up again, this time stirring up (or, more accurately, embodying) the heartbroken rivalry between Torgeir and his brother Roar. In a moment of triumph, Torgeir resists Duncan's imperious commands to shoot Roar, and kills Duncan a second time.

Torgeir, by the last episode in the series, seems set for a happy ending. Birgitte offers a way to a whole new life for them, running an alpaca farm with her sister, who has won funding from a network of women entrepreneurs. When Torgeir goes to Frank to announce his plans to join her, Frank schools him in the traditional Mafia view. 'There's really only one way you resign from this job. That's horizontally' (S3E8). But once the gang war is resolved, Frank softens and gives his blessing, and Torgeir is able to do what is impossible in most Mafia stories – walk away in peace. He goes to bed that night all smiles, whispering his love to his soon-to-be-born child and to Birgitte, full of hope for an idyllic life on a farm near Horindal Lake far from Lillehammer. As he said to Frank, 'I need a new start, like when you came to Lillehammer' (S3E8), and the series seems to have come to a nicely rounded ending as he turns off the light. But then one last thing happens.

Ibsen

After he turns out the light, a new ghost speaks to him, sitting in the same chair next to the bed that Duncan preferred when inciting Torgeir to beat Birgitte. It is not Duncan, whose ghost Torgeir apparently put to rest with a shotgun, but another man that Torgeir caused to die, Duncan's uncle Terry, who proceeds to read aloud two of Hedda's lines from the second act of *Hedda Gabler*: 'Oh, courage! Oh yes. If only one had that. Then life might be liveable. In spite of everything'.[4] We see a look of terror come over Torgeir's face as he listens, which is the final image of the series. It completely unsettles our conviction that good things await Torgeir in his new life, and also seems a bit self-consciously literary, coming at the end of a show that has, by turns been comedy, social satire and gangster thriller. But this moment is not simply a fancy embellishment on a raucous, ribald, action-packed show: it is where the show has been headed all along, and it comes to us like a message in a bottle from the deepest motivations of the series. Henrik Ibsen is, in this context, a touchstone for Nordic noir – the writer who articulated something that is recognizable as the ethos of despair, guilt and agitation that is so central to contemporary Scandinavian crime fiction. The show emphasizes the importance of Ibsen in a scene a bit earlier in this last episode, where Jan, recalling how much he loved acting in his youth, performs one of Nora's speeches from the third act of *A Doll's House*, with somewhat faulty recall: 'I mean that I was simply transferred from Papa's hands into yours. You arranged everything according to your own taste, so I got the same tastes as you – or else I pretended to [...] I see that I have been living in poverty, from day to day [...] It is your fault that I have made nothing of my life' (S3E8).[5] While Nora was speaking of the way her marriage confined and shaped her, Jan seems to be lamenting his life under the Norwegian welfare state, seeing it as something that took much from him in return for its promises of peace and prosperity. As he repeats the last line, 'It's your fault [...] that I have made nothing of my life', Frank's crew sneaks up on him and takes him outside to kill him. Jan is completely accepting of his fate; the move from Ibsen to Mafia retributive killing is seamless.

Conclusion

Lilyhammer is a show of many moods and many genres. Just as its dialogue is bilingual, its ethos is both antic and serious, both satiric and reflective. Frank has his greatest effect on two men: his close associate Torgeir, whom he mentors in the ways of crime, and Jan, the NAV employment counsellor that Frank blackmails in the opening episodes of the show. Each man has a complex trajectory over the three seasons of the programme and each highlights different problems of male violence in Norwegian society. Jan's story reveals the levels of seething anger and resentment under an apparently pleasant façade of a well-intentioned, peaceful and cohesive social system. Torgeir reveals the way ambition, and a will to dominate, can bring a Norwegian man so far from his place in the social order that he no longer knows who he is. With its hectic pace and intricate plotting, it is easy to miss many of the more contemplative moments tucked into the show. One of these is worth remembering. An old man, Frank's roommate in hospital, seems lost in comic dementia – he wanders the halls, he pees on the floor, he tries to read books upside down. But the fog clears for a moment and he says to a rather prim doctor, the one who is obsessed with visitors wearing shoe covers and everyone watching wholesome television, 'rationalistic puritans like you need counterparts like [Frank]' (S3E1). And that line works as well as any to capture what is both funny and serious about *Lilyhammer*.

Notes

1   *Lilyhammer*. Directed by Geir Henning Hopland, Simen Alsvik, et al. Written by Eilif Skodvin, Steven Van Zandt, Anne Bjørnstad, et al. NRK and Netflix. Three seasons, 2012–14. Further references to specific episodes will be included parenthetically in the text as (season number, episode number).

2. *The Sopranos*, 'Pilot', Episode 1, directed and written by David Chase. HBO, 10 January 1999.
3. Karl Ove Knausgaard and Ingvild Burkey, 'I am Someone, Look at Me,' *The New York Times Magazine*, 10 June 2014: M294. Available online: www.nytimes.com/2014/06/10/t-magazine/karl-ove-knausgaard-on-fame-my-struggle.html (accessed 1 March 2017).
4. Henrik Ibsen, *Hedda Gabler*, [1890] trans. William Archer and Edmond Gosse (New York: Charles Scribner's Sons, 1906), Act 2. Available online: www.gutenberg.org/files/4093/4093-h/4093-h.htm (accessed 10 February 2017).
5. Henrik Ibsen, *A Doll's House*, [1879] trans. William Archer (New York: Charles Scribner's Sons, 1906), Act 3. Available online: www.gutenberg.org/files/2542/2542-h/2542-h.htm (accessed 10 February 2017).

Part II

SPACE AND PLACE

Chapter 5

VIEWS FROM *THE BRIDGE*: PANORAMAS, STREETSCAPES AND THE OPTICS OF *NOIR*

Graeme Gilloch

Spatial movements are butterflies
Shadows scatter without a fire
　　　　　　　　　　　　　('Hollow Talk', Choir of Young Believers)

Taking as key points of departure Siegfried Kracauer's pioneering 1922 identification and analysis of the form of popular detective literary fiction, *Der Detektiv-Roman*,[1] and Walter Benjamin's almost contemporaneous exhumation of the 'Idea' of the German baroque play of mourning as the definitive cultural expression of the sorrowful seventeenth-century *Weltanschauung* – his *Ursprung des deutschen Trauerspiels* (1928)[2] – I argue that we can understand twenty-first-century neo-noir as the most acute manifestation of the melancholy and brooding spirit of our own dispirited times.[3] And just as Kracauer and Benjamin pinpoint particular spatial settings as the quintessential scenes of these very different literary forms – the modern hotel lobby in the case of the detective story; ruins and/or the royal court (especially in exotic form: the sultan's palace) in the *Trauerspiel* – so neo-noir narratives also occupy (and are preoccupied with) certain sites and locales. Whether urban or rural, neo-noir has its own characteristic topography (understood literally as the 'depiction of place'). I am concerned here with how the utilization and envisioning of particular metropolitan spaces work to initiate, establish, imbue, inculcate and emphasize particular forms of affect and ambience in the four series of *Bron/Broen* (2011, 2013, 2015 and 2018). Taking its title from the transnational Öresund Bridge connecting Copenhagen and Malmö, this internationally popular and critically acclaimed Swedish–Danish–German television co-production is characterized by the continual use of camera shots and locations that are carefully chosen to foster moods and sensibilities defining the neo-noir imaginary: melancholy, anxiety, haunting and the uncanny.

Bron/Broen is no ordinary example or casual choice, of course. As its very title suggests, the series has a particular penchant for the interplay of space, architecture and visual representation. The object of frequent onscreen depiction and repeated traversal, and fundamental as both the start- and endpoint of the actual narrative itself,[4] the Öresund Bridge is not only a recurrent visual *leitmotiv* throughout, but also an exemplary instance of those liminal and marginal urban structures and sites which proved most attractive – indeed, so seductive – to both Benjamin (as 'thresholds' [*Schwellen*] and 'passages' [*Passagen*][5]) and Kracauer (as 'in-between spaces' [*Zwischenräume*]).[6] Bridges are, so to speak, Janus-faced. As that most astute of observers and essayists Georg Simmel remarked over a century ago, they constitute commonplace symbols of felicitous communication and harmonious collaboration, of co-operation and co-existence, of neighbourliness and mutuality.[7] At the same time, bridges suggest more disquieting aspects: neither here nor there, they are the very architecture of indeterminacy and the uncanny, of the betwixt and between, purely functional structures only ever to be passed over, to be experienced merely and briefly *en passant, en traversant*. Spanning voids, suspended above them, bridges are to be sure meeting points, sites of contiguity and connection; but they are also where the suicidal are to be found, where spies and dissidents are secretly exchanged between governments in espionage thrillers. An in-between for the shady dealings of the go-between, the last resort of those without hope, the bridge is a common no-man's land.[8] *Bron/Broen* is attentive to the most fastidious arrangements of space, bodies and objects – most obviously in the scrupulously composed and staged crime scenes themselves, where anatomy and architecture intersect in the precise location and meticulous articulation of corpses and things.[9] Configured as macabre messages, such crime scenes invite the investigative techniques and testing of forensics and profiling; they are composed as riddles to be solved, picture puzzles to be interpreted, texts and traces to be read; they are the most precise albeit grotesque expression of what Kracauer refers to as 'spatial hieroglyphs' – spaces of and for decipherment.[10]

Given the highly stylized and self-conscious interlacing of the built environment, human *physis* and camerawork, it is perhaps little wonder that the opening credit sequences of *Bron/Broen* introduce a seamless montage of dissolving images envisioning contrasting spatial configurations, conjuring up the modern European city as sprawling, alienating nocturnal technoscape. We are presented with a swift formalist-inspired montage of differing angles and geometries of lines (in parallel, converging in perspective, producing rectilinear forms and orthogonal repetitions and patterns); curvatures and torques (most evidently as instantiated in Santiago Calatrava's 2005 Turning Torso residential skyscraper, the tallest building in Scandinavia and now Malmö's landmark); and, points and flows of light, lens flare, metallic reflections and raindrop refractions. These credit sequences do much more than just present the credits – the who plays whom, the who did what.[11] Firstly, in television series like *Bron/Broen*, the composition and repetition of distinctive theme music and images at the start of each episode – or now more commonly as here, somewhat interrupting and separating the 'previous' from the new by means of an interlude, a little temporal caesura – creates a strong sense of continuity and programme identity, a recognizable signature, an unmistakeable brand. Secondly, these brief sequences should be understood as *establishing shots*, a standard shorthand of film and televisual narrative telling the viewers the where and when of the action that is now about to unfold on screen – in this city, in this neighbourhood, in this particular building. They thus provide orientation and re-orientation; they are imagistic signposts. In the case of *Bron/Broen*, we are treated to a series of intercut scenes of Malmö and Copenhagen, a brief montage of metonymic images, finishing on the most famous monument in the Danish capital, the statue of the Little Mermaid. By the end we are left in little doubt – and Scandinavian viewers are doubtless left in no doubt – as to where we are. Finally, and most significantly, these credit sequences are establishing shots in another, more extended and complex sense: they are not only spatial, they are *affectual* as well; that is to say, they are evocative of particular emotions, sensibilities, dispositions, inclinations and moods. What is *established* then, is not just a sense of a specific time and place – the Scandinavian city today – but also a certain ambience and atmosphere. In short: these credit sequences create – to borrow and re-purpose Raymond Williams' famous definition of 'culture' – a distinctive 'structure of feeling'.[12] How is this done? How do particular representations of the city accompanied by or set to distinctive music invoke and instil, however indistinct and indefinite, a recognizable quality or *air* that is, in the case of *Bron/Broen*, simultaneously alienating, anxious, unnerving, uncanny and melancholy, sorrowful, fretful but also utterly forlorn.[13]

A tale of two bridges

To explore these questions, I begin not with *Bron/Broen* but instead with *The Bridge* seasons 1 and 2 (2013, 2014), the American remake, in which the gridlocked Bridge of the Americas spanning the Texas–Mexico border separating El Paso and Ciudad Juárez substitutes for the – more aesthetically pleasing – Öresund Bridge. I will then, as in the words of the song, work my way 'back to the beginning'. Without wishing to overstate the differences – since they are in any case two sides of the same coin – I propose that the opening credits of *Bron/Broen* and *The Bridge* both demonstrate a degree of loyalty to, and continuity with – be it as contemporary re-working, as pastiche or as homage – the competing visions of the American city found in classic post-war film noir. In his tracing of the complex intersections of rapidly changing post-war American cities and cityscapes, and ever-new and developing cinematic and cinematographic techniques and practices, Edward Dimendberg (2004) posits two concomitant and contradictory tendencies and forces: on the one hand, forms of concentration and intensification producing the characteristic American metropolitan downtown of skyscrapers and verticality – the centripetal city; and, on the other, centrifugal forms of dispersal and distribution resulting in endless low-rise urban sprawl, suburbanization, drive-thrus, malls and the creation of what Joel Garreau termed 'edge city' some twenty-five years ago.[14] Dimendberg writes:

> Tensions between centripetal and centrifugal spatial tendencies provide an important key to understanding the film noir cycle of the 1940s and 1950s. [...] [E]ach reveals distinct modalities of urban anxiety. For if the former elicits the agoraphobic sensation of being overwhelmed by space, fears of constriction, or fear of losing one's way in the metropolis, its fundamental legibility can be assumed ... By contrast, the anxieties provoked by centrifugal space hinge upon temporality and the uncertainty produced by a spatial environment increasingly devoid of landmarks and centers and often likely to seem permanently in motion.[15]

These tendencies are, of course, epitomized by two American cities in particular: on the one hand, or rather, on the one coast, the Gotham City verticality of New York; on the other, the suburban spread and satellites of Los Angeles. But whether their architectural trajectories are upwards or outwards, these cities nevertheless share certain characteristics rendering them – ensuring them – as unhomely homes to the dystopian noir imagination: a monstrous scale which reduces the human individual to an insignificant, alienated, isolated atom; a sense of the labyrinthine, be it a warren of unlit alleyways or the bewildering criss-crossing concrete of tangled freeway systems; the co-existence and clandestine contiguity of obscene wealth and wretched poverty, where the rich invariably get the poor to do their dirty work for them. The noir narrative typically starts out with the humble investigator standing in the lobby awaiting the elevator to the Manhattan penthouse, or turning up the long driveway and passing the manicured lawns of the Beverly Hills mansion; it will wind its way through menacing backstreets, seedy bars, clubs and fleapit motels; eventually, it will make its weary way back again to where it all began. In so doing, the detective will traverse the worlds of the powerful and the powerless – bridge them – so as to disclose the intricate and intimate connections between them, bringing into view unseen, unsuspected 'bridges' of cause and effect.[16]

Set to the jangling, twanging guitar and tobacco-stained voice of Ryan Bingham intoning 'Until I'm One with You', the opening credits of *The Bridge* stress the notion of the 'centrifugal city' by means of a thirty-second fragmentary odyssey, a car journey through the desolate and dispersed vernacular architecture and loci of Tex-Mexicana. This is sunshine and noir.[17] Starting with a desert landscape at first light, and culminating in arrival at the traffic-clogged Bridge of the Americas after dark, the concrete structure itself illuminated by the red tail lights of queuing vehicles, the route takes us through a montage of intercut scenes from both sides of the border, featuring a motley array of ramshackle buildings and shabby settings all bearing the unmistakable marks of dilapidation and destitution. Strung out along the roadsides and shot primarily *en passant* through the passenger window of a moving car, the images dissolve ever more quickly into each other to produce a veritable 'mythology' – as Roland Barthes might term it – of 'Tex-Mexicanicity': low-rise housing and shacks; shopfronts in disrepair bearing signs and murals in English and Spanish ('Horses Welcome' one proclaims; humans maybe not); the brutal functionalism of pylons and power lines, raised water tanks and girder bridges; billboards, traffic signs and overhead lane markers; a makeshift shoe-shine at work; chain-link fencing which fences off nothing but crumbling concrete; a bullfighting arena looming behind stalled traffic; a static fairground big-wheel; the worn faces of busking street musicians; a populated junction with cheap corner-stores; boys kicking a ball with a dog in tow; shiny star decorations, the tattered left-overs of some forgotten street festival; a boarding bus; a group of youths hanging out, up to no good; indistinct female figures, backs turned on a nocturnal street; night-time bars of dubious repute; and finally: a pathetic huddle of grave markers bearing the names of disappeared girls.[18] With its accelerating visions of dereliction and decay, of poverty and prostitution, this is the sordid streetscape of border towns as contemporary 'ruinscape'. El Paso and Ciudad Juárez: as Bingham's plaintive song intimates, the images of these twin cities melt into one another suggesting simultaneously separate identities and physical indivisibilities, one huge sprawling metropolitan mass/mess conjoined by the bridge itself. Significantly, throughout this montage, our vantage point is distinctive: the camera (and hence we the viewer) pass by and pass through these scenes like an automotive observer, a freeway *flâneur*. This is fundamentally a street-level vision, an intimate but ephemeral glimpse of, and into, the insalubrious underside of the corrupt city as witnessed by the watchful occupant of the circulating police patrol-car.[19] Here, the viewer is immediately and inescapably positioned as already embroiled, involved and implicated in this corrupted and corrupting world.

Notwithstanding the variations between the four series, and the clear overarching trajectory of increasing abstraction,[20] the credit sequences of *Bron/Broen* provide a very different vision of the city, though one arguably still in keeping with the conventions and traditions of classic American film noir and the centripetal city.[21] Borne aloft by the camera, the viewer is treated to numerous panoramic aerial shots of the city at night. It is akin to that vision of the city, beloved of planners and architects, that Michel de Certeau, standing atop the World Trade Center in New York, famously designates as the 'Concept City'.[22] Leaving the confusion and cacophony of everyday street-life far below, from up here the entire urban setting is silently laid out before the observer, the all-seeing eye, so that its concentrations and distributions, patterns and grids, nodes and radial routes can be surveyed at a single glance. This is the perspective of the panoptic gaze. In this montage sequence – at just on the minute mark twice the length of *The Bridge* – the viewer no longer circles the city in a car, but rather in a helicopter. We are presented with bird's-eye shots from directly above static structures and moving vehicles, and slow tracking shots following cars speeding along highways and byways; time-lapse images of accelerated traffic flows through busy streets and crowded junctions; a functional rectilinear office building is intercut with a factory stack smoking into the night; we take a turn around the illuminated 'Turning Torso'; we fly over one stanchion of the Öresund Bridge, looking down vertiginously upon the tarmacked deck below.

There are other points of view presented here as well: the bridge's innumerable cables are shot from below through the windscreen of a moving car; a static camera captures a train gliding across the bridge's lower level into the distance; a final shot sees cars wending their way back and forth diagonally across the screen and into the distance in a shot emphasizing perspective; series 2 offers us a couple of day-time images, of Saga Norén's distinctive mustard colour Porsche – shot here in a discoloured monochrome – pictured from behind, as if we were in a pursuing vehicle. Indeed, by series 3 and 4 this car has become an increasing focus, albeit one ever more fragmented into its constituent elements. We are not invested as passengers and treated to the passing scenes of the cityscape as in *The Bridge*, but rather afforded glimpses of the wing-mirror; of tail-lights; of headlights circulating in the nocturnal city and the darkness of urban ring-roads, junctions and interchanges; of the play of lights on a rain-speckled windscreen and bonnet.

What, then, is one to make of these sequences? Firstly, the emphasis here is on cityscape – not streetscape – as rational totality and as geometric abstraction, or rather, as Kracauer puts it in his key 1926 essay on the 'The Mass Ornament', as the epitome of 'abstractness'.[23] The dance routines of the Tiller Girls, he suggests, involve choreography in which the bodies of the performers are first fragmented into the non-stop movement of legs, arms, heads, feathered headdresses, colourful costumes and faces with fixed smiles, and then recomposed so as to form intricate patterns and figures which are then themselves only perceptible and appreciable when viewed at a distance/ from on high. These are performances whose sole artistic purpose is to put on show mechanical synchronization and military precision, the integration of the individual and eradication of the idiosyncratic into a functioning composite whole: the mass. As the very embodiment of disembodiment, of de-individualization and de-personalization, the Tiller Girls thereby constitute for Kracauer the most eloquent and in this sense wholly legitimate 'surface-level expression' of the triumph of instrumental reason, of the ratio, in modernity. There is something similar here in *Bron/Broen*: to be sure, not the industrial machinery and Taylorized rhythms of the 1920s, but rather of the clean, silent circuitry of frictionless flows, feedback loops, moebius strips and recursive systems, of screens and swift soundless pulses and impulses, of sleek, metallic surfaces; clean, polished and hard. This is not the machine and the mechanized body, but rather synapses and the nervous system. This is an envisioning of the digital uncanny, the melancholy of the microchip, the cybernetic city.

Secondly, these are fundamentally de-populated images: in none of the four opening credit sequences do we distinctly see anyone, any human beings. These seem to be vacant cities, habitats utterly bereft of their inhabitants, or rather, whose citizens are reduced to – and only visible as – tiny pinpricks of light, pixels, scurrying hither and thither in their cars, locked in their offices and apartment buildings. The use of time-lapse images in series 1 is both conventional and key here: the accelerated movements of traffic and crowds give them the air of a panic-stricken evacuation, a frantic rush for the urban exits. This is more than just the empty city; it is the emptying of cities. Moreover, it is this absence of the human that accounts in part for the sense of quietude which pervades the credit sequences. These cities are not only unoccupied, they are eerily silent as well. The camera glides smoothly, seamlessly, and we hear only the curiously ethereal, haunting 'Hollow Talk' with its gentle, repetitive chords and hushed, perplexing lyrics. These images and the signature music are insistently but quietly disquieting.

Finally, there is an intriguing mimetic relationship between the urban fabric and the work of the camera in these opening credits. The camera is continuously in motion, reproducing that upon which it is trained, not just through its images but also by means of its own movements. The camera copies, imitates, re-enacts its object. It is as restless as that which it depicts. And so we follow Saga's car as it crosses the Öresund Bridge or speeds through a tunnel, tailing her; a car crossing the bridge is tracked from above, the camera keeping perfect pace with its object below; dramatically, in circling the Turning Torso, the camera arcs too, spinning around and with the skyscraper, mimicking its contours and torque, almost caressing it; finally, the camera looms vertically over the Öresund Bridge, leaping and looping over its towering stanchions. Car, helicopter and camera – these are synchronized, integrated, inextricable; they are complicit and colluding in the surveillance of the Concept City as both perpetual flux and infinite totality.

It would be tempting to conclude that, as heirs of classic noir visions of the city, *The Bridge* and *Bron/Broen* present images of the centrifugal and centripetal city respectively in their credit sequences, but this would clearly be an oversimplification. The opening shots of the very first episode of *The Bridge* are, for example, very much akin to those nocturnal, aerial images of *Bron/Broen*. And the notion of perpetual motion is central to both the Scandinavian and American versions: one roams the streets, the other the skies. Instead of pursuing these contrasts and comparisons with respect to the relationship between camera and cityscape, I would like to add and explore a third complicating term: the car. What distinguishes *The Bridge* and *Bron/Broen* is a different positioning of the viewer, not just in relation to the city, but with respect to the car in the city.

Driven

As I have already suggested, *The Bridge* treats the car as a cruising vehicular refuge from which we, the viewers, glance out onto the city – onto two cities indeed – whose very form and fabric is a response to the advent of the car itself, that 'ordinary and ugly' architecture of gas stations, motels, diners and strip malls first identified and celebrated by Robert Venturi et al. almost half a century ago.[24] The cityscape is not studied or surveyed but merely glimpsed *en passant*. This is the optics of the automotive *flâneur* in a drive-thru world of Americana.[25]

In *Bron/Broen* there is a very different and ever more insistent configuration of city–car–camera. Instead of being ensconced as passengers in the car, we now watch the vehicles from on high as they circulate the city, negotiate the complex of curves and junctions, rush hither and hither in time-lapse rush-hour shots, criss-cross the bridge itself. The car is no longer a mobile vantage point but rather an itinerant object of our gaze. This is no longer the city seen from the car, but instead the car in the city seen from the drone. And, as such, it seems utterly restless, in perpetual motion. It is not so much patrolling the streets of the city – checking up on the neighbourhood, on the look-out, so to speak – rather, it is prowling. Here we see just driving, driving to be cocooned and alone, driving for its own sake.[26] This is driving as a vision of alienation, isolation and loneliness – no longer a 1940s Hopperian nighthawk pensively perched on a bar stool in Phillies bar, but now a nocturnal nomad in the driving seat, at the wheel, a wandering albatross. Nor is this a freeway *flâneur* taking in the sights. Rather, this is a new incarnation and inflection of Edgar Allan Poe's enigmatic and ultimately inscrutable 'man of the crowd'.[27] While the seductive, uncanny figure of this curious short story seeks continual asylum amidst the night-time crowds of London, to lose himself within and amongst them, this car driver – let us name her, Saga, for we have recognized her Porsche already – seems to be searching for nothing, or, at most, seeking out only the emptiness of the road ahead. Here, driving is not geared towards a destination, but is itself unmasked as compulsion. Perhaps this driven driver has simply forgotten how to stop. In any case, this 'woman at the wheel' is, I suggest, an unmistakable and exemplary figure of Lukácsian 'transcendental homelessness' and/or the 'spiritually shelterless' condition of the modern metropolitan identified by Kracauer.[28] From on high, we watch the headlights of cars like lost souls doomed to wander without rest and for ever in the gloom, like fireflies flitting in the darkness.

The sequences I have discussed articulate and invoke different notions of the menacing and the melancholy: the sadness stimulated by *The Bridge* is that attendant upon the corrupted and corrupting city as a site for the disintegration and decay of buildings, of bodies, of blighted lives. This is a twenty-first-century ruinscape – architectural, social, economic, political, personal. Impoverished, bereft, this is a locus that laments what has been and what is still lost. It is haunted by the girls whose names have been etched on the humble crosses in that final, fleeting image to which all the others inexorably lead, to which we have been driving the whole time even if we did not know it. The mood of *Bron/Broen* is of a rather different order. There are other fears, other sorrows here of an existential kind. Gone are the dirt and detritus, the despair and desperation of Tex-Mexicanicity. Copenhagen and Malmö – not twin or *doppelgänger* cities, but rather dual or binary ones – appear as technospaces from which not just the victims of kidnap and murder have been taken, but the human itself has been abducted, extracted, subtracted. The multiple clusters of lights, like miniature galaxies, may be signs of terrestrial life, but switches can also turn themselves on and off. They will no doubt continue to do so in our absence. The lights will go on without us. What happens when we humans have become surplus to requirements; when there is precious little left of the human at all, when there are so few human remains? This is the post-human void of artificial intelligence into which *Bron/Broen* peers. No longer old-style Southern Californian 'sunshine and noir', nor even the crisp chill of Scandinavian 'snowscape and noir', but now only the absolute dystopian soullessness of 'cybernetics and noir'.

Such melancholy thoughts may seem at odds with the seemingly benign and optimistic ending of the final season of *Bron/Broen*. After all, the ghosts that have been haunting Henrik Sabroe have now been laid to rest. He has been reunited with his surviving daughter Astrid and at least learned the fate of his wife Alice and other daughter Anne. And this knowing means that the grieving process for them may now at last begin. Moreover, Frank, the man responsible for all this pain and death, has been arrested and awaits trial for his crimes. But, then again, one wonders: how will Henrik reconcile himself with all this knowledge? It is one thing to discover the truth; it is quite another to live with it. He is now haunted, not by what he doesn't know, but precisely by what he does. And that will not go away. The pills may help: after all, they have got him this far. But will they be enough to last a lifetime? And there is another matter: will justice be done? Will Frank's long-term imprisonment or institutional incarceration suffice? One is reminded that such punishment did not satisfy Henrik's predecessor, Martin Rohde, who himself now sits in a Danish prison, having taken it upon himself to kill his son's murderer. Will Henrik, too, eventually be driven to exact his own retribution?

And what of Saga? *Bron/Broen* duly ends where it all began on the Öresund Bridge. Driving across it one more time – perhaps one last time – Saga pulls over to the side and steps out of the car. She takes out her Malmö police ID and casts it into the waters below, relinquishing what has been hitherto her all-consuming identity as a police officer. Then, resuming her seat at the wheel, she speaks her name for the first time shorn of any official title. Saga Norén. No more, no less. She puts the car in gear and drives off towards an unknown, uncertain future. This also seems to be a moment of both resolution and anticipation: she too, has discovered the harrowing truth about her past, and now a new life beckons. But I would suggest a more equivocal reading of this denouement. Saga does not so much escape in her car as escape into her car. Yes, she has jettisoned one oppressive identity, but another remains: as driven driver, as one who finds sanctuary only in the car. She remains as wedded to her Porsche as she once was to her work.[29] So what exactly is this open futurity to which she finally speeds off? What will Saga do, how will she live, when cars start driving themselves, when she, like the rest of us, becomes a mere passenger? Such days are still a long way off. Indeed, there is a more immediate and pressing matter: where will she be tonight? Will the darkness find her still driving, still circling those empty ring-roads and highways, just a pair of headlights moving in the silence of the nocturnal city? If so, then the opening credit sequence not only sets the disquieting tone for the fateful events that will unfold onscreen, but provides a foretaste, a foresight, of what will become Saga's lonely vehicular vigil.

Notes

1. Siegfried Kracauer, *Der Detektiv-Roman: Ein philosophischer Traktat* (Frankfurt/Main: Suhrkamp Verlag, 1979).
2. Translated as *The Origins of German Tragic Drama*. Trans. John Osbourne (London: Verso, 2009).
3. This is part of a wider project which draws upon Benjamin and Kracauer for the purpose of exploring the contemporary European (neo-)noir imaginary as instantiated in both Scandinavian and Celtic televisual and literary fictions. For more on this see my '*Noir sans frontiers*: Reflections on the transnational *flaneur*-as-detective'. *Sociétés* 1, no. 35 (2017): 31–42.
4. This is true not only of individual seasons, (series 1 for example) but also and most significantly across the whole four series: the overarching narrative begins with the mid-point of the bridge as the crime scene and eventually concludes there as the site of Saga's final self-affirmation. The Öresund Bridge thus spans not only space but also time, returning us inevitably, inescapably to where it all began.
5. Most famously, of course, in his study of the Parisian shopping arcades. See Walter Benjamin, *The Arcades Project* (Cambridge, MA: Harvard University Press, 1999).
6. See Siegfried Kracauer, *Strassen in Berlin und Anderswo* (Berlin: Das Arsenal, 1987).
7. See Simmel's 'Bridge and Door' in *Simmel on Culture: Selected Writings*, eds David Frisby and Mike Featherstone (London: Sage, 1997), 170–3. It is in this benign spirit, one assumes, that the notes of the euro currency feature various generic bridges.
8. Were it not imbued with such multiple and conflicting qualities, and values, the bridge would constitute a veritable 'non-place' (*non-lieu*) to use Marc Augé's term for all such bypassed/sped through sites of contemporary supermodernity. See his *Non-places: Introduction to an Anthropology of Supermodernity* (London: Verso, 2009).
9. The first series begins, of course, with the discovery of parts from two bodies precisely arranged to form a single corpse at the exact centre point of the Öresund Bridge, hence the involvement of both the Malmö and Copenhagen police. This

spatial mid-point of the crime scene also has a temporal corollary: the crime itself occupies a chronological central moment in detective fiction. The investigation that is set in train progresses as the detectives work systematically backwards to the antecedent events and causes of the crime. How has it come to this? – to this act, this moment, at this place? This is what the detectives come to uncover as their enquiries and the narrative move forwards. In conventionally starting with the crime, detective fiction thereby always inserts the reader/viewer into the middle of things, so that we find ourselves inextricably *in media res*, half-way along the bridge.

10 See Siegfried Kracauer, *Strassen,* 52.
11 Indeed, even if they were limited to the mere listing of such information, the typography and colour schemes used would still be of significance in the creation of expectation and mood, a point demonstrated by Robert Porfiro's study 'The Noir Title Sequence' in *Film Noir Reader 4: The Crucial Films and Themes,* eds A. Silver and J. Ursini (New York: Limelight/Proscenium Publishers, 2004), 277–86.
12 See Raymond Williams, *Marxism and Literature* (Oxford: Oxford University Press, 1978), 128–35. For a further discussion of this term see Devika Sharma and Frederik Tygstrup (eds) *Structure of Feeling: Affectivity and the Study of Culture,* (Berlin/Munich/Boston: Walter de Gruyter GmbH, 2015), 1–29.
13 This careful integration and synchronization of image and music to create a particular urban affect is reminiscent of the thematic concerns and techniques of the 'city symphony' genre of films. For a discussion of these see, for example, the essays by Carsten Strathausen and Martin Gaughan in Mark and Tony Fitzmaurice (eds) *Screening the City* (London: Verso, 2003), 15–40 and 41–57. The credit sequences of both *Bron/Broen* and *The Bridge* constitute city symphonies in miniature: micro-symphonies, or city minuets.
14 See Joel Garreau, *Edge City: Life on the New Frontier* (New York: Anchor Books, 1992), 4.
15 Edward Dimendberg *Film Noir and the Spaces of Modernity* (Cambridge, MA: Harvard University Press, 2004), 171–2.
16 *Bron/Broen* and *The Bridge* are no exceptions. Indeed, it is this very juxtaposition of the elite and the destitute that is supposedly symbolized by the conjoined body parts which open the first series of both.
17 In his classic study *City of Quartz : Excavating the Future in Los Angeles* (London: Verso, 2006), 15, Mike Davis critically interrogates how this boosterist city has marketed itself variously in terms of 'sunshine or noir'.
18 I am thinking here in particular of his classic interpretation of the signifiers of 'Italianicity' in 'The Rhetoric of the Image' in *Image Music Text* (London: Fontana, 1987), 32–51.
19 For an insightful discussion of the privileged position of the car-bound spectator see Jude Davis in Shiel and Fitzmaurice (eds) *Screening the City,* 216–38.
20 It is striking how, across the four series of *Bron/Broen,* the conventional establishing shots of place, no longer needed by audiences now familiar with the setting, are increasingly displaced by establishing shots of mood in the form of abstract and geometric patterns of light and lines.
21 Indeed, in many respects, Dimendberg's characterization of how the centripetal city is depicted provides a most apt summation of these opening image sequences: 'one can recognize centripetal space in film noir in a range of contents. These

include characteristic architectural forms (skyscrapers, mass transportation facilities, public landmarks, residential neighbourhoods); spatial practices (crowd movements, police surveillance, strolls and routines); spaces of representation (darkness, skylines, landmarks, cityscapes); and representations of space (the urban core, the grid, maps, photographs)', *Film Noir*, 108.

22 See Michel de Certeau, *The Practice of Everyday Life* (Berkeley: University of California Press, 2011), 91–110.
23 See Siegfried Kracauer, *The Mass Ornament: Weimar Essays* (Cambridge, MA: Harvard University Press, 1995), 75–88.
24 See Robert Venturi, et al. *Learning from Las Vegas: The Forgotten Symbolism of Architectural Form* (Cambridge, MA: MIT Press, 1977).
25 For a discussion of the reconfiguration of the *flâneur*-as-pedestrian to the *flâneur*-as-driver see Nigel Thrift's reworking of de Certeau in Mike Featherstone, Nigel Thrift and John Urry (eds), *Automobilities* (London: Sage, 2005), 41–60.
26 For a discussion of the car itself as a locus of transient 'dwelling' see John Urry's *Mobilities* (Cambridge: Polity Press, 2007), 124–30.
27 See Poe's story 'The Man of the Crowd' in *The Portable Edgar Allan Poe* (Penguin: London, 2006).
28 See Georg Lukács, *The Theory of the Novel* (London: Merlin Press, 1971). See also Kracauer's *The Salaried Masses: Duty and Distraction in Weimar Germany* (London: Verso, 1998), 88. These terms are attempts to articulate the profound crisis of the modern human condition as instantiated in the pre-eminent modern literary form (for Lukács, the novel) and manifested in the increasingly dominant occupational strata of the metropolis (for Kracauer, the white-collar workers). While not wishing to efface their differences, nonetheless 'transcendental homeless' and 'spiritual shelterlessness' seem to share and invoke both a sense of displacement (we, moderns, are at home everywhere and hence nowhere in particular), and disenchantment (rationalization as the diminution of inner life and consolation).
29 On the theme of (pathological) automotive attachments see Mimi Sheller, 'Automotive Emotions: Feeling the Car' in Featherstone, Thrift and Urry (eds), *Automobilities*, 221–42.

Chapter 6

COMPLEX NOSTALGIAS: NORTH, PASTNESS AND COMMUNITY SURVIVAL IN ARNALDUR INDRIÐASON'S *STRANGE SHORES* AND ANN CLEEVES' *BLUE LIGHTNING*

Daisy Neijmann

Ideas of North continually shift: they are multiple and relative. Those who have written on North all agree that it is an unstable descriptor: there is always a 'truer' north, as Peter Davidson puts it.[1] Even as a geographical locus, North is malleable: it always points elsewhere, to a further north, somewhere else, a direction rather than a location.[2] Everyone carries their own idea of North with them. Yet there is also, as Davidson points out, 'a whole tradition of historical, literary, and visual thinking about the concepts of north and northness'.[3] While ideas and stereotypes about North tend to occur and re-occur with remarkable consistency, imaginations about North are as much shaped by specific cultural contexts and adapted to suit the ideologies prevalent in particular time-periods.[4] As Daniel Chartier argues, these multiple and varied ideas oscillate between the universal and the particular, imagination and experience, each influencing the other.[5] The lived experience of daily life in a northern location is coloured by these discourses of North, both shaping the imaginary as local individuals adopt and co-opt 'foreign' ideas, while readers and travellers absorb particular experiences through textual representation and local interaction. These composite imaginaries shape depictions and representations of North, which in turn are used to serve specific needs, to communicate or illustrate a particular message or to fulfil a desire for an alternative, exotic place.

The crime genre brings a particular focus to such an examination, shaped as it is by distinctive formulas, conventions and expectations. In this chapter, I provide a comparative analysis of the representation and function of North and northness in two crime novels which have their inception in different national and cultural traditions, but in which North plays a prominent role. The novels in question are Arnaldur Indriðason's *Furðustrandir* (2010; *Strange Shores*, 2013) – featuring detective Erlendur Sveinsson – and Ann Cleeves' *Blue*

Lightning (2010), fourth in the Shetland series featuring detective Jimmy Perez. The former, written by an Icelandic author for an Icelandic readership, provides an Icelandic perspective on North and northness, while the latter, written by an English author writing about the UK's northernmost periphery which views all of mainland Britain as South, brings a complexity to the perspective of North. The two authors are differently situated: Ann Cleeves hails from Yorkshire which, although very solidly northern in an English context, is still 'doubly' south from a Shetland perspective, with Scotland in-between. Indriðason on the other hand is from Reykjavík: south by Icelandic standards, but still Iceland. Does this matter for the way North is represented in these works, and for the function of these representations, and if so, how? Particularly intriguing in this respect is the fact that both novels centre around the return of the detective to their place of origin, about which they have complex and ambiguous feelings. In both instances, these places of origin are remote even by the standard of their already remote northern places of work. My analysis will include an examination of the function of this theme of return to a remote northern community.

The Shetland Isles form the remote northern periphery of the United Kingdom (UK) and are ambiguous, both geographically and culturally: they are located halfway between the British mainland and Norway, and have a Viking past that has left its traces in the local language and culture. They, like the Hebrides with their Gaelic culture, have been viewed as 'exotic' in their singularity, as well as their continuing connection to a cultural identity located in the past.[6] Iceland meanwhile has, for most of its history, been peripheral to Europe, an island out in the North Atlantic ocean on the far north-western European fringe, with its own colourful history in the European imagination as a locus of the bizarre, primitive and exotic, as Sumarliði Ísleifsson has argued.[7] Unlike Shetland, however, Iceland has been an independent republic since 1944, with its capital, Reykjavík, the centre of power, government and culture. While it is internationally known as Europe's northernmost capital, from wherever else in Iceland you are other than the larger Reykjavík area, Reykjavík is South. Going to Reykjavík in Icelandic is 'going south', not geographically in many instances, but culturally: the direction of the centre. In the two novels, both detectives return to their places of origin. In the case of Jimmy Perez, this is Fair Isle. While the island actually lies to the south of Shetland's mainland, it is the most remote inhabited island in the UK. In the case of Erlendur, it is Eskifjörður, located on the far-eastern shore of Iceland. Again, this is not geographically north, but about as far away as one can get from Reykjavík, on the other side of the central highlands, behind glaciers and mountains. Both locations can thus be viewed as what Davidson terms an 'honorary north', a place 'that has been perceived to embody an idea or essence of north, or northness'.[8] In this chapter I consider what comprises North in the two novels, and how it functions in their cultural imaginary.

Representations of North and northness

The word 'North' does not occur as a concept or idea in *Strange Shores*. North is simply there as a fact of life not far from the Arctic Circle: in the weather, the northern seasons, the landscape and the power of the elements. Erlendur arrives in the autumn, and experiences the onset of winter: the increasing cold, the growing darkness, the first snow. It is ultimately the weather that is the absolute governing force. For how long will Erlendur still be able to camp out in the isolated ruins of the family farm? The northern winter weather is also a determining factor in the crime that Erlendur investigates: the tragedy of the British occupying soldiers caught out in a blizzard during a mountain hike in the Second World War provides a way to hide the first murder, while a bad storm at sea provides the occasion for the second. Erlendur himself belongs to the northern winter: 'Winter is Erlendur's area of choice, he is at home in the dark and the cold which characterize most of Arnaldur's works from the very first novel'.[9] As Úlfhildur Dagsdóttir points out, this characterization of Erlendur is intimately connected with the prominent role of winter in Indriðason's oeuvre as a whole, not only creating a dark and chilling atmosphere, but revealing the darker aspects of Icelandic society. In the Erlendur novels, Iceland appears true to its name.

This close connection between Erlendur and the northern winter has a deeper personal meaning, however, which has importantly shaped Erlendur as a detective as well as a person. As a child, Erlendur lost his younger brother in a blizzard in the mountains. The guilt and grief resulting from this tragedy have never left him, and the almost unbearable uncertainty of his brother Bergur's fate is a driving force for Erlendur as a detective: to provide closure for those who have lost a loved one. Erlendur is obsessed with the stories of those who suffer accidents or get lost in the Icelandic wilderness, a literary genre known in Iceland as *hrakningasögur*, and he has also become a specialist in the effects of cold. This knowledge helps him solve the second murder in *Strange Shores*. That novel is the final one in the Erlendur series, at least chronologically (later novels feature a younger Erlendur), ending with Erlendur's disappearance into the northern landscape and the mountain in whose shadow Bergur was lost. This ending echoes Bergur's fate, as the reader does not know what becomes of Erlendur (although it is implied that he has finally joined his brother). It also alludes to the end of the last of Halldór Laxness' great social-realist epic trilogies, *Heimsljós* (1940; *World Light*, 2002): the main character, Ólafur Kárason Ljósvíkingur, famously disappears into the northern landscape in a similar manner, walking into the mountain, the newly fallen snow and, ultimately, into the glacier; 'And beauty shall rule alone'.[10] This image is powerful but also ambiguous: while it may be interpreted as romantic, a joining of man with sublime nature, there is in fact nothing romantic about the description of the northern climate and landscape in either Icelandic novel. Rather, it is the description of a realistic experience of North where the destructive power of nature and the power of the elements is absolute; a reminder of human frailty and mortality. In the end, it overwhelms us and we disappear into it, all traces erased.

This view has its basis in Icelandic history and culture: a centuries-old experience of poverty, cold and darkness with people trying to survive and wrest a living from this northern land. The locals Erlendur speaks to still display this attitude of stoic resignation in the face of a superior force. As one fisherman's daughter says: 'The fishermen here often used to go out in bad weather. Some of them didn't come back. That's life in a fishing village. I don't think my father allowed himself to get sentimental', while the murder victim's nephew puts it thus: 'Naturally she was beside herself with grief – I can remember that – but it goes with the territory when you live in Iceland. People accept it.'[11] Even small children need a basic knowledge of survival against the elements, as shown by the fact that Erlendur as a young boy knew to dig himself into the snow during the blizzard and to avoid falling asleep. The harsh reality of life in the North is a fact that the inhabitants have learned to accept.

In *Blue Lightning* too, the emphasis is on the northern landscape and the elements, which not only form the background to the story but are crucial to it. The storm that hits Fair Isle just as Perez and his fiancée Fran arrive creates the claustrophobic conditions that allow the first murder to take place and create the isolation in which the murder investigation has to happen, culminating in two further murders and profound tragedy for Perez. Despite these similarities in emphasis and function to the narrative, there are, however, obvious differences in the representation of North and northness in the two novels. Most perceptibly, the northern island, its landscape, climate and community, are recreated here for a more southern, metropolitan readership. The focalizer for this audience is Fran, who is English and hails from London. Fran has a daughter by a Shetlander and has recently moved to mainland Shetland, but despite her love for the islands she is consistently described as an outsider and a southerner: she is bohemian, stylish, an artist who is used to the temperate climate, the lifestyle and conveniences of urban southern England. It is Fran first and foremost who translates Fair Isle for a more urban and southern consciousness. It is her first visit to the island, to meet Perez's family and the place where he grew up, and throughout the novel she grapples with the underlying questions of whether she could ever live there and whether she could ever belong: she 'loved the idea of that, the drama of being in one of the most remote places in the UK', but now 'she wasn't sure how that would work out in reality'.[12]

While in *Strange Shores* the landscape and climate are there as a matter of fact and on their own terms, in *Blue Lightning* we are continuously reminded of the island's location on the remote northern periphery, with the emphasis very much on the dramatic extremes of the elements, the coldness, the bare landscape shaped by frost and beaten by wild winds and waves. This is enforced by the title and cover of the novel.[13] Local conditions are specifically explained, such as the lack of trees, and 'the time of day Shetlanders called "the darkenin"' (313). In Shetland, hail, sleet and rain pelt down with a terrible, destructive force. The storm, which lasts for days, is so ferocious that it creates an extremely tense, fraught atmosphere. The island's sparse population huddles against the elements in small crofts, underlining the limits of human power against the absolute forces of nature in this place of extremes, 'the utter north from civilization', as Davidson puts it.[14] Fair Isle is considered remote and extreme even by Shetland standards, as the reaction of Shetland police officer Sandy Wilson on his arrival makes clear: 'I couldn't take this. It would drive me crazy after a week' (210). Fair Isle is clearly 'other' in its peripheral northernness and remoteness; indeed, the Field Centre, a scientific birdwatching centre on the fringe of the island community, capitalizes on this attraction by providing accommodation 'for people who were interested in experiencing the UK's most remote inhabited island' (9-10). On several occasions the difference is highlighted between the local population, which knows that the weather constantly needs to be negotiated, and the outsiders, who seem both unable and unwilling to understand that, here, nature rules, and everyday life as they know and expect it is simply on hold.

The perspective in *Blue Lightning* is not, however, exclusively with the southern outsider. The insider-outsider dynamic is foregrounded in the novel, partly through Fran, who wants to belong for Perez's sake, but is also acutely aware of her outsider status; partly through the occasionally tense relationship between the islanders and the visitors in the Field Centre; and partly through Perez, who, after having gone south to become a policeman and returned, provides a mediating perspective. Scottish birdwatcher Dougie for instance, thinks that the islanders are all 'strange bastards' (55), while the islanders describe the birdwatchers as 'obsessed', although they do provide 'business for the shop' (20). Jane, the English cook at the Centre, is completely in love with Fair Isle but at the same time keeps her distance from the islanders (10), while Perez, the islander, cannot understand her passionate attachment to the island (70): as a local, his connection to the place is not by choice. It is, in fact, the relationship between Perez and his parents that forms Perez's main connection with the island: the expectations that come with being the only son to carry on the Perez name, to continue the family tradition as crofters and skipper on the ferry to and from the island: 'There's been a Perez in Fair Isle since the first one was washed ashore from a ship during the Spanish Armada' (10). These expectations weigh him down and are an important source of his guilt, but they also provide a sense of continuity and belonging and form 'a connection he had no way of breaking' (181). Perez's paradoxical relationship with Fair Isle thus crystallises the impossible position he finds himself in which lends his character a necessary melancholic depth, while at the same time providing the narrative with an intermediating focalizer.

The extremity, remoteness and wildness emphasized in the novel is of course an important part of the attraction of North for those who would escape urban life, if only temporarily, and seek an antidote to modernity. Kerstin Bergman suggests that, for audiences from the densely populated areas of many countries, the sparsely inhabited landscapes of the north, the open spaces and natural elements, the cold and dark winters all seem far removed from daily life and exotic: '[i]t is the exotic and foreign that is expected to generate desire in readers ... a dream of a different place'.[15]

Northern communities: Fictional and real

Community clearly plays an important role in both novels. Remote northern communities are small, shaped by local conditions, and rely on co-operation for survival, as people try to make a living in close proximity to an awe-inspiring but unpredictable and dangerous nature where cold, darkness and the elements rule, and where survival is difficult. This sense of mutual dependence and survival shapes northern communities, where 'no fellow-citizen is more an enemy than the weather'.[16] Community identity and culture is based on a life characterized by a sense of precariousness and transience, and on the support structure of a strong network of local and family ties. At the same time, it is derived from its distance from the metropolis, the centre of power in the South. In Nordic noir, the representation of these remote, rural northern communities, as many critics have pointed out, relies importantly on their connection with ideas of North as 'other'. North has often had ascribed to it a pastness and cultural authenticity which the crowded, anonymous, multicultural southern centre has lost – a kind of reality vis-à-vis a spoiled present and the artificiality of the metropolis.[17] Remote northern communities are often romanticized as colourful and living a desirable existence closer to nature, as Bergman indicates, and the Nordic noir genre shows a strong tendency to rely on a perceived contrast between northern place and community on the one hand, and violent crime on the other, frequently appearing on book covers in images such as blood in pure, white snow.[18] Such imaginings of remote northern communities obviously rely on popular stereotypes and take little account of the particularities of diverse cultural contexts.

Strange Shores, like all other works by Indriðason, is firmly set in an Icelandic context, and addresses an Icelandic readership first and foremost. The intended readership is a northern one, familiar with the conditions, past and present, of living on an island close to the Arctic Circle, and for whom this setting thus holds no particular attraction other than a daily environment.[19] The main opposition in the North–South binary in this instance is thus one of relation to the centre of power and of urban versus rural consciousness in an Icelandic context. Erlendur has a difficult relationship with modernity and the present. He is in many ways not just a man out of place, but out of time. In this respect, he embodies an important aspect of Icelandic twentieth-century history: he is representative of the generation that lived the sudden and profound change of a traditional rural society catapulted almost overnight into modernity. It has left him rootless. On a personal level, the trauma of the loss of his brother has meant that time for Erlendur has not really moved forward since the accident. He lives in that time period, not the present. For Erlendur, the return to the east is a return to his past: it is a place in memory. He camps out in the ruins of the old family croft, and the focus of his investigation is a case from the past. He speaks mostly with older people who remember that time. This is where, and *when*, Erlendur is most at home.

The East Fjords community in the present only exists on the fringes of Erlendur's perception. He no longer knows anyone there, has not kept in touch with relatives, and he deplores the changes that are taking place, in the form of the big aluminium plant and the dam that provides it with electricity. To the younger local people, he is a stranger, an outsider – the community culture he relates to is in the past. The community itself appears as rather fragmented in the novel. People are in constant transit, and ties are broken. Many have moved away south and lost contact with family and friends. Outsiders have moved in. The main players in the old murder case Erlendur is investigating were all incomers, and in the present, the aluminium plant and the dam have brought in many outsiders, both Icelandic and foreign. Even families that have remained local are not in contact much: everyone is too busy trying to stay in work. As a result, there is a loss of community cohesion and collective memory. People do not remember local events or people. The stories are dying out with the elderly, and books and collections containing local knowledge are cleared out and disappear on the rubbish heap.

This representation of a remote northern community, as well as of the detective at the centre of the novel, reflects both historical attitudes and contemporary developments in modern Iceland. As Marion Lerner points out in her work on Icelandic national identity in relation to nature in the North, this self-identity has largely been based on a pioneer mentality: conquering the land and taming the wild.[20] This drive to conquer the northern landscape and assert man's power over an awe-inspiring nature provided Icelanders with a positive self-image during the nation-building era of the late nineteenth and early twentieth centuries, while at the same time offering an ideology leading towards progress and modernity after centuries of poverty and hardship. Erlendur's obsession with *hrakningasögur* is particularly noteworthy in this respect. This Icelandic literary genre developed, as Lerner argues, alongside the development of national identity and a change in attitude towards wild nature from a raw, dangerous and frightening force to a challenge, and human encounters with the forces of the northern wilderness as a demonstration of the unique qualities which life in the North has fostered in the national character.[21] These stories of people battling the force and perils of the landscape and the elements, although showing a healthy respect for nature, certainly do not praise or glorify it, and the focus is firmly on the heroic human struggle.

Throughout the twentieth century and into the twenty-first, Iceland has demonstrated a determined national effort to embrace modernity, including sustained developments to exploit the natural resources of the northern landscape. Having lived for centuries at the mercy of nature, it remains, to many Icelanders, a source of great pride to assert not only their dominance over it, but to be able to turn it into a money-making resource. This attitude towards the northern landscape is neither new nor particular to Icelanders. As Davidson points out, the North as a source for treasure hunting is as old as other ideas about North, a fact that has received more international attention in recent years which have exposed the fragility of the North in the face of an increased hunt for resources as well as of other damaging effects of modernity, notably pollution.[22] While the voice of those who believe the North needs protection from human exploitation is gradually being heard more than it used to be in Iceland, an instrumental attitude towards nature has so far remained a part of hegemonic nationalist discourse in Iceland. Anne Brydon argues that reason and rationality continue to be used as identity markers, including what is seen as rational management of a non-sentient, raw material used as a capitalist economic resource, as opposed to an aestheticism perceived as dangerously naive, irrational, protectionist and sentimental.[23] The exploitation of its northern resources becomes an issue of sovereignty, Iceland's right to control its own territory without interference from those who live in urban environments and do not have to make a living in and from the difficult northern landscape.

The remote Eskifjörður community in *Strange Shores* demonstrates the effects of this sustained advance of modernity. The big dam and the aluminium plant provide much-needed employment opportunities to replace the loss of traditional fishing and farming that are necessary to stem the tide of those moving south for work, and to keep the community alive, not least with an influx of newcomers, both from elsewhere in Iceland and from abroad (41). However, this has resulted in the disintegration of community ties and traditions, the loss of local memory and lore, emblems of an 'experience of modernity as separation and loss', in Brydon's words.[24] This experience of separation and loss is most poignantly expressed in the character of Erlendur and the elderly people he talks to. They have all become separated in the present from what they knew, or remember, as home. This is not necessarily criticized in the novel. While it is presented in a slightly nostalgic way, it is ultimately seen as a process that is entirely inevitable. Bóas, the local fox-hunter, says in relation to people moving away: 'The countryside was uninhabited when we arrived, so why shouldn't it be abandoned again when we leave? [...] People come and people go. I ask you, what could be more natural?' (10). The main concern for a remote community is how to survive in the changing times. The new aluminium plant run by a foreign multinational has become a focus for this concern.

The cultural alterity that Erlendur is seeking, distinct from modernity and the south, is in the past, while the community in the present is fighting for survival by aligning itself with the centre by joining the national effort of welcoming modernity, industry and newcomers. It is thus entirely appropriate in this respect that Erlendur eventually disappears into the mountains, the northern wilderness. It, rather than a community he no longer recognizes or relates to, constitutes his home: it is in this way that he re-joins his brother, his family, as well as the place that originally fostered them in all its destructive force. This rejoining is not a romantic reunion of man and nature or a restoration of the past to heal the destructive effects of modernity. No such return is possible. Rather, it is a slightly melancholic farewell to a time that is gone, although it should not be forgotten, as well as a homecoming for someone unable to separate himself from that time in the past, joining instead the timeless northern landscape which, it is indicated throughout the novel, will continue to be there long after the human settlement and its efforts to survive through domination and exploitation are gone.

In *Blue Lightning*, it is the insider–outsider dynamic that reverberates throughout the novel. This dynamic works on several different levels that can all be read in the larger cultural and political context of Great Britain, which is made up of a number of different countries and a plethora of local cultures, all united by a central British parliament and government located in the metropolis in the south of England, added to which is a history of colonization and empire. In the Shetland series, a picture emerges of Shetland as the remote northern periphery of the UK, with Shetlanders forming a local community. In this context, 'outsiders' or 'incomers' refers to anyone not from Shetland. In certain instances, urban centres in Scotland function as South, as the location of higher educational institutions, the head offices of the Highland and Islands police force and so on. The main polarity set up in the novels, however, is that between Shetland and metropolitan England (notably London). The Shetland community, meanwhile, has its own identifications. While to the outsider this community may seem small and close-knit in itself, Shetlanders distinguish by island, 'a Fetlar woman' (221), 'a Whalsay man' (238), while Mainland and Lerwick serve as the centre in a Shetland context. Language forms another marker of insider–outsider status. In the UK, cultural identities are commonly constructed and acted out not only through local identification but also through accent. The description of most characters in the novel includes accent as an indicator of where they hail from originally, as well as social class, education, etc. Perez needs to adapt his Shetland way of speaking when communicating with outsiders who would otherwise not understand him (57), but uses his Shetland accent when interviewing locals to earn their trust, while even Fran cannot understand him when he speaks with his parents (95). These identification markers and boundaries all play a role in negotiating the complex web of relationships in the Shetland Isles.

It is the community of Fair Isle in *Blue Lightning* that is at the centre of this web of relationships. Fair Isle is remote even by Shetland standards, and the local community is very small indeed, bound closely together by kinship ties and by its very remoteness. As a result, the insider–outsider binary becomes even more pronounced. Perez himself feels very much both on the inside, and on the outside of his home community. The community is portrayed as extremely tight knit, held together by family history, traditions and religion. Like most other outsiders, and as a representative of modern city life, Fran arrives with 'romantic ideas about rural harmonious community life', as Perez himself observes (240). At the same time, she is anxious about her status as the outsider who is engaged to a local son: 'This place, Fair Isle, was a part of who he was. He'd grown up here and his family had lived here for generations. What would they make of her?' (2). She quickly begins to experience the other side of romance, however. The house where Perez grew up is small and cramped, northern weather is harsh and keeps people indoors, and island life is dictated by community ways, local gossip and religion. Everything is pre-determined, static, and soon Fran starts to feel trapped and afraid she will go mad with boredom: '*Oh, Jimmy*, she thought. *I'm really not sure I could live here, not even with you*' (emphasis in original; 17). Clearly, breaking through the insider-outsider binary is not only a matter of overcoming community boundaries but of boundaries within oneself.

People who are not part of the island community feel their status as outsiders very strongly. The incomers in the Field Centre do not really interact with the locals, while the community accepts them primarily for bringing business. People are identified by their origins: Fran is 'this Englishwoman' (15), a jewellery maker is 'that Scottish woman' (214). When Perez starts his murder investigation, these boundaries become quite confusing to him. He feels this is very much 'his island', his home territory, yet in the Field Centre he feels like 'an imposter in his own land' (88), and he feels he has to 'shift the balance of power' (113). Significantly, his feelings are expressed in colonial terms when he likens the centre to 'an outpost of Empire during the time of the Raj; he felt like a native official bridging the gap between both cultures' (107). This reveals a view of Shetland as a colony rather than a periphery, which is political in itself if we accept Heidi Hansson's distinction between the two in her discussion of travel writing in the Nordic North: 'Colonies are more likely to be viewed as extensions of the colonizing centres and therefore insufficiently civilized in comparison. Peripheries, on the other hand, are unattached to the European centres, with their own distinctive backgrounds and histories'.[25] Hansson argues that, while the North consistently appears in travel writing as a place of nostalgia where escape from the ravages of industrialization and modernity is still possible, some travel writers present it less as a rural Arcadia and more as a social and cultural counterspace where an alternative version of modernity is possible. It is noteworthy in this respect that Cleeves very much downplays the Nordic (Viking) history and heritage of the Shetland Isles throughout the entire Shetland series, to the point where these are virtually absent. Instead, the Isles are portrayed exclusively as a part of Great Britain, and not as a peripheral region with its own independent history and culture. This echoes

James Boswell's description of the Scottish Western Isles as a remote place yet so near to home that, in Sturgeon Thompson's words, he 'could go to encounter alterity without risk or confusion to the self'.[26] The outsiders in Fair Isle are there primarily because they desire an escape from modernity, a temporary or more permanent alternative to life in the metropolitan south, like Jane, the English cook. This alternative, however, is still recognizably and comfortably British, only in a wilder, more natural setting without the excesses of industrialization and urbanization, where cultural traditions have been preserved and people still croft, knit, cook, bake, play the fiddle and dance. As such, it becomes a place of nostalgia where an urbanized readership can still access a more rural, traditional Britain.

As an English author, Cleeves shows great awareness of her own 'outsider' view, which is often handled with great sensitivity, wanting to get things right by the Shetlanders and careful not to idealize or judge them, while at the same time providing the outsider perspective as a counterpoint. However, it is also clear that an important part of the attraction of the novels lies in readers' desire for a locale that is exotic in its singularity, its difference from the centre, yet also familiar enough to be comfortable and provide a nostalgic appeal. The remote northern island community of Fair Isle is portrayed as relying on its traditions and its strong ties to the past for its cohesion and cultural survival. It is these which form a barrier against outsider influence, thereby preserving its pastness, curiosity and nostalgic appeal. The question of whether survival is in fact possible without change and outside influence is never really raised.

Homecomings and endings

The ties that bind remote northern communities make the notion of home and homecoming, at least for those who grew up there, a particularly potent one. The two novels share the central theme of the main detective's homecoming. Both Erlendur and Perez are loners, quiet, thoughtful, melancholic – what many critics have identified as the classic temperament of the Nordic noir detective.[27] Both are also driven by guilt – although their guilt has a different origin. Erlendur suffers from survivor's guilt, Perez's stems from his father's strict kirk teachings and a sense of failure with regard to family and community obligations. In both novels, though, this guilt has a crucial influence on their work as detectives: the need to find answers, to set things right. Detectives in Nordic noir tend to function in many ways as a social conscience.[28] Their compulsion to uncover secrets and reveal the truth makes both Erlendur and Perez incurably, at times even distastefully, curious, as they themselves admit.

Both Erlendur and Perez have a difficult relationship with 'home'. They have 'gone south' and become cops. Their work and living away has changed them. Erlendur moved away with his parents when he was twelve years old. Nothing was ever the same after his brother was lost in the blizzard, and his parents could no longer bear to live so near the northern wilderness. The family moved to Reykjavík, where Erlendur felt rootless and out of place. At the same time, he lost all ties with his home community, ending up neither here nor there, living only with the guilt, the loss, and the lack of closure. He long avoided going back to his village, as the memories were too painful, but in *Strange Shores* Erlendur feels compelled by an earlier case to return. For Perez, it is family that forms the main connection, and the main problem. Perez is the only son of a proud family of Fair Islanders who trace their origins back to a survivor from a Spanish Armada ship, and he feels the weight of his parents' hopes and expectations on him to continue the family line and traditions on the island. His attachment to his family and home is strong, and although he has chosen to follow a different path in life, he feels unable to sever the connection. He feels guilty about disappointing his parents, but struggles at the same time with family expectations to live a life not of his own choosing, weighed down by tradition. He, too, has been trying to avoid going home.

The meaning of home in the context of 'a transnational experience of modernity as separation and loss' in an increasingly globalized world is described by Brydon as 'a physical place as well as a state of being – a place of nurturance, refuge and ease [...]. It is against this threat of disconnection and dislocation that the idea and ideal of home is rendered desirable in Western modernity'.[29] The nostalgia attached to the idea of home and especially the idea of the return, however, proves complex. In the two novels, the detectives are confronted with crimes they did not expect to find, which are perhaps indicative of the larger fact that home as a place no longer corresponds with their idea of home – and possibly never did. Instead of refuge and ease, Erlendur and Perez not only end up solving murders, but also come face to face with their own personal tragedies. For Erlendur, this is the eventual confrontation with his past and his guilt – the shadows or ghosts that have haunted him for so long – as well as the realization that his home is in fact not in the present, but in the past. For Perez, it is the unexpected confrontation with the dangers of his profession, and the fact that even his own community is not free from the evils of modern society to which his fiancée falls victim.

Davidson describes the journey north as 'a journey into a kind of truth', an inner journey connected to emotional cleansing and transformation: North 'intensifies the experience of the individual who goes there'.[30] Fair Isle and Eskifjörður become the focus for a confrontation with complex and painful emotions which shed light on the detectives and their methods, and what motivates them in their work as detectives. In the remote home setting of these communities we see their distinctive character traits crystallized and contextualized – while at the same time representing great personal tragedy which Erlendur finally has to face, and which completely transforms Perez.

Remoteness, extreme weather and personal tragedy shape the characters and role of the two sleuths in *Strange Shores* and *Blue Lightning*, who both originally hail from and finally return to communities moulded by survival in the North. In *Strange Shores*, survival as a modern northern nation means that peripheral communities must adapt and become more like the centre. In *Blue Lightning*, on the other hand, the emphasis is on the outermost northern fringe of the UK as an antithesis to the metropolis, an escape from the limitations of civilization: remote rural community identity is strong and has its attractions, even if that identity is ambiguous. The main concern of the Fair Isle community is the preservation of local tradition through kinship and continuity based in survival in the North, and at the same time forming a barrier that keeps outside influences on the margins. The remote community in *Strange Shores* on the other hand is portrayed as fragmented and threatened with disintegration. The only answer to survival comes in the form of a polluting industry that fills the coffers of foreign multinationals while destroying the fabric of the traditional community. A gentle note of melancholic nostalgia is detectable in *Strange Shores*, and modernity is described as a 'strange beast', but ultimately the past is in the past.[31] The furthest the novel comes to deploring this development is in its critique of the accompanying loss of memory and lore that provide continuity with the past and into the future, as well as of the dominant focus on an industrial attitude to nature to ensure survival. Nature thus appears as ultimately the more powerful, lasting force in *Strange Shores*, while community identity based on tradition appears as the surviving force in *Blue Lightning*.

The nostalgia for community and home in the North in *Strange Shores* is an important link in a necessary connection with the past to understand the present – a link that is in danger of being lost, but it is not a basis to build a future on, certainly not if that community is part of a larger, national effort to join a global community. In *Blue Lightning*, cultural conservatism, while ambiguous, is portrayed as an important way to preserve a continuity and authenticity which serve as a desired refuge, whether temporary or permanent, from the trappings of metropolitanism, a playing ground for urbanites who desire a return to a past and more 'natural' way of life. While Erlendur is granted a homecoming of sorts by becoming one with the past and the landscape, Perez leaves his home community at the end of the book utterly distraught: his return, rather than providing connection or refuge, has only enhanced his sense of separation and loss. He has experienced, in the most painful way possible, that no community, no matter how remote, far north and conservative, is completely detached from the dark side of life in the modern world. This experience does not provide a way out of the complexity and ambiguity, however, for, although he tells the Fiscal 'I'll never be able to go back there', he is in fact back on his way home two days later.[32] The appeal remains: for Perez, for outsiders, for readers. It is this nostalgic appeal, despite its complexity, that informs the representation and function of North and community in *Blue Lightning*. *Strange Shores*, written by and for Icelanders, provides an alternative perspective of an independent northern nation which is still relatively new to modernity and continues to see it as the main road to progress. In this novel, the way to survive as a modern nation in the North leaves little room for nostalgia: 'And so the years passed, time crawling on inexorably into a future that no one from the obsolete past would recognize' (275). This future orientation and instrumental approach creates the wealth and foreign influx necessary to ensure survival, but also brings about loss of memory and community cohesion, the accompaniments of modernity. The two novels do convey one shared message about the North: no matter how remote, it cannot escape the influences of modernity and provide the purity, pastness and refuge that have traditionally been associated with it in the imagination.

Notes

1 Peter Davidson, *The Idea of North* (London: Reaktion Books, 2005), 234.
2 Peter Davidson, 7; Sumarliði Ísleifsson, 'Introduction: Imaginings of National Identity and the North' in *Iceland and Images of the North*, eds Sumarliði Ísleifsson with Daniel Chartier (Québec: Presses de l'Université du Québec, 2011), 3–22, 9; Daniel Chartier, 'The "North" and the Idea of "Iceland": Contemporary Cross-Cultural Construction of Representations of Iceland' in *Iceland and Images of the North*, 515–30, 521–3; Sherrill Grace, *Canada and the Idea of North* (Montreal: McGill-Queen's University Press, 2002), 16.
3 Peter Davidson, 7.
4 Sumarliði Ísleifsson, 17–18.
5 Daniel Chartier, 528–9.
6 Sturgeon Thompson, 'Writing the Fringe: Eighteenth-Century Accounts of the Western Islands of Scotland' in *Beyond the Floating Islands*, eds Stephanos Stephanides and Susan Bassnett (Bologna: Cotepra/University of Bologna, 2002), 106–14, 106.
7 Sumarliði Ísleifsson, *Ísland, framandi land* (Reykjavík: Mál og menning, 2006).
8 Peter Davidson, 19. Until very recently, the communities in the Icelandic East Fjords were not connected to the national ring-road around the island and featured the only part of the road system not yet asphalted, underscoring its remoteness from 'civilization' in the national consciousness. The 'real' north in Iceland meanwhile is its uninhabited interior, the central highland, in the sense that it is the region in Iceland that has had attributes of 'Far North' assigned to it. See Marion Lerner, 'Images of the North, Sublime Nature, and a Pioneering Icelandic Nation' in *Iceland and Images of the North*, 229–53, 230. The language and culture of the geographical north in Iceland have, however, also been associated with conventional ideas about North, particularly vis-à-vis the South of Iceland. See Margrét Guðmundsdóttir, '"Það er drift í henni" Um viðhorf til máls og manna', Lecture, *Friday Seminar Series*, Faculty of History and Philosophy, University of Iceland, 16 October 2015.
9 Úlfhildur Dagsdóttir, 'Reykjavíkurdagar og nætur', *Bókmenntaborgin: Bókmenntavefur: Arnaldur Indriðason*. Available online: https://bokmenntaborgin.is/bokmenntavefur/hofundar/arnaldur-indridason (accessed 11 April 2018). My translation.
10 Halldór Laxness, *World Light*, trans. Magnus Magnusson (London: Vintage, 2002), 598.

6. *Complex Nostalgias* 99

11 Arnaldur Indriðason, *Strange Shores*, trans. Victoria Cribb (London: Harvill Secker, 2013), 198 and 128. Further references to this novel will be to this edition and in the text as page number in brackets.
12 Ann Cleeves, *Blue Lightning* (London: MacMillan, 2010), 15. Further references to this novel will be to this edition and in the text as page number in brackets.
13 All books in the Shetland series in fact carry elemental two-word titles and feature evocative covers of northern land- and waterscapes: *Raven Black* (2006); *White Nights* (2008); *Red Bones* (2009); *Blue Lightning* (2010); *Dead Water* (2013); *Thin Air* (2014); *Cold Earth* (2016).
14 Peter Davidson, 29.
15 Kerstin Bergman, 'The Captivating Chill: Why Readers Desire Nordic Noir', *Scandinavian-Canadian Studies* 22 (2015): 80–9, 86.
16 Peter Davidson, 132.
17 Ibid., 188 and 208.
18 Kerstin Bergman, 86.
19 Given the frequency with which northern scenery is used on the covers of Nordic noir books, including the international translations of Indriðason's novels, it is noteworthy in this respect that the covers of his novels in the original Icelandic do not feature any particular references to North. The original cover of *Furðustrandir* is sepia-coloured and shows a window behind which are the shadowy contours of someone or something, directing the reader to the past and the mysteries it holds, rather than to the northern setting of the novel. Particularly ironic, at least in relation to this novel and in light of my argument, is that, on the cover of the UK publication by Harvill Secker, the novel is marketed as 'Murder in Reykjavik'.
20 Marion Lerner, 229–53.
21 Ibid., 234–8 and 236.
22 Peter Davidson, 51 and 66. Also Ísleifsson (2011), 9 and 18.
23 Anne Brydon, 'The Predicament of Nature: Keiko the Whale and the Cultural Politics of Whaling in Iceland', *Anthropological Quarterly* 79, no. 2 (2006): 225–60, 232–3.
24 Anne Brydon, 240.
25 Heidi Hansson, 'Between Nostalgia and Modernity: Competing Discourses in Travel Writing about the Nordic North' in *Iceland and Images of the North*, 255–82, 272.
26 Heidi Thompson, 107.
27 Paula Arvas and Andrew Nestingen, 'Introduction: Contemporary Scandinavian Crime Fiction' in *Scandinavian Crime Fiction*, eds Paula Arvas and Andrew Nestingen (Cardiff: University of Wales Press, 2011), 1–17, 9; Kristín Árnadóttir, 'Hverra manna er Erlendur?', *Tímarit Máls og menningar* 64, no. 1 (2003): 50–6, 51–2; Bergman, 81–3.
28 Arvas and Nestingen, 2; Bergman, 84; Barry Forshaw, *Death in a Cold Climate: A Guide to Scandinavian Crime Fiction* (New York: Palgrave Macmillan, 2012), 14.
29 Anne Brydon, 240.
30 Peter Davidson, 113 and 193.
31 'Modernity is a strange beast' is my translation of the original Icelandic: *Nútíminn er kyndug skepna* (*Furðustrandir*, Reykjavík: Vaka Helgafell, 2011: 28). The published English translation offers a slightly different interpretation of the elderly woman's words which limits their scope and impact: 'What extraordinary times we're living through' (24).
32 Ann Cleeves, 351.

Chapter 7

NORDIC NOIR AND THE 'POST-COLONIAL' NORTH: THE LEGACIES OF DANISH COLONIALISM IN THE NORDIC REGION

Christinna Hazzard

Since the Danish detective series *Forbrydelsen* (*The Killing*) first aired on BBC4 in 2011, Nordic noir television dramas have become increasingly popular, both in the UK and internationally, and have undoubtedly shaped ideas about the Nordic region and what it means to be Nordic in the twenty-first century. With the austere visual representation of land and cityscapes, plots of murder, political corruption and social exploitation, inaugurated by crime fiction writers in the 1960s and 1970s, Nordic noir has recently reinforced the image of the Nordic region as bleak, grey and crime-ridden. However, this portrayal of the region contrasts starkly with the image of the Nordic nations as safe and socially cohesive, cemented by publications such as the UN's annual 'World Happiness Report', which has consistently ranked the Nordic nations in the top ten since publication began in 2012. These two very different images of the region have each contributed to what one UK journalist has termed 'the All Nordic Everything trend': a recent proliferation of books, documentaries, travel and cookery programmes exploring the culture, landscape, food and languages of the Nordic region.[1] A significant contribution to the trend has been the discovery of *hygge*.[2] Although the Danish word supposedly has no equivalent in the English language, there has been a wealth of articles and books published in the UK on *hygge* since 2015 describing it variously as an 'appreciation of the small things in life', a 'wellness trend' and even an 'attitude'.[3] In 2016 *hygge* was awarded second place in the Collins Dictionary 'Word of the Year' competition, only narrowly losing out to 'Brexit', illustrating the impact of Nordic culture on the British popular imaginary.[4] The fascination with *hygge*, however, and its frequent misinterpretation, epitomizes the largely uncritical engagement with Nordic culture in the UK, which has resulted in the widespread tendency to idealize and homogenize the region and its peoples.

'Nordic' designates a region which is both multilingual and multiethnic, with territories spanning from Continental Europe to the Arctic, and across the

Atlantic. It is comprised of the constitutional monarchies – Norway, Sweden, Denmark – that make up Scandinavia, the independent republics of Iceland and Finland, and the autonomous territories of Greenland, the Åland Islands and the Faroe Islands. Despite overlapping political, religious and cultural histories, the distribution of economic and political power amongst the Nordic territories has historically been, and remains, uneven.[5] This is due in part to the involvement of the Scandinavian nation-states in the European imperialist project, with Denmark in union with Norway, and Sweden having had colonies both within the Nordic region and overseas. Although limited in terms of territory and population size compared to the British, French, Spanish, Dutch and Portuguese empires, at the height of its power the Danish-Norwegian empire had colonies in Africa, Asia and the Caribbean, as well as in the North Atlantic (Greenland, Iceland and the Faroe Islands), and participated fully in the slave trade throughout the seventeenth and eighteenth centuries.[6] Despite this, Denmark, the focus of this chapter, is rarely associated with colonialism and imperialism, and its colonial history continues to be a 'disregarded part of the nation's story', even as questions about independence and secession continue to dominate the national politics of Greenland and the Faroe Islands, the last vestiges of the Danish Empire.[7]

Although the history of colonialism is frequently excluded from popular representations of the region, recent publications such as *Whiteness and Postcolonialism in the Nordic Region: Exceptionalism, Migrant Others and National Identities* (2012), *The Postcolonial North Atlantic: Iceland, Greenland and the Faroe Islands* (2014), and the special edition of *Moving Worlds* on 'The Postcolonial Arctic' (2015) indicate a burgeoning scholarly interest in the political, social and cultural legacies of Nordic colonialism, which have previously received little critical attention. The Danish political drama *Borgen* (2010–13) and the Icelandic crime drama *Ófærð* (*Trapped*, 2015–), have also recently challenged the image of Danish colonialism as 'innocent and benign' by highlighting the continued impact of Danish dominance on Icelandic and Greenlandic society.[8] There has so far, however, been little attention given to how Nordic noir engages with Nordic colonialism. In this chapter, I situate the colonial history of the Nordic region amongst current discussions about the parameters and definitions of Nordic noir and provide close readings of *Borgen* and *Trapped* to explore how the two TV series represent the post-colonial politics of the region. The fourth episode of the first season of *Borgen* is set in Copenhagen and Nuuk (the capital of Greenland), and engages directly with the problems of the contemporary Danish *grønlandspolitik* (Greenland policy) and the challenges facing the future of the Danish commonwealth. The first episode of season 1 of *Trapped* illustrates how Iceland's history as a Danish colony continues to impact relations between the two nations. The two episodes speak to both the unequal power relations between Denmark and its former colonies, and I consider how *Trapped* and *Borgen* tackle the jointly urgent problems of acknowledging historic colonialism and new forms of imperialism in the region. In doing so, I explore the cultural, geographical and linguistic parameters of both post-colonial studies and traditional notions of noir.

Nordic noir and the politics of post-coloniality

Drawing on a range of influences from Anglo-American noir to Scandinavian social realism, Nordic noir is best understood as a composite genre. The name itself reveals two distinct lineages: 'Nordic' designates geographical specificity, and 'noir', an international aesthetic tradition. The term came into use to describe the recent televized crime dramas from across the Nordic region, but has also come to encompass the longer tradition of Scandinavian crime fiction by authors such as Liza Marklund, Henning Mankell and Stieg Larsson from Sweden, Anne Holt and Karin Fossum from Norway, Peter Høeg and Leif Davidsen from Denmark, who have enjoyed international success with serialized and standalone novels, several adapted for film and TV, since the 1990s. With series such as *Borgen*, a political drama, and *Arvingerne* (*The Legacy*, 2014–17), a family saga, also increasingly categorized as examples of Nordic noir, the term has been stretched beyond the confines of the police procedural. Despite moving away from the traditional rubrics of crime fiction, Nordic noir has maintained the element of social and political critique, first introduced by Sjöwall and Wahlöö in the Martin Beck series (1965–75), which has become a defining feature of the genre. It is this social and political impetus of Nordic noir that makes it particularly interesting to think about how the colonial past and present are represented (or not represented) in popular culture, and for raising questions about the legacies of Danish colonial rule in the North Atlantic.

It is easy to assume that the culture of national self-criticism characteristic of Nordic noir results in an engagement with the region's colonial history, however, this has largely not been the case. In her work on Danish colonial history and journalistic practice Bolette Blaagaard argues that Denmark's involvement in colonialism and the slave trade have been so thoroughly 'concealed in the social imaginary', that 'Danes have been able to blot out consciousness of those others who helped to accumulate the wealth through colonialism'; wealth, she adds, that allowed Denmark to construct the modern welfare state.[9] A notable exception of where crime fiction has engaged in post-colonial criticism is Peter Høeg's *Frøken Smillas fornemmelse for sne* (1992; *Miss Smilla's Feeling for Snow*, 1993), in which Høeg offers a sustained critique of the Danish state's involvement in colonialism and poor treatment of the Greenlandic population who reside in Denmark. However, the fact that critical reviews contemporary with the novel's publication evaded Høeg's critique of Danish colonialism almost entirely highlights, the 'curious neglect' of the nation's colonial history within Danish society.[10] Although there has been a recent increase in scholarly publications on Nordic colonialism (see above), texts such as *Miss Smilla's Feeling for Snow* are also still rarely taught on post-colonial literature courses, despite the novel's critical and commercial success outside Denmark.[11]

There are a number of reasons for this lack of engagement with Nordic colonialism in mainstream post-colonial studies, some of which have to do with how the field has developed since the late 1970s. Post-colonial studies emerged as a consolidated field of study at the same time as post-structuralist modes of critical analysis rose to dominance in the 1980s, and several scholars have suggested that this led to a shift in intellectual energies from anti-colonial struggles and national independence movements, to a focus on deconstructive literary and cultural theories.[12] The result has been that the field has solidified around a relatively narrow set of theoretical 'assumptions and investments', which include: 'a constitutive anti-Marxism; an undifferentiating disavowal of all forms of nationalism and a corresponding exaltation of migrancy, liminality, hybridity, and multiculturality'.[13] The post-structuralist bias of post-colonial theory has meant that post-colonial literary studies has privileged modern and post-modern texts, with authors such as Salman Rushdie, J. M. Coetzee and Toni Morrison taking their place firmly within the post-colonial canon.[14] This might go some way in explaining why Nordic authors such as Halldór Laxness and William Heinesen have rarely been addressed in post-colonial studies.[15] Both authors published novels throughout the twentieth century which dealt with the impact of Danish colonialism and national independence in Iceland and the Faroe Islands, and although they experimented both with modernist and surrealist representational modes, they are best known for their works of social realism. A further challenge to studying authors such as Laxness and Heinesen from a post-colonial perspective is that questions about race and ethnicity are quite different in the Nordic region compared to other colonial and post-colonial contexts, as, at least in the case of Iceland and the Faroe Islands, the colonized and the colonizers had a shared ethnic heritage, and both are part of Europe and the West, even if they are semi-peripheral in relation to imperial centres such as London and Paris.

In paying close attention to the problems of the welfare state, Nordic noir TV dramas appear ideally positioned to highlight both the region's colonial history, and new forms of imperialism constituent of the current era of globalized capital. However, Nordic noir, like *hygge*, is easily transformed and adapted to different markets, with different political interests, and the malleability of the term, both as a concept and category, points to its primary purpose as a marketing brand.[16] This risk is, as Bruce Robbins has remarked in a recent essay, that the anti-statism of Nordic noir, traditionally left-wing in the Scandinavian crime genre, also offers an outlet for the 'broader and deeper anti-statism' constituent of the current neoliberal climate.[17] It is with the political ambiguities of both post-colonial theory and Nordic noir in mind, that we turn to the close reading of *Borgen* and *Trapped*.

Historical responsibility and Grønlandspolitiken in Borgen

When Adam Price's *Borgen* launched on BBC4 in 2012 it became popular almost immediately in the UK, with more than 600,000 viewers watching the first episode. The series soon took its place alongside *The Killing*, and was later joined by *The Bridge*, as pinnacles of international success for the Danish Broadcasting Corporation (DR).[18] The story centres on the rise and fall of Birgitte Nyborg, a centrist politician who has unexpectedly become the first female prime minister of Denmark at the start of season 1. Episode 4, season 1 titled '100 Days', first released as '100 Dage' in Denmark on 17 October 2010, deals with Birgitte's one-hundredth day in office, and coincides with the first international diplomatic crisis of the new coalition government. The episode opens with a furtive meeting between a former military intelligence officer, Carsten Ockles, and TV journalist Katrine Fønsmark. Carsten is in possession of photographs proving a long-standing rumour that the CIA is using the Thule Air Base in north west Greenland to transfer illegal prisoners. The US air base has been a controversial issue in Danish politics since it was built in 1951 under the US–Denmark Defence Agreement, in the first instance because the building of the base led to the forced re-location of the local indigenous population from the village of Uummannaq in 1953, which was ruled as unlawful by the Danish Supreme Court in 2003, after legal proceedings were launched by Hingitaq 53 (an Inuit organization) against the Danish state.[19] Further controversy was caused in 1968, when the crash of a US bomber carrying hydrogen bombs led to widespread contamination of the area, despite the ban on nuclear weapons within Danish territory.[20] This episode of *Borgen* draws on both of these historical crises, but also on the anxieties caused by the continued presence of the US military on Danish territory and the ongoing issue of Greenlandic self-determination and independence. Despite officially being granted Home Rule in 1979, and increased political independence from Denmark since the 2008 Self-Government Act, Greenland's foreign affairs and defence are still presided over by the Danish government, making Greenland's changing role within *rigsfælleskabet* (the Danish commonwealth) an active and ongoing problem in Danish politics.

When the story breaks a week after Carsten's meeting with Katrine, Birgitte and her team act quickly to de-escalate the issue, inviting the Greenlandic prime minister, Jens Enok Berthelsen, to Denmark, and arranging a meeting with the Security Committee to investigate the source of the leaked photographs. Before arriving at the meeting, Birgitte suggests to her permanent secretary (senior civil servant to the government), Niels Erik Lund, that the first course of action must be to apologize to the Greenlandic prime minister, to which he responds: 'we are historically reticent to apologise when it comes to Greenland. It presupposes liability and often results in unexpected expenses'.[21] The statement sets the tone for the government's attitude towards Greenland in the episode, and epitomizes the rejection of historical responsibility for the consequences of colonialism typical of the Danish state. As the episode progresses Niels continues to use patronizing language in relation to Greenland and the Home Rule government, which illustrates the colonialist attitude ingrained in the Danish *grønlandspolitik*. Consider, for instance Niels' response to Birgitte when she asks if the Greenlandic prime minister has knowingly been kept waiting before their first meeting: 'Yes, but he is used to it. The Greenlanders have huge problems running their own affairs. They need us. We have just given them the rights to their own underground resources. Imagine if there is oil there. They can't have it both ways can they? I'd give him fifteen minutes at most'. Niels is referring to the 2008 referendum which, as well as granting Greenland increased independence from Denmark, included a new agreement on the distribution of future oil revenues, and his answer reveals the lingering colonialist culture of profiteering from Greenland's natural resources which remains present in the Danish government despite the changes brought about by the referendum.

During the meeting, Birgitte, armed with vague statements offering 'no apology and no money', is completely undercut by Jens Enok's refusal to engage in diplomatic jargon:

> Birgitte, its fine. We have done our duty already just by meeting like this. You can't tell me a thing, and you can't apologise because you're not the one who violated Greenland. We are locked into our old positions. Greenland is small compared to Denmark, just as Denmark is small compared to the USA. *Kalaallitt Nunaat* is what Greenland is called in Inuit. It means 'Land of the Greenlanders'. That is more an expression of hope than reality.

His wearied acceptance of Greenland's fate within the global order seems to strike a chord with Birgitte's progressive centre-left politics, but as a prime minister of a coalition government, she has to negotiate with right-wing factions who consider the idea of Greenlandic self-determination ludicrous. In the meantime, the Danish foreign secretary has been in touch with Washington to try and find out more about the photographs of the prisoners landing at Thule. They have been issued with the embarrassingly clichéd statement, that what happens at Thule is 'on a need to know basis, and you don't need to know', leaving the Danish government in exactly the kind of position described by Jens Enok in his conversation with Birgitte.

As new facts emerge which prove the prisoners on board the American plane were listed as 'missing' by human rights organizations, and therefore likely illegal, the Ministry of Defence respond by producing a 'landings list' which supposedly proves the landing was in fact due to an emergency caused by a technical problems. Birgitte uses the information during her TV interview with Katrine to deny the government's knowledge of whether the landings are a regular occurrence. On the way home Birgitte expresses her disappointment that her one hundredth day in office is marked by her first lie to the Danish public, and to make up for the bad press surrounding the landings at Thule, it is decided she will fly to Nuuk the following day as a gesture towards future co-operation with the Greenlandic Home Rule government. In a similar diplomatic gesture, the US ambassador announces that the president has planned a state visit to Denmark in the summer.

Birgitte arrives in Nuuk with a tight schedule of meetings and publicity events, and only ninety minutes dedicated to discussing the Thule landings with Jens. However, Birgitte's expectations are once again subverted as her 'gesture' of a ninety-minute meeting 'to resolve the matter together' is mocked by Jens: 'It is just that this "matter" started 300 years ago when Hans Egede colonised us and you expect us to resolve it in an hour and a half?' Jens Enok's speech during the meeting not only embeds the recent Thule controversy in the longer history of colonialism in the Arctic, but shows both Danish colonial rule and American imperialism to be part of a 'larger, enfolding historical dynamic, which is that of capitalism in its global trajectory'.[22] The speech thereby lends immediacy to the Greenlandic quest for self-determination which has been so patronized by the politicians in Copenhagen throughout the episode. Birgitte is moved, and accepts Jens' invitation to extend her stay for twenty-four hours, to speak to ordinary Greenlandic citizens and get a real insight into Greenlandic society. Despite her promise to Niels that she would not let her guard down and compromise the party's *grønlandspolitik*, in the end Birgitte realizes the flawed logic behind Danish policy towards Greenland – 'we give them home rule with one hand, but then we overrule them when it really counts' – and agrees to include Jens in future meetings about military and foreign policy when Greenland is involved.

Although the episode both highlights Danish imperial anxieties in relation to the Arctic and takes a critical stance towards the so-called 'benign' colonialism of the Danish government's *grønlandspolitik*, it remains problematic in a number of ways. Firstly, there is a complete lack of engagement with Carsten's motivations for leaking the photographs which set the events of the episode in motion in the first place. His whistleblowing it transpires, comes not from a desire to support Greenland against illegal activities being carried out on its soil by the US military, but instead, as he explains to Katrine, he is doing it for 'honour', because he 'loves Denmark', and feels that for the last ten years the Danish government have 'forfeited any kind of sovereignty when it comes to the US'. Carsten views the activities of the US military in Thule as an affront to the Danish people, to whom he ultimately believes this land belongs. His troubling nationalism is left unchallenged in the episode, overshadowed by the threating presence of the Danish Secret Police and the suspicious circumstances of his suicide at the end of the episode. Moreover, the complicity of the Danish state in the illegal activities of the US is obscured by the positive image Birgitte manages to create through her interactions with Jens. The episode ends with a news story presented by Katrine, announcing that new talks between Denmark and the US government are taking place over expanding radar facilities at Thule, and for the first time they are being carried out on Greenlandic soil.

The Danish government is thus cleansed of any guilt, appearing benign and innocent in comparison with the illegal activities carried out covertly by the US military. As the prime minister of Denmark, Birgitte is a direct representative of the Danish government, and her conciliatory offer of greater inclusivity of the Greenlandic Home Rule government exemplifies precisely the benign guise of Danish imperialism which continues to subject Greenland to its rule.

National sovereignty and global capitalism in Trapped

The Icelandic crime drama *Trapped*, originally titled *Ófærð*, first aired in the UK on BBC4 in February 2016. The ten-episode series was created by the award-winning Icelandic actor, director and producer Baltasar Kormákur, and was the first Icelandic drama to be purchased by the BBC. The plot centres on a murder investigation in a remote town in northern Iceland called Seyðisfjörður, led by the local chief of police Andri, and his officers Hinrika and Ásgeir. The series opens with the discovery of a mutilated torso in the town's harbour, which coincides with the arrival of a Danish passenger ferry and a blizzard which traps everyone in the town for several days. During the course of the investigation, a series of related criminal activities come to light, including a transnational people-smuggling operation, insurance fraud and the corruption of local officials. The history of colonial domination in Iceland reaches back to the mid-thirteenth century, and remains a deeply embedded feature of Icelandic national identity. In 1944, after almost seven centuries of foreign rule, the Icelandic population voted in favour of secession from the Kingdom of Denmark, and Iceland emerged as an independent republic. The first episode of *Trapped* draws on the national history of both colonialism and self-determination, and deals directly with the residual colonial tensions which continue to shape relations between Iceland and Denmark in the twenty-first century.

When the blizzard descends on Seyðisfjörður at the start of the episode, the national homicide detective team are stranded in Reykjavík, leaving chief of police Andri and his officers to conduct the murder investigation on their own. After the dismembered torso has been transported for safe storage at the local fish processing factory, Andri attempts to halt the passengers disembarking from the ferry until the body has been identified. He boards the ferry to speak with the ship's captain, a Dane by the name of Søren Carlsen. In what is clearly an attempt to be diplomatic, Andri starts by addressing the captain in English, requesting a list of crew and passengers. When the captain raises concerns about delaying the ferry, Andri explains that the murder may have taken place on-board the ferry, to which the captain responds, now speaking in Danish, and with some aggression: 'you will not search the ship'. As both characters switch between Danish and English, it becomes clear that the reason for altering the language of interrogation is not because of their limited vocabulary or language abilities, but as a means of asserting authority and control over the situation. That the captain uses Danish when asserting his authority, relying on the assumption that Andri will understand him, can be read as an implicit reference to Denmark's history as an imperial power in the region, and the lasting impact of Danish colonial rule on the relations between the two countries. However, the scene ends with a more explicit challenge to Andri's authority as a representative of the Icelandic state. When Andri informs the Captain that the ship must stay in the harbour to be searched, the Captain, in Danish, demands a warrant: 'You're going to need a court order. A Danish court order. This ferry is registered in Denmark'. As the episode progresses, the captain's unwillingness to co-operate escalates, and he deliberately switches off the ferry's heating later in the episode, causing uproar amongst the passengers and forcing Andri to release them from the ship. The captain's attitude and actions not only mark him out as a suspect in later episodes, but are intended to touch a nerve with Icelandic audiences, who would share the collective cultural memory of centuries of deferring to Danish authority on important Icelandic matters. This short scene illustrates how the legacies of Danish dominance in the North Atlantic are subtly manifest in everyday interactions, but also how Danish imperialism has shaped and continues to shape the region's complex linguistic landscape.

Conforming to the generic expectations of Nordic noir, the episode also introduces a political subplot, which becomes increasingly significant as the series progresses. The episode features a meeting between the town's mayor Hrafn, the town's former chief of police, local business owners Guðni and Leifur, and Friðrik Davíðsson, a local politician, in which they discuss plans to build an international trading port in Seyðisfjörður. The town has been identified as a potential site for the port, which would act as a stop-over between Chinese and US Arctic trading routes. The town's local political and business elite see the port as an opportunity for personal profit, but at the cost of a number of local residents having to sell their land to make space for the development. The series once again draws on historical themes which would be clearly identifiable to Icelandic audiences. The effort by politicians and businessmen to 'sell' Seyðisfjörður for personal profit is not only reminiscent of the negotiations between the Icelandic and US governments to build a military base at Keflavik after the Second World War, the subject of Halldór Laxness' well-known political satire *Atómstöðin* (1948; *The Atom Station*, 1961), but also draw on more recent memories of the 2008 financial crisis which saw the failure of Iceland's three major banks (the largest suffered by any country relative to the size of its economy).[23] In both cases the Icelandic establishment, like the businessmen and politicians of Seyðisfjörður in *Trapped*, were criticized for their actions, which were viewed both as a betrayal of the Icelandic people and a threat to the nation's hard-fought sovereignty. Before *Trapped*, Kormákur directed an award-winning stage adaptation of Laxness' novel *Gerpla* (1952; *The Happy Warriors*, 1958) which re-constructed Iceland's past by employing the Icelandic saga to address and comment on 'contemporary brutality and behaviour patterns that ultimately led to Iceland's financial collapse in 2008'.[24] In this – as in *Trapped* – Kormákur managed to reference the historical narratives of past political and economic threats to Icelandic independence, such as the trade monopoly of the seventeenth and eighteenth centuries, the 1940s Keflavik affair and the 2008 financial crash, to link the history of Danish colonialism and American imperialism to the contemporary crisis of Iceland's recent financial collapse.

As season 1 of *Trapped* progresses, it transpires that the dismembered corpse was a local man named Geirmundur, the son of the fish factory owner Leifur, and that his murder did not take place on-board the ferry, but was carried out in Seyðisfjörður by Maria, a local woman who was raped by Geirmundur seven years previously. The murder is covered up by Hrafn and his associates to protect their own interests, and it becomes clear that they are involved in a web of criminal activities, including the covert negotiations to sell the town to international developers for their own profit. In the end their efforts are shown to be utterly pointless as the developers choose another location to build their port. The series thus illustrates the reach of global capitalism, in which even an isolated Icelandic fishing town is implicated in a transnational criminal network. Rather than deferring responsibility for the illegal actions of the local elite to an external corrupting force, *Trapped* presents the Icelandic state as complicit in an unequal and imperialist system. Amidst the tension and claustrophobia of being trapped in a remote location with a murderer on the loose, the series thus engages in a critique of both the town's local elite and of the structures of power which link the small harbour town to a global system of exploitation.

Between hygge *and noir*

Both *Borgen* and *Trapped* activate the 'disabled' colonial history of the Nordic region in different ways, highlighting the uneven and unequal power relations between Denmark and its former colonies.[25] By engaging directly with the contemporary Danish *grønlandspolitik*, *Borgen* tackles the problems of Danish political hegemony in the region, including the sensitive issue of Greenlandic independence and self-determination. However, as the only episode in the four season drama to deal with the issue of Greenland's position within the Danish commonwealth, *Borgen* exemplifies the tendency identified by Lars Jensen to consider Denmark's colonial history as episodic, as 'a phase we have always already passed through, or as a moment we have always already lost', truncating its relevance to the contemporary moment.[26] In connecting the history of colonialism with contemporary forms of imperialism *Trapped*, on the other hand, goes beyond merely diagnosing a condition of post-coloniality, to criticize Iceland's complicity in an exploitative economic system, and in doing so, raises important questions about the complex and uncertain place of Iceland in the wake of the 2008 crisis.

I wish finally to return to the paradoxical images of *hygge* and Nordic noir, around which most popular representations of Denmark and Danish culture outside the region have been structured. In *Whiteness and Postcolonialism in the Nordic Region* (2012), Jensen and Loftsdóttir suggest that residual notions and structural inequalities from the colonial period are continually 'recreated or projected onto different groups in the contemporary Nordic countries' resulting in the reification of 'whiteness, and notions of Nordic-ness' which feed directly into the construction of Nordic identity today.[27] In the recent commodification and exportation of *hygge* and Nordic noir to the UK and US as a consumer trend, both might be considered examples of precisely such reifications of 'Nordic-ness'. I argue that the apparent incompatibility of *hygge* and noir aesthetics points to the representative dilemma colonialism continues to represent to the Danish national imaginary, and to the way, largely unacknowledged and unchallenged, Nordic colonialism continues to shape Nordic identity and notions of Nordic-ness. It therefore remains the urgent task of post-colonial criticism in the Nordic context to challenge the cultural, ethnic, linguistic and territorial boundaries of the category 'Nordic' in order to illustrate the connection between the region's colonial history and contemporary forms of imperialism.

Notes

1. Filippa Jodelka, 'Fortitude: "not another chunk of Nordic noir"', *The Guardian*, 29 January 2015, Available online: www.theguardian.com/tv-and-radio/2015/jan/29/fortitude-sky-atlantic (accessed 13 March 2019).

2. The Swedish word *lagom* and the Finnish word *sisu* have also been the subject of articles and self-help books. See for example Dunne (2017) and Nylund (2018) both published by Gaia Books, an imprint of Octopus Publishing Group specializing in wellness and wellbeing: Linnea Dunne, *Lagom: The Swedish Art of Living Well* (London: Gaia, 2017). Joanna Nylund, *Sisu: The Finnish Art of Courage* (London: Gaia, 2018).

3. See Michael Booth, 'Hygge – why the craze for Danish cosiness is based on a myth'. *The Guardian*, 4 September 2016. Available online: www.theguardian.com/world/shortcuts/2016/sep/04/hygge-denmark-danes-cosiness-wealth-antidepressants-scandinavians (accessed 13 March 2019); Justin Parkinson, 'Hygge: A heart-warming lesson from Denmark'. *BBC NewsMagazine*, 2 October 2015. Available online: www.bbc.co.uk/news/magazine-34345791 (accessed 13 March 2019; Helen Russel, 'Get cosy: Why we should all embrace the Danish art of "hygge"'. *The Telegraph*, 24 October 2015. Available online: www.telegraph.co.uk/health-fitness/mind/Danish-cosy-hygge-lifestyle-cosiness-winter-warmth-Nordic-Danes-Scandi-home-interiors/(accessed 13 March 2019).

4. Alison Flood, 'Brexit named word of the year, ahead of Trumpism and hygge', *The Guardian*, 3 November 2016, available online: www.theguardian.com/books/2016/nov/03/brexit-named-word-of-the-year-ahead-of-trumpism-and-hygge (accessed 13 March 2019). The annual competition is run by Collins Online

Dictionary. A winning word is selected from a shortlist of ten words that have been added to the Collins Online Dictionary and come to prominence in the UK during the course of a year.
5   Paula Arvas and Andrew Nestigen, 'Introduction: Contemporary Scandinavian Crime Fiction', in *Scandinavian Crime Fiction* (Cardiff: University of Wales Press, 2011), 6.
6   Lars Jensen, 'Postcolonial Denmark: Beyond the Rot of Colonialism?' *Postcolonial Studies* 18, no. 4 (2015): 449.
7   Bolette Blaagaard, 'Remembering Nordic Colonialism: Danish Cultural Memory in Journalistic Practice', *KULT-Postkolonial Temaserie* 7 (2010): 102.
8   Magdalena Naum and Jonas Nordin (eds), 'Introduction: Situating Scandinavian Colonialism', in *Scandinavian Colonialism and the Rise of Modernity: Small Time Agents in a Global Arena*, (New York: Springer, 2013), 4.
9   Bolette Blaagaard, 'Nordic Colonialism', 103.
10 Prem Poddar and Cheralyn Mealor, 'Danish Imperial Fantasies: Peter Høeg's *Miss Smilla's Feeling for Snow*', in *Translating Nations* (Aarhus: Aarhus University Press, 2000), 161.
11 The novel was published in Denmark in 1992, and translated to English the following year, winning the Crime Writer's Association Silver Dagger Award in 1994.
12 Aijaz Ahmad, 'The Politics of Literary Postcoloniality', *Race & Class* 36, no. 3 (1995): 1–20. See also, Neil Lazarus, 'What Postcolonial Theory Doesn't Say', *Race & Class* 53, no. 1 (2011): 3–27; Benita Parry, 'The Institutionalization of Postcolonial Studies', in *The Cambridge Companion to Postcolonial Literary Studies*, ed. Lazarus, N. (Cambridge: Cambridge University Press, 2004), 66–80.
13 Neil Lazarus, 'The Politics of Postcolonial Modernism', *The European Legacy* 7, no. 6 (2010): 771.
14 Joe Cleary, 'Realism after Modernism and the Literary World-System', *Modern Language Quarterly* 73, no. 2 (2012): 256.
15 Halldór Laxness (1902–98) was an Icelandic novelist, poet, playwright and essayist, awarded the 1955 Nobel Prize for Literature. Laxness was an advocate for Icelandic independence, and his works deal with questions about nationalism, national identity and Iceland's place in the modern world. William Heinesen (1900–91) was a Danish-Faroese writer and artist. His novels *The Good Hope* (1964) and *Den Sorte Gryde* (1949) respectively explore the oppression and exploitation of the Faroese people in the era of the Royal Danish Trade Monopoly (1529–1856), and the occupation of the Faroe Islands during the Second World War, and engage with issues around Faroese nationalism, religious sectarianism and independence.
16 Kim Toft Hansen and Anne Marit Waade, *Locating Nordic Noir: From Beck to The Bridge* (Basingstoke: Palgrave Macmillan, 2017).
17 Bruce Robbins 'The Detective Is Suspended: Nordic Noir and the Welfare State', *Post 45* (2015), available online: http://post45.research.yale.edu/2015/05/the-detective-is-suspended-nordic-noir-and-the-welfare-state (accessed 13 March 2019).
18 John Plunkett, '*Borgen* Begins with 629,000 Viewers', *The Guardian*, 9 October 2012, available online: www.theguardian.com/media/2012/jan/09/borgen-begins-viewers (accessed 13 March 2019).

19 Pia Krüger Johansen, 'Thule', in *A Historical Companion to Postcolonial Literatures*, Prem Poddar, Rajeev D. Patke and Lars Jensen, eds (Edinburgh: Edinburgh University Press, 2008), 97.
20 Thorsten Borring Olsesen, 'The Dilemmas and Limits of the "Neither Confirm nor Deny" Doctrine in Danish-American Relations, 1957–1968,' *Journal of Cold War Studies* 13, no. 2 (2011): 117.
21 Adam Price, *Borgen* Season 1 (DVD. DR1, 2010).
22 Neil Lazarus, 'What Postcolonial Theory Doesn't Say', *Race & Class* 53, no. 1 (2011): 6–7.
23 'Iceland: Cracks in the Crust', *The Economist*, 11 December 2008, cited in Steven Earnest, 'Clash with the Vikings: *Gerpla* and the Struggle for National Identity in Iceland', *Theatre Symposium* 21, no. 1 (2013): 69.
24 Steven Earnest, 'Clash with the Vikings', 70.
25 Laura Ann Stohler, 'Colonial Aphasia: Race and Disabled Histories in France', *Public Culture* 23, no. 1 (2011).
26 Lars Jensen, 'Postcolonial Denmark', 449.
27 Lars Jensen and Loftsdóttir, *Whiteness*, 2.

Part III

POLITICS AND MORALITY

Chapter 8

CRIME'S CARTOGRAPHY: USING SJÖWALL AND WAHLÖÖ'S *STORY OF A CRIME* TO MAP SWEDEN'S CO-ORDINATES WITHIN GLOBAL NEOLIBERALISM'S UNEVEN SPREAD

Patrick Kent Russell

It has become commonplace to trace Nordic noir's emergence as a twenty-first-century global phenomenon to Stieg Larsson's *Millennium Trilogy* (2005–07). Larsson's novels were popular in both the UK and the United States, where his pessimistic interrogations of the modern Swedish welfare state fit well with neoliberal logic made mainstream by the elections of Margaret Thatcher and Ronald Reagan. In particular, Larsson's view of the welfare state as inadequate, overburdened and corrupt gelled with neoliberalism's guiding logic that the most effective method for promoting social good comes from individual exchanges in free markets, rather than from the state's distribution of resources. Certainly, Larsson's Lisbeth Salander does not find much good in the welfare state she interacts with, as she is forced to commit non-consensual sex acts to receive resources rightfully belonging to her. Arguably, the only 'social good' in this relationship comes when Salander maximizes her own well-being – violently – by tasering her abusive social worker, tattooing 'I am a Rapist Pig' on his chest, and setting terms for future allocations. Such crimes 'committed in the name of justice', as Ian MacDougall puts it, demonstrate the genre's potential for a socio-political critique that reveals corruption and maps the 'comprehensive failure of the world's most comprehensive welfare system'.[1] This critique has become Nordic noir's defining critical feature.

Nordic noir's method of socio-political critique did not begin with Larsson, however; this potential was inaugurated by Maj Sjöwall and Per Wahlöö's ten-book Swedish *Story of a Crime* series (1965–74), which the pair is generally credited with adapting from the police-procedural format so useful to Nordic noir's critique from American Ed McBain's *87th Precinct* series (1956–2005).[2] Sjöwall and Wahlöö wanted their critique of the Swedish welfare state, the so-called 'People's Home' (*folkhemmet*), to reach as wide an audience as possible; realizing more people read police novels than political pamphlets, they decided to use a fictionalized version of the newly nationalized Swedish police force to draw attention to the state's failures. By setting their novels around Martin Beck's unit – the only competent unit in an increasingly inept force – the pair is able to establish the police bureaucracy as a metonym for the welfare state.[3] Through Beck's unit, the series explores social and political conditions throughout Sweden, revealing systematic dysfunction within the People's Home and demonstrates that it no longer expresses the people's will.[4] In an overtly Marxist view, the series connects the welfare state's failure to embracing capitalism: According to Sjöwall, capitalism made Swedish society colder and more inhumane, and created a 'layer of poverty, criminality, and brutality' beneath the welfare state's façade.[5] Scholars generally take this view and read *Story of a Crime* as castigating the welfare state for abandoning its principles.

This chapter, however, argues that the series does more than just lay the blame on the state for abdicating the people's will. Instead, I argue that by using the police as a metonym for the welfare state separated from the people whose lives it impacts, the series also provides a view of the welfare state as it was being re-made in neoliberalism's image. This view models the process through which Sweden became a neoliberal state that segmented its people according to economic value, and subsequently mismanaged public good by promoting market solutions for social need, rather than the welfare state's universalized social safety nets; the state reduced the resources put into social safety nets and consolidated remaining resources into protecting the markets and market-based solutions. This not only fosters greater inequality – doing more harm for the general public than good – but ends with financial institutions, rather than citizens engaged in civic life, being treated as if they are the cornerstone of society. Consequently, wealthy capitalists and financiers are given a disproportionate influence on the state.

In real-life Sweden – which underwent similar, albeit slightly less apocalyptic shifts than Sjöwall and Wahlöö represent – this influence not only helped make neoliberal ideology mainstream in Swedish civic life, but also provided a crucial foothold for its global spread: Swedish financiers consolidated their power over the Swedish Academy of Sciences to ensure that the 1974 and 1976 Nobel Prizes in Economics – awarded to the 'Father of Neoliberalism' Friedrich von Hayek and to Milton Friedman, the chief architect of neoliberal economic policy – signalled neoliberal ideology as mainstream.[6] *Story of a Crime* asks readers to question the growing role of financial institutions at the expense of everyday citizens. By engaging with the logics that were entering civic consciousness during the decade Sjöwall and Wahlöö were writing, *Story of a Crime* invites its readers to contemplate the causes and consequences of the social, economic and political changes in the Swedish welfare state as it embraced neoliberalism. By reacting to uneven, inconsistent and often contradictory policies – hallmarks of neoliberal ideology that David Harvey and Lisa Dugan show make mapping its global spread difficult – *Story of a Crime* establishes the Nordic welfare state as important coordinates in neoliberalism's path to global hegemony.[7]

Police bureaucracy as metonymy: Sweden's 'circumscribed neoliberalism'

Story of a Crime introduces Martin Beck's unit as they investigate the death of an American tourist, Roseanna McGraw. The same year *Roseanna* (1965) was published, Sweden nationalized its police force, putting one centralized bureaucracy in charge of all Swedish institutions of law and order. This nationalization allows Sjöwall and Wahlöö an opportunity to send their fictional police all over the country during the series, rather than confining them to their native Stockholm.[8] The crimes they investigate through the ten-book series are then able to respond to country-wide social, economic and political conditions – or, at least, to show that tensions created by changing conditions are not solely regional problems. During the decade these novels cover, Sweden was going through a tumultuous set of changes that had a drastic impact on citizens across the land.[9] Since 1928, Sweden had been ruled by the Social Democratic party, which was elected under the 'People's Home' plan advocated by Albin Hansson, promising to improve a society mired by class divisions.[10] The social democratic model was premised on the idea that the state was a 'good actor,' acting in the best interests of society, and provided citizens with adequate resources for a secure life, mainly through universalized programmes for housing, childcare, education, retirement, healthcare and infrastructure – leaving them free to pursue meaningful lives and civic participation.[11] In the post-war period, this plan's success in creating a happy and prosperous nation was used to justify the welfare state as an alternative to both communism and capitalism.

Changes during this decade have, however, also contributed to what David Harvey has called Sweden's 'circumscribed neoliberalism'.[12] While universalized programmes and growing economic equality became hallmarks of Sweden before the Second World War, rationing during the war led to a post-war emphasis on individual consumption. A wave of labour unrest and wildcat strikes precipitated a wave of regulatory reforms that included the Rehn-Meidner Plan, a failed attempt to re-direct corporate profits into collective ownership; at the same time, Swedish industry began shifting from manufacturing to more service-based industries, increasing labour tensions.[13] On top of this were intermittent energy crises, the radicalization of both mainstream political parties, the loss of social democratic hegemony in 1972, and subsequent state programme rollbacks. Though Swedes today generally trust their institutions, there is evidence of growing distrust during this period, including the IB Affair, when journalists uncovered government-sponsored tracking and punishment of dissenting views, and the Norrmalmstorg robbery – where the term

'Stockholm Syndrome' originated – in which victims of a bank robbery sided with the robber over the police.[14] These crises began sowing distrust, acting, as Danish economist Ove Pederson explains, as seeds for the growth of neoliberalism in the welfare state.[15]

Though not investigating these issues directly, Beck's unit's cases reveal myriad social, economic and political tensions surrounding the growing cracks. Sjöwall and Wahlöö were correct to turn to crime fiction, as it is useful for interrogating democracy through the cracks and fissures that cause disorder – most often represented through a crime – challenging readers to contemplate causes and consequences of a crime and the implications of punishing the criminal or determining that no punishment is necessary. Through crime fiction, society itself is put on trial. As such, crime fiction is the most political genre, according to Andrew Pepper, as it thematizes and makes visible the institutional bodies, policing practices, legal processes and judicial norms that make up the legal justice system; this visibility not only draws attention to the system's flaws, but also shows how individual lives are shaped by the push and pull of larger social, political and economic forces.[16] Through their investigations, Beck's unit encounter myriad causes and consequences, as well as numerous people whose lives are impacted by the tensions surrounding them. These people – whether criminal or victim, young or old, rich or poor, native-born or immigrant, urban or rural – are united by little besides their connection to a crime, yet together they contribute to the sense that the welfare state seems to be falling apart.

The police procedural, in particular, is useful for revealing systematic dysfunction rather than attributing disorder to individual dysfunction.[17] Utilizing a police unit also allows multiple perspectives from a rotating cast of officers who – like the citizens they encounter – hold varying opinions, viewpoints and perspectives. Through the entangled perspectives of leftist Lennart Kollberg, left-leaning Beck, the neutral Fredrik Melander, right-leaning Einar Rönn and right-wing Gunvald Larsson – characters who work together but do not always get along, who share a sense of the growing problems but not a common solution – the series makes one thing clear: the state is not working as it should. This set of distinct personalities generates dialogue about society, and provides multiple observations highlighting social tensions created when the state changes its outlook.[18] Through this unit, Sjöwall and Wahlöö ask readers to contemplate the nature of the changing welfare state, and to think about the causes and consequences of its changes.

These causes and consequences are best explored by contrasting Beck's unit with the entire force. Beck's unit is competent; the rest of the force is not. In *Roseanna*, the unit's progress is hindered by the sheer amount of bureaucracy they must navigate thanks to nationalization – little gets done because no one is sure who holds the responsibility to act. By the series' finale, it becomes clear that those who have this responsibility should not. Beck's first chief, however, a competent and dedicated policeman, is replaced by a man who knows little about practical policework or capable administration (*Murder at the Savoy*, 57). His promotion is purely political, and he feels pressured to solve cases deemed important by the political establishment, demanding Beck solve them 'on the double' without providing any extra resources or suggestions for how to do so – an approach common in neoliberalism, which demands that workers produce more with fewer resources, insisting on cost-cutting efficiency, and threatening accountability or austerity measures for those unable to do more with less. Beck even has qualms about his *own* promotion, fearing that being labelled a 'good policeman' would likely put him in the company of those who lack imagination or a moral code; they might be 'good cops' because they follow protocol, but are not 'good guys' who see any connection between their work and the people they serve.[19] The series bemoans the force's homogenization along these standards, as Beck's unit increasingly stands out for including various imaginations and moral codes – occasionally in conflict about how to best protect people, but often agreeing that serving the people is the state's most important function.[20]

Their approach to people, in fact, is what most clearly shows the bureaucracy as wanting: despite growing violence and disorder, Beck's unit retains the ability to see people as human beings. For example, Beck sees Roseanna as a person, rather than a statistic; he asks Kollberg to re-do the initial victimology report to describe her 'not ... as a corpse, but [as] a human being' (29). Doing so allows him to gain an understanding of her killer, whom the unit still treats as a human being despite his crime, since a murderer is still a 'regular human being, only more unfortunate and maladjusted' (38). This sentiment is mirrored by each unit member throughout the series, who often feel sorry for victim and criminal, alike, as 'it's not their fault that everything goes to hell and they don't understand why'.[21] Despite this view, Beck's unit loathes actions that breach the social contract, especially if those actions harm other citizens. Beck, for instance, tells his own attempted murderer that he does not take the attempt personally, but that he cannot forgive the crime because it is a 'breach of a basic rule of life and an important principle'.[22] Even worse are those who breach that basic rule in order to further their own social, political or economic status, especially if they do so by preying on those of lower status.[23] Beck's unit is what the series argues the welfare state should be, and their character development models ways the system can once again fulfil its welfare state goals.

By contrast, the rest of the force invites readers to contemplate what the welfare state has become. Whether a cause or consequence of growing tensions – perhaps both, as responses to one crisis often cause the next – this metonymy shows the state as run by a homogenized group isolated from the people whose lives it impacts.[24] This distance causes the state to move away from its principles; if it no longer sees itself as part of the people, then the principles for providing public good shift in a way more conducive to state power than to individuals. This is especially true if the state representatives like those in Sjöwall and Wahlöö's metonym see themselves at odds with the people. This view – especially when combined with growing cracks in the welfare state's façade, growing hardships for individuals, and growing distrust for institutions caused by policies enacted in isolation – creates conditions in which neoliberalism thrives and a state like Sweden can be re-made in its image.

Sweden remade in neoliberalism's Image: Public consent and mismanaging public good through militarised police and market solutions for social ills

In addition to drawing attention to the state's failures born of homogeneity and isolation, *Story of a Crime* demonstrates the state's changing perspective about who it serves and how to best provide public good: the state begins to see both in terms of consumption and economic value. Historically, this change in Sweden resulted from an explicit propaganda campaign organized by the Swedish Employer's Federation, which reacted to the Rehn-Meidner Plan by trying to weaken faith in the welfare state; indeed, they convinced the public that their woes resulted from institutional overreach, and that the best solution was to reduce state services and liberalize markets so that citizens could maximize their own good.[25] *Story of a Crime* does not deal with this directly, as the propaganda campaign came more than halfway into Sjöwall and Wahlöö's writing process. Instead, the series interrogates the less obvious means by which the public was made comfortable segmenting people: police tactics for fighting crime, which Marx would suggest is a method of demanding citizens justify themselves as worthy of the state, rather than the other way around. In so doing, the series exposes latent fascist tendencies in the welfare state.[26] It also reveals an important feature of these tendencies that make tracking their spread difficult: they are not necessarily the result of precise or deliberate directives. Instead, they are the result of a gradual and uneven re-interpretation of welfare state ideals through neoliberal logics.

Story of a Crime models this gradual and uneven re-interpretation through the bureaucratic response to crime, revealing how consent is built for state actions that segment the populace by economic means. While the population may not support segmentation along economic means, they *do* support police tactics that result in that separation; these tactics are then often pointed at those on the margins, perpetuating their hardships while making the mainstream feel safer and as if their measure of 'good' has been maintained. *Story of a Crime* models this throughout the series, but the most telling example comes from *The Man on the Balcony* (1967), in which police respond to threats of future crimes, rather than solving crimes already committed. After a series of muggings and child sex murders, the public is angry and afraid, and demands state action. The police respond by showing force – rounding up potential suspects – which is meant to pacify the people by assuring them that everything that can be done to protect them will be done, that the bureaucracy has heard their pleas and is providing public good accordingly. Not surprisingly, the bureaucracy fails to find either the criminals or information that might lead to their arrest; all they manage to do is to 'stir up the dregs – the homeless, the alcoholics, the drug addicts, those who had lost all hope, those who could not even crawl away when the welfare state turned the stone over'.[27]

Not only is this police tactic ineffective, but it also targets those on the fringes of society, making their life more difficult and perpetuating social tensions. As the series progresses, Beck's unit notices police tactics often result that way: the poor are targeted for minor infractions like drugs or alcohol – which Beck's unit attributes as the only available release some have from the drudgery of daily life.[28] While those of means have more resources to hide their 'dirty laundry'.[29] Crime, it seems, is only a temporary shortcoming for the wealthy, rather than the natural condition assumed of the poor. As such, the rich in Beck's world are rarely considered for crimes that do not happen in their households. In fact, the wealthy are more often thought of as victims who need protection, especially since those with higher status are more likely to receive the media attention that drives public anger, fear and pressure for police action.[30] In short, their visibility as victims increases public consent for state action, often against those on the margins.

The police respond accordingly, but this also promotes neoliberal economic-based segmentation. Nowhere is this clearer than in the case of Viktor Palmgren, a wealthy industrialist murdered by a former employee. Beck's unit eventually realizes that Palmgren's murder was a crime of opportunity: his murderer randomly encountered Palmgren and decided to exact revenge for having been demoted in Palmgren's company and evicted from an apartment building that Palmgren owned. Beck's unit, of course, is outraged by the obvious wealth gap between Palmgren and those who work for him or live in his properties, as well as the legal means that Palmgren used to make other people's lives harder. They understand that the killer's actions, while an unforgiveable breach of the social contract, were the result of understandable frustration as everything was taken away from him 'bit by bit'.[31] This murder could have been avoided if the opportunity for capitalist exploitation was reduced. Rather than addressing the exploitation that led to the crime, the bureaucracy responds to political pressure and concentrates their resources on avenging Palmgren's death, as his fortune gave him inordinate influence over his society, including the upper echelons of wealth and government.[32] Though their investigation reveals that Palmgren gained his wealth through shady and sometimes illegal practices, the fact that he had it made him important, both as a consumer and as a producer of goods that people use to maximize their well-being. The state did not necessarily start out with the goal of directing its resources to protect markets or market players, but as the public conception of what they need protection from shifts along neoliberal lines, the state's tactics for providing public good are focused there anyway.

Not only does *Story of a Crime* demonstrate one of the ways in which the consumer – and by extension, the producer – replaces the citizen as the privileged political figuration, it also models twin processes for the neoliberal mismanagement of public good that results from and furthers this segmentation: a militarized police to respond to public anger and fear, and market solutions to fulfil all other aspects of public good as the state consolidates its resources into security.[33] The series shows militarization as a complex process: after the police disrupt the lives of those on the margins, those on the margins respond. The police use that response to justify greater spending on weapons and training. In *The Locked Room* (1973), the bureaucracy starts this process by stopping a protest against the US war in Vietnam. Though the protest is peaceful, the police respond with violence that they argue is justified because the protesters 'resisted arrest' by not immediately turning away (55). This leads to more police weapons and training, scare propaganda and harsh responses to even minor offences. By the series' conclusion, the Swedish police are armed with helicopters, tear gas, SWAT teams, automatic weapons, sharp shooters, armoured shields, bulletproof vests and American military training.[34] Each measure is justified by suppressing the violence created by the previous measure. By the series' end, Beck realizes the cascading wave of violence might have actually *begun* with the police.[35]

Equally important, however, is how militarization facilitates neoliberal logics by directing resources towards security and away from social safety nets. While demanding that state entities take larger roles seems like a paradox within neoliberalism – which demands the reduction of the state – it actually works hand-in-hand with that reduction. Even as the public demands more security to combat new threats that were, ironically created by the state's security, they still support an overall reduction in the state's role. As a result, increases in the security budget often lead to decreases in welfare spending; this only perpetuates the divides already made larger by militarization, as well as panic, fear, and the need for protection. Beck's unit draws attention to those divides throughout the series: not only are the poor targeted while the rich are protected, but the average citizen sees their voices suppressed, their civic rights diminished and a greater number of people like them incarcerated.[36] In addition, increased budgets to support militarization result in cuts to pensions, housing and other forms of social safety nets.[37] Though the public did not necessarily support the segmentation of wealth and power, it was the methods of state action they did support that had this result.

This situation is amplified when the state relies on market solutions to fill gaps the left when militarization depletes the resources that could otherwise have addressed the underlying problems that the police are militarized to solve. The series takes this on in a number of ways, but the most telling example comes through gentrification. On the surface, gentrification fulfils the welfare state's goals by providing comfortable and adequate housing for its citizens. *Story of a Crime*, however, illustrates the harm that this can do when left to market forces. First, the city awards private builders with housing contracts. As Beck and his colleagues see, however, new residential buildings are put together haphazardly and are not well-maintained. As landlords incrementally raise rents, those who relied on social safety nets are forced to make difficult decisions between rent and adequate nutrition or leisure.[38] These people are eventually driven out, and the landlords sell the property for either luxury housing or office buildings with higher rents.[39] Those who used to live there are no longer welcome – in fact, their presence invites a response from the militarized police – and their new residences are often 'deleterious to their health' because they are closer to pollution.[40]

While the police bureaucracy sees this as a means of promoting public good, thanks to their new neoliberal interpretation, Beck's unit demonstrates how far these actions are from the welfare state's original intent. Not only do they notice that chaos is created more often than order is restored, but they lament the impact that this has on social cohesion and unity. Vibrant communities are uprooted and people lose their connections to each other. On top of this, people lose some of their ability to act within free markets, as increasing rents push out family-owned businesses like bakeries and restaurants. What's left is mass-produced food lower in nutrition and restaurants that cater to businessmen or people with credit cards.[41] The quality of life decreases for those on the social periphery while wealth and power flow upwards. As people are crowded out, those at the top retain the greatest amount of influence. Subsequently, public good tends to be defined by their needs, and state policies shift in their favour, even though the state does not necessarily intend to foster inequality.

Financial institutions viewed as society's cornerstone: Sweden's co-ordinates in neoliberalism's global hegemony

While growing tensions between a segmented people and an isolated state are the most prominent impact that *Story of a Crime* documents, the most interesting consequence might be what Sjöwall and Wahlöö hint is the inevitable next step: the state values financial institutions more than people, and tailors its methods for public good accordingly. Police responses to property crimes are present throughout the series, as one might expect in a political system that rewards accumulation. In later Beck novels, it becomes apparent that the state treats crimes against property more seriously than crimes against people – especially if the victim is a financial institution. Sjöwall and Wahlöö provide an opportunity to evaluate this shifting logic; along with arguing that many social ills stem from inequality and legal exploitation caused by decreases in welfare, the pair argue that treating people as inferior to financial institutions is representative of the state's abdication from its values, which creates the layer of hardship beneath its facade. This is especially clear in *The Locked Room* (1972) and *The Terrorists* (1974), which juxtapose the bureaucracy's handling of crimes against a citizen and against a financial institution. In both, the institution is given priority and the consequences of segmentation and separation are more obvious. Through this proximity, *Story of a Crime* tracks the state's movement away from its principles, and also provides co-ordinates for Sweden's role in making neoliberal thought globally hegemonic.

The Locked Room deals primarily with two crimes: a classic locked-room murder mystery and a bank robbery. The latter gets the bureaucracy's full attention and resources, while the former is only investigated as a rehab assignment for Beck, who is returning from medical leave. The murder is committed by Filip Mauritzon, a thief who shoots a former associate through an open window, knocking him down with such force that the window closes and latches itself, making the room appear locked. The robbery is committed by Mauritzon's former romantic partner, Monita, who needs money for a fresh start for herself and her daughter, but has no legitimate means of accumulating it. The bureaucracy concentrates on the robbery, which it falsely assumes has been committed by professional robbers – as protecting banks becomes their priority, organized bank robbers become the bogeyman; promoting fear of this bogeyman then inspires public pressure to stop this bogeyman in levels unrelated to its actual existence. Owing to this false assumption, the investigation is a comedy of errors: the police arrest Mauritzon for the crime he did not commit, but assuming he is connected to professionals leads them to concentrate on the wrong bank, allowing those actual professionals to steal half a million kroner.[42] Then, since the police need to show that everything that can be done has been done – so banks can recover their losses through insurance – the police prosecute Mauritzon for the robbery he did not commit, but not for the murder he did. The financial institution's stability seems to matter more than does the loss of individual life, dignity or freedom.

If the bungled operation reveals the separation between state and citizens, then what the state misses by putting banks first reveals what happens to citizens from whom the welfare state slowly retreats. Unlike in other novels where Beck's unit determines the context that contributed to the crime, Beck's team does not make any meaningful contact with Monita. Instead, her plight is revealed through moments of omniscient narration; through them readers witness a plight Sjöwall and Wahlöö suggest is becoming typical for the Swedes caught in neoliberalization's push-and-pull dynamic: already hard lives are made more difficult. Monita married young, starting a family instead of completing her education. When her husband leaves, her lack of education means little opportunity for stable employment, a hardship compounded by the state's decision to roll back expenditures on childcare, making maintaining wage labour jobs impossible for young single parents with no formal qualifications. Like those experiencing gentrification, she has to make hard choices about nutrition, living arrangements and community engagement – she withdraws from her friends because she cannot afford to leave the house. Monita descends into depression, and decides to leave Sweden, so her daughter can grow up in a land where 'buy' and 'own' – two things they cannot do in newly neoliberal Sweden – are not treated as synonymous with 'happiness'.[43] Thanks to Sweden's transition to a service economy dependent upon marginal labour and the diminishment of state services, Monita loses her ability to secure the meaningful life project guaranteed by the welfare state.

The parallel between Monita and Mauritzon is telling, as is their eventual outcome: Mauritzon is jailed for a crime he did not commit, while Monita escapes to a happier life outside Sweden. This ironic outcome is possible only because this society puts protecting its banks ahead of protecting its people, a decision that not only makes people's lives more difficult, but simultaneously renders their hardships invisible – in other novels, Beck and his unit might sympathize about a plight like Monita's, but in this novel it does not even come to their attention. Such a story begs the question: if the welfare state prioritizes financial security, can it even imagine the hardships its citizens suffer in any other terms? Will the state be able to offer any solution other than protecting neoliberal institutions to secure 'access' to maximizing individual well-being? Though it has not explicitly abandoned its principles, it is clear that this radical shift to the militarized protection of consumers, producers and financial institutions has moved further afield from those principles as first imagined.

This is even more apparent in the series' finale, *The Terrorists* (1974), in which the threat of assassinating an American politician on Swedish soil is contrasted with a young woman, Rebecka Lind, who is falsely accused of bank robbery. The bureaucracy again concentrates on the threat to neoliberalism, and thwarts the American's assassination. This time, however, the hardships made invisible through neglect have more drastic consequences, as Rebecka grows so frustrated from her inability to navigate the system – and afraid her daughter will be taken as a result – that she assassinates the Swedish prime minister. The neoliberal way of life is protected, but at the expense of the state's figurehead. Like Monita, Rebecka is a young, uneducated, single mother who has difficulty finding secure work. Whereas Monita robs a bank, Rebecka turns to the state for help to secure safer and more comfortable living arrangements, including avoiding the accommodation made less safe by the increased pollution and bad nutrition that are a by-product of neoliberalization. When asking friends and family for help yields nothing more than temporary relief, Rebecka visits a financial institution for help, but she is turned down because she cannot offer enough collateral; when she asks for a bank 'owned by the people', the bank manager tells her 'mostly in fun' to go to a state bank which is owned by the people, at least in theory.[44] There, the teller erroneously assumes a robbery, having mistaken a gardening tool that Rebecka is carrying for a weapon. Rebecka is arrested owing to prejudice.

Although she is acquitted, Rebecka is not provided with any better tools to navigate the system – not only do her hardships grow, but so does her frustration and fear. She asks her lawyer to write to the prime minister for help; her letter is ignored and Rebecka is on the brink of the kind of desperation that leads to a desperate act of violence. The novels do not condone her violence – her own lawyer suggests that she should be jailed – but they do suggest that such violence only happened because of the hardships that were created when the state re-evaluated its principles. This is crystallized in Rebecka's explanation of why she was so desperate: 'I don't think you can trust any authorities in this country. They don't care about ordinary people who aren't famous or rich, and what they mean by helping isn't what I call help. They just cheat you.'[45] Her lawyer's defence likewise makes concrete Rebecka and Monita's invisible hardships, arguing that Rebecka's actions were the result of having been 'confronted with a system whose arbitrariness we all have to submit to,' especially as it emphasizes materialism and ruthlessness, which overwhelms those at the bottom of hierarchies with 'despair and mindless hatred'.[46] Beck's unit, then, is left with an increasingly complex set of tensions solidified in escalating violence and counter-violence from the state, both of which only make life worse.

While the real-life Swedish context that Sjöwall and Wahlöö were writing in did not experience the same cataclysmic violence – Sweden today still registers the least robberies in Europe, a high measure of happiness, general satisfaction with government and a conspicuous lack of the mass incarceration epidemic seen in the US – it did undergo many of the shifts in thought about 'public good' that the pair narrativized. As the importance of manufacturing decreased alongside the increase in a service-based economy, the financial sector accumulated an inordinate power for its relatively small size. Through a well-financed public campaign, the banking sector was able to change public opinion about the causes of turmoil in the mid-1970s, effectively convincing the public that reducing the state's role would reduce people's hardships. In reality, this only reduced hardship for the financial sector, and actually increased hardship for everybody else. To achieve this shift, the financial industry also used its collective power to ensure that the work of neoliberal thinkers was made mainstream, which it did through the Nobel Prize. Although neoliberalism may have been spread more by British or American post-war foreign policy, including by the World Bank and International Monetary Fund (IMF), this was only possible, in part, because the underlying thought supporting these processes were legitimized through prizes. As such, Sweden's role is crucial for understanding neoliberalism's global spread, as it legitimized the foundational doctrine that would then become hegemonic. Sweden did not pioneer neoliberalism, yet neoliberalism would not be what it is today without the role that Sweden played.

Nordic noir might not be able to solve the world's problem's connected to neoliberalism. In fact, its global spread as seen through the *Millennium Trilogy* and *Story of a Crime* was really only possible because of the process of globalization that neoliberalism relies on. Its socio-political critique of the welfare state is, however, useful in interrogating neoliberalism's global spread. By exposing audiences to people's lives beneath the façade of the welfare state, Nordic noir is not only able to show cracks and fissures within the welfare system, but can provide opportunities for audiences to think about the origins of its underlying tensions. It is easy to blame the evils of capitalism, especially if one shares Sjöwall and Wahlöö's Marxist ideology; but to lay the blame solely on the economic system, or on the political system that capitulated to it, is to miss the complexity of how that system became hegemonic by a drastic re-interpretation of its founding principles through a neoliberal lens – a re-interpretation that makes it seem far removed from those principles, even as it still endeavours to uphold them in one fashion or another. Through Nordic noir, we can not only spend time thinking about the opposing forces that ordinary people might face, but we can also perceive how neoliberal logics facilitated their hardship.

Notes

1. Ian MacDougall, 'The Man Who Blew Up the Welfare State', no. 1, 27 February 2010. Available online: https://nplusonemag.com/online-only/book-review/man-who-blew-up-welfare-state/ (accessed 1 June 2018).
2. McBain's procedural, *Cop Hater*, was published in 1956. Sjöwall and Wahlöö translated it into Swedish, along with several other McBain novels. While most scholars acknowledge McBain's influence on *Story of a Crime*, Sjöwall insisted that she had not heard of him until a review compared their work. She said it was only after that – when the series had been outlined and the first novels completed – that the pair was asked to translate McBain. Charlotte Beyer, 'Death of the Author: Maj Sjöwall and Per Wahlöö's Police Procedurals', in *Cross-Cultural Connections in Crime Fiction*, eds V. Miller and H. Oakley (New York: Palgrave Macmillan, 2009), 141–59, 145.
3. Andrew Nestingen and Paula Arvas (eds), *Scandinavian Crime Fiction* (Cardiff: University of Wales Press, 2011), 3.
4. Rohan Maitzen, 'Martin Beck Has a Cold', *Los Angeles Review of Books*, 8 May 2011. Available online: https://lareviewofbooks.org/article/martin-beck-has-a-cold/#! (Accessed 28 May 2017); Nestingen and Arvas, 3.
5. Louise France, 'The Queen of Crime', *The Guardian*, 21 November 2009. Available online: www.theguardian.com/books/2009/nov/22/crime-thriller-maj-sjowall-sweden (accessed 28 May 2017).
6. Perhaps some pushback against neoliberalism's spread can be read in the fact that Hayek shared the 1974 prize with the Swedish economist Gunnar Myrdal, whose work connected poverty to racial exclusion and other social, demographic and institutional conditions that individuals face.
7. David Harvey, *A Brief History of Neoliberalism* (Oxford: Oxford University Press, 2005), 115; Lisa Dugan, 'Neoliberalism', in *Keywords for American Cultural Studies*, eds B. Burgett and G. Hendler (New York: NYU Press, 2014), 181–4.
8. Sjöwall and Wahlöö, *Roseanna*, trans. Lois Roth (New York: Vintage Crime/Black Lizard, 1965); Arvas and Nestingen, 3.
9. Far too much happens during this period to adequately be covered here. For more, see David Harvey, 112–19; Nestingen and Arvas, 2–9; Andrew Nestingen, *Crime and Fantasy in Scandinavia: Fiction, Film, and Social Change* (Seattle: University of Washington Press, 2008), 23–34; Kerstin Bergman, *Swedish Crime Fiction: The Making of Nordic noir* (Milan: Mimesis International, 2014), 33–4; Steven Peacock,

Swedish Crime Fiction: Novel, Film, Television (Manchester: Manchester University Press, 2014) 29–34; Jakob Stougaard-Nielson, *Scandinavian Crime Fiction*, (London: Bloomsbury, 2017), 1–3; 7–10.
10 Jakob Stougaard-Nielson, 14.
11 Paula Arvas and Andrew Nestingen, 6–8; Jakob Stougaard-Nielson, 19; Paul Thomas, 'State' in *Keywords for American Cultural Studies*, eds. B. Burgett and G. Hendler (New York: NYU Press, 2015). Available online: http://keywords. nyupress.org/americancultural-studies/essay/state/ (accessed 29 October 2016).
12 David Harvey, 115.
13 Jens Lapidus, 'Introduction' in Maj Sjöwall and Per Wahlöö, *The Abominable Man*, trans. Thomas Teal (New York: Vintage Crime/Black Lizard, 2009) vii–x, ix.
14 Barry Forshaw, *Death in a Cold Climate: A Guide to Scandinavian Crime Fiction* (New York: Palgrave Macmillan, 2012), 11.
15 As cited in Jakob Stougaard-Nielson, 10.
16 Andrew Pepper, *Unwilling Executioner: Crime Fiction and the State* (Oxford: Oxford University Press, 2006), 17.
17 Maitzen.
18 Andrew Nestingen, 218.
19 Maj Sjöwall and Per Wahlöö, *The Fire Engine That Disappeared*, trans. Joan Tate (New York: Vintage Crime/Black Lizard, 1969), 7.
20 Maj Sjöwall and Per Wahlöö, *Locked Room*, trans. Paul Britten Ausin (New York: Vintage Crime/Black Lizard, 1972), 55.
21 Maj Sjöwall and Per Wahlöö, *The Laughing Policeman*, trans. Alan Blair (New York: Vintage Crime/Black Lizard, 1968), 211.
22 Maj Sjöwall and Per Wahlöö, *The Man Who Went up in Smoke*, trans. Joan Tate (New York: Vintage Crime/Black Lizard, 1966), 121.
23 Maj Sjöwall and Per Wahlöö *Laughing Policeman*, 211; Peacock, 85.
24 Maj Sjöwall and Per Wahlöö, *Murder at the Savoy*, trans. Amy and Ken Knoespel (New York: Vintage Crime/Black Lizard, 1970), 110.
25 David Harvey, 113.
26 Andrew Nestingen and Paula Arvas, 3.
27 Maj Sjöwall and Per Wahlöö, *The Man on the Balcony*, trans. Alan Blair (New York: Vintage Crime/Black Lizard, 1967), 118.
28 Maj Sjöwall and Per Wahlöö, *Cop Killer*, trans. Thomas Teal, (New York: Vintage Crime/Black Lizard, 1973), 154.
29 Maj Sjöwall and Per Wahlöö, *Murder at the Savoy*, 96.
30 Maj Sjöwall and Per Wahlöö, *Locked Room*, 27.
31 Maj Sjöwall and Per Wahlöö *Murder at the Savoy*, 203–04.
32 Ibid., 106.
33 Andrew Nestingen and Paula Arvas, 8.
34 Maj Sjöwall and Per Wahlöö, *The Abominable Man*, trans. Thomas Teal (New York: Vintage Crime/Black Lizard, 1971), 194–5, 214; *Cop Killer*, 117, 238.
35 Maj Sjöwall and Per Wahlöö, *Cop Killer*, 115.
36 Maj Sjöwall and Per Wahlöö, *Locked Room*, 57–62.
37 Ibid., 68.
38 Maj Sjöwall and Per Wahlöö, *Murder at the Savoy*, 89.
39 Maj Sjöwall and Per Wahlöö, *The Abominable Man*, 15, 44–5.
40 Maj Sjöwall and Per Wahlöö, *Locked Room*, 85–6.

41 Maj Sjöwall and Per Wahlöö, *Man on the Balcony*, 149; Maj Sjöwall and Per Wahlöö, *The Abominable Man*, 12.
42 Maj Sjöwall and Per Wahlöö, *Locked Room*, 275.
43 Ibid., 198.
44 Maj Sjöwall and Per Wahlöö, *The Terrorists*, trans. Joan Tate, (New York: Vintage Crime/Black Lizard, 1974), 28.
45 Ibid., 213.
46 Ibid., 230–1.

Chapter 9

KID STUFF: NORDIC NOIR, POLITICS AND QUALITY

Andrew Nestingen

The child is a key figure in Scandinavian crime fiction and Nordic noir.[1] This chapter argues that a shift has occurred in how the child is represented within this tradition. The child has shifted from a pre-dominantly political figure to a cultural-economic one. Nordic crime writers often depict the child as isolated because of neglect and systemic dysfunction, which leads to victimization, but also criminal violence perpetrated by children. This construction of the child called for political attention and change. Since the 2010s, the child has become a more mannerist figure, shaped by the conventions of family melodrama, and so less isolated and less vulnerable. The child becomes a figure that adds complexity to the personal relationships within Nordic noir. The semantics of childhood – Rousseauian innocence, vulnerability, joyfulness and curiosity – give access to affective and intellectual material that is engaging but requires careful handling by its producers. Increasingly, the child's relationships and transitional, or liminal identity, furnish dramatic potential and positive challenges for writers, filmmakers and television producers, which then become a source of 'quality' drama. The transformation is noteworthy from several angles, but the angle on which this chapter focuses is the child's relationship to the category of 'Nordic noir'. The representation of the child is a definitive feature of the genre, insofar as the child makes evident some of the cultural assumptions, expectations, emotional stances and shared outlooks, that figure centrally in the Nordic states. At the same time, the changes in its representation show how such underpinning notions have changed in recent years, and in particular since the mid-2000s. The world of noir is conventionally a world of deceit, intrigue, cynicism, pervasive criminality and sexuality – a dark world, which rarely includes children. Yet there is a relationship between the child and Nordic noir. In fact, the child figures prominently within it – lying at the heart of all seasons of *Forbrydelsen* (*The Killing*, 2007–11) and *Bron/Broen* (*The Bridge*, 2011–18). As a definitive feature, the child originally figured as a metonymy of welfare-state dysfunction in Scandinavian crime fiction, but since the 2000s and the advent of Nordic noir, the child has come to define domestic space, serving to bring the complexity of family melodrama, and by extension 'quality', into the texts of Nordic noir. While the child's inclusion was initially political, it has increasingly served a cultural-economic function.

The child's ubiquity in contemporary Nordic noir contrasts with the figure's relative absence in the history of crime fiction. The classical detective story is an urbane world of adults, often away from home, in which children are not present. Hardboiled crime fiction and classic film noir are a veritable *nocturama*, and thus not a place where children go. Scholars of film noir such as Vivian Sobchack and Sylvia Harvey have argued that children are definitive figures in noir by their *absence*. Sobchack writes: 'children do not normally (or normatively) find their way into these spaces [of noir.] Women at home in these spaces are rarely mothers […] nor are men fathers'.[2] Harvey writes: '[I]t is the absence of normal family relations (of the network of relationships between mother–father–wife–husband–son) that forms one of the distinctive parameters of film noir'.[3] Sobchak and Harvey argue that a feature of noir is the absence of children, as well as family melodrama. So, too, the spy novel lacks children. It is built around state bureaucracies, surveillance operations and peripatetic operatives.

Children in crime fiction are hived off into their own sub-genre, the whodunnit for young readers, *The Hardy Boys, Nancy Drew, The Boxcar Children, Encyclopedia Brown* and so on. Here, it is the rational super sleuth, whose prodigy is displayed by their good sense, which stands in contrast to the typical depiction of children as tending towards the irrational and gullible. When children do appear in crime fiction, it is not unusual for this irrationality to be the basis of their inclusion. They become monstrous and uncanny, because of their irrationality. As an example, consider Steven King's *It* (1987), in which children's fears materialize as a shape-shifting monster who targets them. Or in the Nordic realm, a good example is the fiction of Yrsa Sigurðardóttir, for example *Sér grefur gröf* (2006; *My Soul to Take,* 2009) and *Ég man þig* (2010; *I Remember You,* 2012); in both children (or their ghosts) are both perpetrators of violence and victims of it. Horror's goal of terrorizing the reader allows for the inclusion of children, while crime fiction's concern with rational understanding tends to keep them out.

The police or legal procedural, in contrast, is a sub-genre of crime fiction in which children turn up sometimes, mostly as an embodiment of the domestic. Domestic scenes tend to involve the police detective or defence attorney at home. Children are typically foils against which the characters of their parents can be developed, supplementing the parents' character development in their professional lives. Children are not perpetrators or victims on their own, but innocent bystanders tugged into the intrigue. If children are present in crime fiction, readers' expectations typically concern how children are insulated from the morally compromised world around them. US crime-fiction critic Janet Hutchings observes: 'I don't like to see crimes against children trivialised by becoming the stuff of entertainment.

The subject will generally only become palatable to me in the hands of a very sensitive writer'.[4] By building her claim on an assumption about the vulnerability and innocence of children, Hutchings' point turns on Rousseauian notions of childhood as innocence. Yet, she also implies, including the child in crime fiction generates the opportunity to write with sensitivity and complexity. An author who writes well about children, in this view, adds to the literary merit of the text, but the status of this merit is more relative than absolute; it comes from, and is generated by way of, differentiation from the representation of children in other crime fiction. This differentiation is a sort-of corollary of Hutchings' point: crime fiction also trivializes crimes against children. This can happen, for instance, when children are included as foils, and crimes against them are included primarily as a conflict or trauma, which a more central, adult character must overcome. A child that is written about sensitively heightens the dramatic quality of the text, for 'sensitivity,' whether primarily realized through style or incorporated through thematic development, is a criterion that entails creating rounded characters whose comprehensibility does not depend on the conventions of the 'cute,' the 'pretty,' or 'the representative of trauma'.

Implicit in Hutchings' comment is a tension between genre and quality. It is tempting to assume that Hutchings is invoking the hierarchical distinction between 'high' and 'low' cultural texts, the more literary the better, the more generic the cruder and lower. This distinction is well known in literary history, as well as in the history of Scandinavian crime fiction.[5] But that would be a mistake, because Hutchings herself is one of the critics who has worked to challenge such distinctions. Rather her point is a relative one, which suggests that the representation of the child can provide a means adding intricacy, complexity and originality. It's not an argument about literary value, but textual richness. The argument here pivots from her point to suggest that as children have come to figure more prominently, and more complexly, in Nordic crime fiction during the last decade, the richness of these representations has led to a kind of mannerism, in which sensitive and dramatic treatment has become the goal, thus outweighing the political concerns that underlay the inclusion of children in Scandinavian crime fiction. There is a connection here to what television studies scholars, following Robert Thompson, have called 'quality' television.[6] I conceive of quality not only in relation to television writing, but more broadly in relevance to genre fiction: quality is a relative term, finding its definition by way of distinction from what is *not* quality. It is not a high-low distinction, but part of an enriched set of distinctions for the analysis of genre. Children, and more broadly the domestic, in Nordic noir in the mannerist phase have become a means of inscribing richness in the texts. But as cultural producers have done this more and more, the child figure has become increasingly conventionalized, part of a quality production strategy, which is a way of drawing on the regionally distinct cultural construction of the child, while also seeking to appeal to an ever-broadening audience of readers and viewers by differentiating these texts from other forms of crime fiction.

The child and the Nordic welfare state

In contrast to the absence of children in the crime fiction genre, the child plays a notably prominent and political role in the development of the police procedural in Scandinavian crime fiction. The child is typically a symptomatic victim or perpetrator. The context for this status is the discourse of childhood in the construction of the welfare state. 'Childhood was in the center for an intensive public debate that formed the ideals of the welfare state,' write sociologists Karin Aronsson and Bengt Sandin.[7] One of the chief aims of welfare state policy in the Nordic countries – beginning in the 1930s, but advancing most rapidly during the 1950s – was to create state institutional systems that supported and protected all members of society. The most vulnerable, such as children and the poor, were a special focus. Universal benefits such as pre-natal care, pre-school childcare, schooling and child allowances are examples of institutionalized programmes aimed at ensuring the health and well-being of children. The implication of such programmes is that a problem exists to be solved, that there is ill health, disease, lack of childcare and schooling, child labourers and impoverished parents without the means to raise their children. In the view of one contemporary Swedish opinion leader, 'the country [was] dominated by poor, unhealthy living spaces, and these [needed to] be replaced by good, hygienic ones'.[8] These would be the homes for healthy children with the resources they need to learn and grow and contribute to society – the welfare state's ideal.[9] This binary so central to the ideal of the welfare state is broadly present in Swedish popular culture, for example in public service campaigns, but also in cinema, popular literature and crime fiction, as we will see.

From the mid-1960s until the mid-2000s, the child serves in Scandinavian crime fiction as a political metonymy; a canary in the coal mine of the welfare state. Initially, the child is an ideological victim of the welfare state, which adds fuel to Marxist–Leninist critique of it. By showing how the state fails in key areas (such as for/with children), crime fiction uses a privileged figure of the welfare state to show its shortcomings. In contrast, since the 1990s and the advent of neoliberalism, the child has increasingly been put forward as a victim whose suffering is caused not by the state, but by a different set of problems, whose source is the retrenchment of state institutions in a globalizing world, which the state is not equipped to deal with. Increasingly, children's victimhood justifies a defence of the welfare state, which must be bolstered in order to handle the problems of a globally connected world. Reading the history of Scandinavian crime fiction in this way emphasizes its history as a socially critical form, and highlights its political dimensions. In this view, children are involved in crime, and detectives' relationships to their children are in shambles, because of welfare-state function and the society produced by it. It is problems with the function of the state that are the root cause of the victimhood. This is why children are present; they are symptomatic characters.

An indicative representation of the child as part of the early political critique can be found in Sjöwall and Wahlöö's novels. Consider, for example, The Man on the Balcony (1967), in which children are victims, because they have been left with inadequate support and attention from the state. Their victimhood stands in contrast to the status of the child in the genealogy of the welfare state. The work of Alva and Gunnar Myrdal, veritable architects of the Swesdish *folkhem* ('People's Home') – the colloquial metaphor for the Swedish welfare state – makes clear the importance of the child. A programmatic text in the Myrdals' theorization of welfare-state institutions was their *Kris i befolkningsfrågan* (*Crisis in the Population Question*, 1934). The book argued that state-provided support for families and children could enhance the rate of population growth, as well as the health of the population, creating a more vital work force and economy. Directly contradicting such discourses, Sjöwall and Wahlöö offer an emblematic episode at Stockholm's Central Railway Station in *The Man on the Balcony*. A fourteen-year-old girl seeks to sell investigator Martin Beck explicit pictures of herself, which she has taken in a nearby photo automat. When the girl approaches Beck, the narrator describes her as 'about fourteen, with blond, greasy hair, in a short batik dress, barefoot and dirty, about the same age as [Beck's] own daughter'.[10] By comparing her with Beck's daughter, the girl is sexualized, for she is implied to be an Other to her domestic, non-sexualized doppelgänger, Beck's daughter. At the same time, she is infantilized; her physical appearance makes evident her inability to take care of herself. The novel calls to mind the debate to which the Myrdals contributed: Karin Aronson and Bengt Sandin write that 'the poor, sickly, undernourished child in the philanthropic propaganda [...] was almost as prevalent during the 1920s and 1930s as are today's images of starving and homeless Third World Children'.[11] Barefoot, dirty and apparently living on the street, the adolescent's appearance is a child of the philanthropic propaganda, and her presence at the station signals the failure of the state, recalling the images of earlier decades. The novel stresses the girl's split identity; she presents herself as an adult, but in so doing figures as a political symptom, for she is truly a child, whom the state has failed, despite its founding commitment to nurture just such children.

Sjöwall and Wahlöö's *The Man on the Balcony* posits that state neglect allows vulnerable children to be victimized by adults. In US crime fiction, the blame for such a situation would fall at the feet of the family, a point made by Sylvia Harvey in her argument about the family in film noir. She argues that, in the ideological construction of modern US society, 'the family is the arena that is sanctified by society for the reproduction and preliminary education of the human race, for the bringing up of children'.[12] If children suffer from neglect, and become vulnerable, the root problem is in the child's family, for socialization and safety, moral and ethical training fall within its sphere. This is not the case in *The Man on the Balcony*. In this novel, the state is blamed. Swedish, and more broadly Nordic, notions of the child were constructed through the discourse and institutions of the welfare state during the twentieth century. One of the major line of arguments was that professionals, doctors, teachers and clergy – that is to say, experts – were better able to secure a healthy childhood for children than the children's families themselves.[13] This argument is founded on the rationalization and social engineering notion of modernity, maintaining as it does that rationality, institutions and experts provide superior guidance than do tradition and deferral to elders.[14] This ideology underlies the establishment of the welfare state in the Nordic countries. Aronson and Sandin point out that, in the Swedish post-war welfare state: 'in a manner of speaking, the children stood alone, without the family, protected by the state and the professionals that worked through its agencies. Childhood (i.e. the good childhood) was a creation of professionals and the state. Institutions were created and new laws passed to support and control childcare in the home'.[15]

The sociologist Gøsta Esping-Andersen has argued that such construction of the welfare state entailed a de-familialization, as the state came to take over many conventional parental functions – including childcare, hygiene and economic provision for the child.[16] This discourse can be seen at work in the colonial history of Scandinavia as well, evident not least in the forced adoption and schooling of children of indigenous Sámi families during the mid-twentieth century. The salience of the child had to do with the urgency of population growth in the post-war period, and the importance of training a competent and healthy workforce. Childhood was often identified as a public health matter, with legislative and institutional solutions put forward as ways to enhance health and education from an early age. Such concerns animated the writings of Alva and Gunnar Myrdal, who envisaged the welfare state as a tool for creating equity, which they viewed alongside others as the foundation of a politically and economically flourishing society.[17] Finland, for its part, put in place pre-natal clinics in 1944, and financial incentives, such as the *äitiyspakkaus* (Baby Box or, literally, Motherhood Package), in 1947. The Baby Box became universally available in 1949.[18] These welfare-state initiatives worked with, but also existed in tension with, conservative and paternalistic views of the working class as in need of discipline and normative guidance. Such views still pre-dominated in primary schools throughout the 1950s, and only school reforms of the 1960s, aimed at enhancing access to basic education, began to reject the earlier moral regime. Corporal punishment in schools was outlawed in 1958 in Sweden, for example.[19] This is the context in which to understand a character such as Pippi Longstocking, or indeed the 'children' of Tove Jansson's *Finn Family Moomintroll* novels.

For the Marxist–Leninists Sjöwall and Wahlöö, the social-democratic agenda that drove the ideas and institutions of the welfare state was a means of buying the consent of the working class, a compromise with capital made by the Social Democratic Party. As such, the welfare state obstructed the development of revolutionary consciousness. Sjöwall and Wahlöö were invested in using their crime novels to foreground the welfare state's failures and the child could figure as an effective political symptom. For Sjöwall and Wahlöö, the free child is apt to be an ideological victim of a nascent consumerism, and if not that, a potential victim of abuse. Left to her/his own devices, the child is apt to harm her/himself, by becoming an ideological dupe. The child is thus political, for it is constructed by the capitalist ideology that determines society more generally, to which the welfare state is necessarily supplicant. For the purposes of my argument, more important than the specific political conflicts that figured in Sjöwall and Wahöö's representation of the child was the installation of the figure of the child as a political touchstone in the socially critical crime novel. In Sjöwall and Wahlöö's novels, the child joined the anti-heroic police investigator, the victim, criminal and the police team of the procedural novel as key semantic units in the sub-genre of the Scandinavian police procedural.

The political figure of the child continued to feature prominently in the Scandinavian crime novel during its 1990s renaissance. Henning Mankell's *Villospår* (1995; *Sidetracked*, 1999) and *Brandvägg* (1998; *Firewall*, 2002) both focus intensely on children as victims and as perpetrators. This theme is also prevalent in Arnaldur Indriðason's novels, for example *Mýrin* (2000; *Jar City*, 2004) and *Vetrarborgin* (2005; *Arctic Chill*, 2009) in which a child of colour is the victim, and children are also the perpetrators of the crime. So too, Jussi Adler-Olsen's *Kvinden i buret* (2007; *Keeper of Lost Causes*, 2011) and his *Flaskepost fra P.* (2009; *Conspiracy of Faith*, 2013) concerns crimes involving children and children as criminals. Lene Kaaberbøl and Agnete Friis' novels, for instance *Drengen I kufferten* (2008; *The Boy in the Suitcase*, 2008) and *Et stille umærkeligt drab* (2010; *Invisible Murder*, 2010), depict a fragmented society through the cutting up and poisoning of children's bodies. A number of Jo Nesbø's novels make childhood traumas the source of criminality, and make the parent-child relationship crucial – *Snømannen* (2007; *The Snowman*, 2010), for instance. Norwegian Anne Holt's Hanne Wilhelmsen series makes parenthood a key focus, first as a point of contention between Hanne and her partner, Cecilie, and later through a child Wilhelmsen has with her second wife: Ellen Rees argues that '[g]ay parenthood is [a] major aspect of Holt's thematic focus'.[20] Such novels by Holt as *Demonens død* (1995; *Death of a Demon*, 2013) and *Løvens gap* (1997; *The Lion's Mouth*, 1999) focus on the consequences of the abuse and neglect of children. Children as criminals and victims are also frequent in Karin Fossum's novels. A Finnish example is Leena Lehtolainen's thirteen-novel Maria Kallio series, which includes both crimes against, and committed by, children, as well as extensive narration concerning the relationship between the investigator Kallio and her children. Then there is *Forbrydelsen* (*The Killing*, 2007–12), which includes both children as victims, and children integrally involved in the investigators' private lives. And, of course, in Swedish and English, it's a girl who is most famous of all: Stieg Larsson's novels narrate and largely turn on the events of Lisbeth Salander's childhood and the intertextual relationships with childhood and children's literature, for instance Pippi Longstocking, as Yvonne Lefler has shown.[21] Salander is herself a version of the child 'standing alone' with the state, only the state has let her down. In this figure we have both a political symptom and an attempt to re-invent the child as a differentiated figure and investigator, all in one. In Salander there is an interesting echo of Sjöwall/Wahlöö's girl in Stockholm Central Station. The ideological lesson offered by Sjöwall and Wahlöö is inflected by Larsson, who of course makes Salander the target of state officials. While Sjöwall and Wahlöö aspire to a kind of social-realist aesthetic, Larsson's depiction of Salander is melodramatic, as he attributes right and wrong, and good and bad to his conflicts, going well beyond a critical position on the welfare state. His state bureaucrats are evil, and seek to destroy young lives. These children belong to a context. Is the context the welfare state discourse? To what extent might we be seeing previous elements of the tradition being re-fitted to suit new production strategies and trends?

Liminality, childhood and representation

Part of the child's political potential is the figure's possibility as a source of 'quality'. This is implicit in what Karen Lesnik-Oberstein designates the liminal status of childhood.[22] The child is defined by their transitional identities, a potential adult, but not yet an adult, moving between categories. The child is physically capable of many adult behaviours, but is rarely capable of holding an adult's emotional worldview, if at all. On the one hand, a pre-dominant view sees the child as a Rousseauian innocent: 'a pure point of origin in relation to language, sexuality and the state'.[23] This is the child who can access 'objects of the real world' unencumbered by mediations of language and institution, writes Lesnik-Oberstein.[24] Yet on the other, the child is always already shaped by the interactions of everyday life – institutions, schools, clubs, apprenticeships – an adult in the making. Whether in Sjöwall and Wahlöö, Nesbø or others, the child introduces contrasts with both political and dramatic dimensions. Is the child being protected by the state? How will the child and the parent resolve their differences? For example, Salander's development is the arc of the *bildungsroman*, as she moves from a figure of physical maturity and emotional stuntedness to a combination of emotional maturity and adult social outlook. The liminality of childhood makes the category political, but also connects it to domesticity and the conflicts that are the sources of the melodramatic tradition.

As a threshold category, we seek to attribute content to childhood through representations of it, giving it value, and dramatic content. Robin Bernstein argues that 'childhood itself [...] is best understood as a process of surrogation, an endless attempt to find, fashion, and impel substitutes to fill a void caused by the loss of a half-forgotten original'.[25] Bernstein's point stresses that because childhood is defined by change, representations of childhood that fix it as 'this thing' or 'that' through image and figure are politically fraught. In her study of

US race politics, and the construction of domesticity and childhood, Bernstein argues that contrasting images of childhood figured in sharply differing political agendas in the nineteenth- and twentieth-century United States: 'White children became constructed as tender angels while black children were labelled as unfeeling, noninnocent nonchildren [...] dyadic divergence, a "melodrama in black and white."'[26] The politics of the representation of childhood are dramatic, indeed, melodramatic. Because childhood itself is a period of continual change and transition, the child is continually re-created through meaningful associations, with strong political and dramatic dimensions. We can see examples of liminality and its politics in Scandinavian crime fiction.

An insightful Nordic example is Mankell's *Villospår*, in which the investigation focuses on the murder of several well-heeled men, who it turns out have frequented adolescent prostitutes, procured for them by Björn Fredman, who is also murdered. In the investigation, Kurt Wallander speaks to Fredman's thirteen-year-old son, Stefan:

> They sat down on opposite sides of the coffee table. A duvet and a pillow on the sofa suggested someone had slept there. Under a chair, Wallander saw the neck of an empty bottle. The boy caught Wallander's eye. His vigilance did not wane. Wallander stopped in his thoughts. Could he interview a minor about his father's death, without a guardian present? [...] He couldn't lose this chance [...]
> What do you enjoy most in school?'
> Nothing. But math is easiest. We've started a club about mystical numbers, three factors, seven-year cycles, that kind of thing.
> Wallander found himself fascinated by the boy sitting opposite. The mature body contrasted with the boyish face.[27]

What makes the boy interesting for Wallander is the continuum of his presence, his vigilance, his physical strength, his cagey handling of the situation, which are all present alongside magical thinking, boyish clubs and a childish face. Layered upon this is the legal status of Wallander's encounter with the child, which the police officer considers as he engages young Fredman. Stefan is double-coded, at once an empty character creating general associations (a child) and, at the same time, a specific political figure, embedded in a particular legal and political context. In the latter sense, Stefan is failed by the state, like the girl in *The Man on the Balcony*, because no institution can protect Fredman or his sister and younger brother from their abusive father. But for Mankell, in contrast to Sjöwall and Wahlöö, the problem is the withdrawal of the state through retrenchment, rather than its failed ideology. While Sjöwall and Wahlöö seek to convey a contradiction between the ideology of the *folkhem* and the real conditions of its citizens' lives, Mankell seeks to show that the diminishment of state institutions through gradual retrenchment allows destructive, indeed evil, dynamics to take root. That seems to be the lesson of Fredman's murderous spree in *Sidetracked*. The violence and abuse in Mankell are the kind of political issue that lend themselves to melodramatic treatment, which I have argued is an important dimension of Mankell's novels.[28] Fredman does not turn to the state for help, but seeks his own justice, albeit as a victim of violent trauma himself, whose perspective is motivated by comic books, indigenous identities and mystical numbers, which he uses to represent himself and his worldview as a child. He does, as Bernstein argues happened in US race politics of the nineteenth and twentieth centuries, use surrogates of himself to pursue justice. When he assumes his alternative identity, he murders the victims in the novel. By making a child the perpetrator, Mankell holds himself to a standard that, for example, Sjöwall and Wahlöö in the example above did not reach. The girl in the train station is a shrill political message, in comparison to the rounded account of Stefan, which seeks to construct him as a traumatized victim, who seeks to create a version of himself and the world which can achieve justice, but in so doing in fact turns himself into an adolescent murderer. In this figure we see the resonance of the child as a political figure, but also a move towards quality aesthetics.

Quality

This political representation of the child has increasingly intersected with an aesthetic of quality. Quality aesthetics make use of the child's liminality within a representational system that is concerned with depicting broad areas of everyday life in a variegated and authentic way, generating moral and dramatic complexity. Quality, here, is an aesthetic and a cultural-economic term, which television studies scholars since the 1980s have used to theorize production practice, textual form and audience address and response. Robert Thompson argues that 'quality TV is best defined by what it is not. It is not "regular" TV'.[29] Against the genres and flow of conventional programming, quality TV offers narrative richness, more elaborate production values (reminiscent of cinema), long-form serialization, modification of conventional TV genres and better writing. Jane Feuer argues that in quality TV's negation of TV, it has drawn extensively on European art cinema production values and writing practices, and the self-reflexivity and intertextuality of auteur cinema.

The connection between quality TV and Scandinavian crime fiction has been documented by Eva Novrup Redvall, Olof Hedling and Anne Maarit Waade, writing about film and television productions in particular.[30] Redvall persuasively traces the advent of quality production and the way this concept drove the conceptualization and production of *Forbrydelsen* and *Borgen* (2011–18), among others.[31] She shows how show runners, writing rooms, script development, development of multiple narrative lines, shooting and editing practice impacted production practices, enhancing organization and co-ordination while also facilitating the vision of show runners, such as Søren Sveistrup, who have guided collaborative processes while ensuring continuity of vision. Hedling and Waade separately show how the Wallander novels were produced as television texts and film adaptations to create a regional franchise, or brand, which carried positively charged associations with crime fiction.[32] Location shooting, casting and the representation of language are instances of such production in Kenneth Branagh's BBC production *Wallander* (2008-16). While these examples concern television, the same issues are present in crime fiction, in which the use of spectacular violence, *rococo* intrigues and investigations, along with a foregrounding of the investigator's domestic life and children, convey a differentiated and branded 'quality' to an international audience.

An interesting example of these aesthetics is the Swedish series *Modus* (2015-17), in which Inger Johanne Vik (Melinda Kinnaman) is a criminal psychologist, trained by the American FBI, who has returned to Sweden and an academic career, seeking to protect her daughters, the older of whom is autistic, from exposure to the criminal world she has come to understand in the United States. The series is adapted from Holt's novels and is strongly shaped around genre convention. Vik calls to mind a cavalcade of female criminal psychologists and profilers who have worked for the 'Bureau' – to name but a few, Clarice Starling (Jodie Foster) in *The Silence of the Lambs* (1991), Dana Scully (Gillian Anderson) in *The X-Files* (1993-2002) and Jennifer Marsh (Diane Lane) in *Untraceable* (2008). In this sense, *Modus* follows genre convention; yet it seeks to engender quality through the casting of Stina Vik (Esmerelda Stuwe), an autistic pre-teen who in the first season is witness to the murder that initiates the investigation. The introduction of disability and trauma, through her witness of the murder, makes the relationship between Vik and Stina weighty and complicated, all the more so when Vik opts to join her former partner to investigate the murder her daughter witnessed. The investigation reveals that the murder is linked to an American religious sect – those wacky Yanks and their crazy religious politics. The political theme does not have the locality and specificity of focus for which Scandinavian crime fiction is known. Yet, the relationship of mother and daughter is intricate and compelling, with strong dramatic dimensions. What we see then is genre elements which are connected to the child in a way that enhances quality, while the political theme diminishes. This is an instance of what I am arguing is 'quality'. While the text is built on a clichéd character, the 'profiler', choices in writing and character development in other areas seek to develop complexity, which is driven by differentiation from other genre material, rather than political or social concerns.

One can draw a line back from *Modus* to Mankell's Kurt Wallander novels and their adaptations, and from there back to Sjöwall and Wahlöö's Beck, and his daughter Inga. In Sjöwall and Wahlöö, Inga remains a minor character, a foil that stands for family, but does not add to the central narrative dimension of the book. By contrast, development of the relationship in *Modus* is the focal point. This dimension is part of a broader trend towards quality in the narration of the investigator's personal relationships in Nordic noir. Whether Sara Lund, Harry Hole, Maria Kallio, Kurt Wallander, Thóra Gudmundsdóttir or Erlendur Sveinsson, each of these investigator's quotidian dramas are extensively narrated. What we note in these characters' depiction is the narration of their relationships to their children, which recurrently feature the focalization of their children's lives. To recall Bernstein, the parents themselves become surrogates of childhood, standing in for their children, but in so doing coming into conflict with some of the notions of children's autonomy, laid out in discussion of the welfare state. In a sense, the emphasis on family makes the series an instance of US-style family melodrama, as the privileging of quality aesthetics, and thereby market identity, and audience address, necessitates the design and writing of these relationships. Stina Vik's autism, and her witnessing a murder, enriches her family life while also making her a dramatic part of the investigation narrative. Quality is putatively the narrative by-product and the difference from Sjöwall and Wahlöö's politicized children is great.

It should be said, though, that quality carries a risk related to 'brand identity'. Too much quality becomes slick, glossy and formulaic, eroding the form's particular appeal. In a global market, cultural texts seeking to transcend national-language readerships and audiences by embracing quality aesthetics risk 'selling out' and losing the specificity of their appeal, emphasized for example by Slavoj Žižek's oft-cited comments on Henning Mankell's novels, in which he argues that the representation of locality is a key aspect of the appeal of globally relevant crime fiction for our age.[33] Žižek seems to suggest that Mankell and crime fiction of the global kind is a generic exoticism, in which location, character and mood are nested within familiar syntactic structures – crime, investigation and resolution. Lars von Trier has argued that efforts to enhance the quality of Danish cinema, by fostering improvements and professionalization in screenwriting education and production practice, exhibit a similar dynamic to what I am arguing occurs with the pursuit of quality in crime fiction. Von Trier remarks that:

> [t]he problem is that a director who turns to a writer comes with an idea for something that has more or less of a heart. And one thing is certain: that when it has been through this very quick dramaturgical treatment there is no longer a heart. Then it is extremely superficial.[34]

Quality aesthetics can mean complexity and revisionist invention, but also, of course, the overproduction of generic elements within an established tradition, with an eye towards market differentiation and audience appeal. Seeking to enhance these semantics by way of quality aesthetics risks losing the particularity that is distinctive, or what von Trier calls 'heart'. The child's liminality makes it a rich figure for the pursuit of quality, providing high moral stakes when Rousseauian associations are in play, but also access to emotionally and morally fraught everyday scenarios. When handled with what Hutchings calls 'sensitivity,' representations of the child can furnish a means of generating dramatic conflict as well as emotional and moral authenticity within everyday situations, distinguishing these representations from other varieties of the genre that lack such complexity. For these reasons, including the child in crime fiction requires a special touch.

Still, this representational use of the child does not eliminate the political. Instead, it emphasizes how the child's liminality can also include political status, in the welfare-state context. This status is part of the social imaginary of the Nordic welfare state. Yet the connection has waned. In more recent texts, the point is more closely tied to liminality, an exploration of the continuum between the family's, state's and child's agency. The exploration of this continuity, and the agency of those involved, is a source to which writers and screenwriters can turn to generate quality. Quality narration has been an aesthetic objective in Scandinavian crime fiction on the screen and on the page for some years now. Quality used as a critical term also opens up some worthwhile perspectives on Scandinavian crime fiction. Quality fosters complexity within genre and also differentiates from other generic texts, while synthesizing with earlier representations of the child. Quality helps explain the child's pervasive presence in Scandinavian crime fiction.

Notes

1. I conceive of Scandinavian crime fiction and Nordic noir as historically distinct categories. Scandinavian crime fiction dates from Maj Sjöwall and Per Wahlöö's first novel *Roseanna* (1965) to 2009, the year of the English-language translation of *Män som hatar kvinnor* (2004), *The Girl with the Dragon Tattoo*. Aesthetically, Nordic noir belongs to the larger category of Scandinavian crime fiction. The intermedial, global phenomenon of Scandianavian crime fiction necessitates the more specific category of Nordic noir, popularized by UK critics since the late 2000s, and focused particularly on texts such as Larsson's novels and the Danish television series, *Forbrydelsen* (2007–11).
2. Vivian Sobchack, '"Lounge Time": Postwar Crises and the Chronotope of Film Noir', in *Refiguring American Film Genres: History and Theory*, ed. Nick Browne (Berkeley: University of California Press, 1998), 157–8.
3. Sylvia Harvey, '"Woman's Place": The Absent Family of Film Noir', in *Women in Film Noir*, ed. E. Ann Kaplan (London: British Film Institute, 1998), 45.
4. Janet Hutchings, 'Child Characters in Crime Fiction', *Ellery Queen Magazine*, 28 August 2013. Available online: http://somethingisgoingtohappen.net/2013/08/28/childcharacters-in-crime-fiction/(accessed 13 April 2018).
5. A concise account of the significance of hierarchical distinctions between cultural difference can be found in the introduction to Edward Said's *The World, the Text, and the Critic* (Cambridge, MA: Harvard University Press, 1984), especially pp. 9–16. On the high-low distinction in Scandinavian crime fiction, and in particular its imbrication with gender difference, see Sara Kärrholm's 'Swedish Queens of

Crime: The Art of Self-Promotion and the Notion of Feminine Agency – Liza Marklund and Camilla Läckberg', in *Scandinavian Crime Fiction*, Andrew Nestingen and Paula Arvas, (eds) (Cardiff: University of Wales Press, 2011), 131–47, as well as Magnus Persson's 'High Crime In Contemporary Scandinavian Literature: The Case of *Miss Smilla's Feeling for Snow*', in *Scandinavian Crime Fiction*, eds Andrew Nestingen and Paula Arvas, 148–58.

6   Robert Thompson, *Television's Second Golden Age: From* Hill Street Blues *to* ER (Syracuse, NY: Syracuse University Press, 1997).
7   See Karin Aronsson and Bengt Sandin, 'The Sun Match Boy and Plant Metaphors: A Swedish Image of 20th-Century Childhood', in *The Global History of Childhood Reader*, ed. Heidi Morrison (New York: Routledge, 2012), 63.
8   Radio personality and author Ludvig Nodström, paraphrased by Thomas Etzemüller, *Alva and Gunnar Myrdal: Social Engineering in the Modern World*, trans. by Alex Skinner, (Lanham, MD: Lexington Books, 2014), 76.
9   Karin Aronsson and Bengt Sandin, 63–4.
10 Maj Sjöwall and Per Wahlöö, *The Man on the Balcony* (New York: Pantheon Books, 1967), 25–6.
11 Karin Aronsson and Bengt Sandin, 62.
12 Sylvia Harvey, 37.
13 Karin Aronson and Bengt Sandin, 64.
14 Thomas Etzemüller, 5–10.
15 Ibid., 64.
16 Gøsta Esping-Andersen, *Three Worlds of Welfare Capitalism* (Princeton: Princeton University Press, 1993), 38.
17 Thomas Etzemüller, 11–12.
18 Lauri Haataja, 'Jälleenrakentava Suomi,' in *Suomehistorian pikku jättiläinen*, ed. Seppo Zetterberg (Helsinki: WSOY, 1987), 737–848, 759.
19 Lundqvist, 98.
20 Ellen Rees, 'Straight Queers: Anne Holt's Transnational Lesbian Crime Fiction' in *Scandinavian Crime Fiction*, eds Andrew Nestingen and Paula Arvas (Cardiff: University of Wales Press, 2011), 100–14, 105.
21 Yvonne Lefler, 'Lisbeth Salander as Pippi Longstocking', *Post45: Nordic Noir: A Series Guest Edited by Bruce Robbins*, 6 July 2015. Available online: http://post45.research.yale.edu/2015/06/lisbeth-salander-as-pippi-longstocking (accessed 13 April 2018).
22 Karin Lesnik-Olberstein, 'Childhood and Textuality: Culture, History, Literature' in *Children and Culture: Approaches to Childhood*, ed. Karin Lesnik-Olberstein (New York: PalgraveMacMillan, 1998), 6.
23 Karin Lesnik-Obertsein, 'Childhood and Textuality', 6.
24 Ibid., 7
25 Robin Bernstein, *Racial Innocence: Performing American Childhood from Slavery to Civil Rights* (New York: New York University Press, 2011), 23.
26 Ibid., 33.
27 Henning Mankell, *Villospår* (Stockholm: Ordfront, 1994), 242. My translation.
28 Andrew Nestingen, *Crime and Fantasy in Scandinavia: Fiction, Film and Social Change* (Seattle: University of Washington Press, 2008), 223–54.
29 Robert Thompson, *Television's Second Golden Age,* 13.

30 See Anne Marit Waade, *Wallanderland. Medieturisme og skandinavisk TV-krimi. Studier i krimi og kriminaljournalstik* (Aalborg: Aalborg Universitetsforlag, 2013), as well as Olof Hedling, 'Murder, Mystery and Megabucks? Films and Filmmaking as Regional and Local Place Promotion in Southern Sweden', in *Regional Aesthetics: Locating Swedish Media*, eds Erik Hedling, Olof Hedling and Mats Jönsson (Stockholm: National Library of Sweden, 2010), 263–90.

31 Eva Novrup Redvall, *Writing and Producing Television Drama in Denmark: From The Kingdom to The Killing* (New York: Palgrave Macmillan, 2013).

32 Olof Hedling, 'Murder, Mystery and Megabucks?'; Waade, *Wallanderland*.

33 Slavoj Žižek, 'Parallax', *London Review of Books*, 25, no. 22 (2003).

34 Qtd. in Redvall, *Writing and Producing Television Drama in Denmark*, 74.

Chapter 10

DARK NIGHTS AND MORAL DIVERSITY: RE-THINKING MORALITY IN NORDIC NOIR

Mary Evans

This chapter's concern is morality, always a central theme of detective fiction. The particular focus here is the way in which that collective fiction known as *Nordic noir* has conceptualized morality. My argument is that in this fiction new lines are being drawn about moral boundaries, as Nordic noir has at its core highly critical views about the contemporary world. At the same time, it has to be said that what Nordic noir has also done, as it has dramatically moved some of the goal posts of detective fiction, is to identify both the very good and the very bad in original but important places, places that are very much part of life in the Global North in the twenty-first century.

It would, however, be wrong to suppose that Nordic noir stands out as unrelated to, and distant from, other contemporary forms of detective fiction.[1] Indeed, Nordic noir has much in common with other forms of noir: particularly that of Tartan noir and what we might see emerging as a distinctly English form of noir which can be called Historical noir. This implies, through the means of detective fiction, the recovery of those hidden aspects of the British Empire that mainstream British culture and politics has not encouraged people to examine too closely. It is only recently that the days of the British Empire have received consistent and public scrutiny, with 'markers' of that empire, such as public statues, acquiring increased criticism.[2] Hiding, the hidden, or what is not said, are central themes in crime fiction. From the earliest days of its genesis, crime fiction has recognized the potency of the need to hide; revelation is often to be feared, although that theme has previously been applied more frequently to individual characters rather than historical events. Agatha Christie in particular was an early exponent of this former tradition. English writers of detective fiction are now seizing on the idea of 'hidden' history. In this, writers encounter a British state that has always maintained an energetic and often effective covering up of unacceptable evidence. A second point which needs to be established here, in linking Nordic noir with other forms of noir, is its presentation of the growing social and political polarization within its own societies and much of Europe and the USA. This recognition of growing social inequality has become commonplace and standard across the political spectrum.³ Equally important are the forms of political and social separation around material issues such as migration and unemployment, topics which are themselves translated into concerns about national and individual identity.

So, whilst Nordic noir has much in common with other recent detective fiction, it also has one important, and in many ways exceptional characteristic. That feature is the articulation of the idea to increase the possible extent of the contexts for moral judgement. This is not to suggest that detective fiction has not always created a wide social range of guilty, murderous individuals; a long line of writers of crime fiction from all over the world have done, and continue to do, this, but the difference is the shift from individual guilt to collective institutional and hegemonic cultural guilt. The latter are now named as the *origin* of murderous intent: motive does not come simply from the various entanglements of personal and family circumstances, but from an impersonal world of increasingly coercive values and assumptions. This might be named as 'normative orthodoxy' or in other sociological terms. The point here is that this shift in the responsibility for the origin of crime (in the case of detective fiction, murder) is towards the collective and away from the individual psyche. But here again the collective intervenes: that psyche which becomes murderous emerges from those circumstances created and endorsed by new forms of social norms. Anyone who has read Tana French or Stieg Larsson or Jo Nesbø will probably recognize this thesis: the articulation of the view that institutions, be they of the property market or various aspects of the welfare state are in themselves morally dubious. All these authors have written of corruption and, more than that, of the corrupting power of institutions and ideas. What emerges is that no longer do some form of the seven deadly sins inform and inspire crime, (most usually greed or envy) but that the very institutions of the world in which we live are themselves morally suspect if not actually indefensible. It is a view which also informed some of the work of the Swedish writers Maj Sjöwall and Per Wahlöö, whose work was published in the 1970s, long before there was any such identification of Nordic noir.⁴ The difference being that the central detective of Sjöwall and Wahlöö's novels, Martin Beck, was not an outsider, and that at least some of the public institutions with which he dealt remained positive.

Yet, the view from the worlds of detection about the growing moral illegitimacy of conventional institutions is also a view which is familiar to watchers of the real-life political scene. In the last five years the two most important political movements in the USA have been the Tea Party and the Occupy movements, whilst across Europe there has been a rise in the number of people supporting political parties on the right of the political spectrum. From very different parts of this spectrum, these groups of individuals have proposed that the very worlds within which we live have to be re-made and re-thought. The most striking feature of these politics is that these radically different movements agree on the entirely unacceptable nature of the contemporary state and conventional politics. One further point to emphasize here is the way in which history, always eager to repeat itself, might be seen to be doing so through the pages of crime fiction. In the 1930s, writers such as Dashiell Hammett and Raymond Chandler in the United States situated the very real possibility of the pursuit of crime and any kind of justice achieved as entirely outside the state institutions of policing. Hammett himself worked as an employee of the Pinkerton National Detective Agency, founded by Alan Pinkerton in the middle of the nineteenth century. This organization was the place that many citizens turned to for a competent investigation of crime because actual detectives and police forces could not only not catch criminals but had little interest in doing so.[5] The absence of intelligence or integrity in the persons formally charged with policing led, inevitably, to the cult of the amateur on both sides of the Atlantic. It was left to the likes of fictional characters, for example, Miss Marple and Philip Marlowe, not just to identify the criminal but to see the social justification for doing so. It took some time for police forces in any part of the world to become even close to the ideal of guardians of public virtue and morality. In the United States, there has always been some ambiguity about whether this would ever be achieved, not least because many police forces have been abusive towards non-white citizens. The work of the journalist Jill Leovy on the absence of formal investigation into the deaths of young male African Americans in California, and the claims of the Black Lives Matter campaign would suggest that the congruence of the pursuit of justice and formal policing structures still has some way to go.[6] In her most recent work of fiction, *Bluebird, Bluebird* (2017) the African American writer Attica Locke wrote that:

> While looking into the cases of men and women, mostly black and Latino, who had been wrongfully accused and often incarcerated for decades, the two investigators discovered a pattern: for every story about a black mother, sister, or wife crying over a man who was locked up for something he didn't do, there was a black mother, sister, wife, husband, father or brother crying over the murder of a loved one for whom no-one was locked up. For black folks, injustice came from both sides of the law, a double-edged sword of heartache and pain.[7]

This comment stands as a telling, and lasting, comment on the operation of the criminal justice system in the United States. But similar patterns, in which race and class impact on the likelihood of criminal prosecutions are found elsewhere.

In raising this question about the ways in which different parts of the world have dealt with questions of morality and its presence or absence in those institutions most centrally concerned with it, we also see some of the larger ruptures between the ways in which different areas construct questions about the origin of evil and the breakdown of the idea of shared morality. There is still, as any reader familiar with Patricia Cornwell will see, a very powerful lobby for the idea that evil lies in the individual. The 'perp', as the wicked person is identified in Cornwell's work, is just that: a person acting alone and apparently not inspired by anything other than by a chaotically violent psyche. But once we start to look at other countries, we see rather different patterns. As suggested, in the last ten years the UK has seen the emergence of detective fiction including very articulate and well-informed accounts of the impact of public and state policies on the lives of individuals. Matthew Frank's *If I Should Die* (2014), the trilogy by William Shaw featuring the detectives Breen and Tozer and the novels by Adrian McGinty, set in Belfast at the time of 'The Troubles' all make apparent the ways in which individuals are made, or unmade, by their times.[8] We do not just live in what Bob Dylan described as 'the times' – the times make us. All these novels have as their central characters people working in the police force doing their best to maintain a sense of policing as viable and to pursue justice as enshrined in the law. That this is often done in the context of a world in which colleagues are corrupt, incompetent or both is a longstanding aspect of global crime writing, which continues to this day. There is almost no crime fiction being published anywhere in the contemporary world in which at least some of the people in the forces of law and order are at least as bad as the people against whom these institutions are supposed to be acting. One of the messages of global crime fiction, quite as much as actual evidence about many aspects of non-fictional policing, is that there is something extremely rotten in this aspect of the nation-state.

This absence of moral certainty is evident throughout Nordic noir and its various themes. A similarity between Nordic noir and Tartan noir began in the 1990s when detective fiction in both geographical areas began to address the same issues. It was a decade characterized in the UK by the continued drip-drip of revelations about corruption, deception and incompetence in what was then John Major's government. A definitive work in this decade was Ian Rankin's *Let it Bleed* (1995), itself inspired by William McIlvanney's novel of 1977, *Laidlaw*.[9] In his novel, Rankin's longstanding central character Detective Inspector Rebus pits himself not against one personal enemy but against an entire Scottish power structure. Towards the end of the novel, when Rebus has begun to realize that he is very unlikely to be able to bring a group of powerful men to anything like justice, Rankin writes of Rebus' views about the men he has been pursing:

> They knew the way the world worked; they knew who – or rather what was in charge. It wasn't the police or the politicians; it wasn't anyone stupid enough to place themselves in the front line. It was secret, quiet men who got on with their work the world over, bribing where necessary, breaking the rules, but quietly, in the name of 'progress', in the name of the 'system'.[10]

The chief villain in Rebus' sights in this novel is a man called Sir Ian Hunter, whom Rebus wanted because, 'He espoused the public good, but lined his pockets with the public's money'. In *Let it Bleed* it is the poor and vulnerable, those on the social fringes who suffer; there is no certainty of retribution for the crimes of the powerful.

Two years after *Let It Bleed*, in 1997, Jo Nesbø published his first Harry Hole novel. The first of the Van Veeteren novels by Nesser had already appeared in 1993.[11] From then on, Nesbø and Nesser pursue themes similar to those of Rebus: that there are seams of deep injustice in all the social worlds that they create: for Rebus this is Scotland, for Nesbø it is Norway and for Nesser a less firmly identified country which is a composite of Sweden, Poland and Norway. It is within these various locations that policemen (and it is largely at this time men) of varying degrees of marginality fight their battles against the conventional world. Even as we have to allow that the description of the 'marginal' policeman covers the considerable distance between Jo Nesbø's Harry Hole and Nesser's Inspector Van Veeteren, the men who constitute the morally aware and admirable in Nordic noir are people who exist in various ways outside conventional culture. Yet this is not in itself an entirely radical departure, since many of the great fictional detectives have very often been outsiders; from Sherlock Holmes to Miss Marple, to Inspector Morse, intelligence and integrity have long been associated with the socially deviant and those at some distance from formal power. Arguably, one of the reasons that crime fiction is so attractive is that its moral compass is very often tolerant, and willing to accept ambiguous human behaviour. It seldom suggests that its heroes and heroines are suffering from the desire to be conventional, or fraught with angst at the sense of their social exclusion. Crime fiction does not do the work of normalization, so longed for by sections of the media. Within these pages it is possible to be a drunk, an occasional heroin addict, a very happy and contented spinster, an unrepentant elitist or a manic depressive, and yet still function as an arbiter, albeit sometimes unwillingly, of ideals about social justice. Here, it is also worth noting that much of crime fiction written in the years after 1970, certainly in much of Scandinavia and the UK, functions as an extended obituary for conventional alpha males: they do not entirely disappear (see P. D. James' Adam Dalgleish, or Ruth Rendell's Chief Inspector Wexford), but the collective account suggests that their days are long gone.

In the characters created by Nesbø and Nesser and other authors representative of Nordic noir, for example, the Icelandic writers Arnaldur Indriðason and Ragnar Jónasson, there is little sense of either the attractions or the existence of normative certainty. In Nordic noir, in large part written after 1980, we can see much of the same kind of critique of the 'normal' world that began in the UK and the United States around the question of suburban, white middle-class life. The existence of a tradition critical of the conventional world was for decades central to much Anglo-American fiction. But in the 1960s, the specific focus of attack by novelists in this realm was the apparent domestic bliss rendered possible by heterosexual marriage and life in the racially exclusive suburbs: Sylvia Plath's *The Bell Jar* (1963) is perhaps the best known example of this theme, although less well known are the novels of Evan Connell and Richard Yates.[12] All these people were saying, loudly, that this created world was maintained by forcing the human into confirming and conformist patterns. 'Not for me' said a later generation, which re-validated urban life and in common with the heroine of John Schlesinger's film *Darling* (1965) departed for what was seen as metropolitan excitement and the social and cultural freedom to be found in the city. It was a flight, in the context of the study of crime, away from the policing of the small community to what was expected to be anonymity and personal privacy. In both the UK and the USA, critical voices defined the suburban life that people were invited to aspire to as the life not worth living and asked why a younger generation should have to conform to the conventional forms of dress or behaviour that had been expected of their parents. The iconic article of clothing from the 1950s and early 1960s was a man's leather jacket. Beloved of Marlon Brando and James Dean, it became and continued to be the archetypal 'sign' of dissent from the 1950s until the years of Nesbø and Stieg Larsson's *The Millennium Trilogy*. The heroine of Larsson's novels, Lisbeth Salander is seldom to be seen without that same jacket. A rapid digression here on the politics of dress in detective fiction: to note that although many of the male characters wear that conventional garment of male respectability, the two-piece suit, they also care little for it. Rankin's Inspector Rebus sleeps in his, and endlessly drops food on it; others abandon it altogether with dress that is as close as possible to the jeans and leather jackets of Brando and Dean. Detecting the signification of clothes in detective fiction is a rich, and as yet largely unexplored, aspect of the study of detective fiction. In the 1960s and 1970s the tables were turned by new cultures of dress and behaviour during the years of Macmillan, De Gaulle and Eisenhower.

Yet, notwithstanding the political shocks of 1968 the Global North maintained much of its political and material authority, even if to do so it had to weaken some of its policing of sexual behaviour. 'Repressive tolerance' as Herbert Marcuse had named it, described with some accuracy many of the shifts in the west in the 1960s.[13] But one remained which was important here: media and print representations of crime still, generally, maintained strict boundaries between the criminal and the rest. Only very gradually did the terms crime and criminals come to lose their certainty. If we then fast forward to the second decade of the twenty-first century we encounter many nation-states that no longer devote much of their time policing many issues around what we might deem private behaviour. But energy once devoted to the imprisonment of homosexuals or the shaming of women named as unmarried mothers is now devoted to other failings of the citizen, most often and certainly in the case of the UK, the status of the individual as an economically independent subject. Alongside the apparent diminution of forms of sexual surveillance there has been the rise of a new form of criminal: the shame and material hardship heaped on the poor and the vulnerable has, in the past decade in the UK and elsewhere, become considerable. Civic virtue, being a good person and an acceptable citizen is now closely associated with the idea of economic independence, both from others and from the state. The only way to be 'good' is to be able to look after yourself.

What emerged by the beginning of the 1980s, across much of Europe and the United States was a new form of capitalism, in which the citizen's private life was subject to much decreased surveillance. But this shift in the state's attention to the sexual behaviour of its citizens did not involve a decrease in its overall activity, but rather a re-direction of its energies towards the population's economic and material lives. Neoliberal and neo-conservative ideas began to take hold of the political imagination and political institutions of the west. It was this new reality which Tartan noir and Nordic noir confronted. New questions were asked; not least how we might live with the damage that those once-praised, and generally legitimated, welfare states were clearly capable of inflicting on the vulnerable. As such, a new generation of anti-heroes were born: Mikael Blomkvist (of the *Millennium Trilogy*) and Harry Hole were to become the morally good 'bad' boys of the twenty-first century. Morality had gone through a seismic shift: no longer the preserve of those representing accepted state institutions, but placed in the hands of those with somewhat fragile connections to the conventional world. These men, and to a certain extent the women who were created within the confines of Nordic noir, went even further towards the truly disenchanted and detached end of the social integration continuum than their counterparts in other parts of the world, and, crucially, previous incarnations of the marginal detective such as Holmes or Marple. The description of these individuals as embodying that Nordic tendency, in all forms of cultural and social life, towards what has been described as 'puritan sparseness and metaphysical intensity' is more than apt.[14] But in addition to this, what heroes or anti-heroes such as Hole and Blomkvist do is to revive aspects of the 'gifted amateur' tradition. Yes, both men are formally employed, but their relationship to formal employment, and their careers within in it, are always tenuous. Not, certainly, as tenuous (indeed non-existent) as the ties of Miss Jane Marple and Lord Peter Wimsey to institutional life, but still maintaining both of those characters' profound scepticism towards formal authority.

Now to the question of why this was the case: the puzzle of the great cultural rebellion that Nordic noir represents. By contrast with many parts of the world, those countries which make up the Nordic world are still and have been in the past shining examples of enlightenment and social justice. There are, throughout this geographical region, universal welfare rights that many citizens of less generous states long for: their policies on health care and state funded provision for parental leave and childcare are just two areas where these countries lead the world. For many of us in the UK, watching as all forms of benefits are eroded or translated into the most meagre and increasingly grudging state provision, the question is that of why these people give voice in their crime fiction to such extreme forms of alienation, disenchantment and *ressentiment*. Emile Durkheim and Max Weber should surely re-appear to flock to these shores to see why some of their various predictions of the modern world have emerged in what would seem to be the most unlikely places. Would they agree with the conservative and right-wing critics of the generosity of some welfare states that this very generosity causes various forms of moral ill health? To these writers, the idea that individual people might actually be supported collectively by other people is deeply suspect. In this view, the world should actually be the place in which we all compete against each other; not to compete is to opt out, to scrounge, to be dependent, to be in all sorts of ways a less than viable citizen.

Yet what Nordic noir asks, is perhaps one of the most fundamental questions of the twenty-first century: that of how to define what individual competition is for, and how that might build social solidarity. The countries in which Nordic noir has its origins are rich in terms of all kinds of resources, not least the level of their inhabitants' formal education. But here, it might be worth unpicking some of the assumptions that surround that last sentence in which formal education is often implicitly assumed to be, if not the key to all mysteries, then at least to the better order of society. Very often invoked as a panacea for all social ills, education carries considerable baggage. For example, in her book *Hard Choices*, published in 2014, Hillary Clinton wrote: 'The global middle class is a natural constituency for America. It's in our interests to see it grow to include more people. We should do everything we can to expand it at home and around the world'.[15] Now on the face of it that sounds all very well and entirely progressive, but a little de-construction allows us to consider critically both the use of the terms 'middle class' and the assumption that this class is so apparently the 'natural' constituency of the United States, given that many observers of the American social structure would point out that the security of middle-class existence is becoming increasingly frail, if not imaginary.[16] 'Precarious' has become the most-often-used description of many lives in the United States. Moreover, and most particularly in the context of the 2016 US presidential election and the Brexit vote in the UK, it has been widely suggested that one of the reasons so many people voted for Trump or supported Brexit was that they viewed the educated middle class as their enemy, and as the reason for increasingly marked social divisions. Michael Gove voiced the view that 'we don't need experts' and Trump said that he loved the 'uneducated'; both absurd statements in terms of our universal and shared needs for people to exercise their specialist, skilled and expert strengths. But perhaps both Gove and Trump were voicing that inarticulate feeling that cannot but accompany much of western education in the twenty-first century: that not to do well in it is a sign of personal failure, of not succeeding, of not being able to compete in what is, in many countries, an increasingly frantic competition for those scarce, well rewarded 'middle-class' jobs. The implicit competition of contemporary education thus becomes one of the sources of contemporary discontent, a shared sense that imperfect performance in these increasingly ruthless systems is to be labelled, as were Brexit supporters, the 'left behind'.

We might therefore go from this de-construction of Hillary Clinton's comment to recognize that her validation of the 'global middle class' is a very problematic idea for various reasons. Clearly, it leaves behind the majority of the population who are not in any sense 'middle class', as at the same time it negates national identity. Notice too, that this middle class is assumed to be on the side of all things progressive, as long as all things 'progressive' are defined in the same terms as those of the United States. But Nordic noir notices that middle-class education might take you to the management of financial markets, to banks, or to the higher reaches of various state or private institutions, whose fundamental purpose is to maintain the structures of privilege and wealth. Nordic noir recognizes that the 'education, education, education' of which Tony Blair spoke in one of his more messianic moments could make an individual utterly supportive of a political and economic system whose rewards are not always equally shared. Almost all detective fiction contains characters that are deeply suspicious of senior management, and the search for both status and financial benefit; in this longstanding tradition, Nordic noir is not breaking new ground. But what it is doing, and what we can see in characters such as Harry Hole and Mikael Blomkvist, are individuals who do not just dislike those more powerful in various hierarchies, but are openly suspicious, if not openly hostile to them. Harry Hole and Mikael Blomkvist both have considerable formal education; in that sense they embody the credentialized work force which was increasingly seen as fundamental to the twentieth century. But more than that, both have skills that are generally absent from the formal western higher education curriculum; in Blomkvist's case an ability to find his way into any computer system, not all of which methods are legal. Harry has a considerable grasp of the cultural and social divisions of urban space: his ability to 'read' that metropolitan space in which increasing numbers of people live is central to his competence. What is being suggested through these characters is the idea of mobile intelligence, an intelligence which is not based in an office, but which can literally, in terms of movement through actual physical space, or in more abstract forms related to computer-based worlds, countenance different forms of reality.

It is Nordic noir that encounters these different forms of reality and recognizes that this contemporary discontent and disenchantment are in part formed by precisely the social policy, education and validation of the idea of a 'skills' society, which are consistently read as necessary and needing to be endorsed by all right-thinking progressive people, even if the acquisition of and rewards for those skills are fundamentally related to social inequality. But, the important question remains of what is absent from those learned capacities. Two writers from Iceland, Arnaldur Indriðason and Ragnar Jónasson, are symptomatic of engagement with the issues raised above. A quotation on the cover of the English translation of Indriðason's novel *Kamp Knox* (2014; *Oblivion*, 2015) hails him as one of the 'greats of modern crime fiction'. Similar endorsements are to be found of Jónasson's work; specifically, his novels *Snjóblinda* (2010; *Snowblind*, 2015) and *Náttblinda* (2014; *Nightblind*, 2016).

Nightblind takes place five years after its precursor, *Snowblind*, and the hero of both books is Ari Thór Arason, a man who is, as is more or less standard for fictional policemen, endlessly conflicted by his personal relations. On the sixth page of the novel the admirable Icelandic childcare arrangements are set against cuts in healthcare and the police; called out into the dark, freezing night Ari finds his seriously injured colleague, a victim of a shooting. The town's mayor is alerted to the incident: this fundamentally 'good guy' as Jónasson describes him, has become, by the end of our introduction to him, someone who is not altogether clear about his moral boundaries and is concerned that Ari, the 'miserable character' is going to wreck everything for him. So, by page 18, we have two men in places they don't much care for, both at odds with their partners, and in one case taking a less enthusiastic view of the other. By the end of the novel, we have discovered that the policeman had been shot by his son, a boy of 19, who had discovered a diary kept by his father in which he voiced his fears that he was becoming like his own father, a man who terrorized and abused his family. The themes of hidden and repetitious forms of domestic violence are central to this book, and relate to two of the murders that are committed in its course. But more than that, the author wants us to consider the origin of that violence and the reasons why it does not disappear. In the final pages of the book, when those guilty of the murders have been identified, the narrative returns to Ari Arason, whose wife and child have by this time left him. He says of their relationship that it was always 'volatile' and that his own anger and jealousy was much to blame for its problems. In this, we encounter again a dynamic of male rage against women; known and recognized in Ari's case and as such, implicitly explaining, and nearly justifying, the murder of the abusive father.

A similar fury and concern with the past is part of the story in Indriðason's *Oblivion*, a novel which takes place early in the central character Inspector Erlendur's career. In common with Jónasson's policeman Arason, (and many others) Erlendur has a less than happy personal life and troubled children. Again, in common with Arason, what is central to the narrative of all these novels is the past: its impact on the present, and the ways in which previous terror, loss and trauma can continue to haunt and damage us. The weaving together in *Oblivion* of a cold case and a murder in the present opens a discussion of the invasion of Iceland, and Icelandic society, by a strange presence, that of the United States. Moreover, it is a presence that constantly attempts to hide, to refuse questions and, in the most comprehensive way possible, refuse the idea of 'speaking truth to power'. Both novels are united by themes of how the complexities of human relationships are worked out, especially through various forms of social power, be they of men over women, or more or less powerful states. In this way it has to be said that Nordic noir, and certainly what was described earlier as History noir, is a powerful argument for the psychoanalytical dangers of refusing to accept parts of both the collective and individual past.

Of course, many societies do not like to return to their past, and if they do, it is done in fragmented and misleading ways. Partial returns to the past all too often involve returns to a fantasy past: consider the endless re-iteration in the UK to a return to the Second World War, when we 'were all in it together' and were united in a common purpose. Consider also, the strength of the case for 'making America great again'; perhaps not a reality which all American citizens would recognize. These kinds of returns are unlikely to be projects that the detectives in much of Nordic and History noir wish to see. Moreover, all of these authors recognize how much of their past many societies refuse to confront when it does not always reflect admirable, or even acceptable episodes of national histories. Writers of detective fiction take a rather different view. At the beginning of the English writer William Shaw's 2015 novel *The Birdwatcher*, which considers the long term impact of the suppression of the Mau Mau in Kenya in the 1950s, there is a quotation from Eric Griffith Jones, later Sir Eric and the attorney general of the British administration in Kenya: 'If we are going to sin, we must sin quietly'.[17] Certainly, the sins were considerable, and the publication of the archives in the early twenty-first century demonstrated exactly how much the British administration had been involved in murder and torture. In this case, the suffering in the past is of the colonized, and what is also clear is that a great deal of effort was put into the suppression of evidence about those years in Kenya. In another recent example of History noir, Matthew Frank's *If I Should Die*, the suffering is that of those soldiers who have to carry out the military campaigns of the state. One of the characters in this novel says:

> Did you know that, on average, a male veteran suffering from PTSD symptoms will not seek help for fourteen years? So instead of appearing on military statistics they get chalked up later as mental health issues, domestic violence, alcohol and drug abuse, unemployment, homelessness, suicide. Two hundred and fifty-six British soldiers died in the Falklands conflict, but more than that have committed suicide since.[18]

Both History noir and Nordic noir recognize the suppression of the different aspects of the past that we do not wish to acknowledge. More precisely, what we do not want to know or to admit is the potential of the state's actual violence and its impact on individuals. In rhetorical accounts of crime, in which the state metaphorically goes 'to war', real forms of violence which occur as a result of state policies are normalized: it is ordinary for the state to take up arms against its enemies. But as detective fiction has recently, so powerfully pointed, those against whom the state takes up arms do not belong at a single place on the moral continuum.

Nordic noir, not just in the work considered here, but in much of the other brilliant and engrossing novels written since the 1980s, sets out a damning indictment of much of the conventional world, an indictment which corresponds with many accounts of the reality of it in the twenty-first century. What this is about is social distance: the growing gap between what we are presented with as a justification and explanation of our times, and the actual reality. At this moment, we can no longer find a moral compass in the places that we expect; it is the world outside the conventional parameters that attracts support, whether from the right or the left of the political spectrum. Harry Hole is in all sorts of ways a nightmare figure to the conventional world; in less dramatic ways so are many of the other detectives of Nordic noir. But the position of 'very bad' is no longer a simple matter of the conventionally criminal, nor is the 'very good' to be found in its typical opponents. We have to begin to look elsewhere for new definitions and understandings of the behaviours and doctrines that we wish to endorse and practise in the twenty-first century. My argument is that Nordic noir sets out the territory of these possibilities.

Notes

1. For full-length studies of Nordic noir see Kirsten Bergman, *Swedish Crime Fiction: The Making of Nordic noir* (Milan: Mimesis International, 2014); B. Forshaw, *Death in a Cold Climate: A Guide to Scandinavian Crime Fiction* (Basingstoke, Palgrave Macmillan, 2012); M. Tapper, *Swedish Cops: From Sjöwall and Wahlöö to Stieg Larsson* (Bristol: Intellect Press, 2014).
2. A recent example of protest against visible memories of the British Empire was the protest against the statue of Cecil Rhodes at Jesus College, Cambridge. In January 2018 the statue remains in place.
3. The material about increasing social inequality in both the UK and the USA is now extensive. See, for example, Stewart Lansley and Joanna Mack, *Breadline Britain: The Rise of Mass Poverty* (London: Oneworld, 2015); Tom Clark, *Hard Times* (New Haven and London: Yale University Press, 2015).
4. The husband and wife team Maj Sjöwall and Per Wahlöö published ten novels between 1965 and 1971. In all of them the central character is Martin Beck.
5. For a discussion of the Pinkerton Detective Agency and its relationship to Dashiell Hammett see Diane Johnson, *The Life of Dashiell Hammett* (London: Pan Books, 1985), 17.
6. Jill Leovy, *Ghettoside: Investigating a Homicide Epidemic* (New York: Penguin and Random House, 2015). The evidence about stop and search policies in the United Kingdom suggests a similar racial bias towards racialized assumptions of criminal guilt.
7. Attica Locke, *Bluebird, Bluebird* (London: Serpent's Tail, 2017), 273.
8. Matthew Frank, *If I Should Die* (London: Michael Joseph, 2014); William Shaw, *The Birdwatcher* (London: Quercus, 2015), *A Song from Dead Lips* (London: Quercus, 2013), *A House of Knives* (London: Quercus, 2014); Adrian McGinty, the Sean Duffy novels, beginning with *Orange Rhymes with Everything* (New York: William Morrow, 1997).
9. The Laidlaw trilogy by William McIlvanney consists of *Laidlaw* (published in 1977), *The Papers of Tony Veitch* (Edinburgh: Canongate, 1983), *Strange Loyalties* (London: Hodder and Stoughton, 1991).
10. Ian Rankin, *Let It Bleed* (London: Orion Publishing Group, 1995).

11 To date there are ten novels by Håkan Nesser all featuring the detective Chief Inspector Van Veeteren. The first (*Borkmann's Point*) was published in 1994 and the most recent is *The G File*, published in 2003.
12 Richard Yates, *Revolutionary Road* (New York: Little, Brown and Company, 1962) and Evan S. Connell, *Mrs Bridge* (New York: Viking, 1959).
13 Herbert Marcuse, *One Dimensional Man* (New York: Beacon Press, 1964).
14 Richard Ruland and Malcolm Bradbury (eds) *From Puritanism to Postmodernism: A History of American Literature* (London: Routledge, 2016), 3–30.
15 Hillary Clinton, *Hard Choices* (New York: Simon and Schuster, 2014), 526.
16 Barbara Ehrenreich, *Fear of Falling* (New York: Pantheon, 1989).
17 William Shaw, *The Birdwatcher*, 2.
18 Matthew Frank, *If I Should Die*, 291.

Part IV

GENEALOGY AND GENRE

Chapter 11

WHAT'S IN A NAME? THE THORNY THREAD OF NORDIC NOIR

Björn Nordfjörd

The name Nordic noir has been swiftly adopted and judged to be a fitting and appropriate term to describe and characterize Nordic crime fiction, film and television. A closer look at the case, however, reveals that the evidence used to support the term is unconvincing if not altogether lacking. In this chapter, I begin by addressing the adoption of the term 'Nordic noir', then trace the origin and specificity of the term 'noir' itself, before finally considering how applicable it is to the Nordic context.

The Crime Scene

It is easy to understand why Nordic noir caught on so quickly for marketing purposes: noir has long been great for advertising and Nordic noir has a very catchy ring to it. After its emergence in 2010 it was quickly adopted as the go-to term in marketing, production, mass media coverage and introductory book titles.[1] A little more surprising, however, was the equally whole-hearted adoption of the term by the scholarly community: largely, I believe, because it is a very practical term as it does not distinguish between media (unlike 'crime fiction'/'crime film') and suggests a regional specificity (Nordic), without excluding Iceland and Finland (which Scandi noir does), while indicating a broader scope (noir). It is a more attractive, practical and inclusive term than Scandinavian crime fiction or its stiff short-hands Scandi crime and Scandi noir. However, in rushing to adopt Nordic noir we forgot to ask ourselves whether Nordic crime fiction, film and television were really noir in the first place, and what the implications might be of uncritically appropriating it for our purposes. Certainly, some questions have been raised about how best to define Nordic noir, its specificity and comparisons made with the 'original' American noir. An etymological study of the noir concept and its applicability to the Nordic region has not, however, been conducted.

When looking at the work of scholars and critics who have tried to define Nordic noir, it soon becomes clear that there is little consensus on the concept's meaning. For example, according to Glen Creeber, Nordic noir 'is best understood as a broad umbrella term that describes a particular type of Scandinavian crime fiction', and drawing upon Steven Peacock's work on Swedish crime fiction considers it a cross between classic English detective fiction, American hardboiled fiction and police procedurals.[2] Not only is this a rather confusing hodgepodge, but it also says little about the noir component. Kim Toft Hansen and Anne Marit Waade rightly point out in their recent work that Creeber's definition is characterized by a contradiction, in that an umbrella term is suggested to describe a particular type of variety that falls under that same umbrella. Their answer to this conundrum is to evoke definitional problems of concepts as such, suggesting that we cannot qualify Nordic noir – at this stage at least.[3] Having put that problem aside they then go on to define Nordic noir as crime fiction plain and simple and use the concepts interchangeably.[4] Conversely, Andrew Nestingen uses the concept in a very demarcated and specific manner in his broad mapping of noir in Nordic cinema in terms of both space and time.[5] Nonetheless, it also reveals many of the problems of adapting the term as Nestingen splits noir into five different categories: 'Classical film noir', 'Nordic noir', 'neo-noir', 'Nordic neo-noir' and 'auteur neo-noir'. It is not only due to regional demarcation that Nestingen must distinguish Nordic noir from 'classical film noir,' but the fact that they differ significantly. According to Nestingen, the Nordic variety has stronger ties to French poetic realism, is more melodramatic, has a stronger moral foundation and is more sympathetic towards its characters, who are also understood as products of their social circumstances; a perspective aligning them with the period's 'universalism of the Social Democratic or Labour parties'.[6] Many of these regional specificities spill into the neo-noir period as Nestingen finds Nordic neo-noir to be characterized by a comparatively stronger 'tendency toward social criticism'.[7] There can be no doubt that Nestingen's mapping does great service to anyone interested in the history of noir in the Nordic region, and that his terminology is both logical and clear. However, in the larger context of studying the concept it becomes confusing or misleading, since what he defines as 'Nordic neo-noir' is analogous to what we typically understand by 'Nordic noir', while in Nestingen's use it refers to films made during the much earlier era of 'classical noir'.

My subject in this chapter is simply that body of texts produced in the Nordic region and which had circulated globally under the banner of Nordic noir.[8] It makes sense to me to trace its origin back to Maj Sjöwall and Per Wahlöö. Among the other conspicuous authors are Swedes Stieg Larsson, Camilla Läckberg, Henning Mankell, Håkan Nesser and Leif G.W. Persson, Norwegians Karin Fossum and Jo Nesbø, Icelanders Arnaldur Indriðason and Yrsa Sigurðardóttir and Dane Jussi Adler-Olsen. The usual televisions suspects include *Wallander* (SVl, 1994–2006; SF, 2005–13; BBC, 2008–16), *Millennium* (2009, also released in film versions), *Forbrydelsen* (*The Killing*, 2007–12),

Bron/Broen (*The Bridge*, 2011–) and *Ófærð* (*Trapped*, 2015–) series. With regards to film there is not much in terms of original material, but numerous adaptations of Nordic crime novels have been made – including a couple of Hollywood productions.[9] Almost without exception these texts fall under the police procedural, and it is my contention that, as such, they are perfectly at odds with the established ingredients and outlook of noir. I will return to these texts after a detour through the origins of the noir concept and its etymological development.

Tracing the evidence

Much more than noir, crime fiction is an umbrella term. Although there is no consensus about the number of sub-groups/sub-genres, the broad strokes are generally agreed upon. John Scaggs splits the field into mystery/detective fiction, the hardboiled mode, the police procedural, crime thriller (includes noir thriller) and historical crime fiction.[10] More recently, Peter Messent has divided it into classical detective fiction, hardboiled detective fiction, the police novel and transgressor narrative (by which he means approximately the same as Scaggs' noir thriller, or what also might be described as the James M. Cain arm of hardboiled fiction).[11] Spy fiction and gangster literature are typically seen as separate, if somewhat related genres. There is also a general consensus about the historical development of the genre: emerging with Edgar Allan Poe, before crystallizing as a genre in England in what we now name classical detective fiction, and then challenged and opposed by American hardboiled fiction during the interwar era, with the police procedural making a rather late arrival during the 1950s, and arguably pre-figured in cinema and television, including the *Naked City* (1948) and *Dragnet* (1950). It is also well known that the noir name itself was introduced in France to first describe translations of hardboiled American novels (from the black covers of the *Série noire*) and later direct and indirect film versions of those very some stories, thus giving us 'film noir'.[12] As French cinephiles and film critics recognized, these films offered something of a counter-narrative to conventional bright and upbeat Hollywood entertainment in their focus on crime, tough-talking and hard-hitting (and sometimes unlawful) private detectives, dangerous femme fatales, untamed passions, dark city settings, etc. As I will ultimately conclude, Scandinavian crime fiction, film and television share few of these attributes.

In the classic 1946 essay 'A New Kind of Police Drama: The Criminal Adventure', which heralds the idea of film noir, Nino Frank singles out four films that ever since have been central to the canon: *The Maltese Falcon* (1941), *Double Indemnity* (1944), *Murder, My Sweet* (1944) and *Laura* (1944). Frank sees these films as deviating from conventional crime films or the film equivalent of classical detective fiction. In fact, he says the films 'belong to that we used to call the crime film, but that would best be described from this point on by a term such as criminal adventures or, better yet, such as criminal psychology'.[13] The difference stems from the hardboiled novelty of Dashiell Hammett, Raymond Chandler and James M. Cain who supplied the original novels for three of the films (not only does Frank altogether ignore Vera Caspary, the author of the novel *Laura* (1943), but considers the film somewhat outdated in comparison with the other three). Frank could not have stated his case any more clearly: 'These "noir" films no longer have any common ground with the run-of-the-mill police dramas'.[14] It is not simply the darker narrative elements, focus on criminal minds and dangerous women, however, that constitute the novelty of noir, but also its formal elements: 'There is another, purely formal, change in expository style, the intervention of a narrator or commentator permits a fragmentation of the narrative'.[15] So, in the very first piece delineating the specificity of noir, the author emphasizes novelty both in terms of narrative (focus and themes) and narration.

In the first book-length study of noir, the classic *A Panorama of American Film Noir 1941–1953*, Raymond Borde and Etienne Chaumeton enforce and elaborate further upon Frank's insight. In it, they describe film noir in terms of a new 'series', in their use, a concept that lies somewhere between a genre and a cycle, and for our purposes it is extremely relevant that they distinguish it from another new series they call 'the police documentary',[16] which translator Paul Hammond notes would now be called the 'police procedural'.[17] This second series is a fundamentally different one and includes films such as *Boomerang!* (1947), *Call Northside 777* (1948) and *The Naked City*. Borde and Chaumeton define the differences between noir and police documentaries thus:

> First and foremost a different angle of vision. The documentary considers the murder from without, from the official point of view; the film noir from within, from the criminals'. [...] The second difference is of a moral, and maybe even more essential, kind. It's part of the tradition of the police documentary to present the investigators as upright, incorruptible, and courageous men. [...] An edifying film, the American police documentary is, in fact, a documentary to the glory of the police. [...] None of this exists in the noir series. If there are policemen, they're of dubious character [... and] even murderous at times.[18]

Thus in the police documentaries/police procedurals, crime is seen from the official perspective of the police, and even though much of Nordic crime fiction, film and television does not outright glorify the police, it typically focuses on members of the force, shows them in a benevolent light and narrates events from their perspective. Conversely, in noir, the perspective typically remains with the criminal or a non-official outsider investigator, and if at all present in noir the police are seen from the outside and likely to be depicted in negative terms.

What Borde and Chaumeton originally defined as a separate series, the police documentary, was later incorporated into the noir family, where it remains. The police documentaries are almost without exception, however, singled out as the black sheep (or good sheep rather) of the genre and not fully noir – shameful exceptions to the true antisocial character of noir. Foster Hirsch, for example, writes:

> The semi-documentary thriller thus had a different tone than the more stylized and claustrophobic *films noirs*. The realistic stories of detection were essentially conservative in their outlook, whereas the studio films tended to be subversive, slyly undermining the middle-class status quo with their depiction of middle America gone haywire. The location stories of police procedures had clear-cut separation between the good guys and the bad, whereas in the stylized *noirs* innocence and guilt, virtue and vice, were presented in much more complex ways.[19]

His description also suggests that it is not only a question of political/ideological outlook, but also form. This is echoed by J. P. Telotte in his ambitious stylistic/formal analysis of noir. Telotte pinpoints four types of noir narration. Two of them stem from attempts to capture the first-person narration of hardboiled fiction: voice-over/flashback structure and the subjective camera. Both of these strategies challenge conventional film narratives, and their concealment of their particular (ideological) point of view by emphasizing and exhibiting 'a single, invariably limited perspective'.[20] Also, the classical narrative form itself can challenge its 'invisibility' through self-reflexivity, as indeed many noirs do in their focus on various forms of mediation and communication. The fourth and final narrative mode or voice is the 'documentary style' and while it is explicitly concerned with perspective, it is also the one, even to a greater extent than classical narrative, that works against the noir emphasis on subjectivity and limited perspective by suggesting 'that the reality it perceives is indeed transparent and true'.[21] Once again, the police documentary, and this time its narrative voice, is singled out as fundamentally opposed to the critical nature of noir proper.

Although the particular evidence may vary, there is clearly a general consensus that noir is somehow different in perspective, theme and form from other crime fiction – especially police narratives. While the focus in this overview has been on film noir rather than roman noir/hardboiled fiction, there is an equally strong consensus on the specificity of the latter, not only in terms of social critique (vs. the more conservative classical detective fiction), but also novelty in form; especially first-person narration and the hardboiled language itself. The shift away from the roman noir to the police procedural is also almost without exception seen as conservative in both form and content. Scaggs states:

> The transition from hard-boiled fiction to police procedural is, therefore, a transition from the private eye, in the sense of personal, small-scale, and

often self-serving investigation, to the public eye, in the sense of civic, large-scale policing that serves society as a whole. [...] Through a project of realism that presents the police as 'credible operatives against crime', the police procedural becomes a powerful weapon of reassurance in the arsenal of the dominant social order.[22]

Thus, literary scholars studying crime fiction have arrived at the exact same conclusion as film critics and scholars analysing cinema. The shift from the private detective (let alone criminal) to the police is seen as a politically conservative shift. A critical perspective from the margins of society has been replaced with a view from the centre – aligning it with the very same state institutions that hardboiled fiction systematically opposed. As Messent argues similarly: 'The police novel is necessarily structured around the protection and re-establishing of the existing social order.'[23] As I will soon make clear, this is crucial in considering the validity of the noir concept in defining and discussing Nordic crime fiction, film and television. Additionally, we find broad differences in form: focus on teamwork rather than individuals, objective vs. subjective narration, and similarly, third person vs. first person narration. The language itself is typically more plain and straightforward as well.

All the key elements of the concept of noir have been established at this point in its history. Despite the increased range of film noir scholarship since the publication of Hirsch and Telotte's work in the 1980s, the foundation I have outlined here remains intact. I do want to address, though, how film noir scholarship has become increasingly inclusive – enlarging the concept's scope in two very important ways. First, noir is no longer limited to stories of private detectives and outright criminals. Instead, noir is largely regarded as a broader term describing anti-social or disturbed characters in conjunction with an overall atmosphere of social pessimism. Lee Horsley, for example, argues that:

> [p]rivate eyes play a part, but so do transgressors and victims, strangers and outcasts, tough women and sociable psychopaths. There are characters who are tarnished and afraid, and who find it difficult or impossible to escape from the 'bleakness, darkness, alienation, disintegration', the 'sense of disorientation and nightmare' that are associated with the modernist crises of culture.[24]

Notably, Horsley includes neither police officers nor the procedural in her broad and inclusive approach.[25]

Second, noir is no longer limited to American cinema and a handful of European films, but understood as an international phenomenon – often with particular ties to emerging modernity and urbanization. Within this global reach, we have seen a focus on East Asian noir and, of course, Nordic noir. The former is much less problematic than the latter. Post-war Akira Kurosawa, and later Seijun Suzuki and Shohei Imamura, are clearly working within the noir realm, regarding both form and critique, during a period of great social upheaval in Japan. Similarly, during the great modernization of Hong Kong, John Woo,

Johnnie To and to a certain extent Wong Kar-wai, self-consciously turn to noir in depicting the turmoil of the period. David Desser sees the neo-noir films of directors such as Takashi Miike and Takeshi Kitano to be 'very much attuned to the so-called "lost decade" of the Japanese economy'.[26] Adding Taiwan and South-Korea to the picture, Mark Gallagher summarizes East Asian noir as follows:

> [Noir films made *under* modernity] use dark materials to register ambivalence or outright alarm about modernity's capacity to jeopardize social contracts. Exported or expanded to include East Asia, noir can register the social experiences and aftermaths of war, colonization, occupation and dictatorship. [...] East Asian noir inhabits spaces that partake of the fruits of modernity and economic growth. Yet as most of our contributors [of the volume] argue, East Asian noir repeatedly represents modernity's casualties, telling stories of the disenfranchised and marginal.[27]

In Nordic noir, however, we find neither a comparable self-reflexive turn to noir, nor the social conditions that Jennifer Fay and Justus Nieland, for example, consider essential to the emergence of noir (and note the similarity to Gallagher's summary of East Asian noir). They consider noir's internationalism to be linked to

> broader conditions of global disquiet with the mobile and dislocated social and cultural relations of modernity itself: of rootless and wandering desire; of chance, accident, and class instability; of local traditions and spaces either imperilled or energized by global flows of culture and capital; and of homelife across the world that has become unsettled, uncanny, or newly foreign.[28]

It is a description at odds with the social stability and regulation of the Nordic region during the welfare period – whose policy changes, or even the later introduction of greater laissez-faire economics, are mere trifles in comparison. Indeed, we should not be surprised that the police procedural rather than noir became the region's token crime narrative – or rather *police* narrative.

My suspicions of appropriating noir for the Nordic region have nothing to do with the national status per se, as I certainly do not consider noir solely or even primarily an American phenomenon. In fact, I will ultimately address certain Nordic films and novels that are indebted to the noir tradition I have outlined here, but first let us take a closer look at what has become the established canon of Nordic noir.

To be noir or not to be noir

In the larger global context of crime fiction there can be no doubt that the major Scandinavian contribution has been in the realm of the police procedural. In fact, the emergence of the form is often seen as stemming from *The Story of*

Crime (1965–74) series by Sjöwall and Wahlöö – even at the cost of the *87th Precinct* (1956–2005) series by Ed McBain that the Swedish authors modelled their series on. In fact, even surveys limited to Anglo-American crime fiction find it typically necessary to make an exception and address the Swedish series. *The Story of Crime*, furthermore, also provided the model and basis for Henning Mankell's Wallander series that arguably instigated and further formulated (at least to a greater extent than any other series) the contemporary phenomenon we now refer to as Nordic noir. It soon become the updated model for many other popular series, including non-Swedish ones, like those of Indriðason's Erlendur and Nesbø's Harry Hole. We can clearly see their influential role in recent surveys of crime fiction where these writers, especially Mankell, follow now on the heels of the parent figures Sjöwall and Wahlöö.[29] Indeed, few, if any, enthusiasts and scholars working in the field are likely to disagree with the key role played by the police procedural within what we now typically refer to as Nordic noir. But, rarely are concerns raised about the applicability of noir in the Nordic context.

However, the question has been raised, although somewhat obliquely, whether hardboiled fiction and procedurals need be mutually exclusive. Messent, for example, points out that some police novels are inflected by the hardboiled tradition in their 'gritty realism where violence and corruption are part and parcel of society as a whole, and in which the police themselves are often affected by such forces'.[30] While I agree with Messent's sentiment up to a point, I do not believe that this applies to the Scandinavian procedural, not even *The Story of Crime*, one of Messent's primary examples. Certainly, the series is intended to offer social critique – if that is not clear enough from the novels themselves, the authors have been quite outspoken about their intentions and adoption of McBain's paradigm: 'In the modern and impersonal society the crime novel is one of the few by which the average reader can get a sense of the computer-controlled and closed-off system that he is forced to be a part of. In simple terms, the crime novel can explain a variety of things in life for people in general'.[31] As such, the novels depict various social problems and injustices while also raising ethical and institutional questions about policing that most procedures do not. Especially towards the end of the series, the entries begin to criticize state surveillance, militarization of the police and the violent suppression of peaceful protests. The novels are not, however, ever antisocial or directed against the state or government institutions as such. Sjöwall and Wahlöö believe in a strong state as a form of government; they want to improve the state, make it better and certainly not do away with it. They are defenders of the welfare state and not its opponents.

In hardboiled fiction (and especially the original American cycle) there is less outright commentary upon the state (or state and federal institutions in American nomenclature), but the role it plays is almost entirely negative. In Hammett's Personville/Poisonville the police are inept and corrupt to a degree unfathomable for Nordic noir and the town's inhabitants live in permanent social breakdown – there is in fact very little society to speak of. The various police forces in Chandler's Los Angeles are apparently too busy beating up Philip Marlowe and stopping him from solving crimes to engage in actual police work, and Cain's Frank Chambers is about to be executed by the state for a crime that he did not commit (although he did get away with murder earlier in *The Postman Always Rings Twice* (1934)). There is no return to normalcy in the typical hardboiled novel as society itself and its institutions are in shambles, including the police force, which often enough has direct ties to the criminal world and adheres to similar rules or lack thereof. We find this tradition alive and well in contemporary authors such as James Ellroy and David Peace whose police novels offer an interesting counterpoint to the Scandinavian variety. The former condemn and reject society, while the latter aim for improvements through social critique. Therein lies a crucial difference between noir and police procedurals. It is as if their vision of society is so bleak that the hardboiled writers see no room for improvements; it is almost a fallen world. Conversely, the social critique of today's Scandinavian crime fiction is typically milder and more optimistic than the wholesale critique of Sjöwall and Wahlöö. Indeed, Stougaard-Nielsen has proposed that Scandinavian crime fiction is united in 'nostalgically longing for the good home and the comforts of a just, egalitarian welfare society',[32] while Bruce Robbins claims that Nordic noir 'contains some affirmation of the welfare state'.[33] In other words, today's Nordic crime writers are not only guardians of the welfare system, but in some cases even look back nostalgically at the era Sjöwall and Wahlöö found so lacking. Their critique is also less likely to be directed at the state itself and instead draws attention to more general social problems, like violence against women or immigrants.

Sjöwall and Wahlöö's main character, Martin Beck, is also in many ways the prototype for the now easily recognizable police figure of Nordic crime fiction. He (and typically it is a he) has become integral to its identity as something specifically Scandinavian and different from more conventionally heroic police figures. Beck faces many difficulties in his private life. He is unhappily married when we are first introduced to him, and divorces late in the series (the typical status for most of his successors), before finally finding a new partner. He has a critical mind and can raise questions about both society and the police force he is part and parcel of. Wallander is clearly modelled upon him, if with his own particular character traits. Erlendur is an Icelandic version of this Swedish model, Carl Mörk a Danish one and Harry Hole is a Norwegian one. They all have difficulties in their private lives, cannot sustain relationships with their partners and drink too much (or used to), and can be stubborn at work, leading to frequent clashes with their superiors. However unorthodox, there is nothing noir-like about this literary Scandinavian policeman. He is of a sound mind, caring, dedicated, hardworking, morally upright, socially conscious and typically a solid citizen overall. Most importantly, he is a policeman and a good and dedicated one at that. The noir protagonist, however, is more likely to be a criminal rather than a policeman and if the latter s/he is an outsider in a force that is itself corrupt and compromising.

As regards form, *The Story of Crime* is told in a third-person omniscient narration. It typically travels smoothly from one police officer to another, and often between criminals and other citizens as well. Even more than the police force itself, the narration is the perfect surveillance machine: it sees and knows everything. The language itself flows without a hitch – hiding almost behind the action it is delivering – avoiding any literary flourishes (it is the equivalent of classical film narration and its invisible editing as analysed by Telotte).[34] In this sense the series is also truly a parent of Nordic noir as all the major series are narrated in the third person – typically omniscient – and chapters focusing on criminal activity, in addition to the detective work of the police, have become a staple of the field. Interestingly, these sections on criminals rarely show any serious interest in their psyche and mental status in the manner of noir texts. Instead, their role is primarily to build up suspense and excitement. This broad, direct, all-encompassing third-person view is the exact opposite of the subjective first-person narration of hardboiled fiction, which is furthermore also often delivered in a stylized or formally interesting manner. Noir of course does not have to be delivered in first person, but it is broadly invested in subjectivity and perspective in a manner that the Nordic police procedural is clearly not.

The biggest success story of Nordic noir, Stieg Larsson's *Män som hatar kvinnor* (*The Girl with the Dragon Tattoo*) and its two sequels, differ from the aforementioned series in that its two main characters are a reporter and a computer hacker rather than police officers. Especially in the figure of Lisbeth Salander, who is notably described in the novel as a victim of the state and goes her own way at the margins of society, the trilogy could be seen to offer a counter-example to the otherwise rampant Scandinavian police procedural. These differences are, however, miniscule and superficial. Mikael Blomkvist and his colleagues at the news magazine *Millennium* function in a very similar manner as the police team in the procedural, with many parties contributing to their work (especially so in the novel), and the magazine itself provides an institutional framework not altogether unrelated to that of law enforcement. Lisbeth is not an official member of the team but she works with them and especially Mikael in trying to solve the case, and she provides her own area of expertise. Her methods are indeed unorthodox and sometimes unlawful, but she is clearly on the morally right side. Thus, even if the film adaptation playfully ties her to the figure of the femme fatale, as pointed out by Nestingen, she ultimately comes to Blomkvist's rescue and remains a devoted partner throughout the trilogy.[35] The men she punishes are guilty of horrible crimes and seen to be deserving of their fate – rather than the semi-innocent victims of the seductive and dangerous femme fatale of noir. Finally, if presented as a victim of the state, its crime is clearly one of incompetence or negligence rather than outright villainy or criminality. Just like Sjöwall and Wahlöö, Larsson is ultimately not against the state, but aims to improve it so that it may serve its citizens better – if anything, the state needs strengthening against outside predators whether they are rapists, serial killers or unscrupulous businessmen (or all three). The trilogy's social critique is thus fully comparable to the run-of-the-mill procedural, and as regards form it is delivered in the same standard third-person omniscient narration.[36] Overall, the trilogy lies much closer to the procedural than noir/hardboiled fiction.

The major Swedish literary series, *The Story of Crime*, *Wallander* and *Millennium*, have all been developed into numerous television series (the last one better known in its film form). I will not be addressing them specifically below, but the same analysis would apply to them, broadly speaking, as to the original novels. Instead, I want to focus on the Danish television series that have begun to rival the Swedish novels for the Nordic noir crown. Although not the first product, it was *Forbrydelsen* that caught the world's attention and paved the way for *Bron/Broen*, a co-production with Sweden that has not only spawned remakes around the world, but further consolidated the formula laid out in *Forbrydelsen* of multiple intertwining storylines. It has been widely followed in the Nordic countries, including the Icelandic series *Ófærð*, and abroad as well, including the UK hit *Broadchurch* (2013–17), not to mention numerous outright remakes. Yet, if there can be no doubt about the importance of *Forbrydelsen* and *Broen* to Nordic noir, we must again raise the question of how noir they really are?

The two series follow the established Scandinavian tradition of being police procedurals and ones that emphasize teamwork to an even greater extent – indeed the novelty of *Broen*'s plot lay in the complex partnership between Danish and Swedish police forces. Numerous scenes in both series show us the team working together, mulling over new leads, delegating work among its members and facing challenges from superiors in the force. The two iconic female leads, Sarah Lund and Saga Norén respectively, may not be conventional police officers, as the series repeatedly emphasize, but it would be hard to find more sincere, dedicated, hard-working and honest officers in any police drama. So if not typical, certainly not noir either.[37] The series' strong focus on domesticity, family drama and children is also completely alien to noir.[38] They flirt with social criticism, find bad apples within the police force and other state institutions, but overall the perspective remains within and fully behind the police, and both laud its increasingly sophisticated techniques of surveillance. As regards the narration, it is strikingly similar to the omniscient third-person narration of its literary counterpart; knowing everything and seeing everything. The presentation is straightforward, the polished cinematography mostly devoid of the subjectivity and stylistic flourishes we typically associate with noir. Although swapping Sarah and Saga for a male figure, *Ófærð* with its unconventional small-town police chief Andri follows this established pattern without a fault (or to a fault).[39]

It is instructive to compare *Forbrydelsen* to the American series *Twin Peaks* (1990–91) on which it is partly modelled. Both begin with the murder of a teenage girl, and then instead of staying solely with the police investigation, in the manner of more conventional crime narratives, focus on the impact upon family, friends and the larger community, and develop therein certain narrative threads with only a threadbare relation to the murder mystery.[40] While in many ways completely different to Sarah, the FBI agent Dale Cooper is certainly no less eccentric, and despite his singularity is able to co-operate with the dedicated – if not always competent – local police force. So as regards plot and the main police character there is much that unites the two series. In terms of narration, style and worldview, however, the series are diametrically opposed, and it is in that distinction that the fundamental difference between conventional police procedural and noir also lies. In *Forbrydelsen* the murder is an anomaly and the characters and the society they comprise are fundamentally benevolent and, plainly put, good. In *Twin Peaks*, on the other hand, the murder of Laura Palmer is reflective of a corrupt and criminal – if not outright evil – society wherein danger lurks in every corner. It is a world filled with ruthless businessmen, gangsters, hitmen, wife-beaters, femme fatales, prostitutes, psychopaths of all sorts and, thankfully, a few good souls amongst them. Everyone is scheming against everyone else and the threat of violence looms over most human interactions.[41] At times *Twin Peaks* draws directly upon classical noir motives like dreams and other subjective riddles, and much of it takes place at night-time and in the dark. No less important is the use of stylized lighting, canted frames, subjective camerawork, expressive colours and hypnotic and eerie soundscapes. The corrupt and evil world of Twin Peaks is appropriately presented through a warped lens. Conversely, the comparatively benign social depiction of Copenhagen in *Forbrydelsen* is presented in a much more straightforward manner (if not without night-time settings) – a precedent that has been followed in all the major Nordic crime series.

Thus noir/*Twin Peaks* and Scandinavian police procedurals/*Forbrydelsen* perceive society and the individual in fundamentally different ways. In the former, crimes are committed out of greed, desire, sadism and outright evil. The fault is the inner nature of the criminal, and not that of society. This is the exact opposite of the Scandinavian tradition that typically approaches the criminal from a sociological perspective. As Nestingen points out 'Nordic neo-noir often seeks to contextualize and make sense of social forces that generate criminality, rather than depicting the criminal as pathological, inexplicable or nihilistic'.[42] The other side of that coin is the view of society itself, which in the noir world is either non-existent or lacking most of the qualities that would aid its members. People are ultimately alone, cannot rely on their fellow citizens, and certainly not social institutions – least of all the police. Again, we find the exact opposite in the Scandinavian tradition. As Creeber argues 'Nordic noir [creates] an overriding sense of hope in an otherwise desolate and desperate world – assuring us that life does have some fundamental meaning, that there is a strange and mysterious force that connects us all and that good will eventually overcome evil'.[43] Conversely, in noir, there is little hope that good will overcome evil and people stand alone without the support of a larger society. They may both deal with crime, but police procedurals and noirs are worlds apart.

The verdict

Despite all of the above, some might still be inclined to ask what does it matter if we call Scandinavian police procedurals Nordic noir? In other words: what's in a name? To begin with, it is most illogical: as an exercise, imagine if we decided not to limit it to the Nordic region but call all procedurals noir – it would be nonsensical. One might just as well call everything noir police procedurals. Critics and scholars coined and developed the concept of noir for a reason – indeed primarily to distinguish the texts in question from such police narratives. The term 'Nordic noir' is therefore highly misleading and politically problematic. To call the procedurals Nordic noir is to give the texts an antisocial flair and stylistic sensibility that is completely at odds with their broad social and aesthetic conformity. Nordic noir's primary crime is to appropriate a concept that was developed to not only distinguish between outsider noir and insider police stories, but to criticize the latter for their conformity.

The naming is guilty of a few other misdemeanours as well. For example, it leaves an actual Nordic noir tradition, and one that importantly predates the current Nordic noir phenomenon, in a conceptual wilderness. It should not surprise us that noir originated primarily in the big cities of California; Los Angeles and San Francisco, during the great upheaval and turmoil of the interwar era, with its relatively weak social institutions and rampant criminality, and that it has emerged around the world primarily in places going through similar social upheaval and transformation.[44] Conversely, it should not surprise us either that the Swedish police procedural originated at the height of the welfare system with its strong social institutions and regulations, and general belief in the state as a safeguard for the well-being of its citizens. However, noir and the North need not be mutually exclusive. Indeed, while the procedural soon became the norm in Scandinavian crime fiction, there also emerged dissenting voices that lay much closer to noir and hardboiled fiction. As I have noted elsewhere, these voices are more likely to be Norwegian, Finnish or Icelandic than Danish or Swedish and that may very well have something to do with their marginality in the Nordic region.[45] Just as *The Story of Crime* drew to a close, Norwegian author Gunnar Staalesen began his series of private detective Varg Veum, drawing explicitly upon the hardboiled tradition, including the first-person narration and wise-cracking detective made famous by Chandler.[46] Many of the Veum novels have been developed into television series (2007–12) that, unlike their better known Scandinavian counterparts, hold onto the separation between the main character and the police. Even more noir-like is the Finnish *Vares* series (2004–) with its down-and-out private detective and his stylized voice-over. It is also striking how Nordic cinema has contributed much more to this noir tradition than its television and literary counterparts. The oeuvre of Finnish director Aki Kaurismäki has a strong noir inflection, whether dealing with crime outright or not, and Danish director Lars von Trier has veered into noir territory numerous times. It is important to note that many of the films in question, including the most self-conscious and original take on noir in the North, the Norwegian film *Insomnia* (1997), not only pre-date the emergence of Nordic noir as an international phenomenon, but are also rarely discussed under its banner.

It would be both misleading and conceptually unhelpful to group all these works within the police procedural tradition, but now that we have named the latter Nordic noir, what are we going to call this tradition of Nordic crime narratives: Nordic noir noir? The term is no doubt here to stay in its current form. I suggest we do not forget, though, how misleading it is. It does matter that Scandinavian crime fiction, film and television consist primarily of procedurals that emphasize teamwork, are supportive of the police and other social institutions, are aesthetically normative, offer a benign view of society and humanity, and champion social control and surveillance in both their subject matter and narrative mode. In other words, it matters that there is precious little noir about Nordic noir.

Notes

1. According to Gunhild Agger the coinage first emerged in relation to a book club and blog at University College of London. 'Nordic Noir: Location, Identity and Emotion' in *Emotions in Contemporary TV Series*, ed. Alberto Garcia (London: Palgrave Macmillan, 2016), 138.
2. Glen Creeber, 'Killing Us Softly: Investigating the Aesthetics, Philosophy and Influence of Nordic Noir Television', *Journal of Popular Television* 3, no. 1 (2015), 21.
3. Kim Toft Hansen and Anne Marit Waade, *Locating Nordic Noir: From Beck to the Bridge* (London: Palgrave Macmillan, 2017), 14–15.
4. Ibid., 19. They are far from alone in doing so. For example, although Jakob Stougaard-Nielsen resists using it in the title of *Scandinavian Crime Fiction* (London: Bloomsbury, 2017), the two are used interchangeably throughout.
5. Andrew Nestingen, 'Nordic Noir and Neo-Noir: The Human Criminal' in *International Noir*, eds. Homer B. Pettey and R. Barton Palmer (Edinburgh: Edinburgh University Press, 2014).
6. Ibid., 163.
7. Ibid., 171.
8. I exclude, though, texts that have closer affinity with gangster (Jens Lapidus, Nicolas Winding Refn) and spy fiction (Leif Davidsen) than crime fiction, for reasons of space and focus, but their presence under the Nordic noir banner strengthens my overall argument. It is certainly not directed at all Nordic crime narratives, however, and especially not those limited to the region itself in terms of translation and distribution.

9   I assume a certain familiarity by the reader with these works, as well as the canonical examples of hardboiled fiction and noir films referenced. It is a matter for a different debate whether to consider American and other non-Nordic adaptations and remakes as part of Nordic noir.
10 John Scaggs, *Crime Fiction* (London and New York: Routledge, 2005).
11 Peter Messent, *The Crime Fiction Handbook* (Chichester: Wiley-Blackwell, 2013).
12 James Naremore, *More the Night: Film Noir in Its Context* (Berkeley: University of California Press, 1998), 13. Naremore does note that there was some precedent for using the concept of film noir to discuss French films in the late 1930s (15).
13 Nino Frank, 'A New Kind of Police Drama: the Criminal Adventure' in *Film Noir Reader 2*, eds Alain Silver and James Ursuni (New York: Limelight Editions, 1999), 15.
14 Ibid., 18. Frank does not give any examples of what he calls 'run-of-the-mill police dramas,' but he clearly has in mind a focus on morally upright detectives (whether they be police officials or not).
15 Ibid.
16 Raymond Borde and Etienne Chaumeton, *A Panorama of American Film Noir* (San Francisco: City Lights Books, 2002), 2.
17 Ibid., 13.
18 Ibid., 6–7.
19 Foster Hirsch, *Film Noir: The Dark Side of the Screen* (Philadelphia: De Capo Press, 1981), 17.
20 J. P. Telotte, *Voices in the Dark: The Narrative Patterns of Film Noir* (Urbana and Chicago: University of Illinois Press, 1989), 16.
21 Ibid., 145.
22 John Scaggs, *Crime Fiction*, 89 and 98. Scaggs is quoting Stephen Knight, *Crime Fiction 1800–2000: Detection, Death, Diversity* (Basingstoke: Palgrave Macmillan, 2004), 161.
23 Peter Messent, *The Crime Fiction Handbook*, 26.
24 Lee Horsley, *The Noir Thriller* (Basingstoke: Palgrave Macmillan, 2009), 3. Horsley is here quoting from Malcom Bradbury and James McFarlane, 'The Name and Nature of Modernism', in *Modernism 1890–1930*, eds Malcolm Bradbury and James McFarlane (Harmondsworth: Penguin, 1976), 26. Horsley's four-part definition of noir emphasizes subjective points of view, shifting protagonist roles, his/her ill-fated relationship with society and a socio-political critique, 8.
25 Apart from briefly discussing James Ellroy's *LA* quartet (1987–92) and David Peace's *Red Riding* quartet (1999–2002), the only exception is Chester Himes' Harlem series that for a long time has been classified with hardboiled fiction rather than police procedurals. The reasons have no doubt to do with the outsider status of its two black police detectives, their violent and often unlawful methods, street language and depictions of a total social breakdown. The series did, however, help to establish many standard elements of the procedural and it is certainly suspect how it is often ignored in scholarship on its early history. I am not claiming that noir/hardboiled fiction cannot include policemen, but that they are handled in a different and much 'darker' manner than in the procedural. For example, even though focused on the police force, Peace's *Red Riding* quartet or *Tokyo Year Zero* (2007) have more in common with hardboiled fiction, not only because of their critique of the force and overall social pessimism, but also their narrative form: first person narration, rough language and formal experimentation.

26 David Desser, 'The Gunman and the Gun: Japanese Film Noir since the Late 1950s' in *International Noir*, eds Homer B. Pettey and R. Barton Palmer (Edinburgh: Edinburgh University Press, 2014), 125.
27 Mark Gallagher, 'Introduction: A Very Rough Guide to East Asian Film Noir,' in *East Asian Film Noir: Transnational Encounters and Intercultural Dialogue*, eds Chi-Yun Shin and Mark Gallagher (London and New York: I. B.Tauris, 2015), 6.
28 Jennifer Fay and Justus Nieland, *Film Noir: Hard-Boiled Modernity and the Cultures of Globalization* (London and New York: Routledge, 2010), xiii.
29 See for example Messent, *The Crime Fiction Handbook*, 43. Notably the only two non-English novels of his fourteen key works of crime fiction addressed in specific sub-chapters are Sjöwall and Wahlöö's *Den skrattande polisen* (1968; *The Laughing Policeman*, 1970) and Larsson's *Män som hatar kvinnor* (2005; *The Girl with the Dragon Tattoo*, 2008). Another Swedish novel, Mankell's *Den orolige mannen* (2009; *The Troubled Man*, 2011), is listed among another eight contenders for such coverage. It speaks to the strength of the Swedish police procedural in the international crime fiction canon.
30 Ibid., 26.
31 Quoted in Michael Tapper, *Swedish Cops: From Sjöwall and Wahlöö to Stieg Larsson* (Bristol: Intellect, 2014), 70.
32 Stougaard-Nielsen, *Scandinavian Crime Fiction*, 11.
33 Bruce Robbins, 'The Detective Is Suspended: Nordic Noir and the Welfare State', in *Crime Fiction as World Literature*, eds Louise Nillson, David Damrosch and Theo D'haen (London: Bloomsbury, 2017), 49.
34 I read most of the novels in English translation so there might be more of a literary investment in some of the original texts. Kerstin Bergman has, however, pointed out the reverse: that some translators try to add a little spice to the original texts: 'Henning Mankell's and Camilla Läckberg's language, in both cases a quite simple language in the Swedish originals, often becomes more aesthetically advanced in the English translations', (84); 'The Captivating Chill: Why Readers Desire Nordic Noir', *Scandinavian-Canadian Studies* 22 (2014).
35 Nestingen, 'Nordic Noir and Neo-Noir', 155–6.
36 It proved especially influential in staging multiple storylines and emphasizing the sadistic torture of women.
37 There is one very important exception to this that has received surprisingly little attention. *Forbrydelsen*'s most outright noir moment occurs at the very end of the series when Sarah executes her primary suspect because she does not have sufficient evidence to put him behind bars. It is a striking moment fully out of character with the social consciousness of the series at large, and has much in common with the most troubling of noir narratives, the vigilante stories of John Carrol Daly's Race Williams and Mickey Spillane's Mike Hammer. Something similar occurs in the *Broen* series when Danish police detective Martin murders an inmate. He is, however, swiftly brought to justice by his upstanding Swedish counterpart – while *Forbrydelsen* concludes with Sarah making her escape to Iceland.
38 See also Nestingen's contribution, 'Kids' Stuff: Nordic Noir, Politics and Quality', to this volume.
39 Conversely, although marketed and often discussed under the banner of Nordic noir, the series *Borgen* (2010–13) has been seen as a problematic fit as it is not a

procedural/crime narrative (Hansen and Wade, *Locating Nordic Noir*, 5–7). While I would not claim that *Borgen* is noir, I have no hesitation in arguing that it is no less noir than its procedural siblings.

40 While the second season of *Twin Peaks* continues where the first left off, the second season of *Forbrydelsen* begins afresh with a new crime, but holds on to the same narrative structure.

41 Even within the core family itself, a place that *Forbrydelsen* is not willing to go, despite briefly flirting with the notion. There is apparently not a single child to be found in the town of Twin Peaks – revealing as well, considering the importance of children for Nordic noir. While both series make extensive use of domestic interiors, *Forbrydelsen* takes place in child-friendly areas, especially the school setting of the first season, while *Twin Peaks* is more at home in conventional noir territory, including hotels, brothels, bars and roadhouses.

42 Andrew Nestingen, 'Nordic Noir and Neo-Noir', 167.

43 Glen Creeber, 'Killing Us Softly', 27.

44 Fay and Nieland, *Film Noir*.

45 Björn Nordfjörd, 'Crime Up North: The Case of Norway, Finland and Iceland', in *Nordic Genre Film: Small National Film Cultures in the Global Marketplace*, eds Tommy Gustafsson and Pietari Kääpä (Edinburgh: Edinburgh University Press, 2015), 61–75. In it, I deal with the noir narratives of Finland, Iceland and Norway in greater depth; in that regard the two essays complement one another.

46 Indriðason and Nesbø have also tried their hand at noir, with *Betty* (2003) and *Hodejegerne* (2008; *Headhunters*, 2011) respectively, while most of their work is procedural. Some authors on the margins of Nordic noir in terms of popularity, also swap police officers for journalists or lawyers, but rarely private detectives, let alone criminals. The perspective and narration also remains very much in the procedural mode. An exception is Finnish Leena Lehtolainen's Maria Kallio series, which is told in the first person, but the language and stylistic flourishes are rather tame in comparison with some non-Scandinavian series. Kallio is also a police detective, despite a brief stint as a private detective early in the series.

Chapter 12

BLEAKNESS AND TENACITY: NORDIC NOIR AND *FIN-DE-SIÈCLE* FRENCH DECADENT LITERATURE

Christopher James

This chapter will investigate a genealogy of Nordic noir that includes late nineteenth-century French novels, specifically those identified with *fin-de-siècle* decadent literature, as both the literary and visual forms employ spatiality in order to foreground personal struggle and cultural critique. By spatiality, I intend more than simply a representation of the characteristics of the physical setting of a narrative – more than a setting, in other words. Spatiality refers to an insistence on the importance of space and place within the world of a narrative; the space or place is granted a primary interpretive role, and significant metaphorical burden is placed on it. While they may seem an unlikely pairing at first glance, Nordic noir and decadence share the fact that they both resist strict definitions. Are they genres, or more precisely moods, or phenomena, for example? If we look at Nordic noir film and television, we see a laundry list of traits: doomed heroes, tough, cynical inspectors, low-key lighting, unbalanced shot composition, systems and institutions as crooked as the criminals themselves, feelings of powerlessness and being worn down, victims and victimizers are often interchangeable – and indistinguishable. This list corresponds rather well with the protagonists of French Decadence when we look back at them. Nordic noir may also include a social conscience where other regional noir does not necessarily. Social conscience is not a principle often linked to the French Decadence, which brings us to the metaphorical choice of genealogy as a way to link the genres. The idea of genealogy is chosen specifically; although it is well worth hesitating before the idea of direct influence, decadent literature might fill a gap between the influence of Poe and the twentieth-century writers who came to influence and provide space for Nordic noir creators. Through the examination of spatiality in the two genres, their resemblances may become more evident, which will be instructive for understanding each on its own, and where Nordic noir situates itself today.

Let us first explore textual spatiality through two representative literary passages. While in Mexico City, the protagonist of Thomas Pynchon's *The Crying of Lot 49* (1966), Oedipa Maas, is viewing an art exhibit in Mexico City, when she is drawn to a triptych whose right and left images are never described, but whose central image makes a profound impact on her. It depicts a room full of girls weaving a tapestry of the world, in which everything is contained, and with which they were trying to fill the world. Maas weeps. 'She had looked down at her feet and known, then, because of a painting, that what she stood on had only been woven together a couple thousand miles away in her own tower, was only by accident known as Mexico'.[1] This passage is reminiscent of Italo Calvino's description of Maurilia, one of the *Invisible Cities*:

> In Maurilia, the traveller is invited to visit the city and, at the same time, to examine some old postcards that show it as it used to be: the same identical square with a hen in the place of the bus station, a bandstand in the place of the overpass, two young ladies with white parasols in the place of the munitions factory. [...] The old postcards do not depict Maurilia as it was, but a different city which, by chance, was called Maurilia, like this one.[2]

Both of these passages have important insights into how literature treats and understands the space of the worlds it creates. This spatialization of vision will prove significant for literary and cinematographic authors emplacing their narratives in order to better situate fictive worlds. Also, Pynchon and Calvino are both essentially visualizing that space for the reader. Finally, both texts' descriptions enter into a broader critical conversation about the representation of space and lived space, along with what Edward Soja terms 'thirdspace':

> a product of a 'thirding' of the spatial imagination, the creation of another mode of thinking about space that draws upon the material and mental spaces of the traditional dualism but extends well beyond them in scope, substance, and meaning. Simultaneously real and imagined and more (both and also ...), the exploration of Thirdspace can be described and inscribed in journeys to 'real-and-imagined' (or perhaps 'real and imagined'?) places.[3]

In this sense of 'both and also', the reader/viewer of Nordic noir is confronted with the complexity of how the fictional North exhibits traits in common, both with what is real and experienced, while adding new layers to what is there. Taking a proper understanding of Thirdspace to a text means constantly referencing and updating cultural understandings of space. This is what Bernard Westphal refers to as a 'stratigraphic' perspective: namely, that all space has its layers of time and experience, and that depth is what impregnates space with cultural meaning.[4] To return to Italo Calvino, it may be useful to consider his spatial understanding of Paris as we turn to consider the use of space in Nordic noir visual media:

> A place has to become an inner landscape for the imagination to start to inhabit that place, to turn it into its theatre. Now Paris has already been part

of the inner landscape of such a huge part of world literature, of so many books that we have all read, and that have counted in our lives. Before being a city of the real world, Paris for me, as for millions of other people in every country, has been a city that I have imagined through books, a city that you appropriate when you read.[5]

In other words, there is a sense of Paris, just as directors of film and television can lean on a visual language of Nordic space in order to situate their stories, and place their detectives in positions to confront the modern world and the human condition.[6]

A few words about French Decadence would be helpful, in order to show connections beyond definitions of genre, mood or phenomenon. It springs up as it is during the second half of the nineteenth century, some tracing it to Baudelaire, others to writers afterwards.[7] Its literature thematically privileges the superficial, the petrified and the aesthetic, yet participating in a nice dialectic with naturalism, driven by much of the same energy, although in decadent works there is much more emphasis on subjective narrative perspective than in naturalistic works of the same period. Asti Hustvedt notes that *fin-de-siècle* writers are obsessed with 'monsters, criminals, savages, prostitutes, syphilitics, hysterics, alcoholics, drug addicts, sexual deviants, madmen, idiots'.[8] As a form, Dominique Rincé writes that decadent literature is stylized using subjective narration, which heavily features internal monologue, in order to internalize the adventure, the struggle; characters are thrust into horrible situations, put to the test, brought to their breaking point. The narrative reshapes itself to conform to rapidly evolving, and devolving, circumstances. The individual is under duress in a violent world, where pain and vice are immediate. All this in order to examine decline, delinquency, neurosis, melancholy, pessimism and losing one's footing in the modern world.[9]

Why all this darkness and pain? To again refer to Hustvedt, via the rise of capitalism, 'all is commensurate with money' – even people, and even what is material and what is abstract, such as ideas, are commodified successfully and without difficulty.[10] A work I will discuss momentarily, Joris-Karl Huysmans' *À rebours* (1884), describes the malady of *fin-de-siècle* France as central to 'all the filthiness of contemporary utilitarian ideas, all the money-grubbing ignominy of the age'.[11] In this light, then, Decadence and all of its fascination with crime, violence, and the underworld is recast as a formal cultural critique, as much as a macabre shock for shock's sake. Instead, Huysmans – among other decadent writers – seek to reflect a deeper, more personal understanding of their surroundings, and the age in which they find themselves. As Matei Calinescu notes, it is 'simply awareness and acceptance of modernity. It will also resolutely and courageously express a progressive creed'.[12] Decadent work is always morbid, but its attraction to death is through art, choosing to boldly present death in realistic and unashamed terms rather than condemning it. This literature is a record of art's failure in the struggle against natural horror, as with the broken lives of the heroes of the noir genre caused by the crimes they – and we – have witnessed. 'Nature fights back and wins, and Decadent writing remains a remarkable account of that failure,' once more in the words of Hustvedt.[13] The French Decadent movement's obsession with death differs from Nordic noir in terms of the vocabulary each genre leans on: in the nineteenth century, to speak this way of 'Nature' was to assign a determining role both to human nature and cosmic, godlike forces, whereas the Nordic noir texts to be discussed below rely much more on institutional forces and the individual's decision to surrender to greed. In terms of the presentation of death, however, the genres can be said to favour both quotidian depictions of violent crime and graphic description (literary or cinematic) of bodies deprived of life.

Quite possibly the most remarkable account of that 'failure' in the face of corrupted human nature, intense violence and crime comes to us in the work of Joris-Karl Huysmans. Arthur Symons called that author's 1884 novel, À rebours, the 'breviary of the Decadence'.[14] Much of the critical attention rightly focuses on its prototypical protagonist dandy, Des Esseintes, who displays a deeply held dissatisfaction with life, a paralysing lassitude to remedy it and a tragic self-destruction and dereliction as he will try to withdraw from the world, and it is through this attempt that the novel makes its essentially spatial observation, that the isolation Des Esseintes finds himself in is related to the psychological deterioration with which he is struggling. In his curation of both the immediate world he inhabits and what will occupy his mind, Des Esseintes fully embraces the decadent ideal of artifice.

After an existential crisis, Des Esseintes has an epiphany: 'When he came to his senses again, he found that he was utterly alone, completely disillusioned, abominably tired; and he longed to make an end of it all, prevented only by the cowardice of his flesh'.[15] Therefore, he chooses the Parisian suburb of Fontenay-aux-Roses to withdraw to, instead of attempting suicide, much in the same way as unwillingness to resort to extreme measures is a common theme that will be seen among the detectives in Nordic noir narratives. The extreme measures need not involve suicide; Nordic noir detectives such as Sorjonen are consistently threatening and wishing to leave police investigative work, yet they never do. Sorjonen's protestations, like Des Esseintes' inability to take his own life, can eventually not be taken seriously. Des Esseintes then attempts to create a new beginning, an artificial world away from the corruption and decay, the fragmentation and the dissonance he saw all around him in Paris. The house at Fontenay-aux-Roses in its rooms, and the novel, reflecting in its chapters the objects of his study and obsessions, would contain all he needed in the world, and as he thought himself in control of its contents and harmony, he could have the choice of every detail. He becomes the ultimate creator, placing before the reader every detail, setting every tone and 'building' a utopian stronghold against modernity. All of this effort, though, takes its toll on his health, and in the end, Des Esseintes is condemned to return to Paris, in order to make a good recovery by leaving behind the solitary life he had crafted for himself in Fontenay-aux-Roses. According to the doctor's orders, he was 'to try and enjoy the same pleasures as other people', to which Des Esseintes replies both: 'But I just don't enjoy the pleasures other people enjoy' and 'So I have to choose between death and deportation'.[16] The book ends with men packing and moving his belongings out of the Fontenay house to return them all to Paris, while Des Esseintes is slumped in a chair. The space in which Des Esseintes is placed by the author turns out to be detrimental, and his mission is a failure in manifold fashion. It is true that Des Esseintes's health is failing, and he is prescribed cod liver oil among other remedies to treat his nervous system, but this is just as much a social diagnosis, and much of the novel's final pages concern the impossibility and inefficacy of retreating from society. The story refuses any single interpretation, yet in general, Huysmans's works reflect the story of learning to understand our need for the company of others, while seeing the world as a decaying place.

Even more so than À rebours, his best-known work, En rade, (The Haven), most effectively embodies this tension occupied by his characters.[17] A 'rade' in French is a haven, a shelter, a temporary home, yet in the story it is shown to be anything but. It is marked by its own permeability, caused by the deterioration inflicted by natural elements. Similar to Poe's House of Usher, the chateau in the countryside in the village of Lourps cannot maintain its integrity. It is exposed, left behind and abandoned in the end as a new place must be sought. And within this spatial crisis, the protagonists find themselves. Despite the heavily-psychologized interior monologue that typifies Huysmans, and which would go on to inform and influence diverse modern narrative conventions like noir itself, it is interesting that his protagonists must be placed in a distinct space to confront their world: in En rade, the chateau; for Des Esseintes in À rebours, his idealised country home; in Là-bas – in the bell-ringer's home at Saint-Sulpice; in En route, a monastery; and in La cathédrale, in Notre-Dame de Chartres. These places are all marked by the past; indeed, they are textual, living spaces where the interior monologue can be externalized and worked out.

Although Huysmans is often regarded as the standard-bearer of the Decadent movement, it is not only in his work that a similar emphasis on spatiality is present. Let us briefly consider a few representative examples of other authors. Octave Mirbeau's Le journal d'une femme de chambre (1900) begins:

> To-day, September 14, at three o'clock in the afternoon, in mild, gray, and rainy weather, I have entered upon my new place. It is the twelfth in two years. Of course I say nothing of the places which I held in previous years. It would be impossible for me to count them. Ah! I can boast of having seen interiors and faces, and dirty souls.[18]

The chambermaid, Célestine, offers her perspective on the faults, fortunes and foibles of the families she serves, and it is from her privileged position as one who sees all that happens behind closed doors that a disturbing image of bourgeois life emerges. Forced by her social station to observe 'interiors and faces', Célestine chronicles the lead-up to and consequences of a mysterious theft of the family's silver, which is worth up to 25,000 francs, all the while falling in love with Joseph, a fellow servant. After Joseph reveals he has come into a small fortune, his plan is to create a seaside space to take advantage of sailors and soldiers on leave: a patriotic, anti-Dreyfus bar, complete with Célestine in an Alsatian outfit feigning an accent from that region, using her eyes that can 'make the men crazy'.[19] Joseph himself is willing to start a brawl when a dissenting voice is heard questioning the anti-Semitic attitudes in the bar at the height of the Dreyfus affair, and Célestine's place in the bar takes advantage of the rallying potential of the Alsace region for the French of the time, in the years after the country's defeat in the Franco-Prussian War. In terms of the spaces of the novel, from impressive chateaux to the bar, which as a setting might well be described as a piece of capitalistic performance art, Célestine and Joseph are able to see the falsity of the bourgeois, nouveau-riche aristocrats that they serve for the first half of the story, in order later, to create a false space to take advantage of contemporary intolerances. The book ends with business booming in the bar, and with Célestine finally revealing that she has long been convinced that Joseph had stolen the silver to set them both up in a new life, a way of diagnosing and clearly embodying the hypocrisy and social mores of *fin-de-siècle* France that the book sought to attack in the first place.

Barbey d'Aurevilly's collection of short stories *Les Diaboliques* (1874) includes the tale 'Happiness in Crime', telling the story of Hauteclaire and Serlon, who conspire to poison the latter's wife, while the former poses as a chambermaid. Barbey's aesthetic can be summed up in two of the collection's other tales, whose characters muse on the following: 'Literature does not relate half the crimes that society commits mysteriously and with impunity every day, with delightful frequency and facility'; 'Would not hell glimpsed through some small window be far more terrifying than if beheld in its entirety in a single sweeping glance?'[20] Allusions to architectural structure and the ubiquity of crime pervade Barbey d'Aurevilly's stories. In the case of 'Happiness in Crime', the lovers' crime occurs in a secluded chateau, described as 'a theater of a crime, of which they have perhaps forgotten the memory in the bottomless abyss of their hearts'.[21] The building is a witness to the crime, without which the lovers would not have found the requisite isolation to carry on their affair, or to live comfortably apart from society.

Briefly, a final example is Jean Lorrain's *Monsieur Bougrelon* (1897), in which tourists visiting the Netherlands are treated to a tour of the 'true' Amsterdam. The titular character introduces himself by happening upon a café frequented by French expats and tourists:

> You have traversed the city, visited the museums, the churches and the girls. Amsterdam is a rather mysterious city, by God; its houses seem transparent, open to all comers; there are but windows, at least one would think that,

and we morons (we are all morons in France) believe we already possess the Dutch, Rotterdam and The Hague, the Zuiderzee and the North Sea, by virtue of only three walking tours. An error, sirs![22]

The city as visited by tourists is insufficient. Bougrelon instead offers tours of bawdy bars and brothels, as well as other seedy visions of *fin-de-siècle* Amsterdam. They traverse the town as he reveals the city's truths to the group.

In all of these literary cases, the author makes use of spatiality in order to reveal a place as fully as possible to the reader, in order to offer access to its innermost secrets, to know and represent the everyday in order to reveal more faithfully the rottenness of those living there. The cities, the country estates, the churches – all of these sites are called to witness, and all of them – significantly – are opened to the reader, and we as readers are given the sense that these places are normally hidden from view, either because the characters wish it so, (as in the case of Huysmans's Des Esseintes) or because otherwise crimes would be revealed (as in the case of the murderers in the work of Barbey d'Aurevilly). All the authors discussed above, along with other writers of the time, make effective use of spaces and places in order to emphasize Decadent ideals of truth in the underbelly, the superficial and dystopic, and most of all within the Third Republic government-supported rhetoric of the time.

As I turn to examples drawn from Nordic noir, in order to examine ways in which the principles of decadence persist in that genre, I will be highlighting the ways space becomes a beneficial convention for directors to innovate with in innovating those principles while codifying their own as a stand-alone regional noir. Examples abound of foregrounding spatiality in Nordic noir television and film. Given the limits of the current chapter, this work will briefly examine three television series: *Fortitude* (2015), *Ófærð* (*Trapped*, 2015–), and *Sorjonen* (*Bordertown*, 2016).[23] Each of these examples participates in noir conventions, incorporates the spatial in a manner that emphasizes representation of the Nordic, and involves links to Decadent motifs that can be said to precede and inform those of noir in the following century. The Decadent literary narratives spatialize sites of domesticity and deviance in order to highlight societal norms and criminal misdemeanours, while the three Nordic noir series examined here emphasize sites of isolation and ruggedness in order to foreground survival, and common bonds as shocking counterparts to greed and crime.

Several facets unite the three series under consideration. First of all, in all three cases, the towns represented are seen as dying and tied to a moribund economic model. The solution in all three cases is land development. *Fortitude* begins with a grisly murder, but one of the first scenes is a meeting where a study of the environmental impact of a glacier hotel is discussed; *Trapped* focuses its investigative gaze on a group of significant local business leaders who are attempting to develop the port town for international trade and tourism, a fact that undergirds their bond, although initially this is not tied to the central murder of the first series; finally, a casino close enough to the

Russian border is what the ruling class of Lappeenranta in *Bordertown* is focused on at the beginning of the series. It is ties to these three building projects that, at best, affects key decision-making throughout the series, and at worst, leads to further murders and crimes in the name of covering up those nefarious ties. In the worlds of these three shows, land development is nothing more than a complete surrender to rampant capitalism and a means by which greed and corruption become more than temptations for those involved. A second connection between the three series is the instability of the police force's situation. If we concede that a detective's role is to uncover truth in order to punish wrongdoing and vice, none of the detectives has a stable environment in which to work. In *Fortitude*, an off-island detective must be sent for due to corruption in the initial investigation; in *Trapped*, the police in Reykjavik do not trust the rural police force to do their jobs properly; and in *Bordertown*, a new serious crimes unit is constantly at risk for being shut down. Finally, the detectives concerned all share an obsessive focus on their work; they are all willing to let family, their towns and social structures collapse around them in the service of their jobs. These institutional questions and the core motivations of both the detectives and the powers that be are tied to the spaces in which the stories take place, and make for a compelling comparison with the Decadent writers' motivations for spatialization. After all, both in the case of the French texts and those of the Nordic noir, the very stories that we are told could not exist without the specific spaces they inhabit, reliant as they are on the spaces and places depicted in order to highlight society's wrongs.

In *Fortitude*, set on the Arctic Norwegian island of Svalbard, the town is corrupted as a murder takes place, seemingly in step with its submission to a future of capitalism and tourism. All the while, some of the town's working class are plotting to profit from nature conservation by selling the centuries-old mammoth carcass that is emerging from the permafrost, but is infected with a fatal illness. When we finally see what really happened to one of those plotters – Pettigrew, whose murder is the one that ignites a British investigation – it is the sounds of Pettigrew's death that are emphasized: his vomiting and gurgling after being stabbed by Elena, his rape victim; the protests as he is dragged to the coast; and finally the sound of him being eaten alive by the polar bear. The sheriff of the town, Dan Anderssen, is left screaming in his car as Pettigrew's murder takes place, and his screams are in sharp relief to the sudden silence of the suffering Pettigrew (S1E11). Bodies are destroyed in this series, and we hear the screams and desperate wailings of the residents of Fortitude.

Throughout the series, the directors make consistent use of the climate's brutality, to frame a place where life is difficult, but crime is rare. Early in the series, one scientist describes the simultaneous harmony of life in the town and the ambiguity of how a darker human nature might be dormant amongst the residents. In the town, even the sheriff is of unknown virtue, and he makes for an interesting case for examining the rottenness of the settlement, when the scientist notes that there has never been a test of his good character: 'Everyone's got a job, no one is poor. So there's no stealing and there's no crime. Everybody's always happy' (S1E1). The answer to the question of plumbing any potential depths to the sheriff's character unfolds over the course of the first series. In many ways, the town's struggle against its mysterious contagion fades into the background against the revelation that the sheriff both failed that test of character (in watching Pettigrew die) and fought to redeem himself (in trying to go to Morton's rescue and not let him die in the wilderness). In this fashion, the climactic scene of the first series takes place in the harshest of conditions, with no horizon and no hope of escape.

Dying together on the glacier, with no gasoline in the snowmobile in order to make their escape to Fortitude, Morton and the old man realize their shared, inevitable fate; at the same time, other characters are literally restrained from escaping the island in a helicopter. The conversation between Inspector Morton and the old man (Henry Tyson) stands out among the episodes of the series as the only one that delves into the truth of matters, with issues such as paternity and guilt being brought to light. Even when the cause of the sickness is discovered, it is done wordlessly, following the scientists' eyes as insects try to escape a laboratory. Within the confines of the town, it is possible to lie to and cheat others. The same is not true in the natural elements. Being there demands recognition of a life and death struggle. Quite literally, the conversation on the glacier could not have taken place had the characters not been in that particular environment, and it could not have happened had they not been dying, for Henry's confessions would never have been voiced. 'You have no right, I don't deserve this,' Morton says as he bleeds out in the snow. 'This is just something that happened,' is the old man's reply (S1E10). For Henry, taking his death into his own hands instead of being forced from the island by an obscure local ordinance, the fatalism of the uninhabitable surroundings aligns perfectly with his assessment of the situation. Red blood on deadly white snow is the image the viewer is left with, a sign of humanity's failure before the harsh natural world whose winds continue to blow. As in the opening sequence of *Bordertown*, to be discussed below, the earth in *Fortitude* bears the reminder of Henry's death on the side of the glacier. The first series' tenth episode ends with the blood spatter beside his body after his suicide, and the eleventh episode begins with the sheriff's (and the viewer's) approach to the corpse. The wounded Morton, without any transportation or possibility of rescue, awaits the sheriff's arrival in the snowy landscape, with everything still and starkly placed: the red parka, the blood around, both made all the more brilliant by the intense white of the snow and the sunshine. Throughout the series, characters understand the space around them, with its concomitant dangers and the questions it asks of them. They enter the wilderness and then come back to civilization, and no deception occurs while in the wilderness.

Iceland's *Trapped* investigates the consequences for Andri, a police chief in a small remote Icelandic town, of leaving a world of urban crime and problems in Reykjavik, without dwelling heavily on the precise cause of that departure, and what is seen as a large professional step down in the show's world. Two characters open the series by leaving their town for the countryside; the beauty of the landscape is meant to harbour them, as they believe their secret place will make for an ideal romantic getaway. They want to be alone, and they are under the impression that the wilderness is safe and approachable. Within minutes, the viewer and characters alike come to know that this is not the case, as their chosen secluded spot catches fire and burns around them. Much of the first series' drama resides in determining the true source of that fire, in which a woman dies; the tension between arson (a human-instigated event) and a horrible accident (the fault of a harsh natural environment) thus frames the show.

In this remote village, there is a constant reminder that danger is all around. The town's location is strategic, both for its harbour and the easy land access for ferries from Denmark, but weather conditions underline its isolation from the rest of Iceland. The village's space drives the plot, when persistent snow cuts the residents off from the rest of the island, and when an avalanche occurs and cuts off electricity and communication with the outside world. The connection between the space of the show's setting and its content is emphasized in the opening title sequence, where the desolate beauty of the Icelandic landscape alternates with landscape-like shots of a corpse. Significantly, the corpse does not appear in the show (as the central murder involves a found torso separated from head and limbs, and the aforementioned woman's corpse would have borne the severe burns of the fire); instead, by decoupling the particular body of the opening credits from the series' narrative and by scoring the visuals with what can be better described as beautiful music than haunting, it invites reflection on the connection between spatiality and the body. The cinematographic choices of the opening titles provide insight into that connection, through intercut transposition of body and landscape over the course of twelve images. Beginning with an aerial view of uneven, snowy terrain and then turning to folds in the skin mirroring the first landscape, allows the viewer to see the body topographically, as a site. This in turn allows the following glacial shot of Iceland to be investigated as a body by the viewer, an impression that may not have been given had the title shots consisted only of landscapes. Iceland becomes a body, and the body becomes a place. A crime committed against that body marks it as a map, and the personified Iceland is suddenly mournful at having seen what it has. It is important to note that the body of the opening title sequence has not been harmed in any visible way, adding layers to the mystery of its demise and the mystique of the landscape. Just as a corpse has a story to unearth, so too does the land itself.

Bordertown's first episode opens with an aerial tracking shot of Helsinki at night, illuminated and alive, before an extended sequence of the dead body of a murdered girl (whom the viewer may at first imagine is the 'doll' of the three-episode arc's title, 'The Dolls' House'). Everything is in motion in these few shots of Helsinki, and life is bustling. That makes a strong contrast with the still corpse, and renders the long, attentive looks that the detective, Sorjonen, gives to the crime scene all the more apparent. Throughout the first series, Sorjonen's colleagues are always hurried, either at a crime scene or in an interrogation. In this way, details are missed, and the divergence between Sorjonen and the rest of the world, including the rest of his division, is stark. At rock bottom, Sorjonen appears to contemplate this contrast – and the necessity of his continuing to do the work that is damaging him so severely. Repeatedly, he sits lost in thought while staring at the light of a flashlight as he clicks it on and off. These are the moments in the series when he is most burdened, and trying to illuminate the physical, lived space he is in seems to allow him to contemplate the duality of metaphorical light and darkness that comprise his world.

Like *Trapped*, in *Bordertown*, the series' opening title sequence does much of the work in establishing the role granted to spatiality in the show, as it describes the journey that the main character takes towards the adoption of his new life, and the idyllic surroundings of the harbour are emphasized. The colours blue and green dominate as the sun shines brightly on a clear day. Significantly, as the title sequence continues, things change. Blood stains the wall of a ravine, but it is right above the road. Earlier shots follow the family's car, from where the blood spreading should be 'visible', the first sign that Lappeenranta will not offer a sought-after and desired escape. Instead, the blood suggests either the violation of an otherwise pristine and ideal, though rough, landscape, or a prevalence of suffering and crime even outside the city. The series asks whether its protagonist can escape the grave crimes that torment him, or whether they exist wherever he might go.

By the time the viewer arrives in Lappeenranta with the Sorjonen family, the sun is setting, and Sorjonen's searching eyes gaze at the viewer in his new surroundings. The viewers have the same questions as he does: namely, can his life be any different here than in the big city? His family will inhabit the same city where his wife grew up, yet the surroundings belie the strains and the state of modern life there. Sorjonen cannot escape his calling, and he cannot find a place to establish the peaceful, family-oriented existence that he craves. The space of his new surroundings calls attention to this. The muted blue and green tones of interior shots are just the same as in the Helsinki hospital at the series' outset; the rain and dark shadows of Lappeenranta's murder victim are similar to that of the house in Helsinki where the little girl, whose murder opens the series, lived, and which directly prompts Sorjonen and his family's move to Lappeenranta; and the crime in Lappeenranta takes place among a set of resort cabins, where vacationers get a break from modern urban life. All of this points to the fact that Sorjonen cannot escape, that the idyllic countryside harbours all the dark possibilities of his former life in the capital and that if he is going to find peace, he will have to find another way. Based on the importance of spatiality, Lappeenranta will offer no solace as a place.

In all of these examples, the past remains present, and threatening, as perhaps it does in all crime serials. The modern world must be navigated, and that must be done alone, as since the late nineteenth century, a sure definition of modernity has included the idea of institutions without character, the loss felt after the broken promises of progress. Huysmans inaugurates this literary tradition with his novelistic oeuvre, exemplified also by Mirbeau, Barbey d'Aurevilly, and Lorrain, as discussed above.[24] One further genealogical connection between *fin-de-siècle* Decadence and Nordic noir bears reflection. In the literary cases mentioned above, the protagonist of each tale is most often an outsider: a dandy, perhaps, or a writer, or at the very least a friend of one of these. Bear in mind, however, what the role of these characters within their texts is: namely, to reveal the world for what it is. Often, it is American hegemony or capitalism that is under attack, because it is those market forces that are coming to define the modern world and all social hierarchies and relationships. In a sense, then, the literary characters revealing the rottenness and greed around them are similar to the detectives of modern Nordic noir. It must be noted, however, that there is a key difference: in the case of the Decadent literary works, revealing the nature and perpetrator of the crimes is enough. That is sufficiently damning for the culture at large; however, justice is elusive. All of the crimes in the French literary samples are solved, but none of them are resolved within the narrative's framework. In a way, then, we have crimes in need of resolution, or in other words, in need of an actual detective. The dandy/writer figure is a cultural critic, but is powerless to right the wrongs surrounding them. On the other hand, the detectives of Nordic noir have as their purpose solving *and* resolving crimes. Exposing what is true must lead to the punishment of crime, and should therefore be more satisfying. In the final analysis, this is not the case, though; even if the perpetrators of the crimes are caught and prosecuted, the spatialized settings of Nordic noir narratives end their respective series living within a society corrupt all the way to the top. Resolving the details of a crime does not change the system in which the detective operates. In both the case of the French Decadence and the Nordic noir, the guiding paradox is that the world is harsh, filled with violence and darkness and corruption. Revealing that is the best course to take, and all that one can do. The French Decadent novels and Nordic noir series both find whatever peace is possible by revealing as much as they can, and both genres end by looking forward to worlds where they might one day have a peaceful and intact social conscience.

To spatialize is a visual code in Nordic noir film and television, whether in urban cases such as *Forbrydelsen* (*The Killing*, 2007–12), *Broen/Bron* (*The Bridge*, 2011–15) or rural series, the climate, the landscape, the geology and generational survival in these conditions make the Nordic countries ideal settings for noir storytelling. It is a similar spatializing code that Huysmans already knew in France at the end of the nineteenth century, space deployed differently in *fin-de-siècle* France, yet still as a charged metaphor for the social world he was writing against. It is a formal innovation which allows the author, or directors, to externalize the interior monologue of the characters. In the case of the three series discussed above, although relying on what is becoming visual cliché in establishing Nordic settings, by placing them within harsh climates, alone and far from so-called civilization, they are at their most bare, their most raw.

In the end, with respect to Decadence, in 1906, shortly before his own suicide, the English poet John Davidson wrote, 'Decadence in any art is always the manure and root of a higher manifestation of that art'.[25] Manure and roots. Transforming rottenness into something hopeful for the future. At the end of *The Girl with the Dragon Tattoo* (2009 – Swedish adaption, directed by Niels Arden Oplev), the first word we see Blomkvist type on a new white screen, signifying a new beginning, is 'Wennerström', fuelled by the discoveries that Lisbeth has made. Kurt ends the British series of *Wallander* saying that although his life no longer 'joins up', but is just 'moments', he is fine, and the above-cited final distant shot shows him with his family bracing the wind, no longer alone, walking into a future where Kurt no longer needs to investigate crime, where the bleakness of life as expressed in the environment can no longer touch him and where successive generations of his family will remember for him. In the same way, Huysmans's novels, especially the early ones, can end quite pessimistically. In *Là-bas*, the protagonist's answer to what will become of an over commercialized, corrupt and aimless generation at the *fin de siècle*: 'They will turn out just the same as their parents. They will stuff their guts with food and evacuate their souls through their bowels'.[26] Alongside this, one of his friends repeats, 'the dawn will be light'. What unites Nordic noir and Decadent literature is a sense of the rottenness of the world, and the harshness of life. In the case of Nordic noir, there is a fixation with the detective's duty to root out that rottenness and call it what it is; in the case of Decadent literature, and especially the work of Huysmans, the characters are civilians, but are also trying to understand – even to detect – what ails society. In both cases, the characters recognize the need to diagnose and treat themselves as well. Yet, what also unites them is a tireless, dogged effort at making a dent in the work ahead, finding a way to survive in such conditions, and it is this tenacity within such bleakness that reveals the commonalities and great promise in encountering both movements today, for readers and viewers alike.

Notes

1 Thomas Pynchon, *The Crying of Lot 49* (New York: Perennial Classics, 1999), 11.
2 Italo Calvino, *Invisible Cities*, trans. William Weaver (New York: Harcourt Brace Jovanovich, 1978), 30–1.
3 Edward W. Soja, *Thirdspace: Journeys to Los Angeles and Other Real-and-Imagined places* (Malden, MA: Blackwell, 1996), 11.
4 Bertrand Westphal, *Geocriticism: Real and Fictional Spaces*, trans. Robert T. Tally Jr. (New York: Palgrave Macmillan, 2011), 140–2.
5 Italo Calvino, *Hermit in Paris: Autobiographical Writings*, trans. Jonathan Cape (New York: Vintage, 2004), 167. This work was cited in Robert T. Tally Jr.'s excellent volume, *Spatiality* (New York: Routledge, 2013), 80.

6   Further study would be welcome about the shorthand of what constitutes Nordic space, especially in terms of clichés and received images that proliferate as works of Nordic noir become more popular throughout the world.
7   Maurice Barrès refers to Decadents as those influenced by Baudelaire, while Rémy de Gourmont also notes Théophile Gautier's usage of the term identifying Baudelaire himself as founding the group. Some point to a later work as serving as both credo and manifesto, with candidates including Paul Bourget's *Essai de psychologie contemporaine* (1883), Paul Verlaine's *Les poètes maudits* (1884) or Joris-Karl Huysmans's *À rebours* of the same year.
8   Asti Hustvedt, *The Decadent Reader: Fiction, Fantasy, and Perversion from fin-de-siècle France*, ed. Asti Hustvedt (New York: Zone Books, 1998), 10.
9   Henri Mitterand, Dominique Rincé and Bernard Lecherbonnier, *Littérature XIXème siècle: Textes et Documents* (Paris: Nathan, 1991), 545–7.
10 Asti Hustvedt, *The Decadent Reader*, 15.
11 Joris-Karl Huysmans, *Against Nature (À rebours)*, trans. Robert Baldick (New York: Penguin, 2003), 179.
12 Matei Calinescu, *Faces of Modernity: Avant-Garde, Decadence, Kitsch* (Bloomington, IN: Indiana University Press, 1977), 176–7.
13 Asti Hustvedt, *The Decadent Reader*, 15.
14 Arthur Symons, *The Decadent Movement in Literature* (London: Constable, 1899), 39.
15 Joris-Karl Huysmans, *Against Nature*, 9.
16 Ibid., 196.
17 A common problem in comparative literature studies is the question of when to settle on a book's translated title. This is the case with *En rade*, translated variously as *Becalmed*, *A Haven* and *Stranded* in new translations since only 1993. I have chosen the title of Hustvedt's 1999 translation, not just because it is the version I prefer, but because as titles go, Hustvedt's is the one that most prioritizes the vital role played in the narrative by the Chateau de Lourps, where much of the story takes place.
18 Octave Mirbeau, *A Chambermaid's Diary*, trans. Benjamin R. Tucker (New York: Benjamin R. Tucker, 1900), 9.
19 Ibid., 210–11.
20 Jules Barbey d'Aurevilly, 'Beneath the cards of a game of whist', (134) and 'A Woman's Revenge', (209) in *Les Diaboliques*, trans. Ernest Boyd, *The Decadent Reader*, ed. Asti Hustvedt (New York: Zone Books, 1998).
21 Ibid., 130.
22 Jean Lorrain, *Monsieur de Bougrelon* (Paris: Librairie Borel, 1897), 26 (my translation). The original French: 'Vous avez déjà parcouru la ville, visité les musées, les églises et les filles. Amsterdam est, palsambleu, une cité assez mystérieuse; ses maisons semblent transparentes, ouvertes à tout venant; il n'y a que des fenêtres, le croirait du moins, et nous autres fats (nous le sommes tous en France) nous croyons posséder en trois tours de ville les Hollandaises et les Hollandes, Rotterdam et La Haye, le Zuyderzée lui-même quoi, toute la mer du Nord. Erreur, Messieurs !'
23 *Fortitude*, originally broadcast on Sky Atlantic (UK), 2015. Interestingly, although set in Norway, the series is filmed in Iceland and the UK; *Ófærð* (*Trapped*, 2015–), originally broadcast on RÚV (Iceland), 2015; *Sorjonen* (*Bordertown*), originally broadcast on Yle TV1 (Finland), 2016.

24 The example of Rachilde's *Monsieur Vénus* and Villiers de l'Isle-Adam's 'Le plus beau dîner du monde' also come to mind, but space here is limited.
25 John Davidson, cited in Holbrook Jackson, *The Eighteen Nineties: A Review of Art and Ideas at the Close of the Nineteenth Century* (New York: Kennerley, 1914), 227.
26 Joris-Karl Huysmans, *The Damned (Là-bas)*, trans. Terry Hale (New York: Penguin, 2001), 209.

Chapter 13

DRAGON TATTOOS, CRIME AND THE CITY: THE CONTEMPORARY EPIC

Giti Chandra

Like much of the crime-fiction-reading world, I, too, pounced on the fourth book in the *Millennium* series – noting, briefly, that it is now called a 'novel' ('A Lisbeth Salander Novel') – praying that it matched up to the original Larsson trilogy. While this is not the place to discuss the relative merits and de-merits of this sequel with respect to the original, there was one aspect of the original that it distinctly lacked: lists. Shopping lists, clothes lists, home improvement lists, window view lists, street lists, other kinds of lists. There are no passages that tell us, for instance, that '[Salander] put on black jeans, a dark pea jacket and matching knitted gloves, cap, and scarf. She took the rings out of her eyebrows and nostril, and put on a pale pink lipstick'.[1] No paragraphs that tell us about:

> an attic flat of seventy square metres right at the end of Bellmannsgatan .... that Blomkvist was able to buy inexpensively. [That] he put money into fixing up the bathroom and the kitchen area but instead of putting in a parquet floor and interior walls to make it into the planned two-room apartment, he sanded the floorboards, whitewashed the rough walls, and hid the worst patches behind two watercolours by Emanuel Bernstone. The result was an open living space, with the bedroom behind a bookshelf, and the dining area and the living room next to the small kitchen behind a counter. The apartment had two dormer windows and a gable window with a view of the rooftops towards Gamla Stan, Stockholm's oldest section, and the water of Riddarfjarden. He had a glimpse of water by the Slussen locks and a view of City Hall.[2]

No passages like this last one that I will indulge myself in, bringing together, as it does, so many lists:

> The bus stop for Hedestad was over the road from Konsum, and Blomkvist started off his exile by carrying out his plans to go shopping in town. He got off the bus by the railway station and made a tour of the centre of town. Along

the way he bought heavy winter boots, two pairs of long underwear, several flannel shirts, a proper thigh-length jacket, a warm cap, and lined gloves. At the electronic store he found a small portable TV with rabbit ears ... He stopped at the library to get himself a card and borrowed two mysteries by Elizabeth George. He bought pens and notebooks. He also bought a rucksack for carrying his new possessions. Finally, he bought a pack of cigarettes.[3]

The Epic List is one of the generic categories that has survived almost intact in literature that carries forward the concerns that animated the ancient epics: among them, the cataloguing of culture that is central to the defining of collective identity. If the epic war is a civilizational one that pits a value system against its 'other', the epic list recognizes and preserves the minutiae of that civilization. In other words, it is as integral to Greek collective identity that they be distinguished from the Trojans in their value systems, as it is that their customs and manners, songs and heroes, games and morning ablutions, items of armour and weaponry, be distinguished from the Trojan as well. Writers who take upon themselves this preservation and propagation of collective identity, have long understood the importance of the epic list. Whitman's *Leaves of Grass*, defining the new nation and people that are America, is organized around such lists. It is a tradition that Bob Dylan follows in the democratic naming of the people. The poem called 'There was a Child Went Forth Every Day' begins thus:

> There was a child went forth every day,
> And the first object he look'd upon, that object he became,
> And that object became part of him for the day or a certain part of the day,
> Or for many years or stretching cycles of years.
> The early lilacs became part of this child,
> And grass and white and red morning-glories, and white and red clover, and the song of the phoebe-bird,
> And the Third-month lambs and the sow's pink-faint litter, and the mare's foal and the cow's calf,
> And the noisy brood of the barnyard or by the mire of the pond-side,
> And the fish suspending themselves so curiously below there, and the beautiful curious liquid,
> And the water-plants with their graceful flat heads, all became part of him.[4]

The poem is a long list of people, places, lands and objects that the child sees every day and which become a part of him. And here is the first verse of 'A Hard Rain's A-Gonna Fall' sung at Dylan's Nobel prize awarding:

> Oh, where have you been, my blue-eyed son?
> Oh, where have you been, my darling young one?
> I've stumbled on the side of twelve misty mountains
> I've walked and I've crawled on six crooked highways

I've stepped in the middle of seven sad forests
I've been out in front of a dozen dead oceans
I've been ten thousand miles in the mouth of a graveyard
And it's a hard, and it's a hard, it's a hard, and it's a hard
And it's a hard rain's a-gonna fall.[5]

The act of listing is also the act of naming, of claiming, of archiving and documenting, of gathering together, the many and disparate parts that make the whole, the sum of which is something greater and different than the parts. George Eliot's loving lists of plants and soils, crockery and linen, books and foods, in *The Mill on the Floss* has a similar compulsion. My contention is that Stieg Larsson's lists are part of this epic tradition, and that, while his plots may be about crime, his theme is collective identity; that while the plot leads us to questions of whodunnit, the theme leads us to questions of 'who are we?' and 'what does it mean to be alive in Sweden in the year 2005?' The very same questions that impel the epic.

When the European realist novel of the nineteenth century took over the nation-building concerns of the epic, and allied itself with social realism, the novel genre lent itself magnificently to the multifarious plots and themes that energized it. Many retained the generic plot characteristics of the ancient epics: long journeys, wars and violence, featured in significant novels from *Don Quixote* to *War and Peace*, *Moby Dick* to *Crime and Punishment*, *The Moonstone* to *A Tale of Two Cities*. My belief is that Stieg Larsson's *Millennium Trilogy* and Arnaldur Indriðason's Erlendur series are the literary successors of this strand of the novel genre: they are the contemporary epics of our time.

In this categorization, some generic characteristics are more self-evident than others. If Joyce's *Ulysses* is a compendium of the minutiae and ethos of life in Dublin at a certain historical moment, then certainly the details of the shape, size, location and value of an apartment in Stockholm, the trends and norms of sub-culture dressing, the contents of a shopping cart and the kinds of coffee machines in the early twenty-first century are no less so. By the time one is done reading *Ulysses*, one should be able to draw a map of a Dublin that Joyce has walked us through. Larsson's painstaking and accurate delineation of the roads and streets, the various districts and parts of Stockholm and his specifying of the routes taken by the various people driving, walking or using public transport through the city in his books, construct a map of it that a visitor could use to make her way in it. From Charlotte Bronte's Villette and Dostoevsky's Raskolnikov, to T. S. Eliot's J. Alfred Prufrock and Woolf's Mrs Dalloway, Larsson's Blomkvist and Indriðason's Erlendur are the latest in a long line of protagonists that trace the outline of their cities in daytime and nocturnal wanderings through their main streets and alleyways.

The figure of the flâneur is, historically, a city-bred one, with specific and evocatively Sherlockian associations with crime fiction. One of the things that the flâneur does, of course, is to turn the reader's attention from the idle human spectator, to the city itself, producing, in Franco Moretti's formulation, a 'literary geography', which allows the reader to 'see how geography may explain the history of culture'.[6] The emergence of the city as protagonist, as the receptacle of 'the history of culture', is, of course, especially conducive to the social realist's art, invested as it is, more often in the forces of social realities that create crime, rather than in the crime itself. 'I don't describe [Reykjavik] in much detail, but it is present in all my books,' says Indriðason; 'its streets, buildings, and history'.[7] Indriðason is specifically interested in Reykjavik, also, insofar as it represents a certain moment in Iceland's history. His protagonist is the detective, Erlendur, whose name means 'foreigner'; almost a prototypical flâneur, you might say. Erlendur 'was born in 1946 and so he has lived through times of great change, and seen Iceland go from being a very, very poor peasant society to a very, very rich modern society'.[8] 'He is born after the war and experiences the great migration from country to urban areas', Indriðason tells Pétur Blöndal:

> As is usual during such social upheavals, there are individuals that are left behind, and Erlendur is one of those. He isn't part of the evolution, he hates the present and he hates Reykjavík. He lives quite a bit in the past, in the sagas and in his own childhood haunts in the east. He often immerses himself in stories of adversity; Icelanders have whole series of books about these, landslides and avalanches, adversities on highland roads, narratives of people that freeze to death, whole groups that are perhaps not even found for half a century. To me this was the only way to make him a believable policeman.[9]

'It worries him', Indriðason says in an interview with Jake Kerridge:

> that people are looking forward without thinking about anything else but the great things they will do, and they don't look back at where they came from, where their roots are. I think that maybe because of how quickly we evolved into this modern society few of us look back now, except for the older generation that lived through these changes and want to look back to simpler times, easier times.[10]

In a 'modern society' centred on the urban, the city is where past and present co-exist, sometimes unacknowledged or unfêted by each other. This location of the present as an integral part of the trajectory from past to future is central to the foundational enterprise of the epic and the realist novel. Insofar as the past is always a construct, and the trajectory leading to the future always a narrative, the idea that those 'simpler, easier times' may never have existed is a given. But what the past actually was, or is, for any given writer or protagonist, is not as important as the fact of positing it as a foundational moment of national identity. In the traditional, European, epic, it is possible to see this use of a historical past in, for instance, Tolstoy's *War and Peace* (1869), but also the evocation of a mythic past set within a real conflict, as in Thomas Mallory's

Morte d'Arthur (1485), written while the War of the Roses was raging outside Mallory's prison walls. More recently, Chinua Achebe's *African Trilogy* (1958–66), especially *Things Fall Apart* (1958), provides a more revisionist take on the past and its relevance to the present collective and national identity of Nigeria.

In Indriðason's books, crime is an effective plot device that connects the past to the present. In a plot device typical of his Erlendur series, cases of crime almost always come paired with an event, or crime in the past that he unravels alongside the present-day offence being solved. Some cases are simply located in the past to begin with – bodies, for instance, uncovered by the relentless, onward march of a city under construction – and are paired with present problems and issues related to them. Such a pairing also allows Indriðason to trace the depths of social issues, and their persistence over time, which have defined Iceland's cultural history, as well as its sense of collective identity.

Individual people are important to him too, insofar as they give the reader a degree of credibility, a hold on reality that is processed through a psychology that is both interesting and familiar. 'I'm always looking for realism', he says. 'Especially in the characterization. You have to have believable characters for the reader to care about'.[11] The issues that propel the plot are similarly believable ones, everyday ones:

> I don't want to preach but there are issues I do want to write about, such as domestic violence, because I think it's despicable. Most of my books are about families as well, and the relationships within families; both the positive and negative sides. I think the family is a very important institution. The fact that we don't have that much crime in Iceland (actually we have all the crimes going, but on a smaller scale perhaps) presents me with a challenge. So my stories tend to be psychological, building on an inner tension, rather than showcasing major atrocities, explosions and fireworks. If there is any one message in my books, and I'm not big on messages, it is this: take good care of your children.[12]

The care of children forms the foundation of a recurring thread throughout the Erlendur series, in the trauma that Erlendur carries within him from losing his little brother in a storm. The boy is presumed dead, because his body is never found, and in various books Erlendur returns to the scene of the storm in search of his brother's body.

Indeed, as has been noted several times, Erlendur has a peculiar fascination with stories of missing persons. His night-time reading consists of books about people who went missing as long as a few centuries ago. Perhaps this fascination has something to do with Iceland's uniquely inspiring geography, its landscapes that are terrifying in both their beauty and their indifference to human life. It has been said that these landscapes are a large part of what is uniquely 'Nordic' in the concept of the Nordic noir. The kind of personal responsibility that Erlendur takes for the incident in which his brother dies is evident in his investment in each of the cases he is given, or which he takes upon himself to solve.

If there is a unique quality to the work of Larsson and Indriðason that lifts it out of the genre of crime fiction and into that of the modern epic, it is the status of the body to which violence has been done, both present and absent, and the self-appointed responsibility of Blomkvist and Erlendur to recognize and comprehend that status. To be able to think our way through this idea, it is as well to remember that the ancient epic (and in this category I include the *Mahabharat* from India, the *Iliad* from Greece, Mallory's *Morte d'Arthur* from England, *The Old Testament* and the Icelandic Sagas, among others) deploys war and violence in very significant ways. The function of war as civilizational divider has been noted. To that literal and symbolic function, I want to add the cipher of the violenced body.

As I have explained more fully elsewhere, the term 'violenced' seeks to avoid the much more specific connotations in the terms 'mutilated', 'injured', 'crippled', etc., which do not carry the connotations of the kind of violence that has been done to them in order to achieve the mutilation, injury or other type of crippling or destruction of the wholeness of the body.[13] For instance, a body may be injured, mutilated, etc., without violence of any kind. Similarly, the term seeks to side step the ideological inflections of 'violated', which sees the body as carrying a degree of sanctity or sacred meaning which is desecrated. The term 'violenced' addresses the body to which intentional violence has been done.

The literary space occupied by the body of Hector dragged by horses, or the body of Duryodhan, torn limb-from-limb so that Draupadi may wash her hair in his blood, Arthur's dying body carried through the hills to the lake and laid in the barge on its way to Avalon, Njal's body laid in symbolic state ready for burning and the many such bodies that punctuate the Sagas and other epics, is central to the fixing of a collective identity. This centrality is not merely symbolic, although powerfully, it is just that; it is central in its physical demand for a narrative. It is a site of trauma that is located, not only by its silence, but also in its insistent witnessing of itself. The violenced body bears witness to the horror visited upon it, commanding both the silence, and the comprehending narrative of its spectator. The narrative that will both understand this body, and contain its horror – that will 'comprehend' it – can be seen as the epic itself, which both contains, and is contained by, the body.

The violenced body's refusal to be contained, or to allow its horror to be captured within a trauma that is then alleviated by the apprehension of the perpetrator of that violence, is part of its very nature. The violence done to the body is, in many ways, violence done to our powers of comprehension themselves – to narrative, to language, to morality, to bodily dignity, to identity. Thus, the missing persons who so occupy Indriðason's work in general, and his protagonist, Erlendur, in particular, carry the accumulated burden of this horror of violence left unspoken, the inarticulable trauma left unarticulated.

The search for the 'disappeared' person signifies the constant deference of meaning in a crime whose violence serves to destroy all possibility of meaning itself. If the detective's job is to find a meaning and purpose for the violenced body, then Indriðason's insistence on the unfindable, the always missing, the never fully apprehended body – or person, or crime or motive – is significant.

It is especially remarkable in a genre which depends on a system of signification for its reason for being. The format of the crime story is, in other words, predicated on a hermeneutic system whereby clues need only to be recognized and deciphered in order for the final meaning to reveal itself. Within such a system, the missing person, in conjunction with the present, violenced, body in Indriðason's work serves as a central, destabilizing motif of his stories – a cipher that forever demands and rejects comprehension. In so doing, it forces the reader towards systems of meaning greater than itself; to a 'meaning' or narrative that is more than the sum of its clues. In my understanding, the greater narrative generated by the missing body, that is more than the sum of the parts of his fiction, is the narrative of collective identity: what Indriðason calls 'a very Icelandic phenomenon' – an emblem of 'Iceland', of 'Icelandic-ness', of a state and way of being that is unique to the country, its geography and its people.[14] I have written more fully, elsewhere, on the process of this narrative through the violenced body.[15] For the purposes of this chapter, I would argue, further, that the need for such an account comes precisely at a time of transition, of change, of upheaval, of social turbulence; a time when a collective's understanding of itself is challenged or is under siege. Indriðason's placing his protagonist, Erlendur, in just such a moment of change, is marked by the presence of these bodies.

In many ways, violent crime is the war that modern societies wage upon themselves, and which the modern hero must fight. In much of contemporary crime fiction, but perhaps especially in Nordic noir, driven as it is, by the last vestiges of social realism, crime is a diagnostic tool: the nature of the crime allows us to determine the nature of the malaise plaguing any given society, community, nation or collective. For Indriðason, issues of crime and punishment are, indeed, central to the conception of society and social justice:

> There shouldn't be crime without punishment, I think. But violence comes in all kinds and shapes, it can be the typical psycho murderer or it can be a 12-year-old boy killing his father because of domestic violence. So what justice do we have there, what kind of justice does he deserve? What is justice, is it the punishment the judge gives to you, or is it something that you give yourself, like in Erlendur's case?[16]

Crimes, with their intricate meshing of human psychology, social commentary and philosophical notions, offer, then, the conditions for the definition and diagnosis of contemporary society – much as marriage did for the nineteenth-century European novel. As Indiðason says to Nicholas Wroe, 'crime fiction is about so much more than just crime', and Indriðason, himself, is extremely aware of the kind of fiction this narrative of violence is, especially its connections to social realism, psychological veracity and collective identity construction.[17] He recognizes that these concerns are what raise the crime novel into the category of 'literary fiction':

> I believe crime novels can be as challenging as literary fiction if you make them believable. I was inspired by the social realism portrayed in the work of Maj Sjöwall and Per Wahlöö; by the way they developed their characters and described the everyday life of policemen who were not superheroes but ordinary people. Like many others, I was fascinated by this. Some of the crime writers in Iceland are journalists and maybe crime writing that deals with social issues is a kind of journalism. Crime novels offer a great way to examine all aspects of society and I think that's what Scandinavian writers are doing so well. And readers are picking up on that. I regard crime novels as literature about the human condition, the things we do or don't do to improve our lives and the lives of those around us. I think that's what all my books are about.[18]

Indriðason's early career was as a journalist (a film critic) for a local newspaper. Stieg Larsson's career as an investigative journalist has been well documented, as well as his own commitment to the crimes and problems that he documented and investigated as a journalist, which form the main plot lines of his *Millennium Trilogy*. In this sense, he, like Indriðason, performs the traditional task of the epic writer: to reflect the character and nature of a people and a society back to those very people and that very society.

That Indriðason's subject, as well as his audience, is the Icelandic people, is clear to him. 'I always write for my Icelandic readership', he says, 'because I don't know how to write for anyone else and the success of my books abroad has not changed that. I think this is why they are successful elsewhere'.[19] That perspective of and for the Icelandic or Swedish people, is – as is so often the case – best given by the insider/outsider character whose role is both to solve the crime and allow the reader to see the world of crime through her eyes. Erlendur and Salander both function as characters whose connection to society is liminal, at odds with the structures and forces that shape it. The quest for justice and meaning, the protector of the vulnerable and disenfranchised, the warrior who survives and triumphs through her wits and unique skills, Salander and Erlendur are the improbable representatives of the people who nevertheless embody the values that their society holds closest to its heart. Imperfect, and transgressional in their own way, it is possible to see the generic traits of the epic hero, as adapted by the realist novel, in both.

Indriðason, himself, speaks eloquently of the importance of Iceland's literary traditions, their place in creating a sense of national identity and culture, and his own emulation of some of the stylistic and thematic characteristics of this tradition. The crafting of collective identity begins right at the beginning, at the moment of creation. In an almost Biblical evocation of naming and new worlds, he says:

> It began at the settlement of the country, because we were newcomers in a land where nothing had a name. We immediately began composing toponyms: names for our mountains and rivers and waterfalls and glaciers, names such as Glóðafeykir (Ember Whirler) and Gullfoss (Gold Falls). Then we began writing our history, not least because we remembered it; we knew its beginnings, which set us apart from many other countries.[20]

The connection with the Icelandic epics, the Sagas, is not incidental. As the archetypal Icelandic hero, Njal, says in Njal's Saga, 'With the law our land shall be built up, and with lawlessness destroyed!'[21] The identification of a land and its people with the upholding of the law is a unique one in the history of nations and epics, and it is perhaps not incidental that the crime fiction novel should follow in the tradition of the location of the epic within such an idea.

This idea that a nation began as a collective, with an already existing history and identity that could be written down, is a powerful one. It gestures to a 'past' more clearly etched in the annals of a people, than most can claim; a unique, almost mystical, construction that can then be looked upon as a foundational enterprise. That the act of naming and writing down, is so intimate a part of the narration of collective identity, is of great significance for Indriðason's own formulation of the function of Icelandic literature. He is deeply invested in a material and ideological history in which 'works, written in Icelandic and in many ways unique, were born. These have,' he says, 'not merely stood the test of time; they are also alive and active within us. A thread, unbroken to this day, runs through the centuries, linking them to us. In the written words of past centuries, we have encountered ourselves'.[22]

I, like much of his non-Icelandic readership, read both Indriðason and the Sagas in translation in English. Even so, it is possible to see the veracity of his assertion that he tries to 'use words sparingly', because the Sagas 'employ a few words to tell a big story, and this is something [he is] always trying to achieve in [his] writing'.[23] 'They get on with the story in a very direct manner, they don't bother with small details. And I try to do this, I try to use as few words as I possibly can'.[24] 'Good crime fiction needs straightforward ideas and short sentences', observes Grant Nichol, writing about Indriðason's recent English translation, *Oblivion* (2015), in his blog on crime fiction.[25] Not merely because it is a stylistic feature that complements his desire for realism, but also because it establishes a linguistic and literary link with the country and its past: 'The Icelandic sagas occupy a huge place in our literature and I don't think any Icelandic writer can escape their influence'.[26]

Indriðason admits to writing for an Icelandic audience, assuming – correctly, I believe – that his work will be more appreciated by an international audience due to this factor, not less; and creates an explicitly and uniquely Icelandic protagonist. 'My first thought when I created him,' he says, 'was that he should be very Icelandic, that's to say, I wanted to celebrate the fact that he was an Icelandic detective and, as such, unique'.[27] That Erlendur is something of a throwback, out of place in a culture that has passed him by – 'an antidote to the madness', he calls him – makes Erlendur the perfect protagonist of novels with this specific 'historical' concern: a man both of, and not of, his times, who is therefore able to see, at a period of transition, the connections and disconnections between the past and present.

His long-term goal, he says, is to 'really understand Erlendur', where understanding Erlendur is itself an effort to understand his own father and the historical moment in Iceland's recent history that he represents:

> My father was of the generation that moved to the city and he wrote about characters who had too. Erlendur comes from the country and never felt at home in the city. His domestic life is either difficult or just bleak. A good-looking man in his 30s with a happy home life and good at his job is a happy ending of a story, not a beginning. The study of family life lets you raise all kinds of questions.[28]

Significantly, many of the Erlendur novels were published during the financial crisis in Iceland, a time of upheaval for the country, in many ways. To my mind, this is the epic impulse that animates the realist novelist: these dragons tattooed on a collective psyche, brought to life through a genre uniquely adapted for the purpose by Larsson and Indriðason.

Much of the focus in this chapter has been questions of genre, tracing features and characteristics of the epic, the novel and crime fiction, and looking at their convergences in Indriðason's and Larsson's fiction. It is interesting, also, to look at the reception of their work. Needless to say, it is popular to an almost unparalleled extent, for Nordic (especially Icelandic) fiction, reaching an international readership that has made their work almost as recognizably Nordic as the Icelandic Sagas. It was, perhaps, to be expected that the lay reader's enthusiasm for their books would, in fact, be used to bolster the argument that they are mere pulp fiction, their popularity proof that they cannot possibly be real 'literature', or have any 'literary' merit.

Apart from the contempt that this shows for many millions of readers across the globe, such a view also exhibits a real ignorance of the history of books that today are considered 'high literature', 'classics', 'canonical works' and so on. Ancient epics, such as the Greek and Indian, were recited to large, heterogeneous audiences before they were written down and became less accessible to a non-literate public. Recitations were held at large gatherings of the populace, where priests or rhapsodes would recite or sing the epic stories to their audiences. The canonical realist novel of the English nineteenth century had a social reception much like television soap operas today. Hardy and Dickens serialized their novels in magazines. The chapters were read out in the town square for the non-literate public, even while aristocratic young ladies rented them from lending libraries. People wrote to Dickens, commenting on his plots and characters and demanding he write in or write out those that they loved or hated in future chapters, and he frequently obliged. Hardy made sure to end each sequel (roughly two chapters long) on a note of suspense to keep his readers interested. Indriðason, indeed, chooses crime fiction specifically because 'the crime novel is an ideal setting for the criticism and examination and dissection of things that are unsatisfactory, not least because it's a genre that is more widely disseminated and more popular than many others'.[29] The point is not a simple correlation between popularity and literary merit, but rather a sense of books written about the people, and for the people; a kind of democratic literary impulse that looks askance, not at the unseemly popularity of certain books, but at our desire to separate a book from its readers, in order to place it on a pedestal. Larsson and Indriðason both posit a real challenge to that impulse; an epic for our times.

Notes

1. Stieg Larsson, *The Girl with the Dragon Tattoo*, trans. Reg Keeland (Canada: Penguin, 2010), 97.
2. Ibid., 16.
3. Ibid., 133.
4. Walt Whitman, *Leaves of Grass* (Philadelphia: David McKay, [c.1900]); Bartleby.com, 1999. www.bartleby.com/142/ (accessed 8 May 2019).
5. Bob Dylan, 'A Hard Rain's A-Gonna Fall' (1962), available online: https://bobdylan.com/songs/ (accessed 8 May 2019).
6. Franco Moretti, *An Atlas of the European Novel 1800–1900* (London: Verso, 1998), 9. Quoted in Christopher Prendergast, 'By the Width of a Street' in *The London Review of Books*, 20, no. 21 (1998): 26–7.
7. Jake Kerridge, 'Arnaldur Indriðason Interview' in *The Telegraph*, 3 September 2013. Available online: www.telegraph.co.uk/culture/books/10283048/Arnaldur-Indridason-interview.html (accessed 8 May 2019).
8. Ibid.
9. Pétur Blöndal, 'Arnaldur Indriðason: The Sound of Creation' interview in *Fabulous Iceland: Snapshots of Modern Writers* (Reykjavik: Fabulous Iceland, 2011), Available online: www.islit.is/en/promotion-and-translations/icelandic-literature/interviews-with-icelandic-authors/nr/3175, (accessed 8 May 2019).
10. Jake Kerridge, 'Arnaldur Indriðason Interview'.
11. Arnaldur Indriðason, speech to international publishers at the Frankfurt Book Fair, 12 October 2011 (Publicity material, Forlagið Rights Agency, 2016).
12. Ibid.
13. Giti Chandra, *Narrating Violence, Constructing Collective Identities: To Witness these Wrongs Unspeakable* (London: Palgrave Macmillan, 2009).
14. Alexander Schwarz, 'Interview with Arnaldur Indriðason', *inreykjavik.is*, 16 November 2012 (Publicity material, Forlagið Rights Agency, 2016).

15 Giti Chandra, *Narrating Violence*.
16 Jake Kerridge, 'Arnaldur Indriðason Interview'.
17 Nicholas Wroe, 'Northern Exposure' in *The Guardian*, 17 June 2006. Available online: www.theguardian.com/books/2006/jun/17/featuresreviews.guardianreview11 (accessed 8 May 2019).
18 Arnaldur Indriðason, speech at the Frankfurt Book Fair.
19 Pétur Blöndal, 'Arnaldur Indriðason: The Sound of Creation'.
20 Arnaldur Indriðason, speech at the Frankfurt Book Fair.
21 *Njal's Saga* (Hertfordshire, Wordsworth Classics: 1998), 138.
22 Arnaldur Indriðason, speech at the Frankfurt Book Fair.
23 Jake Kerridge, 'Arnaldur Indriðason Interview'.
24 Ibid.
25 Grant Nicol, Review: *OBLIVION* by Arnaldur Indriðason, *Crime Watch*, 31 July 2015, Available online: http://kiwicrime.blogspot.is/2015/07/review-oblivion-by-arnaldur-indridason.html (accessed 8 May 2019).
26 Arnaldur Indriðason, speech at the Frankfurt Book Fair.
27 Lynsey, 'Interview with Arnaldur Indriðason' for *Dead Good Books*, 11 August, 2013 (Publicity material, Forlagið Rights Agency, 2016).
28 Nicholas Wroe, 'Northern Exposure'.
29 Julia Holmes, 'Interview with Arnaldur Indriðason' in *Men's Journal Magazine*, USA, July 2014 (Publicity material, Forlagið Rights Agency, 2016).

Chapter 14

THE NEW SWEDISH POLICE THRILLER OF THE 2010s

Kerstin Bergman

Since the 1960s, Sweden has been known for its police novels by authors such as Maj Sjöwall and Per Wahlöö, Henning Mankell and Camilla Läckberg, to mention a few. The police procedurals in the Sjöwall and Wahlöö tradition are characterized by their social and political criticism, their depiction of the disintegrating Swedish welfare state, and their urban settings typical of the big, modern city.[1] In the early 1990s, Henning Mankell moved the Sjöwall and Wahlöö-type novel out into the Swedish countryside, and starting in the late 1990s, this resulted in a division of the Swedish police novel into two distinct types.[2] First, the urban novels in the Sjöwall and Wahlöö tradition, which are inspired by the American police procedural tradition[3] and marked by their socio-political criticism, novels that in the new millennium increasingly deal with transnational crime and international perspectives. This urban tradition is represented, for example, by crime-writer Arne Dahl's first two series: the Intercrime series and the Opcop series. And second, a tradition of rural police novels more inspired by the British police procedural developed.[4] The countryside novels focus primarily on local and personal crimes, and tend to avoid explicit social and political criticism as well as the depiction of anything beyond the borders of the local community.[5] This countryside tradition is represented by novels like those of Camilla Läckberg's Fjällbacka series.

In the 2010s, however, a third type of police novel emerged on the Swedish crime fiction scene. These novels have elements in common with both of the former traditions, but are also significantly different from them in many ways. The new novels are modern police thrillers, written by authors such as Anders de la Motte, Anna Karolina, Kallentoft and Lutteman, Jens Lapidus, Olle Lönnaeus, Jenny Rogneby, but there are many others. This chapter will address the context behind the appearance of these new police thrillers, as well as establish them as a new version of the Swedish police novel by examining their common genre characteristics in terms of protagonists, settings and crimes.

A changing crime fiction scene

The urban tradition and the rural tradition of police novels were both thriving, as they still are, and constituted parallel paths in Swedish crime fiction during the early 2000s. Nevertheless, following Stieg Larsson's success with the Millennium trilogy, published from 2005 to 2007 (the English translation in 2008–09), the Swedish crime fiction scene fundamentally changed. Inspired by Larsson's success, authors realized that they could still be successful crime writers even if they were not writing traditional police novels, which had previously been the norm and had dominated the crime fiction genre in Sweden. The crime writers enjoyed their new-found 'freedom.' Larsson's elaborate playing with crime fiction sub-genres generated a veritable flood of new genre hybrids, as well as crime novels emanating from sub-genres other than the police procedural, and his Salander creation inspired new types of detective characters. The police novel remained important, but became one of many genres.

Some Swedish authors tried to follow the established genre patterns of specific crime fiction sub-genres closely. Representative examples would be Åke Edwardson with *Möt mig i Estepona* (*Meet me in Estepona*, 2011) and Martin Holmén's *Clinch* (2015; *Clinch*, 2016), two novels that revive the American hardboiled crime novel from the first half of the twentieth century, and thus have a strong retro feel to them. Most authors, however, started to mix different crime fiction sub-genres, often including a substantial amount of thriller components, picked up either from the psychological thriller or from the international/political thriller genre. The latter seemed particularly surprising in the Swedish context, where – with the exception of Jan Guillou's *Coq Rouge* series from the 1980s – the political thriller genre had previously been an almost non-existent crime fiction sub-genre, not at all like in modern Danish crime fiction for example, where the political thriller had been an important and very lively sub-genre since the 1970s.[6] However, the psychological thriller has been the sub-genre most influential to the new crime fiction genre hybrids in Sweden post Stieg Larsson. Actually, there are very few Swedish crime novels today that do not display influences from the psychological thriller sub-genre. In the last few years, and inspired by international bestsellers like Gillian Flynn's *Gone Girl* (2012) and Paula Hawkins' *The Girl on the Train* (2015), 'domestic noir' novels by authors like Caroline Eriksson, Elisabeth Norebäck and many others, have also revived the more traditional form of the psychological thriller in Sweden.

Additionally, the Swedish crime fiction scene grew substantially in the 2000s, from around seventy new original Swedish crime novels appearing in 2000, to over 280 new novels being published in 2019.[7] Since the 1960s, crime fiction has been the literary genre in which Swedish society has been examined and discussed, and thus has closely mirrored social developments, and the genre has continuously grown. In a country with only ten million citizens, this growth has today made the crime fiction market quite crowded, something that has resulted in many authors after Stieg Larsson aiming to create unique genre hybrids in an attempt to stand out and differentiate themselves from the competition. Being original is, of course, more difficult than it sounds, and much of what is being published still seems quite similar in terms of e.g. storyline, characterization and style. Nevertheless, the ambition to stand out has contributed to a further diversification of the crime fiction genre in Sweden, and to breaking the dominance of the police procedural sub-genre.

The police novel has, however, remained a popular genre choice among readers and authors alike. Many of the authors have tried to create different kinds of police novel hybrids, mostly by spicing up their police stories with other crime fiction sub-genre elements, but also by introducing other popular fiction genres into the mix. Some examples are Denise Rudberg's police–chick lit mix, Gabriella Ullberg Westin's police–erotica mix, Kristina Appelqvist's police–whodunnit mix, Katarina Wennstam's police–court room drama mix and Lars Kepler's police–psychological thriller blend, to name just a few.

Origins of the new police thriller

One type of genre hybrid that has lately become so popular among Swedish crime writers that it is now possible to regard it as almost a specific 'sub-genre' in Sweden, is the police thriller, a type of police novel that has established itself as the third main type of Swedish police novel in the 2010s, thus complementing the urban Sjöwall and Wahlöö-inspired novels and the rural police novels. The new police thriller has its origin in Jens Lapidus' so-called Stockholm Noir novels, a series that started with *Snabba cash* (2006; *Easy Money*, 2011), which depicted new sides of the Swedish capital and introduced entirely novel perspectives into the national crime fiction scene. Lapidus showed a multiethnic and multicultural Stockholm, where large parts of the stories took place in the city's poorer suburbs, and where most of the main characters were young, petty criminals, often second-generation immigrants, who originated from these suburbs. The protagonists and their social context were then contrasted against the brat culture of rich, upper-class Stockholm, and Lapidus showed how the two spheres connected through criminality.[8]

Lapidus' novels were hardboiled – he himself claims to have been inspired primarily by James Ellroy[9] – and characterized by a fast tempo and plenty of action, but they also included a pinch of social criticism. This criticism was not the central element, as in so many of the novels where authors followed in Sjöwall and Wahlöö's footsteps, but it was still an integral part of Lapidus' stories.[10] His main focus was, however, on the entertainment and suspense factors. Furthermore, Lapidus' novels reached new groups of crime fiction readers, not least younger men, and they are also reported to be among the most checked-out novels in Swedish prison libraries.[11] Lapidus has a background as a criminal lawyer, and his books and stories are often perceived as presenting an authentic image of contemporary Stockholm.[12]

Although the police presence in Lapidus' novels is relatively limited – in his Stockholm Noir trilogy (2006–11) the reader is primarily following criminals and one corrupt police officer, and in his second trilogy (2014–17) the protagonists are a lawyer and an ex-criminal – these novels have been extremely influential on other Swedish crime writers, who have written novels in a similar style but with a stronger police presence. Some of the best examples of the new police thriller writers are Anders de la Motte, Anna Karolina, Jenny Rogneby and the duo of Mons Kallentoft and Markus Lutteman. In what follows, their respective series will be used to describe the characteristics of the new crime fiction sub-genre, as this is where many of the most interesting developments in Swedish crime fiction have taken place in the past ten to fifteen years.

Complex police protagonists on both sides of the law

Anders de la Motte, a former police officer, made his debut as s a crime writer in 2010 with the first part of his *Game* trilogy, a series that had much in common with Lapidus' Stockholm Noir novels. What made de la Motte one of the most important names of the new police thriller is, however, his second series, which so far consists of the two novels *MemoRandum* (2014, *MemoRandom*, 2015) and *UltiMatum* (2015, *Ultimatum/The Silenced*, 2017). The latter book received the Swedish crime novel of the year award from the Swedish Academy of Crime Fiction in 2015, while the former was nominated for the same prize – something that also speaks to the importance and status of this new sub-genre in Sweden.

In de la Motte's *MemoRandum* and *UltiMatum* we meet David Sarac, a police detective who is a handler in the Intelligence Unit of the Stockholm Police Force. His job is to recruit and support informers who can help the police fight organized crime. But when Sarac at the beginning of *MemoRandom* crashes his car into a wall, he wakes up in hospital with no memory of the last few years of his life, and more disturbingly, no memories of his most valuable informant, Janus, whom it becomes urgent to identify and re-connect with. Soon, however, Sarac realizes that he has no idea who he can trust, and that almost everybody around him – and perhaps also he himself – is corrupt in one way or another. The second novel, *UltiMatum*, starts with Sarac escaping from a psychiatric clinic, where he has been locked up after the events of the first novel. Soon his old colleagues are investigating the complicated murder of an unidentified man whose body has been cut to pieces. The story contains many unexpected twists, and spans everything from Stockholm's criminal underground to the country's highest political circles.

Sarac is a typical protagonist of this new type of police thriller. He works for the police, but often crosses the boundaries of the law. The main character of Anna Karolina's police thrillers is a similarly representative example. In her first novel, *Stöld av babian* (2014; *Savage Congress*, 2016), her protagonist Amanda Paller has recently finished her police training and started working as a Stockholm police detective. The reason that she joined the force originally, however, is that she plans to find out what really happened to her estranged sister, who was raped and committed suicide when the police investigation into her rape was disbanded. Without revealing her family background to anyone, Paller seduces the officer who was in charge of her sister's case and who also knew her sister, in order to get information. She also befriends the sister's boyfriend, Adnan Nasimi, who turns out to be a criminal with ties to organized crime. It is with him that Paller eventually falls in love, and their secret and impossible, but passionate, on-off relationship then functions as a driving force throughout the series. The complications of that relationship also lead her to constantly cross legal boundaries, not least since the cases she officially investigates tend to involve the crime gang to which Nasimi is connected. The double loyalties cause trouble for him too, and after events in the first novel, he flees abroad. Upon his return in the second novel, *Står dig ingen åter* (*No One Left for You*, 2015), both the police and Nasimi's former criminal associates are after him, and things turn even more complicated.

Out of necessity or owing to their personality, many of the police protagonists of the new police thrillers are loners, who actually have more in common with the hardboiled private investigators (PIs) of the American tradition,[13] than with well-known Swedish police detectives like Sjöwall and Wahlöö's Martin Beck or Henning Mankell's Kurt Wallander. The new police thriller thus breaks with the classic police procedural tradition of presenting a cooperating police team,[14] as well as with the Swedish tradition of male, 'defective' police detectives by presenting new, individualistic heroes for a neoliberal age.[15] Like their American PI forerunners, the Swedish police thriller protagonists also have their own personal moral codes that they tend to value more highly than the letter of the law, and that is what makes them break the law repeatedly.[16] Police protagonists being driven by personal moral codes has previously been unusual in Swedish police novels, and Dove and Bargainnier note that police officers in British and American police novels are also 'denied the luxury of those private codes of ethics that permit the private eye to violate the standards of society in the light of his own interpretations and loyalties'.[17] While the American hardboiled PIs crossed that line primarily with the greater good in sight, and while their main objective was always to catch the bad guys, this is, however, not always the case with the Swedish police thriller protagonists. Also reminiscent of the classic hardboiled PI's frequent use of violence, is that the protagonists of the new Swedish police thrillers know how to fight and how to use their guns, something that is clearly influenced not only by the American hardboiled novels, but also by the action thriller, not least in the genre's cinematic Hollywood form.[18]

In addition to striving to uphold the law, solve crimes and catch criminals – this being the object of their profession, these new police thriller heroes also tend to have personal agendas that have priority over their role as officers of the law. This makes them constantly use a kind of 'double book-keeping', as they are forced to lie to everyone around them, not least to the colleagues they work with. Additionally, they often end up putting an end to crime and criminals in ways that do not involve handing the bad guys over to the justice system. Dove and Bargainner also note that in British and American police novels it is common for officers to 'take matters into their own hands, often settling cases without an arrest, and handing out rewards and punishments in secret', but then that is primarily due to pressure from 'the police establishment' and the public, and not simply because they have a personal agenda that clashes with that of their employers.[19] Another common denominator of most of these new Swedish police thrillers is that in addition to the 'main' crime the police are investigating, there is another type of crime that has more personal ties to the police protagonists and that runs throughout the different series. The main characters of the new police thriller are thus usually less idealistic than their American predecessors, and in addition, rather pragmatic. Even personal financial gain is often not beyond them. For example, police officer Leona Lindberg, protagonist of criminologist Jenny Rogneby's police thriller series, originally sets off on her criminal path in *Leona: Tärningen är kastad* (2014; *Leona: The Die is Cast*, 2015) in order to amass a fortune, and with that a new life for herself. Money continues to be an important factor for her, even though her reasons for continuing down the criminal path become more complicated as the series progresses. What sets Leona apart are for instance when she in *Leona: Tärningen är kastad* lets a young child rob a bank, and in the second novel, *Leona: Alla medel tillåtna* (2016, *Any Means Necessary*, 2019) teaches a group of criminals how to avoid getting caught by the police, while she coaches them through a series of complicated robberies from which she benefits financially. That the police thriller protagonists are caught in the middle, between their colleagues and the criminals they are supposed to be fighting, contributes to increasing the suspense and thriller aspect of these novels. The double 'loyalties', in combination with other more classic thriller influences also result in the protagonists being subject to threats and danger time and again, and in some cases they are even raped or killed during the series. In the Hercules series by Mons Kallentoft and Markus Lutteman, beginning with *Zack* (2014, *Zack* 2018), the protagonist, Stockholm police detective Zack Herry, has a severe drug addiction that strongly contributes to ordering his priorities.[20] In the opening scene of the second novel in the series, *Leon* (2015), Zack puts a gun to his head and pulls the trigger during a game of Russian roulette. That the protagonist is constantly subject to danger, thus making the reader wonder whether he or she will survive, is perhaps one of the most fundamental elements of all thrillers. [21]

As shown above, an important influence behind the protagonists of the new Swedish police thrillers are the hardboiled (primarily male) private investigators of the American tradition. John Scaggs describes the hardboiled PI as 'a loner, an alienated individual who exists outside or beyond the socio-economic order of family, friends, work, and home', who 'answers to nobody but him- or herself', and who 'is intelligent, but resorts to physical violence and coercion to achieve his goals. He is conspicuously hostile to the forces of law and order, but yet, nominally, at any rate, he shares their aim to restore and maintain social order.'[22] This is also an apt description for one of the modern detective characters to whom the new police thriller heroes, not least the heroines, owe a lot, and that is Stieg Larsson's hacker detective Lisbeth Salander. Salander has been a great inspiration behind numerous Swedish crime fiction heroines in the last decade in many different crime fiction sub-genres, but particularly in the new police thriller. Characters like Jenny Rogneby's Leona Lindberg, Anna Karolina's Amanda Paller and many others are intelligent loners who are excellent at their jobs but socially uncomfortable, with a trauma in their past and a personal agenda that they prioritize above the law. They move on both sides of the law, and they can fight and never hesitate to use violence when needed – especially if they know that they can get away with it. Without Salander, these women characters would not have been possible in Swedish crime fiction, but many of the male heroes of the police thriller also clearly bear traces of Larsson's original hero.

Urban and organized criminality

While many of the new police thriller stories, some of which have been recounted above, might seem a bit over the top – and while the characters can sometimes seem almost a kind of super-hero, surviving the most impossible situations – the settings, crimes and topics addressed in these novels generally constitute realistic portrayals of a multifaceted contemporary Sweden. It is always the urban Sweden that is depicted, primarily big cities like Stockholm and Malmö, and this is something that the police thriller has in common with the typical police procedurals of the Sjöwall and Wahlöö tradition.[23] The crimes of the police thriller are also more similar to those of the urban police tradition, and the protagonists of the new police thriller are mainly dealing with different types of organized crime, not with crimes that are primarily linked to the individual and the personal as in the police novels set in the countryside.[24]

In his crime novels, Jens Lapidus depicts a whole invisible power structure of organized crime lurking under the official surface of Stockholm, and he shows how all power, political as well as economic, lies in the hands of this underbelly of society. In Lapidus' novels it often seems as if the people who are officially in power – politicians, people in finance and business, as well as people working in the legal system – are just puppets, while the criminals are always the ones pulling the strings.[25] The connections between the official and the criminal world are many and complicated in Lapidus' novels, and major sections of society are shown to be corrupt, its officials driven by both greed and fear. In many ways this portrayal of contemporary Sweden is reminiscent of that of the United States in the classic American hardboiled novels by authors like Dashiell Hammett and Raymond Chandler, although there are still some faint remnants of the Swedish welfare state on the surface of the increasingly neoliberal, capitalist society where class differences and segregation are snowballing, and where the real power is held by criminal networks.[26]

The bad guys, whom the police heroes of the modern Swedish police thriller fight, tend to come mainly from the world of organized crime, a world that often has links to a corrupt upper class – something that was also common in the classic hardboiled novels.[27] Moreover, corrupt police colleagues and superiors often turn out to be involved in the crimes and with the criminals that the protagonists are fighting, and a distrust of high-ranking police officers and the security police, as well as people from the upper classes, is also carried over from the police procedural tradition that originated in Sjöwall and Wahlöö's leftist novels.[28]

Much more could be written about the new Swedish police thriller. What is clear after examining protagonists and crimes in this sample of some of the most notable contemporary Swedish police thriller authors, however, is that these novels are similar enough to be defined as a separate crime fiction sub-category on the Swedish crime fiction scene today; a type of crime novel characterized by plenty of action and violence, as well as by very complex plots, protagonists and crimes. The new police thriller is a fascinating and multilayered crime fiction sub-category that simultaneously presents a rather depressing image of both human beings and of modern Swedish society. Nevertheless, it is also a sub-genre that brings about many of the most important new developments in Swedish crime fiction of the 2010s. The authors discussed above are generally considered to be some of the most interesting and promising new writers on the Swedish crime fiction scene today, and they are now being widely translated, even though they are not yet as well-known abroad as the authors who started writing in the 1990s or early 2000s. Similar tendencies could also be found in crime fiction from the other Nordic countries, but so far it is only in Sweden that the new police thriller has developed such a strong and unified presence.

Notes

1 Kerstin Bergman, *Swedish Crime Fiction: The Making of Nordic Noir* (Milano: Mimesis, 2014), 21–2.
2 Kerstin Bergman, *Swedish Crime Fiction*, 105–7; Kerstin Bergman, 'The Well-Adjusted Cops of the New Millennium: Neo-Romantic Tendencies in Swedish Police Procedurals', in *Scandinavian Crime Fiction*, eds Andrew Nestingen and Paula Arvas (Cardiff: University of Wales Press, 2011), 44.
3 Cf. Leroy Lad Panek, *The American Police Novel: A History* (Jefferson, NC, and London: McFarland, 2003), passim; George N. Dove and Earl F. Bargainnier, 'Introduction', in *Cops and Constables: American and British Fictional Policemen*, eds Earl F. Bargainnier and George N. Dove (Bowling Green, OH: Popular Press, 1986), 6.

4 Cf. George N. Dove and Earl F. Bargainnier 'Introduction', 6–8.
5 Kerstin Bergman, *Swedish Crime Fiction*, 111–16.
6 Kerstin Bergman, *Swedish Crime Fiction*, 157; Karsten Wind Meyhoff, *Forbrydelsens elementer: Kriminallitteraturens historie fra Poe til Ellroy* (Copenhagen: Informations Forlag, 2009), 373–5.
7 'Deckarkatalogen', *Svenska Deckarakademin*, n.d. Available online: http://deckarakademin.org/hem/deckarkatalogen-3/ (accessed 15 June 2020).
8 Kerstin Bergman, 'From National Authority to Urban Underbelly: Negotiations of Power in Stockholm Crime Fiction', in *Capital Crimes: Crime Fiction in the City*, eds Lucy Andrew and Catherine Phelps (Cardiff: University of Wales Press, 2013), 65–84, 76.
9 Ingrid Carlberg, 'Min nya bok är mörkare', *Dagens Nyheter*, 27 April 2008.
10 Cf. Joel Åhlén-Nyström, 'Alla har rätt till ett försvar', *The Scholar*, 30 November 2015.
11 Ibid.
12 Ibid.
13 Cf. John Scaggs, *Crime Fiction* (London/New York: Routledge, 2005), 59–64.
14 George N. Dove, *The Police Procedural* (Bowling Green, OH: Bowling Green University Popular Press, 1982), 15.
15 Kerstin Bergman, *Swedish Crime Fiction*, 36.
16 Cf. John Scaggs, 62–3.
17 George N. Dove and Earl F. Bargainnier, 'Introduction', 4.
18 John Scaggs, 64.
19 George N. Dove and Earl F. Bargainnier, 'Introduction', 4.
20 Beginning with the fifth novel in the series, *Falco* (2018), Kallentoft has changed writing partner and is now continuing the series with Anna Karolina as co-author instead of Markus Lutteman.
21 Martin Priestman, *Crime Fiction: From Poe to the Present* (Plymouth: Northcote House, 1998), 43.
22 John Scaggs, 59–61.
23 Kerstin Bergman, 'From National Authority', 71.
24 Kerstin Bergman, *Swedish Crime Fiction*, 115–16.
25 Kerstin Bergman, 'From National Authority', 76.
26 John Scaggs, 57.
27 Ibid.
28 Cf. Kerstin Bergman, *Swedish Crime Fiction*, 44–6.

Chapter 15

'SAFE LITTLE NORWAY': NORWEGIAN NOIR AND THE ROOTS OF SUBVERSIVE SOCIO-POLITICAL COMMENTARY

Nina Muždeka

Introduction: Generic qualms of Nordic and Norwegian noir

Although audiences, publishers and academics in general agree that Nordic noir exists as a separate generic group, defining its generic traits is significantly more difficult. Agnes Broomé considers the corpus of Nordic noir 'too textually diverse to be considered a genre in the traditional sense', yet maintains that it still constitutes 'a functioning and distinct unit'.[1] Writing about Scandinavian noir on television, Glen Creeber focuses on similar genre-defining elements, emphasizing 'bleak naturalism, disconsolate locations, and morose detectives' while simultaneously not excluding its links to 'a tradition of stark social realism'.[2] Translated to Tzvetan Todorov's typology of detective fiction, based not only on the form, but on the themes and styles as well as on the perceived differences in the narrative types, Nordic noir crosses the boundaries of traditional detective genre sub-categorization. It differs from these more traditional versions of the genre – *roman à énigme* (or *roman policier classique*, whodunnit), *roman noir* (or the thriller) and *roman à suspense* (or, *roman à victimes*, the suspense novel) – in that it explores, much more consistently and rigorously, a specific, geographically circumscribed, historical and cultural climate.[3] This climate is characterized, in particular, by some of the premises shared by Scandinavian welfare states, that is, their 'assumptions about ethnic, social, and cultural homogeneity'.[4] Against these assumptions of homogeneity, then, Nordic noir raises questions of Otherness and identity, and attempts to unmask forms and degrees of social injustice – that is, continuing patterns and practices of exclusion. The attempt at generic categorization is somewhat facilitated by the 1970s addition to Todorov's initial classification. This addition, the sub-genre of neo-detective or *néo-polar* novel, 'offered an invigorated critique of social corruption' and a new cast of characters seen as appropriate for social, criminal and judicial milieu of the times.[5] In the choice of protagonists and their identity formation, the chronotope of the quest, the crime that conditions this quest and the resulting socio-political commentary, Nordic noir exhibits significant traits of the latter category. In my analysis of Norwegian noir – as a specific regional variant of Nordic noir – I argue that, as a generic marker, ideological positioning is founded, and played out on the basis of identity construction and the position of Otherness, both on individual and collective levels. This process in turn opens space for the investigation of the wider social, cultural and political reality of Norwegian society through the range of topics that suit the authors' socio-political agenda.

Despite obvious geographical closeness and similarities between the underlying social structure of Scandinavian states, Forshaw maintains that the 'individual identities of Nordic countries are remarkably pronounced'.[6] It is equally easy to distinguish between individual authors of Norwegian noir on account of their topics, the range of socio-political issues they tackle and the setting they choose for such endeavours. Jo Nesbø, for example, portrays Oslo's criminal environment, the drug trade milieu and deprived city-dwellers' lifestyles, with sporadic excursions to exotic places such as Australia or Thailand, which still 'reflect Norwegian society'.[7] Karin Fossum sets her mysteries in the Norwegian countryside, eerily juxtaposing the austerity and the serenity of the landscape with the hidden deviance of criminal minds. Anne Holt emphasizes the position of an outsider in urban Oslo. Her strong socio-political commentary is part of a wider personal and professional framework of social engagement, also exhibited in her other professions – that of a lawyer and one-time Minister of Justice for Norway.[8] Thomas Enger's novels cannot be classified as police procedurals since his Oslo-based protagonist is not a professional police detective, but a renegade journalist. Jørn Lier Horst uses his real-life professional experience as a senior investigating officer in the Norwegian police force to convincingly write about police procedures, and not only the techniques but also the psychology of solving crimes. His approach can be contrasted to that of Jo Nesbø, who readily 'eschews the tradition of real crime police procedurals' in order to take his books 'quite far away from the realism of modern Scandinavian crime fiction'.[9] Horst's novels take place in the Larvik-Stavern area of Norway where harsh weather conditions and the small-city setting not only provide a vivid backdrop, but also direct the police procedures. What all these authors have in common, however, is the subtext of existential issues, reactions to major social changes, and the determinants of criminal, political and social justice.

Characters: Positioning through identity, otherness and liminality

Harry Hole.
The lone wolf, the drunk, the department's enfant terrible
and [...] the best detective on the sixth floor.

Jo Nesbø, *The Devil's Star*

Identity creation in Norwegian noir relates to viewpoints, perceptions and reasoning of the participants in the investigation process, as well as the use of stereotypes in the presentation of hybrid societies and their inhabitants. Because of the inferred polarization between 'self' and 'Other', and the fact that identity is constructed at the watershed between 'familiar' and 'foreign', it has to be explored not as an inherent quality, but as a construct. This construct is highly dependent on the society's attitude towards diversifying concepts such as ethnicity, culture, gender and nation, coupled with how they are represented. The way society responds to these concepts, however, determines not only the issues of identity and Otherness, but also denotes social values and norms. Construction and representation of identity, Otherness and liminality in Norwegian noir, thus, indicate the authors' vantage point in examining sociopolitical issues and contributes to their ideological positioning. Although clearly 'not all heroes of Scandinavian crime fiction fit the stereotypical description of depressed, lonely, middle-aged men with substance abuse problems', Norwegian noir provides the range of characters consistent with the *néo-polar* novel's typical protagonist description: 'broke, marginal, marginalized, unemployed, rejected by society, outraged, etc'.[10] Jo Nesbø's Harry Hole, for example, almost perfectly fits the bill. He is an obsessive yet vulnerable alcoholic and chain-smoker who 'does not have much experience of being happy'.[11] Both his professional and private life abound with demons he needs to confront, and both aspects of his life can be marked as dysfunctional – the first because of his tendency to defy authority and break the rules, the second because of his troubled relationship with Rakel. In Hole's life, with its intermittent episodes of drunken stupor, the only emotional constant is found in his relationship with his mentally challenged sister, Sis. Similarly estranged is Thomas Enger's journalist-investigator Henning Juul, deeply troubled by a personal tragedy, as a consequence of which he has been feeling 'only rage, self-loathing and self-pity'.[12] Juul lives the life of an urban recluse in the utmost self-imposed austerity, in a flat with 'a single mattress, a fridge and somewhere to sit down when the darkness creeps in'.[13] He is no hero – instead, he is haunted by the impression that he 'is taking part in a play where he has been cast as The Victim, the poor soul everyone has to take care of, help back on his feet'.[14]

Both protagonists testify to the changed locus of diversity in Nordic and Norwegian noir. Although the criminal in crime fiction was traditionally seen, in itself, as an Other – the Otherness being imposed on him by his criminality – there are significant differences in the way this Otherness is literalized in different historical periods.[15] Whereas, in the nineteenth century there was a tendency to make Otherness visible through physical traits, in the twentieth century, various national literatures used the concepts of ethnicity, race, culture or nation to mark off the villain as the Other – the choice of the villain's social group depending on the current political and historical circumstances.[16] International crime fiction saw a gradual shifting of the position of Other to other participants in the investigation process. Thus, it has become somewhat common in late twentieth-century crime fiction to treat the figure of the detective as 'the ideal locus in which to foreground and explore difference'.[17] In other words, as a perfect vehicle for exhibiting and familiarizing various aspects of national, cultural, racial, ethnic, sexual or any other Otherness, a detective was also burdened with a liminal, though presumably objective, position of someone who is at the same time an insider and an outsider. This is true for both Nesbø's Hole and Enger's Juul: although Hole is a member of the police force and Juul is a part of a relentless journalistic machine, they do not actually belong in mainstream society. Furthermore, both protagonists strive to emphasize the outsider's position through conflicts with their colleagues and superiors and refusing to comply and conform.

Anne Holt's police inspector Hanne Wilhelmsen is seen by the author as the typical protagonist of Scandinavian crime writing: 'a very dysfunctional person', 'a damaged, psychologically challenged person with a very sharp instinct for police work'.[18] Contrary to the male protagonists of Nesbø's and Enger's fiction, she is additionally marked by her homosexual orientation. As is gradually revealed through the series of novels, although Hanne Wilhelmsen is marginalized and in conflict with her colleagues, it is not because of her lesbianism, but because of her long-standing expectation that, if revealed, her lesbianism will oust her. As Forshaw finds, the very fact that Hanne's lesbianism is 'presented straightforwardly' and not necessarily as 'the defining facet of her persona' holds the subversive potential.[19] Obviously, sexual orientation is not the only criterion to set female protagonists apart as the Other – in a traditionally conceived Western white patriarchal society, they are already made Other through their gender.

The outsider's perspective in Holt's crime fiction does not end with the character of Hanne. Holt's Johanne Vic and Adam Stubø series features an unlikely pair of investigators who end up getting married and starting a family. While Stubø is a police detective, Inger Johanne's profession as a researcher and lecturer at the Institute of Criminology provides her with an outsider position and a fresh, eccentric viewpoint in solving crimes. In Holt's words, the Vik and Stubø books came out of her wish to write about 'a functional family', which she sees as something new in Scandinavian crime writing, precisely because of the traditional representation of protagonists as dysfunctional.[20] She wanted to create a tension between the crime-filled, scary world outside, and the 'cocoon of closeness and love and functionality'.[21]

The family plays an important role in the construction of identity, either through a character's acceptance of the imposed collective identity, or through their rejection of it. In the Hanne Wilhelmsen series, the protagonist's break from her 'neurotic, snobbish, prejudiced, dry-as-dust academic, pseudo-Christian and utterly Norwegian family' brought her 'a resigned, sorrowful certainty that [she] had done something right', but also 'the most dearly bought liberty'.[22] Holt's detective inspector Silje Sørensen also abandons her family's criteria of what acceptable life choices are. Her wealthy family, her upper-class background and her excellent (and expensive) education received in boarding schools in Switzerland and England distinguish her as an outsider in the police department. For her family – and most notably for her mother – a career in the public sector means that she has thrown away her future. Standing out in both worlds, Silje is ascribed a liminal position and ultimately freedom from pre-set social conventions.

The position of the Other is frequently literalized on the physical level and manifested through one or several distinguishing physical traits. While in nineteenth-century detective fiction this was a feature exclusively reserved for villains as a physical label of their criminality, in contemporary Norwegian noir this mechanism applies to investigators and serves to set them apart as the Other. A terrible fire that caught Henning Juul's apartment left him scarred with burn marks – in addition to scarring him for life on a psychological and emotional level. Juul was, however, a castaway even before the accident: he wasn't accepted to the police academy because he 'suffered from every allergy known to man, and had had asthma as a child'.[23] Hanne Wilhelmsen is similarly marked both on the inside and on the outside. In the novel *1222* (2007, *1222*, 2010), for example, in which Hanne finds herself snowed in in a mountain hotel with other rescued passengers from a derailed Oslo–Bergen train, the protagonist's difficult character is markedly presented, but that is not the only feature that sets her apart. Following the shooting that happened five years prior to the events in the novel, Hanne is now in a wheelchair, paralyzed from the waist down. She finds this to be a complex condition: although it symbolizes her entrapment, and obviously adds to her marginalization by physically signifying her Otherness, it also facilitates her utterly voluntary estrangement from other characters through providing a ready – although not truthful – excuse for her distance from others:

> The most important thing about the wheelchair is that it creates distance. Not physically, of course; as I said I am constantly stared at and bombarded with offers of help. I strive more for a kind of mental distance. The chair makes me different. It defines me as something completely different from all the rest, and it is not uncommon for people to assume that I am stupid. Or deaf. People talk over my head, quite literally, and if I simply lean back and close my eyes, it's as if I don't exist.[24]

Furthermore, her disability opens up new perspectives on life, both in a literal and symbolic sense. Observing the world from a different height, Hanne now sees 'things that others miss' but also misses 'some elements that others see' – suggestively, her viewpoint is in many ways similar to that of a child.[25] This change of perspective, however, is twofold as it includes Hanne both as an active and a passive participant: what changed is not only how she sees the world, but also how the world sees her. Hanne is deeply aware of this shift:

'It was as if my stationary sojourn in a room where everyone else was simply coming and going made me so different that I had been accorded the status of oracle; an omniscient authority, a position to which I had never asked to be elevated'.[26]

Karin Fossum expressed Chief Inspector Konrad Sejer's outsider identity through both his background and his physical appearance. Sejer is smart and sharp, thorough, patient, dependable and persistent, with 'a soft spot for little children and old ladies'.[27] Sejer's appearance is remarkable – he possesses 'a natural authority that seemed to come from within, speaking in an impressively deep voice from a height of nearly two metres'.[28] Born and raised in Denmark, he is additionally marked as the Other through a personal tragedy that introduced a 'weak spot' into his 'private universe': 'He had never recovered from his grief at his loss of Elise; it had grown bigger and bigger and then imploded to form a black hole that sucked him in every once in a while'.[29] Sejer's intimate psychological struggles are literalized through his skin condition, psoriasis: these 'patches of scaly skin' lurking 'under his newly ironed shirt' can be seen as symbolizing the battle between the inner and the outer, the hidden and the revealed, the private and public face of a character. Sejer, however, is not a dysfunctional character, and neither is Horst's Chief Inspector William Wisting, also a widower living in a small town, methodical in his work, the psychological aspects of which he cherishes. Both of these characters – along with the aforementioned Inger Johanne in Holt's Vik and Stubø novels – testify to the fact that in Norwegian noir Otherness does not necessarily go hand in hand with dysfunctionality and marginalization.

In addition to the main protagonists of Norwegian noir, other characters – suspects, victims, witnesses, police aides – appear as loci of diversity, challenging assumptions and prejudices. In Enger's novels, for example, Juul's editor Kåre has Tourette's syndrome, yet manages to run a news desk and have a social life. The example of Harry Hole's sister is also significant, since she possesses an almost uncanny ability to pinpoint the simple truth, often elusive in the protagonist's chaotic life. In Fossum's *Den som frykter ulven*, (1997, *He Who Fears the Wolf*, 2003) the focus of Sejer's attention at one point is a group of boys living in a juvenile centre, in which each boy is 'struggling for his own pathetic position in this tiny society of outsiders'.[30] The level of inclusion of such characters in the community varies significantly, depending on the authors' chosen target for criticism. For some of the characters (e.g. Enger's Kåre), some level of mental dysfunctionality does not necessarily entail social dysfunctionality and simply serves to emphasize their Otherness on the basis of their deviance from the perceived standards of 'neuro-normalcy'.[31] For others, on the other hand, the very challenges they are facing in terms of social inclusion are elements used by the author to criticize the malfunctioning of diverse social welfare institutions, as will be discussed in the following section.

Norwegian national identity and socio-political issues

> Perhaps he'll sell the café and move away.
> And it'll become a Chinese takeout.
>
> Karin Fossum, *The Indian Bride*

The construction of identity and parameters of Otherness on an individual level are mirrored on the collective level, opening space for the authors to tackle their chosen range of socio-political topics. Many Norwegian noir authors feel that the size of the country functions as a determining factor for a significant number of social- and criminal-related issues, given that it conditions a specific social milieu. For perpetrators and alleged perpetrators, Norway is 'a country so small that neither he [the alleged perpetrator] nor anyone else would be allowed to forget what had happened'.[32] Such proximity creates a specific climate of closeness: 'Norway is such a small country that everyone is, at most, two acquaintances from knowing everyone else'.[33] In a more optimistic depiction of Norwegian society, corruption 'is more or less unthinkable' in Norway because they 'have no tradition of it' – and 'corruption requires a kind of national tradition!'[34] Paradoxically perhaps, it is frequently tradition and the past that are questioned and problematized in Norwegian noir – most notably, Norway's role in the Second World War and its aftermath. Jo Nesbø's *Rødstrupe* (2000, *The Redbreast*, 2006) tackles Norway's problematic involvement with the Nazis in the past, but also the awakening of national-socialist ideas in contemporary Norwegian society.[35] Similarly, Horst writes about Norway as a safe haven for fugitives – among others, those 'who have committed genocide and other war crimes'.[36] As a result, 'More than 25,000 people in the country were not recorded in any registers, and preferred to remain under the radar'.[37] Through such a portrayal, Norway emerges not as an ordered and transparent society, but quite the opposite – as a secretive society in which the lack of transparency created the sub-class of people living outside the system and its rules. Horst traces contradictory images of a society simultaneously open to immigrants and diversity, but also biased when it comes to its Viking history and the present-day interpretation of that:

> At one time, you Norwegians were poor as well. I think you have forgotten that, but you are so proud of your Vikings that you build museums for them. They were a hundred times worse than the Lithuanian people. They plundered, raped and killed, but now everyone thinks of them as heroes.[38]

Financial aspects feature prominently in the construction of the national identity – specifically with reference to the country's oil wealth – but they also explain Norway's changing demographic structure. The promise of abundance attracts immigrants and Norway is seen as having followed the general

Western trend of becoming an increasingly multicultural and multinational country. Norwegian national identity is juxtaposed with that of immigrants and constructed along the demarcation line between 'us' and 'them'. Similarly, Norway is compared to the immigrants' countries of origin to emphasize its safety and democracy, but also to underline the perceived differences between the first world and the third, or the West and the Global South: 'And if there's one thing I have difficulty in grasping, it's the idea of hatred against groups in a society like Norway. In Gaza, yes. In Kabul, yes. But here? In safe, social democratic Norway?'[39] Immigrants flood to Norway because 'life in Norway was good', because 'Norway's a much better country' than the one they left behind.[40] Conversely, Norway's appeal surpasses the basic level of securing a meagre existence, of acquiring 'food and a job'; it is a country defined by the perceived freedom it grants its citizens, who are 'able to walk in the street without having to show ID papers', and who can 'say what they want and write what they want'.[41] Yet for some of them this dream will backfire. Fossum's *Den onde viljen* (2008, *Bad Intentions*, 2010) and *Elskede Poona* (2000, *The Indian Bride*, 2007) feature, for example, two women who left their home countries (Vietnam and India) to seek this better, Norwegian life. Instead of finding it, one of them became a minority in another man's land, marginalized, different and ultimately bereft through the loss of her greatest treasure – her son.[42] In her experience, Norway proved to be a country in which a Vietnamese kid is 'assigned the role of mascot' at a party where, among the Norwegian youth, he resembles 'a happy little goblin'.[43] In *The Indian Bride* Fossum depicts how 'the Norwegian state has failed to protect women's rights' and the rights of Poona, who found death instead of the safety of a happy marriage.[44] The trust that 'the Norwegian landscape, with its yellow fields' must have instilled in her, the inhabitant of a big city with twelve million people, proved to be fatally deceptive.[45] Her murder is read not only as an example of gendered abuse in a supposedly multicultural, tolerant and affluent society, but also, as in the case of the Vietnamese boy, as an instance of racialized violence. The same kind of violence is featured in the opening of Nesbø's *The Redbreast*, where a neo-Nazi and Norse patriot stands trial for having severely beaten a Vietnamese shop-owner.

Norwegian identity is constructed through these protagonists' emotional profile as well. While Enger sees himself as 'a product of [his] environment', this also applies to his 'burned' protagonist Juul.[46] When defining Juul as 'an introverted man, a thinker, with a pronounced sense of responsibility and justice', Enger also defines these traits as 'quintessentially Norwegian'.[47] Karin Fossum sees Norwegians as 'a little shy, perhaps, and very proud, but friendly'.[48] Horst emphasizes the reticence of Norwegians, who 'keep their doors closed and their curtains drawn. They hide their feelings and keep their secrets'.[49] Holt, however, criticizes her compatriots as 'an ungrateful lot' who still 'reserve the right to stand up for all women, children, foetuses and everything else that forms part of "Norwegian values"'.[50] Yet, when faced with the natural disaster of being snowed in and cut off from civilization, they turn into 'a representative group of Norwegians', 'an almost entirely white collection of individuals', the microcosm of society:

> But otherwise we had most elements. Self-confident young people in horrendously expensive clothes who didn't exchange a single word with dross like Adrian and his miserable girlfriend. Stressed businessmen with top-of-the-range laptops, desperately trying to get an internet connection. Screaming kids and middle-aged women. A handball team of fourteen-year-old girls were completely incapable of grasping the point of showing some consideration for others.[51]

Immigrant and foreign identity in Norwegian society is exposed as having been built on stereotypes and prejudices. In Horst's *Vinterstengt* (2011, *Closed for Winter*, 2013), for example, Lithuanians are seen as itinerant criminals, whereas the role of imported workforce is reserved for Poles in Holt's *1222* and *Det som er mitt* (2001, *What is Mine*, 2006).[52] In *1222*, another outcast character, Dr Streng, explains why Norwegians are feeling threatened by immigrants and not, for example, by other 'different' groups such as little people (to which he belongs). Whereas persons of restricted growth attract only silent curiosity and sometimes disgust, they are never met with fear or hostility because 'there aren't enough of us to make anyone nervous'.[53] Immigrants with 'a little extra skin pigment, different headgear and a different name for God', however, are becoming numerous in Norwegian society in which fear 'is often a question of quantity'.[54] Moreover, there are so many of them that, for example, the Kurds are perceived as a 'new underclass'.[55] This sentiment is also present in Enger's *Burned*: 'What do you think Oslo will look like in thirty or forty years? We'll probably all be Muslims, indoctrinated and well behaved'.[56] Although Norway is traditionally perceived as a democratic and tolerant society, the trend of intolerance towards immigrants and all things foreign is seen as growing, ranging from a plain lack of political correctness and lack of sympathy ('We've some immigrants here, or refugees, or whatever they call themselves. It's not easy for me to tell the difference'.[57]), to the outright display of prejudice and hostility ('"A stoning in Norway?" He shakes his head. "I bet it's those bloody immigrants. [...] There are far too many of them here."'[58]). The demographic fluctuations depicted leave people feeling vulnerable as the established definitions of nationhood and citizenship no longer apply. Social order becomes unstable and the whole society fragile, as the loss of homogeneity is seen as a threat to the notion of uncompromised Norwegian identity.

Alongside national identity, a more universal human identity is also threatened. The aforementioned financial security does not correlate to peace of mind, and this is one of the strands of criticism found in Norwegian noir. Enger's Henning Juul, although living in 'one of the richest countries in the world [...], is not at ease'.[59] Horst's protagonist similarly asks: 'What good does it do us to have all the riches in the world if we no longer bother about one another? We are spiritually backward in this country. Empty shells only concerned with satisfying our own needs'.[60] A link to the angst of living in a modern world, riddled with alienation and estrangement, is evident here. In Horst's *Hulemannen* (2013, *The Caveman*, 2015), the fact that it took people four months to discover – by chance – that one of their neighbours passed away, is seen as a blatant example of how lonely and forgotten people can become in contemporary society. Holt also notices that modern life is taking its toll on people who no longer have time for one another, and feel that they cannot afford to take care of their fellow human beings. Common human courtesy is being markedly replaced by consumerist values, and shopping for unnecessary items emerges as a solace in moments of crisis: 'The kiosk [...] was packed with people who didn't really know what they wanted. The scenario struck me as a confused symbol of western culture: we had all looked death in the eye, and immediately sought consolation in the quest for something to buy'.[61] The Norwegian state and the Norwegian people have become morally problematic on more than one level. As Holt notes, Norway went 'to rack and ruin' with 'the theft of public resources as an everyday occurrence', and greed no longer makes people shudder, but evokes 'a nod of approval' instead.[62] Authorities cook up cover stories in order to hide their misdeeds and deceive the public, undermining the trust in state and public institutions, as evidenced in both Holt's and Nesbø's novels. Particularly sharp criticism is directed towards social welfare services, which should protect those who are most vulnerable – children. Fossum's *Se deg ikke tilbake!* (1996, *Don't Look Back!*, 2002) and Holt's *Det som aldri skjer* (2004, *What Never Happens*, 2008) tackle the coldness and dysfunctionality of these institutions which fail to provide shelter to those who need it most.[63] In these clever vignettes of often traumatized childhood, both authors use marginalized individuals, devoid of the capacity to fend for themselves, to expose a range of social problems that threaten to grow into veritable social pathologies.

Everything is connected: Evil, crime and social responsibility

> You've slogged away year in, year out
> to keep the streets of Oslo moderately safe
> in a country which protects its criminals better
> than it does its own civil servants.
>
> Jo Nesbø, The Devil's Star

As Todorov posits, 'the contemporary thriller has been constituted not around a method of presentation but around the milieu represented; its constitutive character is in its themes'.[64] Ever since Sjöwall and Wahlöö's Martin Beck series, the Swedish branch of Nordic noir has readily followed the tradition of political engagement and strong social commentary given alongside the basic crime investigation plot in the form of police procedurals. This holds true for other regional variants of Nordic noir as well. In Norwegian noir, hence, the investigation of socio-political themes always starts with a criminal act as a disruption of the established order. Writing about noir fiction in general, Cowart found that, 'Every detective story concerns an encounter with vice, inherent or otherwise. The more inherent the vice, the more noir the fiction'.[65] However, what is specific for Nordic noir – and subsequently Norwegian noir – is the fact that vice is present both in the conspiracy and plotting at the highest levels of society and the state, and in actual graphic representations of it, in the form of murders and violence, and that the narrative depicting this vice acts as a vehicle for authors' socio-political commentary. This strategy allows for a simultaneous investigation into vice on both levels: while professional and amateur detectives uncover the details of the murder(s) in question, they also reveal unlawful and unethical behaviour on a higher, more encompassing and more influential level. By resolving the conundrum of the actual initial crime at a micro level of their investigation, the detectives also expose the perpetrators of crimes that have significantly greater consequences for the society and state as a whole. The process of solving the crime thus coincides with the process of rectifying social wrongs and re-establishing the social order, at least for the time being. Herein lies the authors' social – and often political – engagement, for the textual world clearly and poignantly corresponds to the extra-textual one. Sjöwall and Wahlöö 'denounced their Swedish welfare state government as too capitalistic and thus failing to provide an adequate state-supported environment' for its citizens'.[66] Norwegian noir shows that the threatened breakdown of a well-organized and dependable social welfare state and its egalitarian democracy, spawned at the cross-section of the most favourable features of socialism and capitalism, further disrupts the safety and ease of society. By aiming to protect the marginalized and the poor, the Scandinavian welfare-state model is marked by the 'comprehensiveness of social security systems, institutionalized universal social rights, a high level of public support, and a high level of equality'.[67] With the advent of globalization in contemporary society, however, this model is tested.

Anne Holt places her police procedurals in a highly globalized society with an eye on the wider transnational context. Her rendering of crime in Norwegian society reveals that gruesome murders, especially those of children, are inconceivable, while killings are mostly manslaughter: 'The percentage of murderers who reoffend is minimal. Most killings are the result of an ongoing family conflict, terrible jealousy or … pure accident. A drunken brawl'.[68] While one of her characters jokingly states that the most common offence Norwegians are guilty of is 'not notifying the authorities of our change of address', crime fighting still changes due to the financial and managerial measures that lead to fewer staff and the lack of resources.[69] People are feeling less and less safe as the police are losing credibility and trustworthiness:

More and more frequently the papers were running stories about victims of violent crime who had been unable to report the offence because their local police station wasn't manned, rural stations that were closed at weekends, and victims of crime who had to wait several days for the police to turn up and look for any clues. If they turned up at all, that is.[70]

Additionally, the change in demographics leads to a new profile of criminal offences, and hate crimes directed against minority groups, depicted in Holt's *Pengemannen* (2009, *Fear Not*, 2011), are on the rise.

Horst's analysis of exposure to crime in Norway mirrors that of Anne Holt, emphasizing low risk and a relationship between the victim and the perpetrator. Horst also notices the correlation between the welfare state and the rise in crime, however, as well as the link to current international geopolitical events and the influx in imported crime following the Schengen agreement:

After Wisting embarked on his career in the police, the Norwegian economy had grown enormously. With the development of the welfare state, there were fewer poor people in Norway but, at the same time, crime had increased dramatically. The causes of criminality were considerably more complex, with elements other than poverty and need. However, the crime statistics in Norway would certainly look very different if the economy of Eastern Europe showed improvement.[71]

Horst criticizes the complex legal framework that constrains an investigation, and the stricter formal demands on the police force, coupled with the decrease in staff numbers and budget cuts. Similarly to Holt, he investigates society's attitude towards the police, focusing on the public's reluctance to co-operate with them. The roots are, again, found in societal factors, primarily in the public's fear of getting involved, and in the growing distance between fellow citizens. Both Horst and Fossum, through their investigators, emphasize the importance of the nation's image of the police, best evidenced by the police force's co-operation with, and responsibility towards, the press: 'First, the press conference. It robbed them of precious time, but they wanted to look the Norwegian people in the eye and say: "We will take care of this."'[72]

The interest of Norwegian noir authors in the phenomenon of evil does not, however, end with determining the societal factors that condition and trigger it. Their approach transcends the boundaries of their chosen genre niche and resembles non-crime fiction authors – writing in the tradition of William Golding – who investigated the phenomenology of evil as an inherent component of human nature, but also explored its links to the imposed social structures and institutional mechanisms used to control it. Although Karin Fossum identifies the social circumstances that surround the crimes depicted in her novels, central to her investigation of crime is the evil that cannot be divorced from human nature. Even in her Norwegian countryside, 'this tiny spot, a remote corner of the world, peopled by farmers and callous teenagers', evil lurks in the form of 'disdainful people [living] in every single house'.[73] The same is true for Horst's countryside surrounding Oslo, where crime is on the march, more complex and organized than ever before. Nesbø also professes to be obsessed with the question of evil, using the crime genre to ask whether evil exists and to question the nature of both evil and morality. Oscillating between ideas of innate morality and morality imposed through societal rules, he admits to having found no answer.[74] Still, tackling the issues of power struggles and corruption in the police force and heights of government, Nesbø has his finger on society's pulse on one hand, and, on the other, emphasizes the importance of having functioning and trustworthy social institutions in order to (attempt to) quell the evil that is evidently a part of human nature.

While poor working conditions, inadequate staffing and pension cuts represent yet another reflection of the welfare state's breakdown, affecting the police force from the outside, the breakdown – as Enger shows – comes from within as well. It takes the form of disillusionment among young police officers, who were initially bursting with enthusiasm and 'nurturing a vision of making a difference to society, one villain at a time', only to end up 'brought down to earth'.[75] Tragically, this disillusionment also reaches beyond the confines of the police force. In the words of a psychiatrist in Karin Fossum's *He Who Fears the Wolf*, 'You can't be an enlightened, intelligent, involved human being on this earth without at the same time being full of despair. It's just not possible'.[76] *Weltschmerz* aside, this attitude shows the weakening trust in the institutions of the welfare state in the minds and hearts of those who should uphold it – precisely because they are the ones in direct touch with said human nature. Yet, this also perhaps signals their unconscious awareness of the need to try and find new methods to maintain social order, and to keep the ongoing battle with evil alive.

In contemporary analysis, crime fiction is increasingly seen as a suitable arena for exploring and confronting 'some of the tensions of globalized living' in an increasingly multicultural society.[77] As cultural expression, crime fiction 'forms a microcosm of broader social reality through which readers can sharpen their understanding of society'.[78] Norwegian noir exhibits yet another dimension, though. Its world is the one in which everything is connected and in which individual actions, both criminal and otherwise, have irreparable consequences for the community as a whole.[79] Wisting's belief testifies to this: 'Life was best when he felt he was doing something important, when he could follow the interplay of thoughts and actions and knew his efforts were going to make a difference. It fed his belief that his work could help create a better world'.[80] This approach explains the almost philosophical approaches to solving crime taken by Norwegian noir investigators, who are correct to see the wider societal consequences behind individual criminal acts.

Conclusion

> 'What about integration, multiculturalism and all that?'
> 'Save it for the speeches'.
>
> Jørn Lier Horst, *Closed for Winter*

Writing about the social and political seriousness of noir, Wanner concludes that it is 'closely allied to the creation of protagonists marked by their alienation from conventional society – victims who suffer from powerlessness, immobilizing uncertainty, isolation; transgressors who defy a repressive, conformist society'.[81] Not all of the protagonists in Norwegian noir are dysfunctional, yet they are all painfully aware of the zeitgeist and the socio-economic and geopolitical factors influencing their private and professional lives. Constructs of individual and collective identity, serving as a generic marker, reveal a range of topics highly relevant for Norway as a hybridized society. Homogeneity is replaced by differences and inequalities at every step – different financial circumstances, native languages, religious and cultural practices and skin tone – which allows the authors to explore the problems of xenophobia and racism. Murder as a disruption of order symbolizes a much more encompassing and widespread disruption in the community, also signalled by the inclusion of the Other. The police force, who should protect the community and solve the crimes, appear to be hindered by their poor treatment at the hands of the state, which is exemplified by funding cuts, so that the pressure of complex bureaucratic procedures take valuable time away from police work, while the legal system is also deficient. Socio-political commentary given in the frequently subversive subtext unmasks various forms of social and political injustices, enabling Norwegian noir authors 'to settle accounts with *la raison d'état* (interests of the state) and its narratives,' through the process of recovering clues 'that the official narrative has chosen to ignore'.[82] Just like *néo-polar*, which 'paved the way for the *roman noir* to be considered as a significant cultural phenomenon', Norwegian noir appeals to 'an intellectually discerning and politically active audience'.[83]

The construction of Norwegian noir characters, marked off as the Other and assigned a liminal position through their deviance from established norms and expectations, both in rural and urban settings, proves to be important not only for the investigation of fictional crimes but, more importantly, for the current social and political issues that permeate the extratextual world as well. The authors of Norwegian noir peel off the façade of a deceptively idyllic, affluent, equality based and homogenous Norwegian society, to reveal the stark reality of a multinational, though often claustrophobic, society ridden by much of the same illnesses as the rest of the globalized world, with a highly problematized basis for the construction of national identity. With the stable, utopian welfare state continually dissolving right before the eyes of the protagonists and readers alike, the authors of Norwegian noir delve deeper into human nature to establish the true origin of evil. Ultimately, while Norwegian noir confirms the premise that the detective novel can be read as a social one, it also drives home the fact that it can – and indeed, should – be read as a study of the phenomenology of evil and the possibilities of containing that evil through functioning social institutions.

Notes

1. Agnes Broomé, 'The Exotic North, or How Marketing Created the Genre of Scandinavian Crime' in *True North: Literary Translation in the Nordic Countries*, ed. B.J. Epstein (Newcastle: Cambridge Scholars Publishing, 2014), 272.
2. Glen Creeber, 'Killing us Softly: Investigating the Aesthetics, Philosophy and Influence of *Nordic Noir* Television', *Journal of Popular Television* 3, no. 1 (2015), 22.
3. Tzvetan Todorov, *The Poetics of Prose* (Ithaca: Cornell University Press, 1977), 42–52.
4. Andrew Nestingen and Paola Arvas, 'Others Knowing Others: Stieg Larsson's *Millennium* Trilogy and Peter Høeg's *Smilla's Sense of Snow*', in *The Foreign in International Crime Fiction: Transcultural Representations*, ed. J. Anderson, C. Miranda and B. Pezzotti (London: Continuum, 2012), 125. Although it would appear that Nordic noir emerged as a geographically specific sub-category of the detective fiction genre, delineating the exact geographical boundaries is more difficult. The concept of Nordic noir extends to other European – and perhaps even non-European – 'Nordic' zones (e.g. Shetland, a zone historically and culturally linked much more closely to Scandinavia than to the British – or indeed Scottish – mainlands). This suggests that parameters other than strictly geographical ones are relevant when defining the scope of Nordic noir.
5. Jason Herbeck, 'Detective Narrative Typology: Going Undercover in the French Caribbean' in *Detective Fiction in a Postcolonial and Transnational World*, ed. Nels Pearson and Marc Singer (Farnham: Ashgate, 2009), 66.
6. Barry Forshaw, 'New Stars of Nordic Noir: Norway's Authors Discuss their Country's Crime Wave'. *The Independent*, 8 July 2011. Available online at: www.independent.co.uk/arts-entertainment/books/features/new-stars-of-nordic-noir-norways-authors-discuss-their-countrys-crime-wave-2308559.html (accessed 21 April 2020).
7. Jordan Foster, 'Norwegian Noir', *Publishers Weekly* 257, no. 4 (25 January 2010), 94.
8. Although her term as Minister of Justice was short-lived (from 1996 to 1997), Holt has always had an extremely influential public voice as an author, politician and as a general public figure. She also spent two years working for the Oslo police department.
9. 'Crime writer Nesbø Faces up Evil in new Nordic Chiller', *The Sun Daily*, 16 November 2017. Available online: www.thesundaily.my/archive/crime-writer-nesbo-faces-evil-new-nordic-chiller-CUARCH503623 (accessed 22 February 2020).
10. Agnes Broomé, 'The Exotic North', 272; Jean-Pierre Deloux, 'Le Noir new-look', *Magazine litteraire*, 194 (April 1984). Quoted in Herbeck, 'Detective Narrative Typology', 66.
11. 'Crime writer Nesbø Faces up Evil in new Nordic Chiller'.
12. Thomas Enger, *Burned* (London: Faber and Faber, 2011), 36.
13. Ibid., 7.

14. Ibid., 15.
15. Heather Worthington, *Key Concepts in Crime Fiction* (Basingstoke: Palgrave Macmillan, 2011), 86.
16. Ibid., 74.
17. Ibid., 86.
18. 'Intervista a Anne Holt', *Giulio Einaudi editore*, 4 November 2009. Available online: www.youtube.com/watch?v=8SX7PLjTH-0 (accessed 22 February 2020).
19. Barry Forshaw, 'New Stars'.
20. 'Intervista a Anne Holt'.
21. Ibid.
22. Anne Holt, *1222* (New York: Scribner, 2012), 146.
23. Thomas Enger, *Burned*, 35.
24. Anne Holt, *1222*, 23.
25. Ibid., 157.
26. Ibid., 76.
27. Karin Fossum, *He Who Fears the Wolf* (London: Vintage, 2004), 67.
28. Ibid., 30.
29. Ibid., 34.
30. Ibid., 98
31. I have borrowed the term 'neuro-normalcy' from Jacob Stougaard-Nielsen, who uses it in his discussion of deviant female detectives in Scandinavian noir narratives. More in: Jacob Stougaard-Nielsen, 'Deviant Detectives in the Scandinavian Welfare State: *The Girl with the Dragon Tattoo* and *The Bridge*' in *Crime, Deviance and Popular Culture: International and Multidisciplinary Perspectives*, eds Dimitris Akrivos and Alexandros K. Antoniou (London: Palgrave Macmillan, 2019), 13–40.
32. Anne Holt, *What is Mine* (New York: Warner Books, 2006), 24.
33. Jo Nesbø, *The Snowman* (London: Harvill Secker, 2010), 36.
34. Anne Holt, *What is Mine*, 32.
35. The problematic past I am referring to means, in the words of Marek E. Jasinski, 'collaboration with Nazi Germany forces that invaded in April 1940 and occupied the country until 1945', as well as 'the issue of the approximately 140,000 foreign PoWs and forced labourers taken to Norway by Nazi Germany, and exploited not only by the Werhmacht, SS and Organization Todt, but also by many state-owned and private Norwegian companies'. More on this in: Marek E. Jasinski, 'Reinforced Concrete, Steel and Slaves: Archaeological Studies of Prisoners of World War II in Norway – The Case of Romsdal Peninsula', in *Prisoners of War*, eds Harold Mytum and Gilly Carr (London and New York: Springer, 2013), 145–68.
36. Jørn Lier Horst, *The Caveman* (Dingwall: Sandstone Press, 2015), 55.
37. Ibid., 105.
38. Jørn Lier Horst, *Closed for Winter* (Dingwall: Sandstone Press, 2013), 206.
39. Anne Holt, *Fear Not* (London: Corvus, 2011), 143.
40. Thomas Enger, *Burned*, 125; Karin Fossum, *Bad Intentions* (New York: Haughton Mifflin Harcourt, 2010), 200.
41. Karin Fossum, *Bad Intentions*, 200.
42. Karin Fossum's 2000 novel *Elskede Poona* was first translated into English in 2005 as *Calling Out for You*, and then in 2007 (American edition) as *The Indian Bride*. As I used the American edition for this chapter, I used this title as well.

43 Karin Fossum, *Bad Intentions*, 139.
44 Mitzi Brunsdale, *Encyclopedia of Nordic Crime Fiction: Works and Authors of Denmark, Finland, Iceland, Norway and Sweden Since 1967* (Jefferson: McFarland & Company, 2016), 267.
45 Karin Fossum, *The Indian Bride* (Orlando: Harcourt, 2007), 136.
46 Barry Forshaw, 'New Stars'.
47 Ibid.
48 Karin Fossum, *The Indian Bride*, 32.
49 Jørn Lier Horst, *The Caveman*, 117.
50 Anne Holt, *1222*, 29.
51 Ibid., 42.
52 Anne Holt's 2001 novel *Det som er mitt* was also translated into English in 2016 as *Punishment*.
53 Anne Holt, *1222*, 128.
54 Ibid., 129.
55 Ibid., 117.
56 Thomas Enger, *Burned*, 262.
57 Karin Fossum, *The Indian Bride*, 114.
58 Thomas Enger, *Burned*, 171.
59 Barry Forshaw, 'New Stars'.
60 Jørn Lier Horst, *The Caveman*, 177.
61 Anne Holt, *1222*, 122.
62 Ibid., 230.
63 Anne Holt's 2004 novel *Det som aldri skjer* was also translated into English in 2011 as *The Final Murder*.
64 Tzvetan Todorov, *Poetics of Prose*, 48.
65 David Cowart, *Thomas Pynchon and the Dark Passages of History* (Athens: The University of Georgia Press, 2012), 124.
66 Mitzi Brunsdale, *Encyclopedia*, 4.
67 Francis Sejersted, quoted in Steven Peacock, *Swedish Crime Fiction: Novel, Film, Television* (Manchester: Manchester University Press, 2014), 29.
68 Anne Holt, *What is Mine*, 15.
69 Ibid., 24.
70 Anne Holt, *Fear Not*, 37.
71 Jørn Lier Horst, *Closed for Winter*, 207.
72 Karin Fossum, *The Indian Bride*, 37.
73 Ibid., 30.
74 'Crime writer Nesbø'.
75 Thomas Enger, *Burned*, 75.
76 Karin Fossum, *He Who Fears the Wolf*, 118.
77 Jean Anderson et al., 'Introduction' in *The Foreign in International Crime Fiction: Transcultural Representations*, eds J. Anderson, C. Miranda, and B. Pezzotti (London: Continuum, 2012), 5.
78 Katrin Jakobsdóttir, 'Meaningless Icelanders: Icelandic Crime Fiction and Nationality' in *Scandinavian Crime Fiction*, eds A. Nestingen and P. Arvas (Cardiff: University of Wales Press. 2011), 47.
79 E.N. Redvall cites this as 'theory of interdependence'. See more in: Eva Novrup Redvall, *Writing and Producing Television Drama in Denmark* (Basingstoke: Palgrave Macmillan, 2013), 166.

80 Jørn Lier Horst, *Closed for Winter*, 105.
81 Len Wanner, *The Crime Interviews, Volume Two* (Glasgow: Blasted Heath, 2012), 126.
82 Josiane Peltier, 'Didier Daeninickx and Michel de Certeau: A Historiography of Affects' in *Detective Narratives in European Culture since 1945*, eds Anne Mullen and Emer O'Beirne (Amsterdam: Rodopi, 2000), 269.
83 Claire Gorrara, *The Roman Noir in Post-war French Culture: Dark Fictions* (Oxford: Oxford University Press, 2003), 77.

VAL MCDERMID ON NOIR IN THE NORTH

Interview by Lorna Hill

Scottish crime writer Val McDermid reflects on the notion of noir and nationality and the relationship between Nordic noir and Tartan noir. She consolidates her understanding of the genre, making the connections between noir and traditional histories and collective and cultural memory.

What does noir and nationality mean to you?

There is definitive connective tissue between so-called Tartan noir and what is coming out of the Nordic countries. I think part of that is cultural. Historically, there has always been quite strong connectivity between the Nordic countries and Scotland, particularly Norway. Parts of Scotland used to belong to Norway – so there has always been that cultural connectivity. Whenever Scottish football teams get anywhere they always end up playing the Faroe and the Iceland teams. There is something about the long dark nights and the oral traditions of both the Nordic countries and the Scots of storytelling around the fire in the winter. That was how stories were passed on before we wrote them down and put them into books. Those are things we have in common, so I imagine that over the years, with the kind of trade and commerce that has gone on over the North Sea, those stories have been exchanged. That same interest in the darkness exists. And also, there is that political sense Scotland has had for a long time, although, it wasn't always as staunchly Labour in the past as people think it was, I think we've also had a strong sense of egalitarianism and social democracy and meritocracy here. You look back at Robert Burns' writing, 'A Man's a Man for a' That' and that is the kind of substrate of Scottish political consciousness. I think that is also something we feel more in tune with the moderate Nordic countries. There are all these historical and cultural connections and that is probably why there are tonal similarities in a lot of the work.

What about the connections between noir and the landscape?

Scotland and the Nordic countries both share that sparsely populated landscape. We have a few big cities and towns, but a lot of our landscape, like theirs, is empty and startlingly beautiful and changes quite dramatically with the seasons. I think it is fair to say in countries like this the landscape holds a particular place in people's heads. It is a backdrop to what they think about when they think about their country. They think about their city or their town, but they also think about the Highlands or the volcanoes in Iceland or the ice caves or waterfalls. They are just part of your consciousness, of where you come from. I think Scots go out into the wider country more than their English counterparts. It seems to me, having lived a long time in England also, that when the English go out into the country they go on quite manicured country walks, whereas we just head off into the hillside and through the Machair there is a much greater sense of the wilderness, that you also find in the Nordic countries. And, anything can happen in the wilderness.

What are the defining characteristics of Nordic noir for you?

Right from the start, Maj Sjöwall and Per Wahlöö (who pioneered modern Scandinavian crime fiction with their Martin Beck series in the 1960s and 1970s) had a political element and dimension where the novels get used to make social points as well. They are not just about the crime, but the organic nature of the crime and how that arises from the society that you are policing. They also, mostly, have a powerful sense of teamwork among the detectives. I think they are bleaker than Tartan noir. You don't get many laughs in Scandi crime. There is less humour, but very much an understanding of the social conditions that create the seedbed for the kind of crimes they are writing about. They often have that strong sense of community, particularly the ones that are set outside the big cities, which creates very powerful pictures of the interactions in small communities. Karin Fossum is a writer who has a penetrating eye for how small communities cohere and how they fall apart. Arnaldur Indriðason was the first Icelandic writer I read and I was entirely captivated by his portrait of Reykjavik and an Iceland that is the contrapuntal opposite to what the Icelandic tourist board would like us to think of. We are not told about the crimes that Arnaldur writes about in his books. I also like Åsa Larsson. Again, there is that sense of getting out of the big city, but her books also have those tentacles that go back into city life as well. Anne Holt I think is also interesting. Her character Hanne is confined to a wheelchair for most of the books and is also lesbian, so there is a sense there of using the role of the outsider, in a very powerful way, in a character who absolutely confounds pity. You won't feel pity for her, you will feel terrified of her.

What does the notion of Tartan noir mean to you?

There are elements of Tartan noir that run through Scottish literary tradition; that idea of duality, the doppelgänger which you see right from the start in *The Confessions of a Justified Sinner*, that then goes through *Jekyll and Hyde* and so we make great use of this, not just in one character who has two faces, but in the Sherlock Holmes and Watson kind of things. There is a lot of that sense of people in their reverse in the stories. And then, there is that sense of what Hugh MacDiarmid called the 'Caledonian antisyzygy' – the yoking together of two opposing forces. So on the one hand you have Calvinism and Presbyterianism and all that dark, dour duty and that you shouldn't have fun, especially not on a Sunday, and set against that you have all the Gaelic tradition of dance and music and laughter and drink. So those two traditions pull within us individually, as well as a society and so that sets up a strong dynamic tension quite a lot of the time as well. The darkness of being in a country that has had no say in its own direction for 300 years, there are a lot of negatives and frustrations in that. But as someone pointed out to me quite recently, which I hadn't thought of before, is it because the best minds in Scotland were not occupied with running the country that we had the Scottish Enlightenment? We had the tremendous flourishing of Scottish inventiveness in the nineteenth century; Scotland when it built the empire with all the concomitant problems that it has historically for us, but that's what we did. So all the tremendous energies that would be dissipated in running the country were set free for other things. So that is another aspect. What we also have in Tartan noir is black humour. The Scots have gallows humour and we also laugh in the face of disaster because we've had lots of practice and not just with the football team. We are accustomed to things going horribly wrong. We are very much of the 'if you don't laugh you would just put your head in the gas oven' school of philosophy. Really. So that black humour runs like a thread through Scottish crime fiction generally and it is right across the board whether it is the more cosy M. C. Beaton, Hamish Macbeth, or it is the Stuart MacBride and Chris Brookmyre darkness. The humour is still there, we can't help ourselves we have to laugh at it. It is how we have survived as a nation: drink and laughter.

Denise Mina, Louise Welsh, Stuart MacBride and Chris Brookmyre are all writers who have picked up the baton laid down initially by William McIlvanney and then Ian Rankin and I staggered forward with it, and this new wave of writers have come through. But there are an awful lot of good writers out there in Scotland at the moment. Every year I see a fresh crop. At the moment, I would say three of the most creative writers in crime fiction generally are Scots – Graeme Macrae Burnet, Mary Paulson-Ellis and Abir Mukherjee. They are all doing very different things with the genre and demonstrating the versatility of the form. So it is clear that when you look at the long list, for example, for the William McIlvanney Scottish Crime Book of the Year Prize, there are twelve books on that longlist and none were there to make up the numbers. What is happening is a new flowering and there are new Scottish writers coming through all the time. It is a very exciting time to be working in this field.

Crime fiction is used to address questions of morality in society. Do you think it is something that Nordic and Scottish writers do more than other authors?

I certainly think that the wider sense of social morality is a concern, both generally speaking in Nordic noir, and to a large extent in Tartan noir. I don't sense that same thing in many writers outside that circle. There are some notable exceptions, Eva Dolan, for example and Nicci French's Frieda Klein novels, but more generally I think it is less of a burning concern, and I think in a way the Scots and the Nordic writers don't sit down with the idea we are going to go on a moral crusade. I think it is something in the fabric of our community and the concerns we are brought up in. This is not Thatcher's Britain.

In what way are these books shaped by the political contexts of these countries?

Historically there has been a difference, particularly in the past forty years in terms of the Scottish body politic and what happens south of the border. This is not Thatcher's Britain. We still have social concerns and you can see that in the measures taken by the Scottish government to mitigate austerity: free prescription charges, not implementing the bedroom tax, funding social care, not making people pay university tuition fees. These are indicative of the kind of social morality that prevails here, and it is not all about selfishness and grinding the faces of the poor into the dust as you clamber your way to the top of the greasy pole. Yes, sure we are ambitious and there are people who are profoundly selfish and profoundly capitalist here, but there is still an underlying ethos, I think, of trying to create a fairer society.

I moved back to Scotland in 2013 after about thirty years away and have noticed huge changes. We are welcoming of immigrants generally. There was a report recently where Scotland is deemed the best place in Europe to be gay. You certainly couldn't have said that when I was growing up! I think it has become a much more diverse society and at its heart there is a sense of caring. We have 10 per cent of the population of the UK and we took over 30 per cent of the Syrian refugees and they have settled here, communities have welcomed them. I am not saying there aren't pockets of England where these things happen as well, but here there is more of a sense of this is how we are and this is the country we aspire to be.

The Scottish parliament has been a focus for the things that matter to us. I know not everybody agrees with the things the Scottish parliament does. But

I think in general their instincts are right, I just wish they would sort out the education issue. I have that old-fashioned thing of that you teach them to read, you teach them their timestables and you build on that. If you don't have those foundation stones there is not much else you can do. I know it is old fashioned, but it worked for generations of Scots and gave us the best education system in the world allegedly. Solutions seem to be thin on the ground. The First Minister's reading challenge has been a good initiative to promote an interest in reading for pleasure. She is a keen reader herself and she wants to spread that.

And what about the parallels with the Nordic countries?

Well, when Iceland's economy flushed itself down the toilet, it was a lesbian that got them out of trouble which was something I personally found quite satisfying. However, I don't follow Nordic politics closely enough to comment. I was in Gothenburg recently for the book fair and was astonished and appalled to find the book fair brought to a standstill on the Saturday by a neo-Nazi march. It was heartening that 500 Nazis turned up and 10,000 anti-Nazis turned up for the counter demonstration, but nevertheless there was a period of about three hours when the book fair was surrounded by armed police and people couldn't get in or readily out. I am aware of the strong neo-Nazi right wing in the Nordic countries now – certainly you would know that if you read Jo Nesbø and other writers – but it was quite shocking to see it so visibly on the ground. The police did a great job and contained the whole thing. It was shocking nonetheless. The reason it all went off was that the book fair had given a stand to an extremely right-wing publication in Sweden and there was some talk about boycotting it. Some people stayed away and some stayed. After talks with my publisher, I decided to go, as one should always take on these views and visibly stand against them, but it was quite shocking.

You have often spoken of crime novels reflecting social history. What challenges do you think crime writers will reflect on now, in light of Brexit and Trump?

There is so much to occupy front and centre of our consciousness at the moment. I mean there are threats to democracy with the rise of the Right in America, the populism of Trump and the horrors that await us with Brexit. I can't see any other outcome other than a complete car crash of the British economy, and for all the other things – the cultural things and practical things which will be shattered by this. It just makes me profoundly depressed. There is the rise of the Right and we have our own extremely unpleasant neo-Nazi movement in this country, and of course the rise of terrorism. Part of the thing we will have to confront a lot more directly is our own participation in colonialism and slavery.

Louise Welsh and others have been looking at this over the past couple of years with the Empire Café series of events exploring Scotland's indebtedness to the slave trade. Those are things we will have to deal with, and we will have to recognize the fact that a lot of the problems that are happening in the Middle East go back to decisions this country was involved in making in the 1920s with artificial borders and artificial divisions which are well and truly coming back to bite us. These are all things that will colour what we write about. On another level, we will have to deal with the definite effects of austerity on people's lives; the deprivation and the way lives are being de-railed by the dismantling, to a large extent, of the welfare state. There are all kinds of problems waiting for us at home. The fire at Grenfell Tower in London was a terrible reminder of the huge gap between the 1 per cent and the rest of us. If you live in one of those nice high-rise blocks in Canary Wharf or the East of London you have sprinkler systems and fire extinguishers on every floor. But if you live in a tower block in a poor part of town you can just fry.

Danny Dorling, the human geographer, has made powerful arguments that we cannot afford the 1 per cent, the super-rich who come and hollow out the cities with their investment apartments that nobody ever lives in, and all the other influences that has on local population centres. Increasingly, there seems to be a caste system developing in our cities, where if you are really rich you live in the centre with all the amenities and all the empty flats around, so you don't have neighbours to make any noise. And if you are servicing that, you are out in the far-flung reaches of nowhere. I remembered the other day something the writer Sue Grafton said to me in 1994 in Santa Barbara. She said to me: 'There are two groups of people living in Santa Barbara. There are the rich, and the people who service the rich'. It just occurred to me that was a kind of prophetic image of what our cities are becoming.

So there is plenty for writers to think about, and you don't have to sit down with an agenda. I never sit down with an agenda and say this is going to be my immigration book, or this is going to be my homelessness book, but if you have any kind of consciousness of living in the world then you cannot avoid engaging with these things because these are the things that crimes rise from. Ever since the new wave of feminist private eye novels in the 1980s, there has been an increasing sense of crime fiction being much more organic in that the crimes that happen take place because of where they happen. In the golden age, there was a sense of random murders being bolted onto random villages. But now I think the best crime fiction is about the kind of crimes that arise because of the place where they take place, and the lives people have there, the kinds of occupations they have and the concerns they have. That is where the politics creeps in because that is what affects our lives.

So we are looking at consequence rather than political theory in our books. It is quite interesting that writers are being asked these questions now. Journalists and readers are talking about the kind of issues that come up in our books and talking to writers as if we should have an opinion about these things, which is useful.

CODA

Gunnar Staalesen

After having read all of these interesting chapters, I would not be surprised if you are left with at least one question: does Nordic noir really exist? Is there a simple way to define it? Or is it only a way of marketing books from the same geographic area? To begin, I will try to answer two questions, the first one being: where is the North, from which 'Nordic' is derived?

Normally, one would speak about the Scandinavian countries as one entity: Denmark, Norway and Sweden. These three countries have languages that are so close to each other that we can read books in all three languages without having them translated (though they are very often translated and published in the national language of all these countries). When we speak, we can understand each other easily, if we do not speak too fast.

Nevertheless, the three countries have quite a different history, Norway being governed by Denmark for 400 years, and then in a union with Sweden for almost 100 years. Between 1397 and 1905, Norway was not a free country (the reason, I am sure, of why the majority of the population in two referenda decided that Norway should not be a member of the European Union). Sweden and Denmark fought several wars, and some animosity can still be detected between representatives of these two countries.

The two other countries that are usually called Nordic are Finland and Iceland. They both have languages that are not comprehensible in the Scandinavian countries, even though Icelandic is closer to the original Norse language than the other Nordic ones. Iceland has a long history of being governed by (Norway and) Denmark. Icelanders still learn Danish in school and some can speak directly to their Nordic brothers and sisters. A minority of Finns are Swedish-speaking, but usually we have to use English, at least when talking with younger people from these countries.

The history of Norway towards Denmark can be compared to that of Scotland and England. In my opinion, one could easily define Scotland as a Nordic country. I remember Ian Rankin once said that he felt more like a 'North Sea writer' than a 'British' one. Looking at writers like Ann Cleeves in her Shetland series, Ian Rankin and other Scottish writers, it is possible to say that the North should at least include Scotland in the definition of Nordic, even if it lacks the geographic specialty of the Scandinavian countries, Iceland and Finland: the short Nordic summer nights and the long, dark nights of winter. And 'dark' in French is, of course, 'noir'.

This leads us to the second question: what is 'noir'? In my opinion, the original 'Nordic noir' must be the Icelandic Sagas, written mostly in the thirteenth and fourteenth centuries, with Njál's Saga as perhaps the most famous one. If you follow the literary links, there is a path going more or less directly from these sagas to the writing of American hardboiled writers like Dashiell Hammett and Raymond Chandler. They even have the most perfect one-liners. As we all know, the word 'noir' linked to crime fiction was given to writers like Hammett, Chandler and Horace McCoy, published by the Série noire imprint of the French publisher Gallimard from 1945 onwards. The same expression was also used to describe American films based on the same material (*The Big Sleep, The Maltese Falcon, Double Indemnity*, etc.), i.e. film noir. Originally, the meaning of the word was 'hardboiled'. Agatha Christie, Dorothy Sayers and even Arthur Conan Doyle were not looked upon as 'noir' writers, neither was Georges Simenon, even if they were all writing crime novels and short stories. The 'noir' writers are Hammett, Chandler, McCoy, Ross Macdonald, Mickey Spillane (which leaves a bad taste in the mouth), and several others, all of them Americans.

Why was the name 'noir' linked to Nordic writers, then? The big watershed in modern crime fiction happened when the ten novels of the Swedish couple Maj Sjöwall and Per Wahlöö were published between 1965 and 1975, featuring the police inspector Martin Beck as the central character. What they did was to combine very good crime novels with political criticism of the modern Swedish welfare society and the role of the police corps in that period. They wrote about police brutality, prejudice and corruption, and they did it in a way that not only opened the eyes of writers in the other Nordic countries, but since they were being translated into several languages, they influenced writers in many other countries too.

I have already mentioned Ian Rankin as a 'North Sea writer', and he has often pointed to Sjöwall and Wahlöö as at least one of the sources of inspiration when he started his Rebus series. He writes in his own personal style, of course, but the relationship to the Swedish couple is easy to see when it comes to the use of political background in his novels. The same way of telling a story in the form of police procedurals can be seen in most Scandinavian writers in the decades that followed, with Henning Mankell and Stieg Larsson as the best-known Swedish successors. Even if his novels are based on a more thriller-like dramaturgy, the immensely popular Norwegian writer Jo Nesbø definitely writes a modern-day version of the Martin Beck novels, as does Jørn Lier Horst.

In the wake of Sjöwall and Wahlöö, two generations of writers have followed. In Norway, Jon Michelet and I were among the first, and after some years the interest in our books from other European countries grew. My books were translated into English, German and Russian, as well as Danish and Swedish in the 1980s, and I have been able to watch the development of what was later termed 'Nordic noir'. Both Michelet and I were clearly inspired by Sjöwall and Wahlöö, and our first crime novels were police procedurals. Then we changed to a more hardboiled style. Michelet let one of his police investigators, Vilhelm Thygesen, leave the force and start working as a lawyer, freelancing as a kind of private detective, and I created my own version of the classic private eye, Varg Veum.

The first Varg Veum novel was an experiment, and I was not sure if it would work. Was it possible to transfer this American style of crime writing to Norway, forty years later? But no critic protested against this private detective story from Bergen in the 1970s, and the readers loved it. After having finished my third and last police procedural, in 1979, I wrote number two in what was now going to be a long series: *Yours until Death*. Among today's Nordic crime writers, I am one of the very few who write in the direct tradition of Hammett, Chandler and Ross Macdonald: the classic 'crime noir'. Almost all of the other writers are writing in the police procedural style, and I agree with the critics who raise the question: can this really be called 'noir'?

The first world-famous literary detective was of course Sherlock Holmes. He was a private detective, as was Hercule Poirot and several other characters from the golden age of British crime literature. The Norwegian writer Stein Riverton (a pseudonym for Sven Elvestad) had two central detectives, the police inspector Knut Gribb and the private detective Asbjørn Krag, but I would not call the stories about Knut Gribb 'police procedurals' in the modern understanding of the word. In other words: it was the private detective who dominated this genre from the beginning.

Some critics have pointed back to *The Moonstone* (1868) by Wilkie Collins as an early novel describing police work at Scotland Yard. Later on, I would certainly count the 1930s Maigret novels by Georges Simenon as 'police novels' with a realistic description of police work rather than a quest for 'whodunnit'. Nevertheless, it was in the 1950s that the shape of the modern 'police procedural' became highly visible within the genre, with writers like Hillary Waugh and Ed McBain on the front line. Then, in 1965, Sjöwall and Wahlöö published their first book, and the rest is history.

But is a 'police procedural' really a 'noir' novel? Not in the original use of the word 'noir', but it seems today that that term is more and more being used as a synonym for all sorts of crime stories. One might say that it is the meaning of the word that has changed. In other words – writers as varied as Jo Nesbø and Camilla Läckberg, Karin Fossum and Stieg Larsson, Henning Mankell and Håkan Nesser, Kjell Ola Dahl and Yrsa Sigurðardóttir, Antti Tuomainen, Jørn Lier Horst and many others can all represent so-called 'Nordic noir'. What they all have in common is that they are defined as crime writers and that they live and write in one of the Nordic countries. And that, if you ask me, is a rather loose definition.

Final question: will the 'Nordic noir' wave endure? Why not? If the Nordic writers continue to write good enough books to keep the interest of the common reader, what we call Nordic noir might live forever, like the Icelandic Sagas which started it all.

INDEX

24 (TV series) 60

Aalto, Alvar 7
Ackroyd, Peter 13, 14, 20, 39
acting 45, 59, 61, 68, 109, 119, 120, 152, 174
adaptation 3, 10, 43, 52, 55
Adler-Olsen, Jussi 139, 166
 Flaskepost fra P./Conspiracy of Faith 139
 Kvinden i buret/Keeper of Lost Causes 139
adventure 167, 179, 185
aesthetic/aesthetics 2, 3, 7, 8, 9, 18, 19, 41, 42, 53, 103, 111, 140, 142–5, 147, 177, 178, 185, 188, 235
 international aesthetic tradition 103
 noir aesthetic 41
 Northern aesthetic 9
 visual aesthetic 7
Africa 19, 63, 102
African Americans 151
Äitiyspakkaus (baby box) 138
Åland Islands 102
alcoholics 123, 185
alienation 80, 155, 170, 230, 234
America 8, 41, 156, 159, 169, 200, 243
 Latin America 8
Anglo-Saxon hegemony 2
Anna Karolina 211, 214, 219
Appelqvist, Kristina 213, 217
architecture 7, 42, 61, 74, 76, 80
 vernacular architecture 61, 76
Arctic 87, 90, 101, 102, 107, 109, 139, 190
 Arctic Circle 87, 90
Aronson, Karin 137, 138, 146
Arvas, Paula 99, 112, 129, 130, 146, 218, 235, 237

Arvingerne/The Legacy (TV series) 103
Asia 102, 171
Auden, W. H. 8
Aurvåg, Trond Fausa 66

Baltasar Kormákur 108
banks 109, 126–7, 157
Barbey d'Aurevilly, Jules 188–9, 194, 196
 Les Diaboliques 188, 196
Bargainner, Earl F. 216
Barthes, Roland 77
Bates, Quentin xvi, 2
Baudelaire, Charles 185, 196
Beau Sejour (TV series) 2
Beck (TV series) 3
belonging 11, 57, 62, 89, 117
 national belonging 57, 62
Benjamin, Walter 73, 74, 82, 196
Bernstein, Robin 140–1, 142, 144, 146
Blaagaard, Bolette 103, 112
Black Lives Matter 151
blackmail 58, 64
bleakness 170, 183, 195
body/bodies xiv, 26, 33–5, 39, 40, 47, 53, 74, 78, 80, 82, 83, 108, 120, 139, 141, 186, 190–2, 203–5, 214, 242
Boomerang! (film) 168
Borealism 9, 19
Borgen (TV series) 16, 102–5, 110, 112, 113, 142, 180, 181
Bourdieu, Pierre 5
Breivik, Anders 60
The Bridge (US TV series) 3, 42, 73, 75, 76, 77, 78, 79, 80, 83
Bron/Broen/The Bridge (Nordic TV series) 3, 10, 11, 14, 16, 23, 25, 26, 28, 30, 31, 33, 34, 37–8, 39, 73–5, 77–81, 83, 105, 112, 133, 167, 175, 178, 194, 236

Brookmyre, Chris 241
Broomé, Agnes 221, 235
Browning, Christopher 17, 20
Buzard, James 8, 19

Cain, James M. 1, 41, 167, 168
    Frank Chambers 173
    The Postman Always Rings Twice 173
Call Northside 777 (film) 168
Calvino, Italo 184, 195
    Invisible Cities 184, 195
canted frames 176
capital 75, 86, 102, 104, 138, 171, 193, 213, 219
capitalism 41, 107, 108, 110, 118, 119, 128, 146, 155, 185, 190, 194, 231
Caribbean 102, 235
cartography 118
La casa de papel/Money Heist (TV series) 2
Celtic 7, 82
Chandler, Raymond 41, 54, 151, 168, 177, 217, 246, 247
child/children 3, 14–16, 26, 27, 32, 34, 44, 58, 62–63, 67, 87, 88, 122, 133–45, 146, 158, 175, 181, 200, 203, 216, 225–6, 228, 230, 231
    troubled children 158
Christie, Agatha xv, 5, 6, 12, 13, 18, 28, 149, 246
    Hercule Poirot 5, 18, 28, 29, 247
    Miss Marple 6, 151, 153
    The Murder of Roger Ackroyd 4
    The Mysterious Affair at Styles 13, 25, 28, 29, 30
Chronicles of Newgate 4
chronotope 145, 222
CIA 49, 105
cinema (*see also* film) 1, 9, 19, 20, 39, 41, 53, 54, 55, 136, 142, 144, 166, 167, 170, 178
    American cinema 1, 170
    Nordic Cinema (*see also* Scandinavian film) 166, 178
city 9, 13, 15, 52, 58–60, 74, 75–83, 94, 124, 139, 154, 167–8, 183–5, 188–9, 193, 199, 201–3, 208, 211, 219, 222, 228, 240
    concept city 77, 79

cityscape 41, 44, 78–80
Cleeves, Ann 3, 14, 85–6, 94–5, 99, 245
    Blue Lightning 85, 88–9, 93, 96–7, 99
    Shetland series 86, 93, 94, 99, 245
    Wildfire 15
climate 8, 36, 42, 44, 64, 87, 88, 99, 104, 130, 160, 194, 221, 227
    cultural climate 221
    emotional climate 44
Clinton, Hillary 156, 161
cold 5, 7, 9, 64, 87–8, 90, 99, 113, 118, 129, 130, 158, 160, 230
colonial history 102–4, 110–11, 138
colonialism 102–4, 106, 107, 108, 110, 111, 112, 243
    Danish colonialism 3, 101, 104, 110
    Nordic colonialism (*see also* Scandinavian Colonialism) 104, 111, 112
    Postcolonialism 102, 111 (*see also* post-colonial)
colony/colonies 94, 102, 110
    Danish colony 102
Conan Doyle, Arthur 13, 20, 28, 39, 246
    Sherlock Holmes 29, 30, 153, 241, 247
    The Sign of Four 13, 20, 25, 28, 29, 39
constitutional monarchies 102
Copenhagen 10, 26, 43–4, 46, 73, 75, 81, 82, 102, 107, 176, 219
corpse/corpses 74, 82, 110, 121, 191–3
corruption 7, 42, 46–7, 50, 57, 101, 108, 117, 150, 152, 172, 186, 190, 194, 221, 227, 233, 246
    political corruption 101
Creeber, Glen 10, 42, 46, 53, 166, 176, 178, 181, 221, 235
crime fiction
    Anglo-American crime fiction 172
    classic crime fiction 12, 28
    contemporary crime fiction 4, 42, 53, 205
    crime thriller 18, 167
    Danish crime fiction 212
    domestic thriller xv
    English detective fiction 166
    espionage thriller 74
    European crime fiction 12

gangster thriller 67
global crime fiction 152
golden age crime fiction xv, 13
hardboiled crime fiction 134
historical crime fiction 167, 237
international crime fiction 180, 233, 235, 237
modern crime fiction 7, 157, 246
noir thriller 167, 179
Nordic crime fiction 3, 7, 14, 15, 135, 165, 168, 170, 173, 237
police or legal procedural 117, 120, 103, 134, 136, 139, 167–72, 174, 176–8, 180, 211–13, 215, 218, 219, 247
police thriller 211, 213–18
political thriller 212
psychological thriller xiv, 212–13
Swedish crime fiction 2, 5, 129, 130, 160, 166, 211–12, 214, 217–18, 219, 237
US crime fiction 134, 137
crime film 165, 167
criminality 4–5, 50, 118, 133, 139, 174, 176–7, 213, 217, 223, 225, 232
criminals 4, 30, 59, 66, 123, 139, 151, 154, 168, 170, 174, 181, 183, 185, 213–18, 229, 230
crisis 16, 17, 36, 41, 63, 84, 105, 109–10, 121, 137, 186–7, 208, 230
diplomatic crisis 105
criticism xv, 4, 5, 12, 37, 50, 53, 103, 111, 149, 166, 175, 209, 211, 213, 226, 229, 230, 246
literary criticism 4, 5
political criticism 211, 246
social criticism xv, 53, 166, 175, 213
critique 6, 16, 49, 50, 52, 64, 97, 103, 110, 117, 128, 136, 137, 153, 169, 170, 172–3, 175, 179, 183, 185, 221
social critique 6, 169, 172, 173, 175
socio-political critique 117, 128, 179
culture xiii, 5–6, 11–12, 17, 19, 38, 54, 57–9, 61, 63, 65–6, 75, 82, 83, 86, 88, 90, 91, 94, 98, 101, 103, 106, 111, 113, 136, 146, 149, 153, 170, 171, 194, 200, 201, 202, 206, 208, 209, 213, 223, 230, 236, 238

British culture 149
national culture 1, 13
Nordic culture 101
sub-culture 201

Dahl, Arne (*Intercrime* series, *Opcop* series) 211
dandy 186, 194
Danish Commonwealth 102, 105, 110
Danish television 10, 12, 53, 145, 175
darkness 46, 53, 54, 66, 78, 80, 82, 84, 87, 88, 90, 170, 185, 193, 194, 223, 239, 241
Davidson, Peter 7, 8, 19, 85, 98
Dean, Will (*Dark Pines*) 2
death 7, 18, 36, 60, 66, 81, 99, 119, 123, 129, 130, 139, 141, 160, 179, 185–7, 190–1, 202, 228, 230, 247
decadence 3, 12, 183, 185–186, 189, 194–5, 196
decay 77, 80, 186, 187
de Certeau, Michel 77, 84, 238
de la Motte, Anders 211, 214
 Game trilogy 214
 MemoRandum 214
 Ultimatum/The Silenced 214
Denmark xiv, 2, 10, 11, 12, 23, 30, 54, 102–11, 112, 113, 144, 147, 192, 226, 237, 245
depression 126
Dickens, Charles 208, 209
Dicte (TV series) 16
director 1, 41, 44, 53, 108, 144, 171, 178, 185, 189, 190, 194
disappeared 77, 130, 205
disintegration 80, 92, 97, 170
documentary 168–9
 police documentary 168–9
domestic xv, 8, 14, 18, 52, 53, 133–5, 137, 143, 153, 158, 159, 181, 203, 205, 208, 212
 domestic life 53, 143, 208
 domesticity xiii, 47, 140–1, 175, 189
doppelgänger 81, 137, 241
Dostoyevsky, Fyodor 4
Double Indemnity (film) 167, 246
Dove, George N. 215–16, 218, 219

Dragnet (TV series) 167
drama 23, 34, 31, 35, 38–39, 42–4, 54,
    82, 88, 102–3, 108, 110, 133, 147,
    167, 175, 179, 192, 213
    family drama 175
    political drama 102–3
drug addicts 123, 185
Dugan, Lisa 118, 129
Dürrenmatt, Friedrich 6
Dylan, Bob 152, 200, 209
dysfunctionality 226, 230

economy 33, 41–2, 60, 109, 127–8, 137,
    171, 232, 243
education xv, 93, 119, 126, 137–8, 144,
    156–7, 225, 243
Edwardson, Åke (*Möt mig i Estepona/
    Meet me in Estepona*) 212
egalitarianism 42, 57, 239
Eliot, George (*Mill on the Floss*) 201
Ellroy, James 173, 213, 219
empire 93–4, 102, 149, 160, 241, 244
    British empire 149, 160
    Danish empire 102
Enger, Thomas 222, 223–4, 226, 228,
    229, 233, 235–8
    Burned 229, 235–8
    Henning Juul 223–6, 228–9
entertainment 135, 167, 213
    Hollywood entertainment 167
epic 3, 4, 87, 199–209
    ancient epic 200
    contemporary epic 199, 201
Eriksson, Caroline 212
ethical 6, 28, 137, 172
ethnicity 9, 223, 17, 104
exceptionalism 6, 20, 102
    Scandinavian exceptionalism 6
exotic 10, 14, 73, 85–6, 90, 95
expressionism 41

failure 2, 17, 46, 49, 51, 53, 95, 109, 117,
    118, 122, 137, 139, 156, 185–7,
    191
The Fall (TV series) 2, 3, 23, 25, 27, 28,
    30–1, 32, 33, 37–8, 39
family 12, 14–17, 26, 27, 34, 37, 44–5, 47,
    49–51, 53, 57, 59–60, 87, 88–91,
    93, 94–6, 103, 125–7, 133–4,
    137–8, 143–5, 150, 158, 168,
    175–6, 181, 190, 193, 195, 203,
    208, 215–16, 224–5, 231
Faroe Islands 102, 104, 112
Faulkner, William 41
FBI 59, 61, 143, 176
female characterization 43
feminine 12, 38, 47, 146
feminism xiii, 47
    Nordic feminism 47
femme fatale 16, 35, 41, 167, 174, 176
film (*see also* cinema) 1, 2, 7, 12, 16, 19,
    36, 41–2, 45–6, 49, 53–4, 55, 58,
    66, 75–7, 83, 84, 103, 129, 130,
    134, 137, 142–3, 145, 146, 147,
    154, 165–71, 174–75, 178, 179,
    180, 181, 183, 185, 189, 194, 237,
    246
    European film 170
    gangster film 58
financial institutions 118, 125, 127
fin-de-siècle 183, 185, 188–9, 194
Finland xiv, 14, 102, 138, 165, 181, 196,
    237, 245, 246
flaneur 82, 84
flashback structure 169
Flynn, Gillian (*Gone Girl*) 212
folk costumes 61
Forbrydelsen/The Killing (Danish TV
    series) 2, 3, 10, 14, 16, 41, 42,
    43–5, 47–52, 54, 101, 133, 139,
    142, 145, 166, 175–6, 180, 181,
    194
    Sarah Lund 11, 16, 45–7, 175
Fortitude (TV series) 2, 111, 189–91, 196
    Morton 191
Fossum, Karin 103, 166, 222, 226–8, 232,
    236, 237, 240, 247
    Den onde viljen/Bad Intentions 17,
    228, 236, 237
    *Den som frykter ulven/He Who Fears
    the Wolf* 226, 233, 236, 237
    Elskede Poona/The Indian Bride 17,
    227, 228, 236, 237
    Konrad Sejer 226
    Se deg ikke tilbake!/Don't Look Back
    230
Frank, Matthew (*If I Should Die*) 152,
    159, 160, 161

French, Tana 15, 20, 37, 40, 150
  The Wych Elm 15
friendship 25, 48

gangsters 58, 176
gender xv, xvi, 3, 6, 16, 17, 18, 19, 21, 23, 33, 35, 36, 38, 39, 43, 46-8, 51-2, 145, 223, 224
generic traits 206, 221
genre xiv, xv, 1, 3-8, 10-13, 16, 25, 30, 33, 37-8, 39, 41-3, 48, 50, 53, 54, 83, 85, 87, 90-1, 103-4, 120, 133-6, 139, 143, 145, 163, 167-9, 181, 185-6, 189, 201, 204-5, 208-9, 211-14, 218, 221, 232-3, 235, 239, 241, 247
  crime fiction genre 136, 212-13
  subgenre xiv, 212
gentrification 124, 126
ghost 11, 66-7
global transmedia 1, 10, 18
globalization 13, 42, 50, 53, 128, 180, 231
The Godfather 58, 63
Goodfellas 58, 59
gossip 45, 94
greed 14, 150, 176, 186, 189, 190, 194, 217, 230
Greenland 8, 12, 102, 105-8
grief (*see also* mourning) 28, 44, 87, 88, 226
Grønlandspolitik/Greenland policy 102, 106, 107, 110
Guillou, Jan 212
guilt 6, 67, 87, 89, 95, 96, 108, 150, 160, 169, 191

Hammershøi, Wilhelm 7
Hammett, Dashiell 1, 7, 12, 151, 160, 168, 217, 246-7
Harvey, David 118-19, 129, 130
Harvey, Sylvia 134, 137, 145, 146
haunting 73, 79, 81, 192
Hawkins, Paula (*The Girl on the Train*) 212
health 39, 40, 111, 125, 136-137, 138, 159, 186, 187
  mental health 39, 40
health care 119, 155, 158

Heartless (TV series) 11
Hedling, Olof 11, 19, 54, 142-3, 147
Helsinki 192-3
hero 8, 16, 48, 49, 52, 60, 158, 205, 206, 207, 217, 223
heroine 48, 153, 154
heterosexual 53, 153
highlands 8, 86, 240
history 1, 9, 14, 24, 30, 31, 35, 38, 86, 88, 90, 93, 94, 98, 102-4, 107-9, 110, 111, 129, 134-6, 138, 145, 146, 149, 151, 158-9, 161, 166, 170, 179, 202-3, 207-8, 218, 227, 237, 243, 245, 247
  national history 108
Hoeg, Peter (*Frøken Smillas fornemmelse for sne/Miss Smilla's Feeling for Snow*) 12, 103
Holmén, Martin (*Clinch*) 212
Holt, Anne 20, 103, 139, 222, 228, 230-2, 235, 236, 237, 240
  1222 20, 225, 229, 236, 237
  Demonens død/Death of a Demon 139
  Det som aldri skjer/What Never Happens 230, 237
  Det som er mitt /What is Mine 229, 236, 237
  Hanne Wilhelmsen 139, 224-5
  Løvens gap/The Lion's Mouth 139
  Pengemannen/Fear Not 232, 236, 237
  Silje Sørensen 224
  Vik/Stubø series 224, 226
homelessness 80, 159, 244
home rule 105, 106, 107, 108
homogeneity 122, 221, 229, 234
homosexuals 154
horror 11, 33, 63, 185, 204
Horst, Jørn Lier 14, 222, 227-8, 232, 236, 237, 238, 246-7
  Hulemannen/The Caveman 230
  Vinterstengt/Closed for Winter 229, 236, 237, 238
  William Wisting 17, 226, 232-3
human condition 1, 84, 185, 206
humour 43, 48, 240-1

Huysmans, Joris-Karl 185–7, 194–5, 196, 197
  À rebours 185–7, 196
  Des Esseintes 186–7, 189
hygge 101, 104, 110–11

IB Affair 119
Ibsen, Henrik 67–8, 69
  A Doll's House 68, 69
  Hedda Gabler 67, 69
Iceland/Icelandic xiii, xiv, xvi, 2, 8–12, 14, 19, 86–8, 90–2, 98, 99, 102, 104, 108, 110, 112, 113, 153, 157–8, 165, 173, 175, 177, 180, 181, 191, 192, 196, 202–6, 208, 209, 237, 239, 240, 245, 246
identity/identities 10–11, 16–17, 18–19, 20, 23, 30, 36–7, 38, 39, 54, 60–61, 65, 75, 77, 81, 82, 86, 90–3, 97, 98, 102, 108, 111, 112, 113, 133, 137, 140, 142, 144, 150, 157, 173, 178, 200–7, 209, 222–4, 226–9, 234
  collective identity 200, 201, 203–7, 224, 234
  European identity 11
  individual identity 150
  national identity 17, 19, 38, 61, 91, 98, 108, 112, 113, 157, 202–3, 206, 227–9, 234
Iliad 204
imagination 8, 76, 85, 86, 98, 121, 155, 184
Imamura, Shohei 170
immigrants 57, 63–4, 173, 213, 227–9, 242
immigration 50, 58, 64, 244
imperialism 102, 104, 107–11
  American imperialism 107, 110
  cultural imperialist 1
  Danish imperialism 108–9
  European imperialist project 102
independence 14, 48, 53, 102, 104–6, 110, 112, 155
independent republics 102
Indriðason, Arnaldur 3, 86, 90, 98, 99, 153, 157, 166, 181, 202–9, 210
  Erlendur 15, 17, 19, 85–8, 90–3, 95–97, 99, 144, 158, 172–3, 201–6, 208

  Furðurstrandir/Strange Shores 85, 87, 88, 90, 92, 96–7, 99
  Kamp Knox/Oblivion 157, 158, 207, 210
  Mýrin/Jar City/Tainted Blood 15, 139
  Vetrarborgin/Arctic Chill 139
innocence 133, 135, 146, 169
  rousseauian innocence 133
Insomnia (film) 178
integration 16, 51, 64–5, 78, 80, 83, 92, 97, 155, 170, 234
internal monologue 185
intertextuality 142
interwar era 167, 177
intolerance 188, 229
intuition 47
Inuit 8, 105, 106
investigation xiv, 4, 6, 13, 16, 30, 31, 33, 42–50, 59, 83, 88, 91, 94, 108, 120, 123, 126, 141, 143–4, 151, 170, 175, 190, 215, 222–3, 231–2, 234
Iraq War 36, 50
islamophobe 60
Ísleifsson, Sumarliði 9, 19, 86, 98
isolation 9, 39, 80, 88, 122, 186, 188, 189, 192, 234

Jensen, Lars 10, 110, 111, 112, 113
Jónasson, Ragnar xvi, 153, 157, 158
  Snjóblinda/Snowblind 157, 158
  Náttblinda/Nightblind 157, 158
Jordskott (TV series) 11
journalism/journalist/s 16, 17, 53, 101, 119, 105, 151, 181, 206, 222, 223, 244
Joyce, James (Ulysses) 201
justice 4, 31, 36–7, 45, 47, 52, 60, 81, 117, 120, 142, 151–3, 155, 180, 194, 205–6, 216, 222, 228, 235

Kaaberbøl, Lene and Agnete Friis (Drengen I kufferten/The Boy in the Suitcase, Et stille umærkeligt drab/Invisible Murder) 139
Kallentoft, Mons and Markus Lutteman 211, 214, 216, 219
  Leon 216
  Zack 216
Karppi/Deadwind (TV series) 16
Kar-Wai, Wong 171

Kepler, Lars 213
The Killing (US TV series) 2, 19, 41, 43–53, 54
  Sarah Linden 45–6, 48–9, 51–3
Kitano, Takeshi 171
Knausgaard, Karl Ove 65, 69
knitting 45, 62–3, 66–7
Kracauer, Sigfried 73–4, 78, 80, 82, 84
Kristmannsson, Gauti 9, 19
Kurosawa, Akira 170

Läckberg, Camilla 146, 166, 211, 247
Lapidus, Jens 130, 178, 211, 213, 214, 217, 219
  Snabba Cash/Easy Money 213
  Stockholm Noir Trilogy 214
landscape 7–8, 10, 14, 18, 39, 42, 43, 62, 76, 87–8, 91–3, 97, 101, 109, 184–5, 191–4, 222, 228, 240
Lang, Maria 6, 13
Lappeenranta 190, 193
Larsson, Stieg 15, 18, 103, 117, 139, 150, 154, 160, 166, 174, 180, 201, 206, 209, 212, 217, 235, 246, 247
  Lisbeth Salander 117, 140, 146, 154, 174, 199, 206, 212, 217
  Män som hatar kvinnor/The Girl with the Dragon Tattoo 14, 15, 145, 174, 180, 195, 209, 236
  Mikael Blomkvist 155, 157, 174, 195, 199, 201, 204
  Millennium trilogy 117, 128, 154, 155, 174–5, 199, 201, 206, 211, 212, 218, 235
Laura (film) 167, 168
Laxness, Halldór 87, 98, 104, 109, 112
  Atómstöðin/The Atom Station 109
  Gerpla/The Happy Warriors 109, 113
  Heimsljós/World Light 87, 98
legacies 101, 102, 109
  cultural legacies 102
Leovy, Jill 151, 160
Lesnik-Olberstein, Karen 146
Lillehammer Olympics 61–2, 65
Lilyhammer (TV series) 2, 3, 9, 57, 59, 61, 68

Frank Tagliano 57
Giovanni Henrickson 57
Steven Van Zand 57, 59, 68
liminality 11, 31, 33, 104, 140–2, 144–54, 222–23
literature xiii, xv, xvi, 4, 5, 8, 9, 39, 42, 55, 83, 104, 112, 136, 140, 146, 161, 167, 180, 183–5, 188, 195, 196, 200, 206–8, 209, 247
  classics 208
  decadent literature 183, 185, 195
  high literature 208
  travel literature 9
locations 2, 10, 11, 14, 25, 73, 86, 153, 221
Locke, Attica (*Bluebird, Bluebird*) 151, 160
Loftsdóttir, Kristín 10, 19, 111, 113
loneliness 42, 80
Lönnaeus, Olle 211
Lorrain, Jean 194, 196
  Monsieur Bougrelon 187
loss 15, 41, 51, 91–2, 96–8, 119, 126, 140, 144, 158, 194, 201, 226, 228, 229

McBaine, Ed 117, 129, 172, 247
  87th Precinct series 117, 172
MacBride, Stuart 241
McDermid, Val xvi, 3, 239, 241, 243
McGinty, Adrian 152, 160
McIlvanney, William 160, 241
  Laidlaw 152, 160
mafia 57–9, 61, 64, 66–8
Mahabharat 204
Mallory, Thomas 202, 203, 204
  Morte d'Arthur 203, 204
Malmö 10, 12, 26, 34, 73–5, 81, 82, 217
The Maltese Falcon (film) 167, 246
Mankell, Henning 12, 14, 19, 103, 139, 141–4, 146, 166, 172, 180, 211, 215, 246–7
  Brandvägg/Firewall 139
  Mördare utan ansikte/Faceless Killers 12, 13, 15
  Villospår/Sidetracked 139, 141–2, 146
  Wallander series 2, 17, 42, 141, 143–4, 166, 172–3, 175, 195, 215

Marcuse, Herbert 154, 161
market solutions 118, 122, 124
marketing brand 104
masculine 3, 17, 25, 28, 33, 47, 53, 62, 64
masculinity 19, 57, 59
mass shooting 36, 60
media 9, 10, 11, 39, 54, 83, 112, 123, 147, 153, 154, 165, 184
melancholy/melancholia 9, 185
melodrama, melodramatic 14, 16, 20, 45, 50, 133–4, 141, 144
memory 14, 15, 45, 91–2, 97–8, 109, 112, 188, 214, 239
   collective memory 91
   cultural memory 15, 109, 112, 239
metonymy 119, 121, 133, 136
Midnatssol/Midnight Sun (TV series) 2
migrant others 102
migration 12–14, 150, 202
Miike, Takashi 171
militarization 124, 172
Mina, Denise 241
minorities 65
Mirbeau, Octave 187, 194, 196
   Le journal d'une femme de chambre/A Chambermaid's Diary 187, 196
misogyny 23, 31, 37, 65
missing persons 45, 203–5
modernist/modernism 4, 5, 18, 24, 104, 112, 170, 179
modernity 41, 78, 83, 90–98, 99, 112, 138, 170–1, 180, 185–6, 194, 196
Modus (TV series) 143
money laundering 58
monsters 185
montage 64, 74–7
morality 3, 4, 50, 115, 149, 151, 155, 204, 233, 242
Morris, William 8
Morse 153
motherhood 16, 35, 138
mourning (*see also* grief) 73
multiculturalism 65, 234
Munch, Anders V. 8, 10, 19
Murder, My Sweet (film) 167
music 18, 59, 61, 64, 74, 75, 79, 83, 192, 241

mystery xv, 4, 7, 12, 13, 20, 24, 126, 147, 167, 176, 192
Myrdal, Alva and Gunnar 129, 137, 138, 146

The Naked City (film) 167, 168
nation xvi, 38, 39, 50, 65, 91, 97, 98, 102, 119, 152, 154, 200–1, 205, 207, 223, 241
   nation state 102, 152, 154
national politics 102
nationality 237, 239
naturalism 185, 221
neo-conservative 155
neoliberalism 51, 117–22, 124, 125, 127, 128, 129, 136
Nesbø, Jo 15, 139, 140, 150, 153, 154, 166, 172, 181, 222–4, 227–8, 230, 233, 235, 236, 237, 243, 246, 247
   Harry Hole 144, 153, 155, 157, 160, 172–3, 222, 223
   Rødstrupe/The Redbreast 15, 227, 228
   Snømannen/The Snowman 139, 236
Nesser, Håkan 153, 161, 166, 247
   Van Veeteren 153, 161
Netflix 2, 11, 18, 54, 68
New York City 58, 59, 60
nightmare 14, 160, 170
nihilism 41
Njal's Saga 207, 210, 246
Nobel prize 112, 128, 200
Noir
   Anglo-American noir 103
   auteur neo-noir 166
   classical film noir 166
   domestic noir 212
   film noir 7, 12, 16, 36, 41, 49, 53, 54, 75–7, 83, 84, 134, 137, 145, 166–70, 179, 180, 181, 246
   historical noir 149
   Hollywood noir 1, 41
   literary noir 1
   neo-noir 41, 73, 166, 171, 178, 180, 181
   noir philosophy 42
   Nordic neo-noir 166
   Norwegian noir 2, 221, 222–3, 225–7, 229, 231–5

nostalgic neo-noir 41
Scandinavian noir 221, 236
Tartan noir 2, 149, 152, 155, 239–42
transnational noir 1
non-white citizens 151
Norebäck, Elisabeth 212
normalcy 173, 226, 236
Norman, Tanya 5, 18
normative orthodoxy 150
Norrmalmstorg robbery (Stockholm Syndrome) 119–20
North Sea 189, 239, 245–6
Norway xiv, 3, 9, 57, 60–65, 86, 102–3, 153, 181, 196, 221, 222–3, 225, 227–9, 230–4, 235, 236, 237, 239, 245–6, 247
Norwegian Troll Park 60
Norwegian Welfare and Labour Administration (NAV) 58, 60, 64–5, 68
Norwegian/Norwegians 2, 17, 20, 57–66, 68, 102, 139, 173, 177–8, 190, 221–34, 235, 236, 246–7
nostalgia 28, 65, 94–7, 99
novel
 crime novel xiv, xv, 2, 37, 139, 172, 206, 209, 212, 214, 218
 French novels 183
 néo-polar novel 221, 223
 network novel 4, 18
 police novel 117, 167, 170, 172–3, 211–13, 215–18, 247
 Swedish novel 175, 180
Novrup Redvall, Eva 142, 147, 237
nuclear weapons 105
Nuuk 102, 107

Ófærð/Trapped (TV series) 10, 102, 108, 167, 175, 189, 196
 Andri 108–9, 175, 191
omerta 59
orientalism 9
Öresund bridge 25, 28, 31, 35, 38, 73–75, 78–79, 81, 82
Oslo 61, 222, 225, 229, 230, 233, 235
otherness 10, 221–7
outcasts 170

outsider 49, 88–9, 91, 93–5, 150, 168, 173, 177, 179, 194, 206, 222, 224–6, 240

pain 81, 151, 185
past 10, 13–15, 23, 25, 44–5, 52, 60, 64, 66, 81, 86, 90–3, 95–8, 99, 103, 109, 110, 154, 155, 158–9, 187, 193, 202–3, 207–8, 214, 217, 227, 236, 239, 242, 244
 individual past 158
 pastness 85, 90, 95, 98
peace 31, 48, 58, 67–8, 193–194, 201–2, 229
Peace, David 173, 179
peaceful xiv, 52, 57, 68, 124, 172, 193, 194
People's Home (folkhemmet) 117, 118, 119, 137
Pepper, Andrew 53, 120, 130
periphery 11, 86, 88, 93, 125
personal privacy 154
perspective 28, 36, 45, 51, 53, 74, 77, 78, 86, 89, 95, 97, 104, 122, 142, 166, 168, 169–70, 174–6, 181, 184, 185, 224, 225
 outsider's perspective 224
 subjective narrative perspective 185
Persson, Leif G. W. 146, 166
pessimism 170, 179, 185
photographs 31, 84, 105–7
Plath, Sylvia (*The Bell Jar*) 153
Poe, Edgar Allan 80, 84, 167, 183, 187, 219
 "The Man of the Crowd" 84
poker games 58
political satire 109
popular fiction 5, 6, 213
post-colonial 101–4, 110, 111
 post-coloniality 103, 110
 post-colonial politics 102
 post-colonial studies 103–4
postmodern 6
postmodernism 161
poverty 5, 68, 76–7, 88, 91, 118, 129, 160, 232
powerlessness 41, 183, 234
precariousness 90

Pressa/Cover Story (TV series) 16
Price, Adam 105, 113
prison 81, 203, 213
prisoners 105, 106, 236
private detectives 167, 170, 181
prostitutes 141, 176, 185
prostitution 77
protests 172, 190
psychopaths 170, 176
Pulp Fiction 208
punishment 4, 13, 18, 81, 119, 120, 138, 194, 201, 205, 234
Pynchon, Thomas 184, 195, 237
   The Crying of Lot 49 183, 195

quality xv, xvi, 2–3, 14, 33, 75, 125, 133, 135, 140, 142–145, 180, 204, 223
   quality television 3

racism 17, 50, 63, 66, 234
rage 45, 62, 64, 65, 158, 223
   masculine/male rage 62, 64, 158
Rankin, Ian 11, 17, 152, 154, 160, 241, 245–6
   John Rebus 17, 152–4, 246
   Let it Bleed 152, 153, 160
rapists 175
Raynal, Patrick 1, 18
reader/readers xiv–xvi, 5, 14–16, 28, 83, 85, 87, 90, 95, 97, 99, 118, 120, 121, 126, 134, 136, 146, 152, 172, 179, 180, 184, 186, 189, 195, 196, 202–3, 205–6, 208–9, 213–14, 216, 233, 234, 243–4, 247–8
Reagan, Ronald 117
refugees 13, 64, 229, 242
remake 2, 42–4, 55, 75
repressive tolerance 154
responsibility 17, 31, 46, 105, 110, 120, 150, 204, 228, 230, 232
retro 19, 212
Reykjavík 86, 96, 99, 108, 190, 191, 202, 240
rights 16, 106, 124, 146, 155, 209, 210, 228, 231
   human rights 106
River (TV series) 2

Robbins, Bruce 37–38, 40, 51, 55, 104, 112, 146, 173, 180
Rogneby, Jenny 211, 214, 216, 217
Rudberg, Denise 213
rural 213, 232, 234, 7, 9, 10, 12–14, 42, 73, 90–1, 94–5, 97, 120, 190, 194, 211–12

Sagas 202, 204, 207–8, 246, 248
Sandemose, Aksel 65
Sandin, Bengt 136–8, 146
Scaggs, John 167, 169, 179, 216, 219
Scandinavian 5, 6, 8, 10, 19, 37, 42, 48, 49, 53, 54, 62, 65, 67, 75, 79, 81, 82, 99, 102–4, 112, 129, 130, 133, 135–6, 139, 141–3, 145, 146, 160, 165–7, 171–8, 180, 181, 206, 218, 221–4, 231, 235, 236, 237, 240, 245–6
   Scandinavian design 8
   Scandinavian knitwear 62
Schiller, Friedrich 4, 18
Schram, Kristinn 9, 19
Scotland 86, 93, 98, 153, 239–42, 245–7, 8
Seattle 44, 46, 49, 52
self 65, 66, 95, 223
   self-confidence 45, 66, 229
   self-consciously/self-reflexivity 2, 9, 67, 74, 142, 169, 171, 178
   self-contained 12, 13
   self-criticism 103
   self-determination 106, 107, 108, 110
   self-doubt 66
   self-exotication 8, 10
   self-fulfilment 49
   self-Government Act 105
   self-identity 91
   self-image 91
   self-interest 51
serial killers 19, 25, 28, 36–8, 52, 175
Série noire 1, 167, 246
sexual harassment 64
sexuality 33, 49, 133, 140
Shaw, William 152, 159, 160, 161
   The Birdwatcher 159, 160, 161
Shetland 86, 88–9, 93–4, 235, 15

Sigurðardóttir, Yrsa xvi, 11, 14, 134, 166, 247
   Ég man þig/I Remember You 134
   Sér grefur gröf/My Soul to Take 14, 134
silence 44, 59, 82, 190, 204
Silence of the Lambs 143
Simenon, Georges 6, 246, 247
Siodmak, Robert 41
Sirico, Tony 59
Sjöwall, Maj and Per Wahlöö xv, 2, 3, 5–6, 12, 18, 42, 103, 117–22, 125–6, 128–9, 130, 131, 137–44, 145, 146, 150, 160, 166, 171–4, 180, 206, 211, 213, 215, 217–18, 230–1, 240, 246–7
   Det slutna rummet/The Locked Room 124–6
   Mannen på balkongen/The Man on the Balcony 122, 130, 137–8, 141, 146
   Martin Beck 3, 19, 42, 103, 112, 118–21, 124, 125–7, 129, 137, 143, 150, 160, 173, 178, 215, 230, 240, 246
   Murder at the Savoy/ Polis, polis potatimos! 121, 130
   The Story of Crime series 171–172, 174–5, 177
   Terroristerna/The Terrorists 125, 127, 131
Skou, Niels Peter 8, 10, 19
The Snitch 59
snow xv, 8, 9, 12, 15, 20, 57, 61, 62, 64, 66, 81, 87–8, 90, 103–4, 112, 139, 146, 191–2
   snowed in 225–9
soap opera 45, 49, 52, 54, 208
Sobchack, Vivian 134, 145
sociable psychopaths 170
social change 1, 14, 15, 129, 146, 222
social divisions 156, 157
social exploitation 101
social injustice 42, 221
social justification 151
social network analysis 3, 23–4, 28, 30, 35–6, 38, 39

social norms 23, 150
social realism 24, 103, 104, 201, 205, 206, 221
social stability 171
social values 223
socially cohesive 101
socio-political commentary 221, 222, 234
The Sopranos 2, 59, 69
   Maureen Van Zandt 59
Sorjonen/Bordertown (TV series) 189–91, 193, 196
soundscape 176
sovereignty 92, 107, 108, 109
space 8, 11, 14, 17, 18, 23, 30, 31, 33, 44, 71, 73–4, 76, 81, 82, 83, 84, 90, 94, 109, 133, 134, 136, 157, 166, 171, 178, 183–5, 187–94, 195, 196, 197, 199, 204, 222, 227
   liminal space 11, 18, 31
   metropolitan space 73, 157
   urban space (*see also* city) 157
spatiality 183, 187, 189, 192–3, 195
spatialize 189, 194
specificity 12, 55, 103, 143–4, 165, 168, 169
   geographical specificity 103
Springsteen, Bruce 59
Staalesen, Gunnar xvi, 2, 3, 177, 245
   Varg Veum 177, 247
stereotype/s 9, 10, 17, 23, 35, 85, 90, 223, 229
Stockholm 119, 120, 140, 146, 147, 201, 213–17, 219
storyline 64, 175, 180, 213
storytelling 194, 239
Stougaard-Nielsen, Jakob 10, 19, 173, 178, 180, 236
strangers 33, 38, 170
Strindberg, August 4
structuralist analysis 4
struggle/s 16, 37, 45, 69, 91, 96, 104, 113, 183, 185, 191, 226, 233
style xv, 5, 7, 28, 31, 33, 43, 48, 57, 61, 66, 81, 135, 144, 168–9, 176, 213–14, 246, 247
   visual style 7, 31, 33
stylized lighting 176

subjective camera 169
 subjective camerawork 176
subjectivity 169, 174, 175
suburbanization 76
suppression 159, 172
surveillance 14, 54, 60, 79, 84, 134, 154–5, 172, 174–5, 178
 sexual surveillance 154
survival 85, 88, 90, 92, 95–8, 189, 194
survivor 95–6
Suzuki, Seijun 170
Svalbard 190
Sweden xiv, 2, 3, 5, 6, 7, 11, 12, 18, 23, 30, 51, 102–3, 118–19, 122, 126–8, 138, 143, 147, 153, 175, 201, 211–14, 217–18, 237, 243, 245
Swedish Academy of Sciences 118
Swedish welfare state 117–18, 137, 211, 218, 231
sympathy 229
system 49, 50, 60, 68, 78, 98, 110, 112, 117, 120–1, 125, 127–9, 142, 151–2, 157, 172–3, 177, 187, 194, 200, 205, 216–17, 227, 234, 243–4
 legal system 217, 234

tattoo 14, 15, 145, 174, 180, 195, 209, 236
 Dragon tattoo 14, 15, 145, 174, 180, 195, 209, 236
television 1–3, 8, 10–12, 16, 18, 23, 24, 33, 35, 37, 39, 41–3, 45–8, 52–5, 57–8, 60, 68, 73–4, 101, 130, 133, 135, 142–3, 145, 147, 165, 167–8, 170, 175, 177, 178, 183, 185, 189, 194, 208, 221, 235, 237
television series/TV series 2–3, 7, 8, 9, 10, 11, 16, 18, 20, 35, 39, 42–3, 45, 46, 48, 51, 52, 53, 54, 57, 74, 102, 145, 175, 177, 178, 189
 Danish TV series 10, 43, 51, 53, 145, 175
 Icelandic TV series 10
 Finnish TV series 16
 noir TV series 3, 42
 Nordic TV series 2, 8, 10
 Norwegian TV series 57
 quality TV series 2

 Swedish TV series 11
 US TV series 2, 45, 46, 48, 52
territory 31, 36, 85, 61, 88, 92, 94, 102, 105, 160, 178, 181
 Danish territory 105
terror 67, 158
terrorism 50, 60, 243
Thatcher, Margaret 117, 242
third world 137
Thule 8, 106–7, 113
Thule Air Base 105
To, Johnnie 171
Todorov, Tzvetan 230, 235, 237
topography 73
tough women 170
tourism 10, 19, 189, 190
Tourneur, Jacques 41
tradition 1, 2, 4, 6–8, 11–12, 24, 30–1, 33, 42, 47, 60–2, 65, 67, 77, 85, 89, 91–2, 94–8, 103–4, 133, 138, 140, 144, 149, 153, 155, 157, 168, 171–3, 175–8, 184, 194, 200–2, 206–7, 211–12, 215–18, 221–4, 227, 229–30, 232, 239, 241, 247
 countryside tradition 211
 literary tradition 42, 194, 241
 urban tradition 211, 212
transgressors 170, 234
transnational 1–3, 6, 10–13, 16–17, 18, 19, 21, 35, 43, 53, 73, 82, 96, 108, 110, 146, 180, 211, 231, 235
trauma 15, 91, 135, 142–3, 158, 203–4, 217
Trenter, Stieglitz 6
True Detective (TV series) 42

Ullberg Westin, Gabriella 213
Ulmer, Edgar 41
uncanny 20, 73–5, 79–80, 134, 171, 226
unemployment 58, 150, 159
United States 36, 41–3, 59, 117, 141, 143, 151, 153, 155–8, 217
Untraceable (film) 143
urban 1, 5, 9, 12–14, 30, 42, 73–4, 76–9, 83, 84, 88, 90, 92–3, 95, 97, 120, 134, 153–4, 157, 170, 179, 191, 193–4, 202, 211–12, 213, 217, 219, 222–3, 234

US military 105, 107–8
US-Denmark Defence Agreement 105

vice 119, 122, 127–8, 136, 139, 166, 169, 185, 190, 203, 230–1
victimology 121
victim/s 12–15, 25, 28, 30–1, 35, 47, 49, 50, 53, 81, 96, 120–1, 123, 125, 134, 136–7, 139, 142, 158, 170, 174, 183, 190, 193, 223, 226, 232, 234
viewer 24, 27, 48, 77, 79, 83, 184, 191–3
violence 4, 7, 14–18, 23, 31, 33, 36–7, 57, 61–2, 66, 68, 121, 124, 127–8, 133–4, 142–3, 158–9, 172–3, 176, 185–6, 194, 201, 203–6, 209, 210, 215–18, 228, 231
    domestic violence 158, 159, 203, 205
voice 25, 26, 76, 92, 155, 169, 188, 226, 235
    narrative voice 169
voice-over 169
volcanoes 240
Von Trier, Lars 2, 144, 178
    Riget/The Kingdom (TV series) 2

Waade, Anne Maarit 7, 10–11, 18, 19, 42, 53, 54, 112, 142–3, 147, 166, 178
Wallander (TV series) 2, 42, 143, 166, 195
    Kurt Wallander 17, 42, 141, 143–4, 172–3, 175, 215
Whitman, Walt (*Leaves of* Grass) 200, 209
waterfall 8, 207, 240

welfare state 3, 5–6, 9, 40, 42, 46, 51–3, 55, 65, 68, 103–4, 112, 117–23, 126–8, 129, 136–40, 144–5, 150, 172–3, 180, 211, 218, 231–4, 236, 244
Welsh, Louise 241, 244
Wennstam, Katarina 213
white 7, 20, 61, 62, 84, 90, 99, 141, 153, 184, 191, 195, 200, 224, 229
    non-white 64, 151
    Western white patriarchal society 224
whiteness 102, 111, 113
wife-beaters 176
Wilder, Billy 41, 76
wilderness 87, 91, 93, 96, 117, 191–2, 240
Williams, Raymond 5, 20, 83, 180
witness 57, 126, 143, 188–9, 204, 209
witnessing 144, 204
women xvi, 6, 16–17, 23, 28, 30–1, 33, 35, 39, 40, 46, 49, 51, 53, 63, 67, 134, 145, 151, 154, 155, 158, 168, 170, 173, 180, 217, 228–9
women investigator 43, 46
Woo, John 170
Woolf, Virginia 5, 203
    Mrs Dalloway 201
Woolrich, Cornell 41

X-Files (TV series) 143
    Scully 143
xenophobia 65, 234

zeitgeist 37, 234

www.ingramcontent.com/pod-product-compliance
Lightning Source LLC
Chambersburg PA
CBHW072130290426
44111CB00012B/1853